Education and Democracy

Re-imagining Liberal Learning in America

Robert Orrill, Executive Editor

College Entrance Examination Board
New York

THE COLLEGE BOARD is a national nonprofit association that champions educational excellence for all students through the ongoing collaboration of more than 3,000 member schools, colleges, universities, education systems, and organizations. The Board promotes—by means of responsive forums, research, programs, and policy development—universal access to high standards of learning, equity of opportunity, and sufficient financial support so that every student is prepared for success in college and work.

In all of its publishing activities, the College Board endeavors to present the work of authors who are well qualified to write with authority on the subject at hand and to present accurate and timely information. However, the opinions, interpretations, and conclusions of the authors are their own and do not necessarily represent those of the College Board; nothing contained herein should be assumed to represent the official position of the College Board.

Editorial inquiries should be addressed to Publications Services, The College Board, 45 Columbus Avenue, New York, NY 10023-6992.

Copies of this book may be ordered from College Board Publications, Box 886, New York, NY 10101-0886, (800) 323-7155. The hardcover edition is priced at $29.95 per copy; the paperback edition is priced at $22.95 per copy.

Library of Congress Catalog Card Number: 97-76801

International Standard Book Number: 0-87447-588-0 (hardcover)
                                     0-87447-589-9 (paperback)

Printed in the United States of America.
10 9 8 7 6 5 4 3 2

Contents

Authors vii

Editor's Prologue xiii
Robert Orrill, The College Board

Re-imagining Liberal Education. 1
Louis Menand, The City University of New York

From Discipline-Based to Problem-Centered Learning. 21
Ellen Condliffe Lagemann, New York University

Naming Pragmatic Liberal Education 45
Bruce A. Kimball, University of Rochester

Cosmopolitan Pragmatism: Deliberative Democracy
    and Higher Education 69
James T. Kloppenberg, Brandeis University

Pragmatism, Idealism, and the Aims of Liberal Education . . . 111
Charles W. Anderson, University of Wisconsin–Madison

Innovation in the Liberal Arts and Sciences. 131
Douglas C. Bennett, Earlham College

Professing the Liberal Arts. 151
Lee S. Shulman, Stanford University and The Carnegie
    Foundation for the Advancement of Teaching

The American Tradition of Aspirational Democracy 175
Elizabeth Kamarck Minnich, Union Institute

Liberal Education and Democracy: The Case
    for Pragmatism 207
Alexander W. Astin, University of California, Los Angeles

Dewey versus Hutchins: The Next Round 225
Thomas Ehrlich, California State University

The Stratification of Cultures as the Barrier to Democratic
    Pluralism 263
Troy Duster, University of California, Berkeley

Biology, Pragmatism, and Liberal Education 287
Ernst Mayr, Harvard University

Liberal Education in Cyberia 299
Peter Lyman, University of California, Berkeley

Placing Liberal Education in the Service of Democracy 321
Nicholas H. Farnham, The Christian A. Johnson Endeavor
    Foundation

Education for a World Lived in Common with Others 327
Lee Knefelkamp, Teachers College, Columbia University, and
    Carol Schneider, Association of American Colleges and
    Universities

Afterword. Anchoring the Future in the Past: 1931–1997 345
Rita Bornstein, Rollins College

Authors

Charles W. Anderson is professor emeritus of Political Science and Integrated Liberal Studies, University of Wisconsin–Madison. His publications include: *The Political Economy of Mexico, Politics and Economic Change in Latin America, Issues of Political Development, The Political Economy of Modern Spain, Statecraft, Value and Judgment and Income Distribution, Pragmatic Liberalism,* and *Prescribing the Life of the Mind.*

Alexander W. Astin is Allan Murray Cartter professor of Higher Education and Work, University of California, Los Angeles, and director of the Higher Education Research Institute at UCLA. He has served as director of research for the American Council on Education, and the National Merit Scholarship Corporation and is the founding director of the Cooperative Institutional Research Program. He has received awards from the Association for Institutional Research and the American Association for Counseling and Development, among others.

Douglas C. Bennett is president, Earlham College, Richmond, Indiana. He previously served as vice president, American Council of Learned Societies; vice president/provost, Reed College; and associate dean, College of Arts and Sciences, Temple University. He was also on the faculty of Oregon State University, Temple University, the University of Pennsylvania, and Swarthmore College, and has published extensively in the areas of political science and public policy.

Rita Bornstein is president of Rollins College, Winter Park, Florida. Since her appointment, she has published extensively on the college president's role as public intellectual. She has served on the board of the National Association of Independent Colleges and Universities and is currently a member of the board of the American Council on Education.

Troy Duster is professor of Sociology and director of the Institute for the Study of Social Change, the University of California, Berkeley. He has been a visiting professor or scholar at the University of Stockholm, the University of British Columbia, the London School of Economics, the University of Melbourne, Williams College, and Columbia University. He is currently a member of the National Advisory Council for Human Genome Research and chair of the National Institutes of Health/Department of Energy advisory committee on Ethical, Legal, and Social Issues in the Human Genome Project.

Thomas Ehrlich is Distinguished University Scholar, California State University, and visiting professor, Stanford Law School. He has served as president, Indiana University, Bloomington; provost and professor of law, University of Pennsylvania; guest scholar, the Brookings Institution, Washington, DC; director, International Development Cooperation Agency, Washington, DC; and president, Legal Services Corporation, Washington, DC.

Nicholas H. Farnham is director of Education Programs, the Christian A. Johnson Endeavor Foundation. He has also served as executive director of the International Council on the Future of the University, an academic association devised to strengthen university performance and academic excellence with a group of 350 scholars from 21 countries. Recent publications include *Rethinking Liberal Education,* written with Adam Yarmolinsky.

Bruce A. Kimball is professor at the Warner Graduate School of Education, University of Rochester. He has served as dean of Morse College, Yale University; associate director and assistant professor, University of Houston; and assistant dean of Dartmouth College. He is the author of *Orators and Philosophers: A History of the Idea of Liberal Education,* and contributed the central essay to *The Condition of American Liberal Education: Pragmatism and a Changing Tradition.* In progress are: *The Emergence of Case Method Teaching, 1870s-1990s: A Search for a Legitimate Pedagogy;* and, as editor, *American National Biography* and *A Documentary History of Liberal Education.*

James T. Kloppenberg is professor of History, Brandeis University. He previously taught in the French department at Dartmouth and was a visiting professor, *Ecole des Hautes Etudes en Sciences Sociales*, Paris. He is a fellow, Center for Advanced Study in Behavioral Sciences, Stanford. His publications include *Uncertain Victory: Social Democracy and Progressivism in European and American Thought, 1870-1920* and "Pragmatism: An Old Name for Some New Ways of Thinking?" in *The Journal of American History*. A work in progress for Oxford University Press is *Thinking Historically: Interdisciplinary Studies in History and Theory*.

Lee Knefelkamp is professor of Adult and Higher Education and program coordinator at Teachers College, Columbia University. She has taught at the University of Maryland, the American University, and Macalester College and was a senior fellow with the American Association of Higher Education and the Association of American Colleges and Universities. Her work has focused on college students' intellectual and identity development; intercultural issues on the campus; multicultural curricular transformation; and moral and ethical development in the context of race, ethnicity, and sexual orientation.

Ellen Condliffe Lagemann is professor of History and Education and director, Center for the Study of American Culture and Education, School of Education, New York University. She was formerly professor of History and Education and director, Institute of Philosophy and Politics of Education, Teachers College, Columbia University and served as editor of the *Teachers College Record*. She is a member of the National Academy of Education, the History of Education Society, the American Educational Research Association, and the American Historical Association.

Peter Lyman is university librarian, University of California, Berkeley. He has served as university librarian, dean of the University Libraries, and Martha Boaz Library Research Professor, the University of Southern California and executive director, the Center for Scholarly Technology. Publications include *Research in the Global Reference Room: Gateways to Knowledge*, forthcoming from MIT Press and "Public Place and Private Space: The Library in an Information Age," a *Daedalus* special issue on the centenary of the New York Public Library. He is a board member of the Council on Library Resources and the Research Libraries Group.

Ernst Mayr is Alexander Agassiz Professor of Zoology, Emeritus, Museum of Comparative Zoology, Harvard University. He has served as director, the Museum of Comparative Zoology, Harvard University; curator, the Whitney-Rothschild Collection, American Museum of Natural History; and assistant curator, the Zoological Museum, University of Berlin. He was visiting professor or lecturer at Cornell University, the University of California/San Diego/Riverside/Davis, and the College de France, Paris. Recent publications include *This is Biology: The Science of the Living World* and *One Long Argument: Charles Darwin and the Genesis of Modern Evolutionary Thought*. He is a member of the Berlin Brandenburg Academy, the Russian Academy of Science, the Center for the Philosophy of Science, the *Academie des Sciences*, the Royal Society, and the American Society of Zoologists.

Louis Menand is professor of English, the Graduate Center of the City University of New York. He has also served as literary editor and staff writer for *The New Yorker;* associate editor of *The New Republic;* assistant professor of English, Princeton University; and preceptor, Columbia University. His most recent book is *The Future of Academic Freedom*. He has published extensively on the philosophy of education and related issues in publications ranging from scholarly journals to the *New York Times Magazine*.

Elizabeth Kamarck Minnich is professor of Philosophy and Women's Studies, the Graduate School, Union Institute, Ohio. She was formerly professor of Philosophy and the Humanities, Scripps College and has also taught and held administrative positions at Barnard College, Hollins College, and Sarah Lawrence College. In addition to the books *Transforming Knowledge* and *Reconstructing the Academy: Women's Education and Women's Studies,* she has published numerous essays, conference proceedings, and book reviews.

Robert Orrill is executive director, Office of Academic Affairs, the College Board. He has taught History and American Studies at the University of Wisconsin, Madison; Skidmore College; and Empire State College, State University of New York, where he was chair of the Graduate Council and chief administrator of the Graduate Program. At the College Board, he has served as general editor for "The Academic Preparation for College Series" and "The Thinking Series." He has also been responsible for publication of *The Future of Education: Perspectives on National Standards in America* and *The Condition of American Liberal Education: Pragmatism and a Changing Tradition,* produced under the auspices of the Board's National Center for Cross-Disciplinary Teaching and Learning.

Carol Schneider is executive vice president, the Association of American Colleges and Universities (AAC&U). She has also taught History at the University of Chicago, De Paul University, Chicago State University, and Boston University, and headed the University of Chicago Institutes on Teaching and Learning. She is currently responsible for the AAC&U's project on higher education and American pluralism, "American Commitments: Diversity, Democracy and Liberal Learning."

Lee S. Shulman is Charles E. Ducommun Professor of Education, Stanford University and president, the Carnegie Foundation for the Advancement of Teaching. Previously at Michigan State University, he was professor of Educational Psychology and Medical Education, and founding codirector of the Institute for Research on Teaching. He recently completed a five-year research program, funded by the Carnegie Corporation, to design and field-test new strategies for the assessment of teaching at the elementary and secondary levels.

Editor's Prologue

ROBERT ORRILL
EXECUTIVE DIRECTOR, OFFICE OF ACADEMIC AFFAIRS,
THE COLLEGE BOARD

Unless education has some frame of reference it is bound to be aimless, lacking a unified objective. The necessity for a frame of reference must be admitted. There exists in this country such a unified frame. It is called democracy.

John Dewey, 1937

America must be looked upon as either an offshoot of Europe, culturally speaking, or as a New World in other than a geographical sense. To take the latter view is neither brash patriotic nationalism nor yet a brand of isolationism. It is an acknowledgement of work to be done.

John Dewey, 1944

At the beginning of the twentieth century, a troubled state of mind had overtaken many leaders of American higher education. This uneasiness was not about financial resources or student enrollment. Both were increasing, and higher education on the whole was prosperous and looking toward further expansion. Rather, what disturbed educators was an uncertainty about educational fundamentals and their lack of an assured sense of direction. Most especially, they missed the organizing power of a shared and firmly held conception of liberal education. The president of Cornell, Jacob Schurman, wrote forthrightly about this difficulty in his annual report for 1906-7: "The college is without clear-cut notions of what a liberal education is and how it is to be secured, . . . and the pity of it is that this is not a local or special disability, but a paralysis affecting every college of arts in America."[1]

Increasingly, observers attributed this disabling condition to a growing ambivalence about curricular reforms that, by 1900, had been adopted almost everywhere in American higher education.[2]

Often collectively referred to as the "new education," these reforms had effectively replaced a narrow curricular model bounded and defined by the prescribed study of classical languages and literatures with one that, in principle, admitted no substantive restraints and sought to be "coextensive with the reach and interest of intelligence."[3] This new openness had allowed many "modern" subjects to be added to the liberal arts curriculum and, in line with a call for an end to prescription, also afforded faculty more freedom to decide what to teach and students greater opportunity to "elect" what they chose to study. With this expansiveness, however, had also come disarray and disunity. Actions that reformers had promised would result in a much-needed "redefinition" of liberal education were instead producing an all-pervasive "confusion" about exactly what a liberal arts degree signified.[4] If students merely chose as they liked from among an ever-more-diverse array of subject offerings, how then could it be said that one degree was the equivalent of another or that all shared in the educational purposes that an institution thought should be common to every program of liberal study? Under the pressure of this uncertainty, the impulse of many education leaders was to call a halt to further forward movement in the direction of the "new freedoms." Even "some few . . . of the reformers," John Dewey wrote, "are themselves beginning to draw back." They "are apparently wondering," he added, "if this new-created child of theirs be not a Frankenstein, which is to turn and rend its creator."[5]

Such was the unsettled state of mind of liberal educators at the beginning of this century. Some continued to proclaim the future, but others now began to consider how to reclaim the past. As Schurman reported, many simply wavered and were unsure about which direction to commend. Almost everywhere, the prescriptive "classical" model of liberal education was in full retreat, but scarcely anywhere was the "modern" and more freewheeling "elective" alternative wholeheartedly welcomed. In fact, the "elective" approach increasingly was thought not to be a model at all in that it defined an "education" (so critics said) as nothing more than *any* aggregation of studies that might result from the whim of this or that individual student in choosing from among a large assortment of unconnected course offerings. Moreover, these courses themselves were developed and taught by a faculty now more often invested in specialized research interests than in thinking through how what was taught and learned contributed to a broad and comprehensive conception of a liberal education. Overall, then, recent reforms had substantially expanded and diversified the educational enterprise, but, at the same time, they had left liberal education bereft of any forceful theoretical direction or unifying philosophical definition. Dewey described the educational situation this way: "There is no longer any old education save here and there in some belated geographic area. There is no new education in definite and supreme existence. What we have is certain vital tendencies."[6]

As the century unfolded, this condition threatened to become chronic. Left to drift, "vital tendencies" did not take on any definitive shape as Dewey earlier forecast they might. Rather, it became commonplace for educators and lay observers alike to speak of the "malady" or "crisis" of liberal education.[7] Painfully, the recognition took hold that a centuries-old model of liberal education had collapsed without any durable and inspiriting alternative having arrived to take its place. If disorder and bewilderment were not to prevail, there was a great need to construct an approach to liberal education that, as Dewey urged in 1931, would point "the way out of educational confusion."[8] Increasingly, other influential educators spoke of the problem in much the same way. In 1936, for example, Chicago's Robert Hutchins prefaced his own call for the reform of liberal education with very similar words: "The most striking fact about the higher learning in America," he said, "is the confusion that besets it."[9] Also in 1936, Harvard's James Conant likewise proclaimed that intellectual "anarchy" was rife in American education and that it was "the mission of the liberal arts curriculum of our universities" to "bring order out of . . . educational chaos."[10] At the close of that same year, in an otherwise argumentative response to Hutchins, Dewey once again wrote that he fully agreed with the view "that present education is disordered and confused." This left no doubt about what educational problem most needed attention. "The problem as to the direction in which we shall seek for order and clarity," Dewey concluded, "is the most important question facing education and educators today."[11]

But which direction should be taken? Two sharply divergent schools of thought emerged in response to this question. One we can call conservative and "restorationist," the other progressive and "pragmatic" or "experimentalist."[12] The first looked to the past and sought reform through a model of liberal education derived from classical European sources. In most of its versions, this model placed supreme importance on the "exposure" of American students to a selection of "great books," that, at a minimum, included samplings from Greek philosophy and literature as well as Christian scripture and theology (though the latter were usually treated as if they were secular documents). These texts, so the argument ran, projected "the imaginative visions of supreme genius" that all should revere and, as such, also reflected "permanent standards of excellence" that could serve as a basis for discriminating between better and worse, high and low, lasting and transient. Taken collectively, they were said to constitute a binding "Western tradition" or "heritage" that all Americans shared in common and should embrace as their own. Beginning in the 1930s, the most publicly visible advocate of this position was Hutchins, but ultimately the most influential within the academy may have been Conant.[13]

In contrast, the second, or "pragmatic," approach looked to the "living present" for its orientation and advocated an experimental search for distinctively American models to guide the future practice of liberal education. John Dewey and other supporters of this point of view were critical of any educational stance that encouraged reverence toward "ideas and ideals . . . inherited from older and unlike cultures" and argued that, instead, the locus of liberal education must be found within "the dominant interests and activities of the great body of the American people." In effect, viable models for liberal education could not be "borrowed" from across the Atlantic or recalled from the past, but must be newly imagined, made, and tested on American ground. An ally of Dewey's, Horace Kallen, later said of the derivative "restorationist" model that it sought to make of the United States "nothing else than a spiritual colony of Europe, dependent upon the mother-continent for all the meanings that dignify man and ennoble his works."[14]

In the restorationist model, the function of liberal education was the transmission of culture from the past to the present, from Europe to America. For pragmatists, however, the liberal college above all needed to overcome this disposition toward reproducing European culture in an American setting. Pragmatists argued that the aim must be to "make the college count in developing a culture which is more truly indigenous." This could not be accomplished if colleges understood that the work of liberal education should be practiced through a reclaimed, or "equivalent," model of the kind that was previously dominant in the era of the classical curriculum. Such a classical model, the pragmatist George Herbert Mead wrote, was based on a belief that Americans should accept and follow "the forms and standards of European culture." As such, it was "frankly imitative" in intent; neither creative nor productive, "inferior, not different." In consequence, the result was an academic culture that in its intellectual workings could not produce "an interpretation of American life" or organize a learning environment that was other than "sterile in the development of the larger American community." The model of liberal education that some wanted to resurrect, Mead advised, could produce only a "cultivated American [who] was a tourist even if he never left American shores."[15]

From the pragmatic point of view, the sources from the past most useful to the liberal educator were not ancient Athenians or medieval Scholastic schoolmen but rather the likes of Emerson, Whitman, and the problem-solving American pioneer. In Dewey's intellectualized vision, the last especially was an exemplar of one who demonstrated how ordinary people could develop the capacity "to experiment and improvise" when faced with the need to resolve difficulties under "unprecedented conditions." The "creative effort" involved in these tasks did not display the Scholastic "correctness in thinking" admired by Hutchins, but it did evidence intellectual virtues of a sort perhaps even more essential given the pervasive flux of modern conditions. On this score, Dewey wrote of the pioneer experience: "Versatility and inventiveness, ready adaptation to new conditions, minds of courage and fertility in facing obstacles, were the result." For the pragmatist, such were the desired educative outcomes and dispositions that a modern liberal educator had to nurture among students. This was the task that Dewey had in mind when, in the 1930s, he spoke of education as "one of the great opportunities for present day pioneering."[16]

In contrast, the "restorationist" model looked East to the aristocratic "high civilization" of Europe for inspiration rather than West to the American frontier. Even so, this school of thought included both avowed elitists and professed democrats. Many of the former were followers of Matthew Arnold who, in a lecture tour of the United States in 1883, had brought both the philosopher Plato and the prophet Isaiah to bear in warning American democrats against the inescapable "unsoundness" of the majority of their fellow citizens. The only defense against "ruin" in democratic times, he argued, was the continuance of a kind of classical liberal education that, by focusing attention only on a few, could produce a "saving remnant" capable of upholding "true elevation" in the midst of prevailing low practices.[17] Borrowing largely from German sources, Arnold applied the term "culture" to the "holy seed" sewn by this "remnant"; and for some American educators, both then and now, this cultivation of an intellectual elite through close attention to "the best that has been known and said" has provided the defining function of a liberal education. Early in this century, the democratic experimentalist Dewey had disparagingly described this camp's stance within the American college ranks:

> To very many this idea of culture covers adequately and completely that for which the college stands. Even to suggest that the college should do what the people want is to lay unholy hands on the sanctity of the college ideal. The people, the mob, the majority, want anything but culture. The college stands for the remnant. It is the fortress of the few who are capable of upholding high ideals against the utilitarian clamor of the many.[18]

By the middle decades of the twentieth century, however, many "restorationists" had adopted a considerably more democratic stance even if they continued to regard anything remotely "utilitarian" with the utmost horror. Usually, they held to Arnold's view that the content of liberal education should be organized around "the best that has been thought and said" as drawn from Western European literature; but this was advocated along with the stated belief that the ideas gathered together under this rubric were the "common inheritance" of all Americans and the intent was that as many students as possible should have access to them in some measure. The educational issue for the pragmatist, in contrast, was not how to place examples of "rare genius" before students, but rather how to invent an education that would serve to bring forth the creative power that was in each and every individual. Democracy, for the pragmatist, was a fact of nature, not a product of books. So, too, was creativity. The social purpose of a genuinely democratic and liberal education, then, was not to convey that "genius" is exceptional and far above the common lot, but rather it was to bring to full realization the natural fact that resourcefulness and intelligence are widespread. If varied in their outward appearance, these human capacities nonetheless are possessions owned by all and are endowments from which each can contribute to the betterment of associated living and common enterprise. Echoing Emerson and William James, Dewey said about creativity:

> We are given to associating creative mind with persons regarded as rare and unique, like geniuses. But every individual is in his own way unique. Each one experiences life from a different angle than anybody else, and consequently has something distinctive to give others if he can turn his experiences into ideas and pass them on to others. Each individual that comes into the world is a new beginning; the universe is, as it were, taking a fresh start in him and trying to do something, even if on a small scale, that has never been done before.[19]

The debate between restorationist and experimentalist positions was most explicitly joined and intensely argued during the middle decades of this century. From the early 1930s to the late 1950s, there were few attempts to project a unifying model and rationale for American liberal education that did not take their bearings from these two positions. Some took sides, but others tried to have it both ways and broker an accommodation between the two. The most well-known and influential of the latter attempts was the Conant-initiated Harvard Report of 1945. Colloquially known as the Red Book, this report was the result of a three-year effort undertaken by a Harvard faculty committee to develop a guiding "concept" for liberal education that would do no less than serve to unify the whole of the American educational enterprise. One of the authors described the venture in the following way:

> Today, educational theory may be broadly distinguished into two types, the one theological (or quasi-theological), the other naturalistic in outlook. The first stresses architectonic unity and planned control of reason; the second, the spontaneous pattern of growth. The first is rationalistic, concerned to establish fixed premises and to make deductions from them; the second is empirically-minded, inductive, hospitable to innovation. The latter is associated with John Dewey, pragmatism and the scientific temper; the former, arising as a reaction to it, is associated with the names of Hutchins and the St. John's group. The Harvard Report envisages the problem of educational philosophy largely in terms of these two conflicting types; the solution which it offers may be regarded as resulting from the effort to reconcile them.[20]

Reaction to the Red Book, however, indicated that Harvard's attempt at reaching an accommodation had largely failed. Traditionalists for the most part were quietly positive, sensing correctly that the report's advocacy of "compulsory" study of the "Western heritage" and "great texts" placed Harvard solidly in the restorationist camp. Experimentalists, though, fired back with lengthy critiques arguing that the report, in fact, was no synthesis but rather a "Bourbon" document authored by "soldiers of . . . tradition" inescapably committed to a "quasi-theological" version of "neo-classical humanism."[21] Other readers committed to neither position, such as Columbia's Irwin Edman, observed that the attempt of the Harvard committee to appeal to both contending parties had resulted in a report largely made up of "vanilla-flavored homiletics" and "bland abstract double-talk."[22] After all the returns were in, the one thing certain was that American liberal education remained a house divided.

At the close of the twentieth century, have we arrived at a different place? Do we now agree about what function we want liberal education to perform in the United States? Should it be an education, as the Harvard Report proposed, that aims to convey to students an appreciation of a shared "Western heritage" and thereby bestow upon them the "received ideals" needed to achieve a "settled outlook" about who Americans are and what they hold important? Or is it, as John Dewey said, one that views the protagonist of a liberal education as a "perplexed wayfarer" in a new land who requires the skill, energy, and courage to map unknown territories and chart future directions? Is it, the pragmatist would ask, an education that assumes the world is mostly given and already largely made; or is it one that regards ourselves and our surroundings as unfinished and open to both the opportunities and hazards of remaking? And what kind of curriculum models follow from our answers to these questions? Are they ones that should be constructed, as restorationists have argued, with the aim of attempting to reproduce a kind of education presumed to have been practiced in ancient Greece or nineteenth-century Oxford? Or should they be ones developed, as pragmatists urge, through an experimental search for a distinctively American approach to liberal education directly aimed at addressing issues arising from late-twentieth-century realities?

Such questions are not likely to be easily resolved or ever permanently retired. Doubtless, we can expect to hear from both restorationists and pragmatists so long as the debate about the future course of American liberal education continues. It is important to note, however, that many restorationists themselves no longer appear to share the belief of Hutchins and Conant that the model of liberal education they advocate can be practiced on a large scale in the United States. Allan Bloom, for example, acknowledged that the "great books" approach to education is "almost universally rejected" in these times; and he could detect no enthusiasm among faculty in any part of the contemporary university to adopt any such model. Moreover, the kind of education that Bloom eloquently defends can be undertaken, he said, only by a "small number" of "advantaged youths" whose life circumstances are such that they are able to pursue an education free of material concerns and purposes. The relevance of this model in our American democracy, therefore, is not to be found in its capacity to touch and animate the many, but rather in its devotion to the perfection of a small number of the "greatest talents" who, so Bloom claimed, are "most likely . . . to have the greatest moral and intellectual effect on the nation." In Bloom, once again, an influential voice in the restorationist camp has proclaimed Arnold's view that the function of liberal education is to nurture a saving "remnant" who, in the midst of hostile and debased circumstances, can direct attention to "the rare, the refined and the superior." [23]

Among pragmatists, the outlook at present is significantly different and also a good deal more positive about the future prospects of liberal education. Whereas restorationists lament the weakening influence of European traditions on American educational thought and practice, the experimentalist Frank Wong views the same fact as helpful in eliminating long-entrenched assumptions that have "seriously inhibited the possibility of even considering an American model of liberal education." [24] The historian Bruce Kimball goes even further and argues that pragmatic assumptions, in fact, are already powerfully present in attempts to envision a future direction for American liberal education. Based on a close study of the contemporary reform literature, Kimball makes the proposal that, "at the end of the twentieth century, the liberal arts in the United States are moving toward a conception that can reasonably be called 'Pragmatic liberal education.'" If this pragmatic "turn" is fully actualized, Kimball argues, educators in this country for the first time will have "a principled rationale and legitimatization" for the practice of liberal education that is "historically grounded in American culture." [25]

By no means would all educators agree with Bruce Kimball that such a pragmatic "turn" is fully underway. Few, however, would dispute that we need a forceful renewal of the search for a rationale and orientation to guide American liberal education. This perhaps is made all the more pressing by the fact that there are no Hutchins, Conants, and Deweys these days to keep the fundamental importance of this matter at the forefront. However much these academic leaders disagreed among themselves, they were at one in insisting that a concept of liberal education must be the organizing center, not just of the undergraduate curriculum, but across the educational enterprise in the working interrelationships among high schools, colleges, and professional education. They were also in agreement that the answer to how higher education should serve the democratic aspirations of the nation would be realized most vitally through its understanding and practice of liberal education. In contrast, as the philosopher John Searle has pointed out, much recent dispute in the academy has been about a lot less. Often, in fact, it concerns no more than the syllabus of an introductory course in the humanities or some other very small fraction of the curriculum. Such debate may not be insignificant, but its import pales considerably, Searle says, when we consider the larger absence of "any coherent theory of what we are trying to achieve in undergraduate education." In language that would not have sounded at all unfamiliar in 1900, Searle concludes: "Faced with the well-known cafeteria of courses, and obliged to fill very few requirements, a student is more likely to be well educated as the result of chance, or of his or her determination, than as a consequence of planning by the university authorities." [26]

On the threshold of a new century, can we think more ambitiously about reform of the undergraduate curriculum? Can we, in fact, take up Dewey's challenge of re-imagining liberal education from the "ground up" in the United States? Moreover, what bearing might (or should) pragmatic thought have on this undertaking? Does the legacy of American pragmatism in all of its variety provide a moral and intellectual resource that can sustain educators in such an immense work? These are among the questions that the contributors to this book attempt to address in the context of contemporary conditions and in light of current educational issues. Taken together, the essays reflect a remarkably spirited and convergent effort to envision how a pragmatic "turn" in liberal education could be advanced and what the educational and social consequences might be if it were given full effect. At the same time, they also provide a thorough and unblinking discussion of the obstacles to change of any sort in American educational practice. Collectively, the result is as complete a picture of the interplay of trends and countertrends in the American college curriculum at the end of the twentieth century as a reader is likely to find. However, even more than this, say Lee Knefelkamp and Carol

Schneider in this book, the combined contributions constitute "from
a dozen different starting points, and through . . . joining . . . apparently quite disparate standpoints and conceptions, an emerging and
important new direction for U.S. higher education."

The powerful intellectual impetus that emerges from these essays
is owed more than a little to the occasion at which most were first presented and discussed—a colloquy on the college curriculum held at
Rollins College in February 1997. Organized by the College Board
and Rollins College, the colloquy was entitled "Toward a Pragmatic
Liberal Education: The Curriculum of the Twenty-First Century."
Helpfully, the event was also cosponsored by the Association of American Colleges and Universities and the American Council of Learned
Societies. Participants included institutional leaders from more than
50 colleges and universities and the exchanges among participants
that followed the presentation of each paper were invariably intense,
lengthy, and to the point. All of the essays have since been revised to
take into account issues raised in these discussions, and therefore this
book is, in a very real sense, a product of the kind of cooperative activity that the early pragmatists urged upon us.

Acknowledgments are always an enjoyable part of making a book. Special thanks, of course, go to President Rita Bornstein and her colleagues
at Rollins College for their help in all of the work that led to the preparation of this publication. It was President Bornstein who first proposed that a national curriculum conference held at Rollins in 1931,
and chaired by John Dewey, could be usefully reprised at the end of
the twentieth century. Without this suggestion and the attention that
she gave to planning the subsequent event, this book would never have
been conceived let alone brought to completion. Thanks in addition
to my College Board colleagues Dorothy Downie, Jeff Hale, and Geoffrey Kirshner who, as always, made the exceptional look routine. Their
contributions to both the organization of the colloquy and the completion of this book are beyond counting. Once again, also, the expert
editorial judgment of Madelyn Roesch has been a sustaining resource
throughout. Most credit, of course, must go to each individual author.

Above all a collective thanks to them and thanks, too, to College Board President Donald M. Stewart, whose support and encouragement helped make work on this book a special pleasure.

Notes

1. Quoted in Abraham Flexner, *The American College* (New York: The Century Company, 1908).
2. Many of the essays in this volume add considerable detail and insight to the story of the historical developments sketched in this brief stage-setting prologue. Additionally, among secondary sources, the indispensable book on this period in higher education continues to be Laurence Veysey, *The Emergence of the American University* (Chicago: University of Chicago Press, 1965). Veysey, however, must now be supplemented most especially by Julie Reuben, *The Making of the Modern University* (Chicago: University of Chicago Press, 1996).
3. Quoted in Flexner, *American College.*
4. The promise of "redefinition" was perhaps most prominently articulated by Charles W. Eliot, the president of Harvard, in an 1876 address entitled "What Is a Liberal Education?" The address is reprinted in Charles W. Eliot, *Educational Reform* (New York: Arno Press and the *New York Times*, 1969).
5. John Dewey, *The Educational Situation*, in Jo Ann Boydston, editor, *John Dewey: The Middle Works*, Volume 1 (Carbondale: Southern Illinois University Press, 1976).
6. Ibid.
7. Homer Rainey, "The Crisis in Liberal Education," *School and Society* (September 1928).
8. John Dewey, *The Way Out of Educational Confusion*, in Jo Ann Boydston, editor, *John Dewey: The Later Works*, Volume 6 (Carbondale: Southern Illinois University Press, 1989).
9. Robert M. Hutchins, *The Higher Learning in America* (New Haven, CT: Yale University Press, 1936).
10. Stated in an address at the Tercentenary of Harvard College and reprinted in full in James Conant, *My Several Lives* (New York, Harper and Row, 1970).
11. John Dewey, "Rationality in Education," in Jo Ann Boydston, editor, *John Dewey: The Later Works*, Volume 11 (Carbondale: Southern Illinois University Press, 1987).
12. As with all such dichotomies, this one is overly broad and omits important distinctions among individuals that I cluster together in one camp or the other. For certain, Conant would have objected strongly to being placed in the same company with Hutchins (and very probably would have rejected any suggestion that Harvard was following a course set by another institution or individual). Nonetheless, I think it is relatively easy to demonstrate that reform-oriented debate about liberal education in the middle decades of this century was largely organized around these two opposing dispositions.

13. See Hutchins, *Higher Learning* and *General Education in a Free Society* (Cambridge, MA: Harvard University Press, 1945).

14. Horace Kallen, *The Education of Free Men* (New York: Farrar, Strauss and Company, 1949).

15. George Herbert Mead, "The Philosophies of Royce, James, and Dewey in Their American Setting," in *Selected Writings* (Chicago: University of Chicago Press, 1964).

16. John Dewey, "Construction and Criticism," in Jo Ann Boydston, editor, *John Dewey: The Later Works*, Volume 5 (Carbondale: Southern Illinois University Press, 1984).

17. Matthew Arnold, "Numbers," *Discourses in America* (New York: The Macmillan Company, 1924).

18. Dewey, *Educational Situation.*

19. Dewey, "Construction and Criticism."

20. Raphael Demos, "Philosophical Aspects of the Recent Harvard Report on Education," in *Philosophy and Phenomenological Research* (December 1946).

21. See critiques by Sidney Hook, Harold Taylor, and Horace Kallen in *Philosophy and Phenomenological Research* (December 1946).

22. Irwin Edman, "Harvard Ponders Education," *The Nation* (September 15, 1945).

23. Allan Bloom, *The Closing of the American Mind* (New York: Simon and Schuster, 1987).

24. Frank Wong, "The Search for American Liberal Education," in *Rethinking Liberal Education* (New York: Oxford University Press, 1996).

25. Bruce Kimball's full argument can be found in Robert Orrill, editor, *The Condition of American Liberal Education* (New York: College Entrance Examination Board, 1995). The present volume includes Kimball's response to his critics in an essay entitled "Naming Pragmatic Liberal Education."

26. John Searle, "The Storm Over the University," *New York Review of Books* (December 6, 1990).

Education and Democracy

Re-imagining
Liberal Education

LOUIS MENAND

PROFESSOR OF ENGLISH, THE GRADUATE CENTER
OF THE CITY UNIVERSITY OF NEW YORK

What do people imagine when they use the term "liberal education"? The language of education theory is fairly amorphous,
and unavoidably so, because education is a fairly amorphous
process. People become educated; you can't really stop them. Those
who make a profession of educating others believe (against some evidence to the contrary) that it is possible to intervene in that process,
or to participate in that process, in ways that are helpful, rather than
redundant, counterproductive, or futile. They believe that there are
educational outcomes that are more or less desirable, and methods
of achieving those outcomes that are more or less effective. But education requires us to deal with singularities, not regularities—to deal
with persons, not laboratory models of persons—so we can never be
entirely sure in the abstract what will work in the specific case.

"Liberal education" is a term associated with one of the outcomes
of going to college—that is, the outcome of being a liberally educated person. College serves other purposes as well, but most people
agree that becoming liberally educated is the sine qua non of the
experience. A college that fulfilled all of the other purposes of higher education but that failed to provide its customers with a liberal
education would be considered deficient. But what does it mean exactly to have had a liberal education? This is where the amorphousness
comes in. Most people think about liberal education what Gandhi
said he thought about Western civilization: he said he thought it would
be a good idea. People tend to think liberal education is a good idea
without being much more particular about it than that.

Even those who think about the subject for a living—even professional educators—tend to give extremely general descriptions of
the sort of qualities they imagine a liberal education to instill. These
descriptions ordinarily revolve around concepts such as intellectual
well roundedness, cultural breadth, moral imagination, and the ability to think critically, with the idea that these acquirements conduce
to traits such as curiosity, sympathy, a sense of principle, and independence of mind. We could add other terms to this list, but they
would probably not be any less general or uncontroversial.

Let us say that curiosity, sympathy, a sense of principle, and independence of mind are the qualities we want liberally educated people to have. We might debate that particular list, or worry over some
of its items more closely, or come up with a somewhat different list.
But let's just assume that the ability to behave in ways that reflect those
qualities—or qualities equally admirable, it doesn't matter—is the
outcome we have in mind when we imagine a liberal education. The
question is, Is there anything educators can do to achieve this outcome? Can we actually make people of college age more curious, sympathetic, principled, and independent-minded than they would be if
we paid no attention to those ideals? Or to put the question the other way around: Are there things we could do that would actually make
people of college age less curious, sympathetic, principled, and independent-minded than they would otherwise be? In other words, what's
school got to do with it?

The best way to understand what people imagine when they use
the term "liberal education" is to look at the ways that idea has been
instantiated. Believing that liberal education is important, what have
colleges done in order to ensure that students get it? There have been,
historically, two approaches. These might be called the Fluid Model
and the Core Model. With the Fluid Model, liberal education is conceived of as the sea in which the various departmentalized fields of
study, from physics to philosophy, all swim. This fluid is not an actual body of knowledge in itself; it is a background philosophy, a sort
of intellectual DNA, which informs work in any particular field. That
is a more holistic way of putting it than many of the people who support this model prefer. Some supporters of the Fluid Model identify

three distinct types of intellectual DNA: the DNAs of the natural sciences, the social sciences, and the humanities.[1] But the basic idea is the same. It is that instruction in a particular field should be designed in a way that will impart to the student something that transcends mere technique or data—a set of general intellectual skills and attitudes, the acquisition of which constitutes a liberal education.

Bruce Kimball's essay "Toward Pragmatic Liberal Education," for example, can be read as an instance of the Fluid Model.[2] Kimball provides a list of the features of contemporary higher education that he considers "pragmatic"; these include multiculturalism, service, community, citizenship, an emphasis on values, and the belief that teaching is a process of learning and inquiry. This is a list of background elements. These are guides for orienting study; they are not, or not necessarily, objects of study in themselves. Values, citizenship, and so on are the stuff that rubs off when students are busy learning other things. Another way to put it would be to say that the philosophical background of higher education once featured such concepts as knowledge, disinterestedness, and rationality, and that it has recently tended to feature such concepts as understanding, critical thinking, and perspectivalism instead. These sets of concepts are quite different, but they are both imagined structurally in the same way: as transdisciplinary intellectual values, super-skills that all college graduates are expected to have picked up, whatever the field they are studying.

The characteristic institutional consequence of the Fluid Model is the distribution requirement. Distribution requirements are often sneered at as enforced dilettantism, a way of compelling students to dip a toe into uncongenial pools with the notion that even though they are likely to retain next to none of the very little information they soak up, they will nevertheless, by dint of performing this toe-dipping action three times, become well-rounded persons. It is a kind of baptismal theory of knowledge. This is undoubtedly one implication of the distribution requirement system; but the underlying aim is not to parcel out a few differently flavored bits of information. The underlying aim is to enable students to grasp that there are certain common elements to learning in all fields. It's a way of helping them see that the goal of education is not the accumulation of information, but the ability to think like an educated person, whatever the particular context.

The Core Model is the model for people who think that the Fluid Model is not enough. Its institutional consequence is the required core course, or sequence of courses, the most well-known examples of which are probably Columbia's Literature Humanities and Contemporary Civilization courses. (Harvard's core curriculum offers an array of specialized courses, and is therefore, in contrast to Columbia's, more like a formalized version of the distribution requirement.) Core courses are extradisciplinary. They are not taught as introductions to academic fields of study, which is what courses taken to fulfill distribution requirements frequently are. Core courses are generally administered independently of academic departments and they are conceived of as self-contained educational experiences. The Core Model reflects the belief that liberal education is not merely a set of general skills and attitudes, which is the basic assumption of the Fluid Model, but an exposure to, and knowledge about, particular works of art and thought. In the view of the people who endorse the Core Model, liberal education is itself a discrete body of knowledge, whose values penetrate and transcend all the special sciences.

The traditional content of core courses is classical and modern philosophy, with an almost exclusive emphasis on political philosophy, and the major literary works of the European tradition. More recently, core curricula, as in the highly publicized case of Stanford's, for example, have become more global in scope. The idea, though, is the same. It is that certain works of literature and abstract thought, including the major religious texts, constitute the ground from which specific kinds of knowledge spring. The term people tend to use for this ground is "culture," and even in colleges where no core courses are required, "culture" often now takes the place once held by philosophy: it is regarded as the basic template of human achievement. "Culture" is the thing students should know before they can really know anything more particular—about other societies or about their own. The theory behind the Core Model is the theory of general education.

There has, historically, been a split among partisans of general education. It is a split that manifests itself elsewhere in the undergraduate curriculum, particularly in courses in the humanities, but it is most dramatic in core courses. The split is easily seen by contrasting the well-known general education proposals of two university presidents, Robert Maynard Hutchins of Chicago and James B. Conant of Harvard. In Hutchins's view, as he presented it in *The Higher Learning in America* (1936), general education consists of courses in "the permanent studies"—that is, the classics. The classics are "permanent" because their truths are timeless: they continue to underwrite everything we know. "A classic," as Hutchins put it, "is a book that is contemporary in every age."[3]

Conant's idea was quite different. *General Education in a Free Society* (1945)—the volume Conant sponsored, also known as the Harvard Report or the Red Book—endorsed a core curriculum on the grounds that in a meritocratic society, citizens need a common fund of knowledge, a kind of cultural lingua franca, to prevent politically dangerous class divisions from developing. "The problem," as the authors of the Red Book say, ". . . is not merely to foster the skills and outlooks which divide man from man according to their special gifts and different destinies but to develop also the traits and understandings which they must have in common despite their differences."[4] For "open-mindedness without belief is apt to lead to the opposite extreme of fanaticism."[5] It is not flippant to say that the Red Book's prescription for general education was a response to the threat of Communism, for that is precisely the way Conant talked about it. General education was a benign substitute for a national ideology in the Cold War era.

As the Red Book conceives of the matter, the great books are not read because they articulate truths that transcend historical circumstances (although the authors do not, of course, slight the wisdom or the continued relevance of those texts). The great books are read because they have been read. Whether Plato or Rousseau or Mill was right about fundamental human nature is not important, or not determinable; what is important is that we live in a society shaped to some degree by the ideas of Plato, Rousseau, and Mill, just as we live in a society in which we can expect to encounter works of art influenced to some degree by Homer, Shakespeare, and Cer-

vantes. These writers represent a fund of allusion; they are touch-
stones for contemporary culture and debate; but most of all they
constitute a common heritage that bonds each citizen—doctors,
lawyers, and cabdrivers—to each. In the socioeconomically diverse
world the authors of the Red Book imagine, in which cohorts split
off onto different educational paths as their talents and merits allow,
general education is the glue.

These are the two basic rationales for the Core Model. One is substantive, the other is utilitarian. In the Hutchins version, the core is
where fundamental and timeless truths are encountered. In the Conant
version, the truths of the core are not timeless; their significance is
largely a function of their historical role. We can see a more recent
incarnation of this split in two books that rose to prominence simultaneously in the spring of 1987 and chased one another up the bestseller list: Allan Bloom's *The Closing of the American Mind* and E.D.
Hirsch's *Cultural Literacy*. Bloom, who was, of course, a Chicagoan,
echoed Hutchins's claim for the eternal relevance of the canonical
works of Western philosophy. Hirsch, though he was writing about
school, not about college, argued for his list of what might be called
the great words—the words and phrases he maintained that "literate
Americans know"—not because they articulated truths, but simply
because they were part of the vocabulary of contemporary life, things
every would-be educated person ought to know because every educated person does know them. Bloom wanted students to be cultured;
Hirsch merely wanted them to be literate.[6]

Since the time of Hutchins and Conant, the whole problem has
acquired a new edge. This was the result of two developments, one
intellectual and philosophical, the other social and demographic.
The intellectual development is well enough known. It has to do with
the overturning of a scholarly dispensation that met very nicely the
need to combine the disinterested study of the human world (that
is, research and interpretation) with respect for the particular values of the Western tradition (as taught to undergraduates). This was
structuralism, which celebrated cultural difference without invidi-
ousness (at least in theory), and which became, in the decades following the Second World War, a common methodological orienta-

tion throughout the human sciences, from linguistics and anthropology to literary criticism. In the late 1960s, though, structuralism
began to come under assault, first for theoretical reasons and then
for political ones. Its claim to theoretical rigor was disputed; so was
its claim to be unhierarchical, or apolitical, in its understanding of
cultural difference. The transformation of academic thought from
the structuralist to the poststructuralist dispensation is a complicated narrative, but everyone is familiar with the outcome, which is a
widespread and almost rote skepticism among academics about the
value of the sorts of texts typically taught in core courses. What were
once positively charged elements of social cohesion now tend to be
presented as potentially negatively charged elements of social division. What the Red Book celebrated about the books to be read in
general education courses—their gluiness—is precisely what came
to seem either false about them (they did not really stick together:
they deconstructed) or wrong with them (they stuck together things
that wanted to be apart: they were hegemonic).

There is a sense, however, in which this intellectual development
was not a rejection of the values the Core Model was designed to promote, but simply a deepening of their effects. Skepticism about the
tradition is, after all, part of the tradition. That is one of the attitudes
the "great books" teach; and to the extent that discussing the classics
skeptically induces students to raise questions, later in life, about
appeals to "the classics," or to the authority of "tradition," this is entirely in keeping with the spirit of liberal education as the authors of the
Red Book, at least, conceived it.

The other development exerting pressure on the Core Model,
though, is less tractable. This is the demographic transformation of
the American college, a transformation owed, above all, to the growth
of the public university. The number of public university campuses
in America doubled between 1960 and 1990; and although there are
one million more students in private institutions today than there
were 30 years ago, there are nearly 7 million more in public ones.
Half the work force now passes through college. The distinctive feature of this new population is (not surprisingly) its heterogeneity.
When college became just the next rung on the ladder of public edu-

cation, when it became affordable to people who, before the emergence on a mass scale of public two-year and four-year colleges, would ordinarily have entered the work force directly following high school, it began acquiring the variegated character of the typical public school classroom. One set of statistics makes the point rather dramatically. Between 1984 and 1994, total enrollment in higher education increased by about 2 million, or 16 percent. Not one of these new students was a white American male. Seventy-one percent were classified as African American, Native American, Asian American, and Hispanic American. The remaining 29 percent were nonresident aliens (a category that increased by 36 percent) and white women. The number of "white men" in higher education actually declined. People classified as "minority" and "foreign" account for 26 percent of all students in higher education today. Twenty years ago, that figure was 15 percent. Thirty years ago, it was under 7 percent. Student bodies are also more diverse in terms of age. Almost half of all undergraduates today are 22 or older, and 30 percent are 30 or older. Roughly half of the people who attend college never get any degree at all, because they never graduate.

And this new population is more economically diverse, as well. Many are students who cannot afford the tuition at a selective liberal arts college and who do not have the family resources to regard higher education as a resolutely nonvocational experience, an introduction to the liberal arts. Public education is what makes college possible for them. The average tuition and fees at four-year public colleges are $2,860 (as against $12,432 at private colleges) and two-thirds of all students now in four-year colleges—5.8 million people—attend them. Another 5.3 million people attend two-year public colleges. The average tuition there is $1,387. Public colleges and universities enroll 11.1 million of the 14.3 million students now in higher education. That's 78 percent of the total student body.[7]

This new population makes different demands on college than did the population of 30 or 40 years ago. Its members do not all have the same interests or wish to learn the same things. In the typical college classroom today, the social, cultural, and intellectual differences among individual students are usually immediately and persistently

in evidence. Their interest in education is likely to be far more practical than that of the typical college student of 1960, for whom merely having attended college was a cashable distinction. More of today's
students may need work on basic skills—for many, English is a second language—and they may regard college as vocational preparation in a much less abstract sense than students once did.

If colleges continue to offer these students "culture," on either
the traditional model of the great works of Western literature and
philosophy, or on the more contemporary model, in which those
books are read through a scrim of theoretically informed skepticism,
what is being gained? It is possible to see some of the contortions to
which the Core Model is susceptible even at elite institutions by reading David Denby's account of the core curriculum at Columbia, where
literary texts are anachronistically bent out of shape to produce issues
of contemporary relevance for classroom debate.[8] Where the texts
are not compelled to point toward a contemporary moral, the argument is commonly made that they are being read to teach the skill of
reading. But reading a literary text is a *particular* skill, not a generalizable one. Not everyone can do it well; it takes a lot of practice and
experience to get it right; and the skill is nontransferable. Knowing
how to read a poem enables people to do one thing, which is to read
more poems.

The Fluid Model suffers from a similar belief in transferability.
To a significant degree, the contemporary philosophy of higher education has turned out to be what the philosophy of higher education
was back before the rise of the research university in the middle of
the nineteenth century: the philosophy of mental discipline. Learning a scholarly field, any field, well is thought to develop general mental faculties, which may then be applied to problems and issues encountered in life after college. But problems and issues in the academic
world are not always analogous to problems and issues in the nonacademic world; resolving problems and issues in the nonacademic world
usually requires taking into account frictions of a kind deliberately
bracketed in the academy. Work is a spectrum, of course; it doesn't
divide itself up neatly into academic and nonacademic sorts, and there
are nonacademic occupations in, say, government agencies or arts

institutions, that naturally recruit from college graduates who majored in, say, sociology or art history. But many college graduates today will seek work well outside the academic band of the spectrum, and this work will be like all work in that it will require, above all, not research techniques borrowed from the senior thesis, but curiosity, sympathy, flexibility, and so forth—the virtues of liberal education, not the tools of scholarly inquiry.

The chief institutional consequence of the theory of mental discipline, or, as it is now generally called, critical thinking, is the undergraduate major. In most of the humanities and social sciences, the knowledge and skills acquired in mastering the major have fairly little relation to the knowledge and skills people will need in the world of work, with the exception of one group. These are the students who go on to graduate school, either to a professional school, such as law or medicine, where undergraduate training in the sciences, economics, and philosophy may be useful, or to a doctoral program in an academic discipline, where what is learned in the undergraduate major is obviously germane. But most college students don't go to graduate school of any kind; very few attend doctoral programs in an academic field of study; and even fewer actually end up working as scholars or college teachers for a living. Yet colleges are, in many cases, educating their students as though they all intended to become professors.

The major has other problematic implications as well. One is that the undergraduate who majors in English or sociology today is being trained in an academic field that will essentially not exist (except possibly as an object of contempt) 10 or 15 years from now. Anyone who teaches in a university is familiar with the experience of running into someone who graduated from college 30 or 40 years ago, and who happened to major in one's own field. After two minutes of conversation, it becomes clear that this alumnus's notion of the field is frozen circa 1955 or 1960. People who spend their lives teaching and doing research in a discipline tend to forget how much time is expended just keeping up with the changes, and how close to impossible it is for even a nonprofessional with a continuing interest in the subject to follow scholarly developments within the discipline.

One finds, therefore, students who have recently graduated with impressive credentials from Ivy League colleges who know a fair amount about an academic field as it existed around the time of the date on their diplomas, but have little other particular knowledge and few other skills of any kind. They tend to have no more knowledge about how the world works than the average newspaper reader does. It is the ignorance of the well educated. But most people would not say that these students were not liberally educated, for most people are determined to define liberal education as the opposite of anything having to do with knowing in a concrete way how the world works, or how to work in the world. It is true that students who attend Ivy League colleges do not normally need that kind of knowledge; they will move on, almost automatically, to professional school or to high-status employment where their training will be taken care of. But when half the work force passes through college, as it does now, it is worth asking whether the old models of undergraduate instruction continue to serve a useful function.

The debate over the nature of the college curriculum, the debate between utilitarian and anti-utilitarian philosophers of education, is as old as the modern college. Charles William Eliot and James McCosh had this debate in the 1880s; humanists such as Irving Babbitt had it with progressives such as Abraham Flexner around 1910; John Dewey had it with Hutchins in the 1930s; Allan Bloom and his critics repeated it in the 1980s.[9] A certain staleness has crept over the debate, partly because the issues are so familiar, but partly because the stakes have come to seem so small. Whether or not college students should be obligated to devote 2 or 3 of their 32 credits to philosophy and literature courses, or to courses outside their major field of interest, cannot possibly be an education problem of serious import. Yet that is what the debate over liberal education usually boils down to. Is there another way—another model that would not involve merely tinkering around the edges of the departmental major?

The philosopher most firmly associated with the conception of education as social and practical, rather than abstract and book driven, is John Dewey. Dewey's conception of education is distinguished from the conceptions of many of the other writers who have debated the nature of the curriculum because of its intimacy with the concept of democracy. Eliot, Babbitt, Bloom, and the rest were, of course, explicitly interested in the role of education in a democracy, just as Dewey was. But Dewey's idea of the connection was more profound; for he conceived of the educational process as itself democratic. He thought education could prepare people for life in a democracy only if the educational experience were also democratic, only if learning mimicked the processes of living socially in a democracy. Dewey's understanding of the crucial role education plays in preparing students for citizenship, and his insistence on the importance of maintaining access to the whole spectrum of educational opportunity, from early childhood through adulthood, are indispensable in any discussion of American higher education as it has evolved since Dewey's time.

Dewey did, over the course of his long career, make some remarks about higher education,[10] but most of his work focused on the schools. This was a natural emphasis because only a small percentage of Americans in his day attended college, so that the democratizing function of higher education was not dramatic for him. Today, that function *is* dramatic, and this makes it natural and appropriate to consider the extent to which Dewey's understanding of the nature of education in the early years of life might be relevant to the condition of liberal education now.

There is one stage of education in which Dewey's influence has never really waned, and that is early childhood education. Dewey's manifesto on early childhood education, *The School and Society,* was published in 1899. It became a bestseller, it has been translated into many languages, and its tenets seem in many education circles today as fresh and iconoclastic as they did a century ago. The central principle of *The School and Society* is summed up in the catchphrase, still repeated portentously to prospective parents at progressive-minded nursery schools around the country, "Children learn by doing." In Dewey's own formulation, it is the teacher's job to see that the activities and tendencies of the children

> are organized and directed through the uses made of them in keeping up the cooperative living [which Dewey felt ought to characterize

the classroom experience], taking advantage of them to reproduce on the child's plane the typical doings and occupations of the larger, maturer society into which he is finally to go forth . . . . [I]t is through production and creative use that valuable knowledge is secured and clinched.[11]

Is it possible to spin this still-golden oldie, "Children learn by doing," in thinking about the future of higher education? The argument against it rests on the reasonable point that while preschool and school education coincide with a period of rapid cognitive development in people's lives, postsecondary education is designed for people who are, developmentally, pretty well formed, and whose main sources of socialization are no longer either the school or the family. College teachers are dealing with biological grown-ups, whose most basic habits of inquiry are already established and whose learning environment extends well beyond the classroom and the professor's control. Obviously people continue to learn, and to learn how to learn, in college. But we know a lot less about the psychology of this stage of education, and what we do know is probably much less generalizable across all 18- or 20-year-olds than what we know about early childhood development is generalizable across all 4- and 5-year-olds. There is, too, as studies of the predictive accuracy of SAT scores for college achievement suggest, apparently a switch in learning patterns between the first half of college and the second half; and this makes it even more difficult to come up with a pedagogical theory of undergraduate education that has anything like the cognitive basis that theories of early childhood education have.[12] Still, Dewey did not think that the connection between learning and doing became less intimate or less effective as people grew older. That is because he didn't think of this connection as simply an educational strategy. He thought human beings learn by doing because that is the adaptive behavior of the organism. He regarded the symbiosis of knowledge and action as a philosophical premise, and although college students don't work with manipulables (or not in the classroom, anyway), that doesn't mean that the general principle doesn't still apply.

The mistake in attempting to re-imagine undergraduate education along Deweyan lines is to assume that meaningful reform can be

carried out within the college alone, and without a recognition of
what is going on both before and after college in the education system. Dewey argued, in *The School and Society,* that reform of one stage
in the education system necessarily implied reform of all the stages,
from nursery school through graduate school. The extent to which
these stages in his day were regarded, theoretically and practically, as
discrete distressed him; they continue to be regarded this way today.
There have been a number of suggestions for improving the effectiveness of undergraduate education that emphasize the importance
of the links downward, between college and grades K through 12. But
there is also the matter of the links upward, the links between college
and graduate education. A couple of issues seem important regarding this link. The first is an old issue, one William James complained
about back in 1903 in "The Ph.D. Octopus," which has to do with the
lack of a correlation between the ability to perform research and the
ability to teach.[13] The undergraduate major is the tentacle of the octopus that reaches down into the lives of college students. To the extent
that the design of the major reflects the research interests of the professors, it seems, for reasons already stated, an inefficient vehicle for
liberal education. But there is also the problem that, in many areas,
the academic discipline is no longer a useful rubric for scholarly
research, which makes the major an inadequate introduction even
to much scholarly activity.[14]

A second issue related to the link between college and postgraduate education is the monopolization of the professional areas of
knowledge. It is, in most American colleges, impossible to take a course
on the law (apart from an occasional legal history course), because
knowledge of the law is the preserve of people who go to law school.
Yet a knowledge of the law is one of the keys to understanding the
political and economic system in which Americans live. Many college
students, similarly, never take a class in business, or even in economics. Most take no classes in architecture, education, or engineering,
unless they are in a special, and usually segregated, architecture, education, or engineering program. Few students who do not intend to
become specialists take courses in subjects touching on health or technology. These are all matters adults have to deal with throughout life,

but people who have attended college generally have no more sophisticated an understanding of them than people who have attended only high school.

The suggestion that an understanding of matters of immense practical importance, such as law, business, technology, and health, should have a more central place in the college curriculum smacks of vocationalism, and it is customary to think that nothing could sound more illiberal than that. But the purpose of education is to empower people, to help them acquire some measure of control over their own lives. Some of this empowerment consists of learning how to think critically, how to communicate clearly, how to pose theoretical questions about practical issues. But some of it also must consist in knowing about the way the world works. Critical theory doesn't empower people. Self-esteem doesn't empower people. Knowledge empowers people. You can't dictate what people will do with it, but you can at least give them access to it. That an exposure to the way the world works can be presented in an appropriately high-level curricular setting can be seen in innovative programs underway at a number of private and public colleges. Bradford College, for example, a private college in Massachusetts, offers what it calls a "practical liberal arts" curriculum, in which students combine general education (nonspecialized study) with a "comprehensive" (that is, cross-disciplinary) major and a "practical" (that is, vocationally oriented) minor. Students do internships (called "practical learning experiences") in their junior year. And they are assessed, in part, through portfolios, rather than through individual papers for individual classes. The Bradford program is not vocational. It offers a general education in areas such as "Wellness" and "The Nature of Work" because it presumes that these are matters all college graduates should know something about.

The Bradford model manages to incorporate into its general education curriculum a good deal of exposure to scientific knowledge and methods. One of the drawbacks of the Core Model is that it either omits science completely, or presents it in the form of "culture," as some of the "classic texts." For Dewey, the scientific method was the type for all learning and inquiry. One need not go quite that distance to concede that science and technology do require formal education for nonspecialists to understand, and that most liberal arts colleges do little or nothing to ensure that students receive it in any programmatic way. The modern research university arose in response to the preeminence of scientific approaches to knowledge. The problem of how to put the humanities in proper institutional relation to the sciences has persisted since the turn of the century. The solution has been for scholarship in the humanities to be practiced on a more or less scientific, or positivistic, model (dissertations that constitute "original contributions to knowledge," peer review, and the like), while undergraduate instruction in literature and philosophy stresses moral issues and "human values." It is a divide, between fact and value, that inheres in both prevailing models of liberal education today; and one merit of imagining a fresh model is that it might make this division less antagonistic, an accomplishment that was the aim of nearly everything Dewey wrote.

Innovations similar to Bradford's—particularly out-of-the-classroom, or "service," experience and cross-disciplinary teaching—are becoming standard elsewhere. Twelve Pennsylvania colleges calling themselves the Commonwealth Partnership now advise new Ph.D.s that they must have interests that extend beyond their disciplines, be able to teach "communication skills," be socially involved, and teach by personal example. Candidates for jobs at Evergreen State College in Washington, a public institution, are required to complete a questionnaire about their views on pedagogy and other matters. Professors today have to be able to teach basic skills courses and a much wider range of much-less-specialized courses than they once did.

This may give rise to a market-driven change in the character of graduate education that has nothing to do with the persuasiveness of theoretical models. When Harvard surveyed the 1995 recipients of its Ph.D., it discovered that only 27 percent had found teaching positions.[15] For, in many cases, the top-ranked programs are the ones having the most trouble placing their graduates. One reason may be that their students' training is perceived as too specialized and their teaching experience as too narrow, by many of the schools where jobs are available. Harvard graduate students teach Harvard undergraduates. Most classrooms are very different. A recent internal study at the University of Chicago reported that graduate students there are concerned that their training is not preparing them for jobs at schools with more heterogeneous classrooms. It also reported that Chicago undergraduates are asking for more vocationally related courses in the curriculum.[16] If graduate training at Harvard and the undergraduate curriculum at Chicago alter in the direction of greater attention to pedagogy and less attention to specialization, the whole character of higher education will begin to change. This will not be a matter of tinkering with a few reading lists.

Let us suppose that the undergraduate curriculum were transformed in a way that eliminated the proto-professional major and that replaced the "culture"-based core requirements with general courses in law, business, government, the arts, and technology—that did not abandon exposure to literature and philosophy, which everyone should have, but that did abandon the idea that literature and philosophy are the mandatory bases for specialized knowledge. What would happen to liberal education? How could it be re-imagined in a way that would enable colleges to produce students who were well rounded, who had cultural breadth and moral imagination, and who knew how to think critically? How would it help students develop the capacity to display curiosity, sympathy, a sense of principle, and independence of mind?

The Deweyan answer to questions like these would be that you cannot teach people a virtue by requiring them to read books about it. You can only teach a virtue by calling upon people to exercise it. Virtue is not an innate property of character; it is an attribute of behavior. People learn, Dewey insisted, socially. They learn, as every progressive nursery school director will tell you, by doing. Dewey believed that the classroom was a laboratory in which to experiment with the business of participating in the associated life. American higher education provides almost no formal structure, almost no self-conscious design, for imagining pedagogy in this spirit. But the only way to develop curiosity, sympathy, principle, and independence of mind is to practice being curious, sympathetic, principled, and

independent. For those of us who are teachers, it isn't what we teach
that instills virtue; it's how we teach. We are the books our students
read most closely. The most important influence on their liberalism
is our liberalism.

Notes

1. See, for example, Christopher J. Lucas, *Crisis in the Academy: Rethinking Higher Education in America* (New York: St. Martin's Press, 1996), 157–67.
2. Bruce A. Kimball, "Toward Pragmatic Liberal Education," in Robert Orrill, editor, *The Condition of American Liberal Education* (New York: College Entrance Examination Board, 1995), 3–122.
3. Robert Maynard Hutchins, *The Higher Learning in America* (New Haven, CT: Yale University Press, 1936), 78.
4. *General Education in a Free Society: Report of the Harvard Committee* (Cambridge, MA: Harvard University Press, 1945), 94.
5. Op. cit., 78.
6. Allan Bloom, *The Closing of the American Mind: How Higher Education Has Failed Democracy and Impoverished the Souls of Today's Students* (New York: Simon and Schuster, 1987); E.D. Hirsch, Jr., *Cultural Literacy: What Every American Needs to Know* (Boston: Houghton Mifflin, 1987).
7. Figures are for a variety of years from 1993 to 1996. They are drawn from the Almanac Issue of the *Chronicle of Higher Education,* September 2, 1996, and the National Center for Education Statistics, *Digest of Education Statistics 1996* (Washington, DC: U.S. Department of Education, 1996). This paragraph and the one above it are adapted from my article "Everybody Else's College Education," the *New York Times Magazine,* April 20, 1997, 48–49.
8. David Denby, *Great Books: My Adventures with Homer, Rousseau, Woolf, and Other Indestructible Writers of the Western World* (New York: Simon and Schuster, 1996).
9. See "Charles William Eliot Expounds the Elective System as 'Liberty in Education,' 1885" and "James McCosh Attacks the New Departure and President Eliot, 1885," in Richard Hofstadter and Wilson Smith, editors, *American Higher Education: A Documentary History* (Chicago: University of Chicago Press, 1961), 2: 701–30; Irving Babbitt, *Literature and the American College: Essays in Defense of the Humanities* (Boston: Houghton Mifflin, 1908); Abraham Flexner, *The American College: A Criticism* (New York: The Century Co., 1908); John Dewey, "President Hutchins's Proposals to Remake Higher Education" and "'The Higher Learning in America,'" in Jo Ann Boydston, editor, *John Dewey: The Later Works 1925–1953,* Volume 11 (Carbondale: Southern Illinois University Press, 1987), 397–407; Robert Maynard Hutchins, "Grammar, Rhetoric, and Mr. Dewey," in ibid., 592–97; Allan Bloom, "Western Civ," in *Giants and Dwarfs: Essays 1960–1990* (New York: Simon and Schuster, 1990), 13–31; and Robert L. Stone, editor, *Essays on "The Closing of the American Mind"* (Chicago: Chicago Review Press, 1989).

10. See Dewey, "The Way Out of Educational Confusion," in *The Later Works,* 75–89, and "Statements to the Conference on Curriculum for the College of Liberal Arts," in ibid., 414–23.

11. Dewey, *The School and Society,* in Jo Ann Boydston, editor, *John Dewey: The Middle Works 1899–1924,* Volume 1 (Carbondale: Southern Illinois University Press, 1976), 82.

12. See Neil L. Rudenstine, "Diversity and Learning," in *The President's Report 1993–1995* (Cambridge, MA: Harvard University, n.d.), 29.

13. William James, "The Ph.D. Octopus," in *Essays, Comments, and Review,* in *The Works of William James* (Cambridge, MA: Harvard University Press, 1987), 67–74.

14. See Stanley Katz, "Do Disciplines Matter? History and the Social Sciences," *Social Science Quarterly* 76 (1995), 863–77, and Louis Menand, "The Demise of Disciplinary Authority," in Alvin Kernan, editor, *What's Happened to the Humanities?* (Princeton, NJ: Princeton University Press, 1997), 201–19.

15. See "Beyond the Ph.D.," *Harvard Graduate School Alumni Association Newsletter* (Summer 1996), 1.

16. See "Report of the Task Force on the Quality of Student Experience," the *University of Chicago Record* (May 23, 1996), 2–11.

From Discipline-Based to Problem-Centered Learning

ELLEN CONDLIFFE LAGEMANN
PROFESSOR OF HISTORY AND EDUCATION, DIRECTOR,
CENTER FOR THE STUDY OF AMERICAN CULTURE AND EDUCATION,
SCHOOL OF EDUCATION, NEW YORK UNIVERSITY

A s is well known, undergraduate enrollments in professional programs increased significantly between the mid-1970s and the mid-1980s. Although that trend has moderated, it warrants careful scrutiny and reflection. In part, the trend reflected economic realities and the widespread belief that professional education would offer more immediate and greater economic returns. In part, too, though, the preference reflected a continuing sense among undergraduates that the liberal arts are lifeless, while professional programs allow them to interact more directly with "the real world."

If matters of student preference are important in a system of higher education that is as competitive and consumer-driven as ours in the United States is, so is the possibility that pragmatic approaches to liberal education could be especially effective in nurturing the habits of mind most needed today. Because they might demonstrate new possibilities for developing and testing knowledge in relation to the problems of meaning and social connection that confront us today, pragmatic approaches might help solidify the drawing power of the liberal arts. At a time when change has become constant, it is important to be able to think in action, to understand the indeterminacy of knowledge, and to be able to articulate, test, and revise one's thoughts in conversation with others. Though the two are not entirely separable, *what* one knows matters less than *how* one approaches experience. Because pragmatic approaches to liberal education would, by definition, acknowledge that priority, they might have greater value than approaches built around the mastery of a canon, core, or discipline. Despite the appeal of liberal learning expressly designed to join thought and action, history indicates, I believe, that fostering this kind of education will be enormously difficult and will require fundamental, strategically planned change.

In what follows, I would therefore like to suggest something of the challenge I think history will present to people interested in developing and institutionalizing pragmatic approaches to liberal learning. I will do that by turning, first, to two early advocates of such education, the philosopher, John Dewey, and the settlement leader, Jane Addams, in order briefly to explore both their ideas and the fate of their efforts at education reform. Then, I should like to recall a number of the most important lines of development in higher education over the last 100 years, in order to point out how those have militated against wide acceptance for the kind of education Dewey and Addams, among others, favored. Finally, I should like to turn that perhaps disheartening story on its head by venturing the thought that, difficulties notwithstanding, efforts to foster more problem-centered modes of learning within programs of liberal education might be helpful in overcoming some of the dilemmas now central to American higher education and American society. In important ways, therefore, efforts to define and advance pragmatic approaches to liberal education could further strengthen what is indisputably the finest system of higher education anywhere in the world.

Possibilities Lost: John Dewey and Progressive Education

According to John Dewey, liberal education was "the sort of education that every member of the community should have: the education that will liberate his capacities and thereby contribute both to his own happiness and his social usefulness." [1] Implicitly in the entry on "liberal education" he prepared for Paul Monroe's *Cyclopedia of Education* in 1912–13 and more directly in other comments, Dewey suggested that liberal education could not be given an *a priori*, universal definition because it did not involve any fixed set of subjects. Liberal education could not be identified "with the linguistic, the literary and the metaphysic," he observed.[2] Beyond that, liberal education could not be opposed to scientific, technological, or even professional education, Dewey insisted. Once, but no longer, a privilege reserved for upper-class gentlemen, liberal learning for Dewey had to do with matters of method and direction and not with any distinctive body of knowledge. Regardless of subject matter, a liberal education, Dewey believed, should evoke certain qualities of mind and character. To be liberally educated, he stated, was to demonstrate a "hospitality of mind, generous imagination, trained capacity of discrimination, freedom from class, sectarian, and partisan prejudice and passion, [and] faith without fanaticism."[3]

Despite statements such as these, which clearly set forth his vision of liberal learning, Dewey wrote relatively little about higher education. He did this by intention, being convinced that "the college problem is primarily not a college problem, but . . . is in what we call the grades and high school."[4] Obviously, therefore, Dewey saw the reform of elementary and secondary education as a necessary precondition to more pragmatic approaches to higher education, and it is in relation to reform at those levels that his impact as an education reformer must be appraised.

Having graduated from Johns Hopkins in 1884, Dewey spent 10 years teaching at the University of Michigan and then, in 1894, moved to the University of Chicago, where, during 10 enormously happy and productive years, he developed a philosophy of education that remained essentially constant throughout the remainder of his very long career.[5] As described in contemporary writings, for example, *The School and Society* (1899), and in subsequently published works, notably, *Democracy and Education* (1916), Dewey's philosophy entailed active, problem-centered learning. In interaction with astutely observant, highly knowledgeable, and autonomous teachers, children were to be helped to extend the knowledge and experience they brought to school by discovering and mastering new knowledge and skills relevant to the projects they were undertaking collaboratively with their classmates, projects such as planning and growing a garden, building a clubhouse, or learning a foreign language. In this way, Dewey believed, knowledge could be psychologized—made accessible through

its relation to the interests of the child—and learning could be socialized—directed toward understanding and being able to act in the
kind of social situations that actually existed in the world.[6]

Although many of Dewey's education writings were widely circulated and his name was associated with a great variety of education
reforms, the little-known fact is that his philosophy of progressive education had relatively scant influence on actual practices. Dewey himself expressly disassociated himself from many self-styled progressive
innovations, thereby indicating that even in schools that professed to
be "Deweyan," his ideas had been, at best, only partially understood
and implemented.[7] More important, despite often negative rhetoric
about the great influence of Dewey and Teachers College, where
Dewey had an affiliate appointment after leaving the University of
Chicago for Columbia, few public schools tried to institutionalize progressive ideas, and those that did tended to do so very superficially
and selectively.[8] Beyond that, the influence Teachers College did exercise had far more to do with the ideas of Edward L. Thorndike, the
psychologist whose work supported bureaucratically organized, sub-
ject-centered forms of schooling, than with those of John Dewey.[9]

That Dewey's name became an icon widely associated with education reform is indisputable. More likely than not, that was because
popular writers such as Randolph Bourne lionized him, and influential educators such as William Heard Kilpatrick of Teachers College
claimed to derive their actually quite different ideas (for example,
those having to do with the so-called project method of instruction)
from Dewey. Despite that, however, there is little concrete evidence
to suggest that Dewey was able to change the course of schooling in
the United States and there is a lot of evidence to suggest how rare
Deweyan practices are even today.[10] However brilliant Dewey's ideas
were, he was not a strategic thinker, and the impact of his ideas on
institutionalized education practice was unfortunately slight.

Possibilities Lost: Jane Addams and the Social Settlement

Sadly, the same point can be made about Jane Addams. Well known
as an unusually humane social activist, Addams was also a brilliant

intellectual of distinctly pragmatic bent.[11] At Hull House, the settlement she established with Ellen Gates Starr in 1889 on Chicago's west side, Addams produced a continuous stream of incisive social commentary, and much that she had to say pertained to education. In style, Addams's writings were often autobiographical and, as Jean Bethke Elshtain has observed, always filtered through the particulars of "concrete human experience."[12] In them, one finds brilliant analyses not only of public schooling, but also of many more experiential forms of education, even what Addams aptly called "education by the current event."[13]

That education should have been a central theme in Addams's speeches and essays reflected the purposes she believed essential to settlement work. In her writings about the settlement, Addams often described it as an educational institution. In fact, she frequently argued that the settlement was an antidote to the college. Bent upon bringing "into the circle of knowledge and fuller life, men and women who might otherwise be left outside," Hull House was the setting for a wide range of lectures and discussions on science, politics, literature, and art.[14] In addition, one resident led a Plato Club to discuss philosophy and, while he served on the faculty of the University of Chicago, John Dewey gave Sunday lectures on social psychology. All this was vital, Addams believed, because, like Dewey, she thought liberal learning should and could be both accessible to all people and liberating in effect. Writing of the early years of the Hull House Shakespeare Club, she once said, for example:

> I recall that one of its earliest members said that her mind was peopled with Shakespeare characters during her long hours of sewing in a shop, that she couldn't remember what she thought about before she joined the club, and concluded that she hadn't thought about anything at all. To feed the mind of the worker, to lift it above the monotony of his task, and to connect it with the larger world, outside of his immediate surroundings, has always been the object of art, perhaps never more nobly fulfilled than by the great English bard.[15]

Despite such praise for the inspiring power of liberal culture, which certainly tended toward the romantic, Addams was very much a real-

ist and keenly aware of the pedagogical problems involved in offering liberal learning in ways that could connect with the large, general interests of diverse audiences. For that reason, she and her Hull
House colleagues took the development of new, more popular methods of adult education as an essential challenge of settlement work.
They were well aware that the academic orientation of most college
and university teachers could have a deadening impact on potentially
eager students. "A course of lectures on astronomy . . . will attract a
large audience the first week," Addams once observed. But too often,
the audience, which comes hoping "to hear of the wonders of the
heavens and the relation of our earth thereto" is instead "treated to
spectrum analysis of star dust, or the latest theory concerning the
milky way." Addams astutely concluded: "The habit of research and
the desire to say the latest word upon any subject often overcomes
. . . sympathetic understanding of [an] audience." Having seen this
happen on many occasions, Addams became convinced that popular adult education required "the most direct forms of expression"
rather than "the dull terminology of the classroom" as well as a focus
on "large and vital subjects."[16]

In addition to disseminating liberal learning, Addams believed
settlements should be "sociological laboratories" where social theories could be applied, tested, and refined. In 1895, she and some of
her Hull House colleagues published one of this country's earliest
social surveys, *Hull-House Maps and Papers.* Seven years later, she published a text entitled *Democracy and Social Ethics* that was widely used
in philosophy classes, including ones taught by Dewey at the University of Chicago. A remarkable book, *Democracy and Social Ethics* considered traditional ethical concepts in relation to contemporary, everyday problems of life in an urban, industrial society. As was true of her
classic autobiography, *Twenty Years at Hull House,* it exemplified the
way in which a settlement, in Addams's view, could serve not only to
help bring knowledge to its neighbors, but also to disseminate knowledge derived from life in that neighborhood to people in other locales.

Despite the emphasis Addams placed on education and research
as well as on their intimate connection, and despite the fame she
achieved across the United States and throughout the world, settle-

ment work as she pioneered it did not long survive her death in 1935.[17] Often claimed as a founder of the social work profession, Addams was, in fact, a sociologist in the nineteenth-century sense of someone who studied social problems in order both to understand and act on them. Her brilliance was acknowledged by many people, including John Dewey and other scholars at the University of Chicago. And yet, the styles of research many of the same people were beginning to pursue were increasingly rendering obsolete the synthesis Addams sought between theory and action, study and discussion.[18]

As a result, settlements such as Hull House increasingly became settings in which a university-based (usually male) sociologist might collect data, but they no longer served as primary centers for social research. Increasingly, too, as social work became a profession rather than an extension of one's obligations as a resident neighbor, which was how Addams always conceived it, settlements became centers for charity or welfare administration and not for discussion and debate about the sources of common social problems. Finally, of course, as an emphasis on individual reformation, which derived not from settlement work but from the charity organization movement, moved to the center of social work practice, liberal learning was displaced.[19] Hull House still stands today, but settlement work as defined by Jane Addams has generally been superseded. As with Dewey, Addams is an icon to practices she did not support, and, though her ideas are still available for study, their influence in the domains of study and practice she straddled—sociology, social work, and education most important among them—has, in the end, been remarkably slight.

The Transformation of Higher Learning

As Dewey and Addams were both well aware, they were living at a time when knowledge was increasing at an enormous rate and becoming more and more specialized. In considerable measure, it was specialization, especially as manifested in increasing professionalization and discipline formation within newly emerging research universities, that limited the institutionalization of their ideas.[20] In Dewey's case, for example, the emergence of a professional cadre of education researchers, bent on developing a professionalized science of education, helped to undermine the kind of collaborative, practice-based approach to the study of education that was essential to his conception of progressive education.

Despite common misconceptions concerning Dewey's advocacy of child-centered education, extraordinary teachers, freely interacting on an equal basis with university scholars as well as with parents and many other members of the public at large, were indispensable in Dewey's formulation of progressive education. Teaching and learning in classrooms of the sort Dewey envisaged would require constant, collaborative study and discussion of problems of curriculum, social organization, and student behavior.[21] As professionalization advanced, however, such cross-role, cross-field study and discussion became more and more difficult.

Scholars of education within university schools and departments of education, which were just being founded at the turn of the century, believed they could formulate laws of learning that would have universal application across school settings. Thus implicitly diverging from Dewey's understanding of the unique, constantly shifting context of each and every classroom, early university educationists also believed that laboratory experimentation rather than classroom observation, let alone conversations with teachers, should serve as the empirical basis for their formulations. Fitting well with models of scholarship then developing across the range of university schools and departments, these beliefs about education scholarship made Dewey's views seem romantic and prescientific.[22] Edward L. Thorndike suggested this when he observed, in 1911, that "what physical science has to do with the cosmologies of the early philosophers, the science of education has to do in comparison with the first generalizations of Herbert Spencer or Dewey."[23]

Beyond that, status issues related to professionalization necessitated that scholars of education demonstrate their expertise by generating knowledge that appeared to be superior because it was more theoretical than the tacit, idiosyncratic knowledge of classroom teachers. Absent such knowledge, there would be little to legitimate their supposedly superior university rank. That, too, militated against the kind of free-flowing, reciprocal conversation between teachers, university-based scholars, and other interested parties that Dewey thought essential. The point is not that professional scholars of education purposefully set out to go in a different direction from Dewey—although that was, indeed, the case in a few key instances, including that of Dewey's successor at the University of Chicago.[24] The point is rather that, as it was manifested in the development of education scholarship, the trend toward specialization that made the research university home to an ever-multiplying array of professional fields and disciplines ran counter to Dewey's most essential beliefs about the nature and social relations of science.

Obviously, as I have already suggested, Addams's conception of the social settlement fell victim to the same tendencies. Advancing professionalization fostered more and more rigid divisions between the development and application of knowledge. Those were compounded by gendered assumptions concerning male inclinations to be inventive and female inclinations to be intuitive, malleable, and always disposed to take on roles involving nurture and care. Such beliefs easily supported expectations that men would generate new knowledge and women would apply it. Owing to all this, as universities came to hold a virtual monopoly on knowledge creation, social settlements were redefined. No longer regarded as "sociological laboratories," they became places of charity to which scholars might go to document the problems of the poor, the deviant, or the newly arrived.

Although the dissemination of knowledge in the form of adult education never came so definitely and exclusively within the orbit of universities as research did, specialization also fostered a tendency to assume that education should proceed under the auspices of professional teachers and scholars.[25] This did not obviate the need for the cultural offerings once so central to social settlements such as Hull House. But, as credentials became more important tickets for entry to graduate study and a wide array of jobs and professions, and as credentialing became a more important function of colleges and universities, adult education came to be a more important part of university-sponsored programs of continuing education and a less important aspect of settlement work. Combined with complicated nationwide changes in social welfare policy, professionalization thus narrowed and transformed what a social settlement could be. In the process, much that was essential to Jane Addams's vision got lost.

Closely related to specialization, professionalization, and discipline formation, the emphasis on expertise that was so essential to the rise of the university was yet another factor in both the emergence of the twentieth-century U.S. system of higher education and the marginalization of approaches to education that were compatible with Dewey and Addams's pragmatic orientation. This emphasis revealed an important difference in belief between genuinely populist progressives such as Dewey and Addams, on the one hand, and many of their contemporaries, on the other, both mugwump types such as Harvard President Charles W. Eliot and younger progressives of technocratic persuasion such as Walter Lippmann.

Via his championing of the elective system as well his public statements about government, the professions, education, and much else, Eliot did a great deal to popularize belief in the notion that leadership in a modern society should require, along with a tested sense of character, high levels of unusual knowledge and skill. Central among the many different reasons that prompted him to champion course election at Harvard was the prospect that election would allow students to develop their particular talents to higher levels and at younger ages than would be possible if they were required first to master a broad spectrum of knowledge. Arguing that the public schools should foster a deference to experts in all their students, Eliot maintained that colleges should be institutions through which the most able would become the best trained and most cultivated and rise to positions of power, responsibility, wealth, and fame.[26] "Civilization means infinite differentiation under liberty," Eliot once said.[27] If education in a democracy should offer equal opportunity, it should also ensure that the most talented had the opportunities necessary to prepare themselves to lead the nation.

More than is often remembered today, Eliot's views were unusually important early in the twentieth century. This was partly because Eliot purposefully and very skillfully turned himself into a schoolmaster to the nation. Even before he put together the five-foot shelf of Harvard Classics, which was said to represent all one needed to read (in 15 minutes a day) to be liberally educated, Eliot had traveled widely, spoken everywhere, and published extensively. Once such an obscure figure that a California news reporter called him "Dr. Eliot of Dartmouth College, [in] New Haven," by the end of his long tenure at Harvard (1869–1909), Eliot had become so well known that he was called the "first private citizen" of the nation.[28] Beyond that, Eliot was as strategic a thinker as John Dewey was not. He purposefully set out to dominate all the organizations that could have an impact on the reforms he favored. Gaining the ear of many of the nation's influential leaders, Eliot helped shape some of the organizations that were most important to the turn-of-the-century transformation of higher education. Among these, few were more important than the Carnegie Foundation for the Advancement of Teaching, of whose board of trustees Eliot was first chair.[29] Established in 1905 by Andrew Carnegie to be a pension fund for professors, the Carnegie Foundation, in fact, became what its first president once described as a "Great Agency . . . in standardizing American education."[30]

Through the eligibility rules established for its pension fund as well as a series of opinion-shaping reports such as the famed Flexner study of medical education, the Carnegie Foundation helped define the standards that differentiated types of institutions, for example, universities and colleges, and levels of quality, for example, good medical schools and bad barber colleges. Those definitions helped set patterns of giving at many of the philanthropic trusts organized to dispense new post–Civil War wealth. Equally important, Carnegie Foundation activities helped to connect old ideas concerning equality, mobility, and just rewards to individuals for hard work, honesty, and frugality, to new expectations concerning higher education, social efficiency, and social stratification. The result was an ideology of meritocracy that supported belief in the likelihood that, even if one did not come from a family of established prominence, with talent and character, one could rise up the ladder of educational opportunity into leadership roles in government, business, or the professions.[31]

As was true of many of their contemporaries, Dewey and Addams concurred in aspects of this ideology and they also recognized the

importance of expertise. However, their thinking ran counter to Eliot's
in rather subtle but important ways. Eliot was much less concerned
than Dewey and Addams were with finding ways deliberately to foster equal relations between and among different people. Contra-
vening the social Darwinist and libertarian assumptions that guided
his thinking, such efforts would, in Eliot's view, subvert the natural
order of things. Rather than promoting equality, the challenge to
Eliot was removing whatever barriers stood in the way of those possessing natural talent. This would give everyone a fair chance, while
guaranteeing that "the best men" would rise to positions of responsibility and power.[32]

Of course, Eliot wrote and spoke about democracy just as frequently as Dewey and Addams did. However, when he did so, he
referred to something that was more narrowly political than broadly cultural. In his view, democracy had more to do with having an
equal vote than possessing and being able to exercise an equal voice.
Eliot applauded the fact that in the United States there was "no class
legislation, feudal system, dominant church, or standing army to
hinder or restrain" and that instead there were "public schools,
democratic churches, public conveyances without distinction of
class, universal suffrage, town-meetings, and all the multifarious
associations in which democratic society delights."[33] He was not troubled, as Dewey and Addams were, that freedom from restraint might
no longer be sufficient to ensure equal rights for all people. Finding new ways not merely to allow, but positively to promote free communication and universal participation in the definition of common goals and policies was a concern of Dewey and Addams that
Eliot simply did not share.

The same could be said of younger progressives who also subscribed to a belief in the efficiency of expert leadership. Often situated in research institutes such as the Brookings Institution and the
National Bureau of Economic Research, these younger progressives
were intent upon counteracting the problems of public opinion and
public intelligence that Walter Lippmann so brilliantly analyzed in
many of his writings, and most especially in *Public Opinion* (1922).
They shared Lippmann's worries about the capacity of ordinary peo-

ple to decipher the "news" and hoped to provide a corrective through disinterested expertise. On occasion, they focused attention on the difficulties involved in disseminating expertise or countering what they took to be false propaganda or outrageously ill-informed popular ideas. More often than not, however, progressives of technocratic persuasion focused most intently on the challenges involved in financing and otherwise supporting scientific research. Rarely, if ever, did they pick up on Dewey and Addams's deep-seated belief that the most important challenges for a large, heterogeneous, complex, democratic society involved going beyond the disseminating of expertise to identify more effective means of public education.

A constant theme in Addams's writings, this point was also forcefully expressed in a review of *Public Opinion* Dewey wrote for the *New Republic*. Having associated himself completely with Lippmann's belief that finding ways to capture and communicate public events and issues was coming to be *the* problem of democracy, Dewey concluded nonetheless that Lippmann had reached the wrong solution. Education of experts who could then inform and lead the public was not sufficient, Dewey insisted. "Democracy demands a more thoroughgoing education than the education of officials, administrators and directors of industry," he said. What is more, he continued, just because "fundamental general education is at once so necessary and difficult of achievement, the enterprise of democracy is so challenging. To sidetrack it to the task of enlightenment of administrators and executives is to miss something of its range and its challenge."[34]

Unfortunately, Dewey's criticism did not proceed to a full elaboration of how he thought one could move to what he called here "fundamental general education." And that shortcoming, which was not fully corrected in any of Dewey's writings, has limited possibilities for extending, building from, and testing Dewey's vision in actual social experiments. That notwithstanding, Dewey's criticism of Lippmann did suggest the degree to which a focus on promoting high levels of knowledge, apart from an equal focus on inventing ways to universalize the capacity to understand, appreciate, and criticize such knowledge, could lead—and indeed, has led—to profound political inequalities.

In addition, Dewey's criticism forced one to see the degree to which Lippmann's willingness to countenance delegated conceptions of democracy made it unnecessary to work to create new forms and media of education that might promote fully equal and participatory communication and deliberation. Because Lippmann's political values, as those held by Charles Eliot, were less radically democratic than those held by Dewey and Addams, he did not worry as they both did that liberal education would remain an exclusive, elite preserve rather than the common experience Dewey and Addams wished it to be. In a society of expert governance such as that imagined by Lippmann and a little differently by Eliot, it was more important to promote specialization and course election than open communication and common learning.

Obviously, there were many other forces involved in the turn-of-the-century transformation of higher education in the United States that were also important in limiting the institutionalization of Dewey and Addams's ideas. There was, for example, the matter of the secularization of knowledge. By the early decades of the century, it was coming to be widely believed that "scientific" knowledge had to be "objective" and that "objective" knowledge had to be value free. What this really meant was that scholars working in the social sciences were expected to engage in research that avoided explicit consideration of the ethical implications of their findings.[35]

To Albion Small, first chair of the Department of Sociology and Anthropology at the University of Chicago, who was a contemporary of Dewey and Addams, science was "sterile" unless it contributed "to knowledge of what is worth doing."[36] But to William F. Ogburn, one of Small's prominent Chicago successors of the next generation, sociology conceived as a science was "not interested in making the world a better place in which to live, in encouraging beliefs, in spreading information, in dispensing news, in setting forth impressions of life, in leading the multitudes, or in guiding the ship of state." Science, Ogburn maintained, was "interested directly in one thing only, to wit, discovering new knowledge."[37] The difference in view expressed by these two sociologists derived from changing perceptions concerning the relation of research and reform that clearly ran counter to the seamless conception favored by both Dewey and Addams. That, too, diminished the impact of their ideas.

The Dilemmas of Preeminence

Even leaving aside all the rest that was important to the development of research universities, most with liberal arts faculties situated within them, as well as to the creation of discipline-based departments and, despite continuing variation, the formation of a nationally standardized "system" of higher education, the point may be clear. As a result of developments at the turn of the century, especially the increasing specialization and secularization of knowledge and the increasing hold of social and political values favoring trained expertise in government and mobility through education, the vision of pragmatic liberal education one can discern in Dewey and Addams's writings did not gain wide assent. Even if parts of that vision were incorporated within the progressive colleges, it remained an alternative fundamentally at odds with the central tendencies of U.S. higher education.

It is also important to note, I think, that during the century that has followed the turn-of-the-century transformation of higher education, any number of developments have, if anything, reinforced the forces militating against acceptance of pragmatic approaches to liberal education. For example, the discipline-based research orientation of most universities was mightily strengthened by the contracting and grant system developed after World War II for federally supported scientific research. In addition, the identification of faculty members with disciplinary colleagues across the nation became more and more pronounced as institutional competition and a "star" system of recruitment grew over the years. As this occurred, attention to local problems and local neighborhoods, as well as participation in local as opposed to cosmopolitan communities of knowledge, dwindled and more and more institutions, including independent liberal arts colleges, were pulled into the orbit of the research university.[38]

To a considerable extent, of course, the forces that produced the modern U.S. system of higher education were logical, if not inevitable, counterparts to the rapid and continuously accelerating development of knowledge that has characterized modern industrial society. Since the colonial era, when nine colleges were founded, U.S. higher education has always been remarkable in quantitative terms. The United States has long led the world in the number of colleges and universities it supported and the number of students those institutions enrolled. After World War II, its system of higher education also became outstanding in qualitative terms. Beginning in the 1950s and continuing until today, U.S. colleges and universities have been a magnet for students from many countries. More students choose to come to the United States to study than choose to go to any other nation. By the mid-1970s, the United States also led the world in Nobel prizes and in most world rankings of universities.[39]

In light of all this, the reforms that produced today's colleges and universities must be seen as abundantly successful. They resulted in a system of higher education that is considered preeminent around the globe, and that preeminence should be proudly acknowledged. More than that, at a time when realized and anticipated declines in funding threaten the quality of U.S. research and development activities, ways must be found to protect and enhance the qualities that have made for excellence.

At the same time that we celebrate its stellar achievements, however, we must concede that the U.S. system of higher education faces a number of challenges that are, in a sense, the very obverse of its strengths. Understood as the downside to the positive developments of the last 100 years, these challenges are evident in a number of difficult, and, in the long run, dangerous dilemmas that have arisen as some priorities for higher education have been advanced more effectively than others. By way of example, consider just two.

As historian Thomas Haskell has recently argued, strong disciplines are necessary to the "professional autonomy and collegial self-governance" that is "the heart and soul of academic freedom."[40] The continuous criticism generated through internal disciplinary reviews and peer evaluation processes helps justify the exemption from external regulation and oversight that academic freedom brings. Valuable in maintaining the conditions necessary to free and critical inquiry, disciplines can nevertheless make it difficult to address the problems that exist in the world outside the academy. Problems of health, poverty, or arts support rarely parse themselves along neatly drawn disciplinary lines. If that might suggest the value of cross-disciplinary training or a team approach, actual experience with such remedies indicates that disciplinary knowledge is itself now too specialized and disciplinary thinking too well ingrained to be easily susceptible to cross-disciplinary ventures.[41] For the moment, therefore, we must live with a dilemma. If we want to maintain academic freedom, which has proven value to creative teaching and research, we need disciplines to guarantee standards and rigor; and yet, if we bind ourselves to the distinctive questions and logics of the various disciplines, we may not be able to address the world's most important and complex problems as effectively as we would like to do. Though, on the upside, disciplines foster intense critical interaction within a community of scholars, disciplinary thinking can make it difficult to generate sure links between knowledge and reform.

Another current dilemma with turn-of-the-century origins has to do with expertise. Who could say they were against expertise? And yet, who could not share Dewey and Addams's concern that, in a democracy, expertise must be combined with common access to knowledge. This was what John Gardner was worried about, I think, when he subtitled his book, *Excellence*, with the classic question, "Can we be equal and excellent too?"[42] Whether that dilemma can ever be resolved, at the moment we know much more about how to cultivate expertise than we do about how even to conceive of problems of public education in the broad, not-school-limited sense Dewey often wrote about. Once again, therefore, we live with an impossible choice, this one pertaining to the political consequences of education. Should we acknowledge different levels of education by explicitly countenancing different levels of political enfranchisement, which we now do, but only implicitly; or, regardless of education, should we instead find ways to insist on absolute equality in matters of public deliberation or choice? Neither alternative is desirable, but our current state of educational competence and political imagination has left us with this sorry choice.

What, then, might we do? The challenges implicit in the two dilemmas I have described are hardly unknown, and yet, little that is enduringly and widely effective seems to have been done to address them. Perhaps, therefore, we need more historically self-conscious ways of thinking about the problems and possibilities we face. Because the system we have today emerged from the turn-of-the-century trans- formation of higher education, we may need to return to the choic- es made and patterns set at that time in order to identify ways to redress the imbalances and resulting dilemmas that are a legacy of that era. This would involve taking up where Dewey, Addams, and others of their ilk left off and thinking through questions they never addressed or perhaps even formulated. Central among these, I believe, are questions of technology, strategy, and philosophy.

The questions of technology I have in mind do not necessarily have to do with the Internet, although, someday, it may provide part of an answer. They have to do with inventing new ways for people to communicate well across social distance so that together they can reach common understanding and generate knowledge that may help resolve common problems. It may be, for example, that not only the idea of a college set in one geographic place, but also views of col- lege-going as a predominant preoccupation for a number of years are dated. It may be that liberal learning should be reconceived and redesigned as a constant aspect of adult life. However that may be, the point is that, while sustaining and improving the delivery systems we already have for uncommon learning, for the development of expertise, we need also to invent new delivery systems that will pro- mote engagement in common learning. Whether those delivery sys- tems take the form of new college curricula, new interactive pro- gramming for PBS, new funding for library outreach, new corporate personnel services, or new services to match people with one anoth- er and with educational resources, the goal must be to balance our established capacity to train people for highly skilled occupations with a new capacity to nurture critical and yet collaborative dispositions and habits of mind. Already the stated goal of many institutions, this balance must now be realized in the experience of more people, and for that to happen ways will have to be identified to ask bold ques- tions of technology and institutional redesign in determined, sus- tained, and daily ways.

Closely related to that, efforts to correct historic imbalances in American higher education will require attention to questions of strategy. It is all well and good to suggest that common learning must assume a priority equal to uncommon learning, but we live in a world full of hierarchies that are built on credentials and standards, most of which reflect choices and values that encourage excellence at the expense of equality. In addition, we live in a world where it is impossible to separate the higher education system from business, the professions, the military, government, and any number of other "systems." That makes it very difficult to initiate fundamental, systemic change. Given how difficult it is merely to change a college curriculum, which, relative to changing the balance among the purposes of higher education, is barely tinkering at the margins, it is hard even to imagine how one might go about the kind of truly radical change that would be necessary if liberal education were to be reconceived as a means to promote problem-centered ways of thinking and to better combine those with discipline-based styles of thought.

In recent years, any number of scholars have turned their attention to the reform of undergraduate education and some have advanced plans that build on the ideas of earlier advocates of pragmatic approaches to liberal education. Charles W. Anderson did this in the curriculum he described for instilling what he called "practical reason," and so did Kenneth A. Bruffee in his analysis of collaborative constructivist learning.[43] In addition, there have been some extremely interesting experiments with new curricula, for example, those associated with the cross-discipline faculty workshop and experimental seminars initiated with Andrew W. Mellon Foundation support at Syracuse University in the middle 1980s.[44] Thinking strategically, the question is, assuming there is value in such problem-centered, pragmatic approaches to liberal learning, how can discrete, somewhat different, and yet essentially compatible proposals and experiments be reviewed, criticized, revised, and perhaps synthesized, and then, how could the resulting ideas be translated into experiments that could illuminate not only the pros and cons of the plans being tested, but also the implications those plans would have for further, related changes in professional standards, business practices, government regulations, and the like.

Doubtless, there are many committees, commissions, and study groups already considering such questions. But the burden of my argument is that isolated, intermittent efforts, however creative, will not be sufficient to the challenge. Indeed, ways need to be found to make the recalibration of U.S. higher education a central, shared interest of the nation's colleges and universities. As silly, not to mention impracticable, as it may sound, there might be value in thinking through how such institutions could imitate the town of Farmington, Connecticut, which sponsored a month-long "television turn off" some years ago to protest excessive TV watching and insufficient reading and conversation. What would happen if a college stopped its business as usual for a week to study and debate what it was doing and why it mattered?

Whether such a scheme could have merit, questions of strategy and of technology will need to be combined with questions of philosophy—or perhaps I should say politics—if the difficult dilemmas facing U.S. higher education are to receive not only the persistent, but also the honest, and even soul-searching, attention they require. Do we really want to see ourselves and to be seen as equal to our neighbors? Do we really want to educate all young people to be fully and equally enfranchised citizens, or, in the end, do we want to train them for the world that exists? Do we want to liberate with all that could suggest for independent thought and even social change, or do we merely want to "furnish and discipline" young minds? Do we really want to "work" on problems of poverty, or are we content merely to study them?

These questions are no more rhetorical in the United States today than they were at the time the modern system of U.S. higher education came into being. And along with questions of technology and strategy, philosophical questions of the kind posed above are important today. They will have to be debated honestly and fundamentally, if the possibilities for democracy and common learning that were at least glimpsed by progressives such as Dewey and Addams are to be recovered and combined with the beliefs and practices of reformers such as Charles Eliot and Walter Lippmann. To advance pragmatic approaches to liberal education, many people will have to engage in pragmatic liberal education. Finding ways not merely to talk about that, but, more important, to translate more balanced priorities into the lived purposes and practices of colleges, universities, and the surrounding institutions with which they interact may seem like a daunting task. And it is. But, if ways can be found to collaborate for that purpose, the preeminence already achieved by U.S. colleges and universities will be sustained and enhanced. Understood that way, the challenge is no larger than the gains to be had.

Notes

1. John Dewey, "Liberal Education" [1912–13], in Jo Ann Boydston, editor, *John Dewey: The Middle Works, 1899–1924*, Volume 1 (Carbondale: Southern Illinois University Press, 1976–83), 274.
2. John Dewey, "The Problem of the Liberal Arts College" [1944], in Jo Ann Boydston, editor, *John Dewey: The Later Works, 1925–1953*, Volume 15 (Carbondale: Southern Illinois University Press, 1981–90), 278.
3. John Dewey, "The Prospects of the Liberal College" [1924], in *Middle Works*, Volume 15, 201.
4. John Dewey, "Statement to the Conference on Curriculum for the College of Liberal Arts," in *Later Works*, Volume 6, 415.
5. Robert B. Westbrook's biography, *John Dewey and American Democracy* (Ithaca, NY: Cornell University Press, 1991) remains the best overall portrait; Andrew Feffer, *The Chicago Pragmatists and American Progressivism* (Ithaca, NY: Cornell University Press, 1993) describes the community of thinkers in which Dewey as well as Jane Addams were situated in Chicago.
6. John Dewey, *The School and Society* [1899], in *Middle Works*, Volume 1, 3–109; and *Democracy and Education* [1916], in *Middle Works*, Volume 9. Dewey's philosophy of education can also be gleaned from Katherine Camp Mayhew and Anna Camp Edwards, *The Dewey School* (New York: D. Appleton–Century, 1936).
7. John Dewey, *Experience and Education* [1938], in *Later Works*, Volume 13, 1–62.
8. Arthur Zilversmit, *Changing Schools: Progressive Education Theory and Practice, 1930–1960* (Chicago: University of Chicago Press, 1993), 20, 167, and passim; Peter L. Buttenweiser, "Unfulfilled Dreams: Thoughts on Progressive Education and the New York City Schools, 1900–1978," in Diane Ravitch and Ronald K. Goodenow, editors, *Educating an Urban People: The New York City Experience* (New York: Teachers College Press, 1981), 171–86.
9. Ellen Condliffe Lagemann, "The Plural Worlds of Educational Research," *History of Education Quarterly* (Summer 1989), 186–214.
10. Larry Cuban, *How Teachers Taught: Constancy and Change in American Classrooms, 1890–1980* (New York: Longman, 1984).
11. Charlene Haddock Seigfried, *Pragmatism and Feminism: Reweaving the Social Fabric* (Chicago: University of Chicago Press, 1996).

12. Jean Bethke Elshtain, "Civic Identity and the State: From Hegel to Jane Addams . . . and Beyond," in Michael Brint and William Weaver, editors, *Pragmatism in Law and Society* (Boulder, CO: Westview Press, 1991), 190.
13. Jane Addams, *The Second Twenty Years at Hull House* (New York: Macmillan, 1930), chap. 12.
14. Jane Addams, "Moral and Legal Protection for Children," in Ellen Condliffe Lagemann, editor, *Jane Addams on Education* (New York: Teachers College Press, 1985), 203, 205.
15. Jane Addams, "Socialized Education," in ibid., 176.
16. Ibid., 174, 175.
17. Judith Ann Trolander, *Professionalism and Social Change: From the Settlement House Movement to Neighborhood Centers, 1886 to the Present* (New York: Columbia University Press, 1987).
18. Mary Jo Deegan, *Jane Addams and the Men of the Chicago School, 1892–1918* (New Brunswick, NJ: Transaction Books, 1988).
19. Ellen Condliffe Lagemann, "The Challenge of Jane Addams: A Research Note," *History of Higher Education Annual* 6 (1986): 51–61.
20. Burton R. Clark, *The Academic Life: Small Worlds, Different Worlds* (Princeton, NJ: Carnegie Foundation for the Advancement of Teaching, 1987), chap. 2.
21. John Dewey, "School and Society," in *Middle Works*, Volume 1, 39–56; Ellen Condliffe Lagemann, "Experimenting with Education: John Dewey and Ella Flagg Young at the University of Chicago," *American Journal of Education* (May 1996) 171–85.
22. Ellen Condliffe Lagemann, "Contested Terrain: A History of Education Research in the United States, 1890–1990," An Essay for the Twenty-Fifth Anniversary of the Spencer Foundation (Chicago: Spencer Foundation, 1996).
23. Edward L. Thorndike, "Quantitative Investigations in Education: With Special Reference to Co-operation within this Association," in Ellwood P. Cubberley, et al., editors, *Research within the Field of Education, Its Organization and Encouragement* (School Review Monograph #1; Chicago: University of Chicago Press, 1910), 35.
24. Lagemann, "Plural Worlds of Educational Research," 204–10.
25. Joseph F. Kett, *The Pursuit of Knowledge under Difficulties: From Self-Improvement to Adult Education in America, 1750–1990* (Stanford, CA: Stanford University Press, 1994), esp. chap. 6.
26. Charles W. Eliot, "The Function of Education in a Democratic Society," in *Educational Reform: Essays and Addresses* (New York: Century, 1898), 401–18.
27. Quoted in Hugh Hawkins, *Between Harvard and America: The Educational Leadership of Charles W. Eliot* (New York: Oxford University Press, 1971), 144.
28. The quotes are from ibid., 159, 290.
29. Hugh Hawkins, *Banding Together: The Rise of National Associations in American Higher Education, 1887–1950* (Baltimore: Johns Hopkins University Press, 1992) describes the full universe of organizations.
30. Quoted in Ellen Condliffe Lagemann, *Private Power for the Public Good: A History of the Carnegie Foundation for the Advancement of Teaching* (Middletown, CT: Wesleyan University Press, 1983), 37–38.

31. Although he does not focus on the Carnegie Foundation, David O. Levine, *The American College and the Culture of Aspiration, 1915–1940* (Ithaca, NY: Cornell University Press, 1986), provides an excellent account of this.
32. Hawkins, *Between Harvard and America*, chap. 5, and W.B. Carnochan, *The Battleground of the Curriculum: Liberal Education and American Experience* (Stanford, CA: Stanford University Press, 1993), chap. 2.
33. Quoted in Hawkins, *Between Harvard and America*, 146.
34. John Dewey, "Review of *Public Opinion*" [1922], in *Middle Works*, Volume 13, 344.
35. There is a rich literature on this subject, two rather different recent examples being George M. Marsden, *The Soul of the American University: From Protestant Establishment to Established Nonbelief* (New York: Oxford University Press, 1994) and Julie A. Reuben, *The Making of the Modern University: Intellectual Transformation and the Marginalization of Morality* (Chicago: University of Chicago Press, 1996).
36. Quoted in Douglas Sloan, "The Teaching of Ethics in the American Undergraduate Curriculum, 1876–1976," in Daniel Callahan and Sissela Bok, editors, *Ethics Teaching in Higher Education* (New York: Plenum, 1980), 17.
37. Ibid., 19.
38. Hugh Davis Graham and Nancy Diamond, *The Rise of American Research Universities: Ethics and Challengers in the Postwar Era* (Baltimore: Johns Hopkins University Press, 1997), chaps. 1 and 2. In briefer compass, this story is also presented in Thomas Bender, "Politics, Intellect, and the American University, 1945–1995," *Daedalus*, Winter 1997, forthcoming.
39. Graham and Diamond, *Rise of American Research Universities*, 9–10. For an earlier positive appraisal see *Three Thousand Futures. The Final Report of the Carnegie Council on Policy Studies in Higher Education* (San Francisco: Jossey-Bass, 1980).
40. Thomas L. Haskell, "Justifying the Rights of Academic Freedom in the Era of Power/Knowledge," in Louis Menand, editor, *The Future of Academic Freedom* (Chicago: University of Chicago Press, 1996), 54.
41. David Easton, "The Division, Integration, and Transfer of Knowledge," in David Easton and Corinne S. Schelling, editors, *Divided Knowledge: Across Disciplines, Across Cultures* (Newbury Park, CA: Sage Publications, 1991), 7–36.
42. John W. Gardner, *Excellence: Can We Be Equal and Excellent Too?* (New York: Harper, 1961).
43. Charles W. Anderson, *Prescribing the Life of the Mind: An Essay on the Purposes of the University, the Aims of Liberal Education, the Competence of Citizens, and the Cultivation of Practical Reason* (Madison: University of Wisconsin Press, 1993); Kenneth A. Bruffee, *Collaborative Learning: Higher Education, Interdependence, and the Authority of Knowledge* (Baltimore: Johns Hopkins University Press, 1993).
44. Peter T. Marsh, ed., *Contesting the Boundaries of Liberal and Professional Education: The Syracuse Experiment* (Syracuse, NY: Syracuse University Press, 1988).

Naming Pragmatic Liberal Education

BRUCE A. KIMBALL

PROFESSOR, WARNER GRADUATE SCHOOL
OF EDUCATION, UNIVERSITY OF ROCHESTER

Editor's note: The following paper is Bruce Kimball's rejoinder to responses addressed to his 1995 essay entitled "Toward Pragmatic Liberal Education." Both the original essay and the responses are printed in Robert Orrill, executive editor, The Condition of American Liberal Education: Pragmatism and a Changing Tradition *(New York: College Entrance Examination Board, 1995).*

In the pages that follow, I intend to reconsider and extend the argument that I made in an essay, "Toward Pragmatic Liberal Education."[1] In the precise summary of Thomas Green, that essay "describes a situation and the elements of a consensus in response to that situation, and then . . . gives that consensus a name."[2] This approach of heuristic naming, which I adopted as well in my history of liberal education,[3] aptly conveys the nature of my proposal that, at the end of the twentieth century, the liberal arts in the United States are moving toward a conception that can reasonably be called "pragmatic liberal education."

In this paper, I would like to do three things. First, I wish to restate my argument while adverting to some of the original responses and other commentary that have appeared. Part of the intention here is to explain myself in view of these interpretations. Second, I wish to consider why this argument about liberal education, which I still find persuasive, has been regarded by a number of respondents and reviewers as not only unpersuasive but rather implausible or, if plausible, fairly repugnant. Another way of posing this was stated by Rita Born-

stein, when she first spoke with me about holding a colloquy that would
recall the 1931 Rollins College conference on liberal education that
was chaired by John Dewey. President Bornstein wondered why it was
that many academics seem to like pragmatic ideas, but avoid associating themselves with pragmatism at all costs. The third issue to be
addressed is to explain why any of this matters. "What difference does
it make if you're right or not?" as a college president asked me after
a recent talk I gave on pragmatic liberal education. I ought to start
with this question perhaps, because my first two points presuppose
that the discussion will make a difference to someone in some way.

I

The question of what difference it makes echoes the famous query
posed by William James in his 1907 work *Pragmatism*. To ascertain the
meaning of any notion, James said that one should ask: "What difference would it practically make to anyone if this notion rather than
that notion were true?" This question requires us, in James's words,
"to interpret each notion by tracing its respective consequences";[4]
and the consequences, as I conceive them, of my proposal about pragmatic liberal education are that, if I am correct, then certain changes
that we are seeing now in liberal education will likely endure. They
are not ephemeral shifts that will soon pass away. These consequences
follow from the fact that the changes are being legitimated by a sophisticated, philosophical rationale that is historically grounded in this
culture.

   To put the matter conversely, I would say that if I am wrong—if
the recent changes are ephemeral responses to adventitious economic
or demographic forces (as they are often portrayed), or if the recent
changes can be rationalized by German idealism or French existentialism, as two respondents to the original essay maintained[5]—then
the recent proposals and modifications in liberal education offer little or no indication about what might be coming in the next decade
or even next year. But if we are seeing changes in liberal education
converging with a sophisticated, philosophical rationale that is historically grounded in American culture, then it follows that the changes

are likely to persevere for some time. This is what is at stake; this is what matters. Whatever their immediate stimuli and origins, the changes in liberal education are likely to endure if pragmatism is providing a principled rationale and legitimation; and I turn now to reconsider this proposal, which was the central argument of my original essay.

That argument about pragmatic liberal education is founded on three basic propositions. The first, which I call here the "consensus thesis," maintains that a consensus is emerging around some seven points in discussion about liberal education in the United States. These seven points are that liberal education should

- first, become multicultural;
- second, elevate general education and integration, rather than specialization;
- third, promote the commonweal and citizenship;
- fourth, regard all "levels" of education as belonging to a common enterprise;
- fifth, reconceive teaching as stimulating learning and inquiry;
- sixth, promote the formation of values and the practice of service;
- seventh, employ assessment.

The second proposition of my argument—called here the "warrant thesis"—maintains that there is some philosophy or theory or metarationale that makes coherent and thereby legitimates the emergent consensus. In short, there is some rationale that warrants the consensus. The third proposition—the "pragmatism thesis"—proposes that pragmatism is this metarationale, that pragmatism is now, for the first time, converging with liberal education.

II

I do not want to say much more about the seven individual points, aside from observing that greater attention should perhaps have been given to interdisciplinarity, as Julie Thompson Klein, Louis Menand, and George Shields have urged.[6] What I wish to address

briefly here is why a number of readers have been unpersuaded by
the consensus thesis.[7]

One kind of objection stems from regarding the consensus as a
universalization that admits no exceptions, rather than a generalization or approximation, much as one might say that today there is a
consensus in the United States that the health care system should be
reformed. Asserting this does not deny exceptions. Hence, responses pointing out that Rush Limbaugh would disagree or that "higher
education in this country is hardly monolithic" deny the claim by
exaggerating it.[8] The sense I had in mind is expressed in Arturo
Madrid's observation, "Multiculturalism, although under severe attack,
has been affirmed on most U.S. campuses." Madrid proceeds to grant
five of the seven points. This is the kind of approximating judgment
that the consensus thesis involves.[9]

Thus, the consensus thesis is an inductive generalization drawn
from the evidence about the discussion and practice of what is currently called "liberal education." It is not the result either of an "earnest
desire" for a consensus, or of a "search" for a consensus.[10] Rather, the
consensus thesis intends to describe what is actually happening; and
this starting point is in sympathy with Green's, Carnochan's, and pragmatists' suspicion of "deductively generated programs"[11] that begin
with principles and elegantly infer their implications.[12] The validation
for the consensus thesis therefore lies in the evidence of the discussion and practice of liberal education.

Another challenge to the thesis lies in distinguishing between
opinion and practice. In the words of Richard M. Freeland, "it is far
from clear that most [of the seven points] have gained significant
acceptance at the operational level within the academy."[13] This "operational objection" seems excessively stringent, however. After all,
most would agree that there is a consensus on the need to reform
the health care system in the country, notwithstanding the fact that
it has not "gained significant acceptance at the operational level"
within hospitals.[14]

Beyond these rejoinders, what requires emphasis here is that the
consensus thesis presumes a long historical process. My original essay
refers to the century-long battle over the reformulation of the liber-

al arts, in line with Aristotelian philosophy, that occurred in the medieval universities and then persevered for the next 400 years. The consensus over the convergence of the liberal arts and Aristotelian philosophy, to which Robert M. Hutchins said he wished to return at the University of Chicago, was statutorily adopted at the University of Paris in the year 1255. However, it is important to observe that in 1210 and 1215 the liberal arts faculty at Paris was expressly prohibited from teaching the major texts of Aristotle or commentaries upon these works.[15] Consequently, the convergence between the liberal arts and Aristotle was worked out slowly and fitfully over nearly a century, beginning in the late 1100s.

This struggle tends to be forgotten or minimized by those looking back from a much later time, as we do today. We tend to be more impressed by the dominance during the subsequent four centuries of the Aristotelian-Scholastic formulation of the liberal arts. As a result, there seems to arise an unstated assumption that the emergence of a consensus around a formulation of the liberal arts occurs fairly rapidly and unanimously. This unstated assumption underlies many objections to the consensus thesis, and it must be emphasized here that the putative consensus has emerged in the course of a century-long process of transformation that proceeds at different rates in different communities and includes false starts and retrenchments along the way. This point can be seen by recalling briefly the context of Charles W. Eliot's paper "What is a Liberal Education?" (1884), which anticipates several important changes in liberal education appearing over the next century.

Writing as the president of Harvard University, Eliot himself discusses how "some of the studies now commonly called liberal, have not long held their present preeminence; and . . . . new learning has repeatedly forced its way, in times past, to full academic standing, in spite of the opposition . . . of established teachers and learned bodies."[16] Eliot's account of the contentious process whereby "new" sciences have cyclically displaced established disciplines within the liberal arts applies to the subsequent fortunes of his own proposals, which took the first major step away from curricular prescription based upon a belief in monocultural preeminence.[17] It was this step,

I believe, that led eventually to a consensus around the idea of multiculturalism in liberal education, but it took a century to unfold.

Eliot's step away from monocultural preeminence was taken far out of the mainstream of liberal education of his time.[18] In the 1890s, the leaders of Catholic colleges and universities, particularly the Jesuits, loudly challenged the expansion both of the canon and of curricular choice in liberal education.[19] A decade later, W.E.B. du Bois, who was then serving at the N.A.A.C.P., and Professor Augustus Dill of Atlanta University published their study of African-American colleges in the United States. This study called for expanding choice in modern subjects and reducing the curricular requirements in Greek and Latin that still held fast in African-American colleges.[20] Also at that time, A. L. Lowell succeeded Eliot as president of Harvard with the charge to pull the university back from the excesses that Eliot had introduced.

Meanwhile, Princeton President James McCosh had made a pointed response to Eliot's conception of liberal education. Lamenting Eliot's departure from requiring classical studies for a liberal arts degree, President McCosh expressed great frustration that Harvard's prominence provided Eliot such a bully pulpit for his outlandish ideas.[21] McCosh's belief that Eliot was a renegade was, in fact, the common view of the time.[22] McCosh's most fervent complaint against Eliot's expansion both of the canon and of curricular choice was that Harvard was fostering what McCosh called "dilettanti courses" pitched "down to the level of those . . . who do not wish to study deeply or study hard." Among the "dilettanti courses" that McCosh identified were botany; seventeenth-, eighteenth-, and nineteenth-century French literature; medieval history; and modern European history.[23]

Coincidentally, medieval history was the course of study that Henry Adams had been appointed to establish at Harvard, in line with Eliot's vision of a university devoted to rigorous, free, and scientific inquiry. Now, I suggest that very few professors today, when confronted by an advisee saying that she wanted to study medieval history with Henry Adams, would respond by shaking a finger and saying: "As long as I am your academic adviser, you are not going to escape from the tough part of the curriculum into such facile dilettantism." Instead, we seem far more likely to agree that there are many paths up the mountain, indeed, that there are many mountains to climb, from which the view is equally breathtaking. In short, we are agreed on multiculturalism, whether that means offering courses or programs addressing a range of cultures or requiring all students to be exposed to different cultures.

To be sure, attacks upon multiculturalism can still be found amid what Robert Orrill appropriately called the "literature of lamentation" regarding higher education.[24] Prominent among these attacks is the recent jeremiad against multiculturalism by Robert Bork.[25] Meanwhile, leading figures in the academic establishment, such as the dean of Yale College, caution that multiculturalism can lead to superficiality, just as McCosh did, although the Yale dean today refers not to "dilettantism" but to the "Epcotization" of the study of culture.[26] Nevertheless, the Yale dean today makes this warning as a qualification upon his enthusiastic endorsement of multiculturalism. In fact, general agreement on multiculturalism has been noted by another leading figure and keen observer of higher education, Francis Oakley.[27]

The relative consensus existing today that liberal education should be multicultural becomes apparent if one looks at developments over the course of a century. To be sure, the process occurred at different rates in different communities and involved false starts and retrenchments at various points. The overall pattern, however, indicates that curricular prescription based on a belief in monocultural preeminence began to break down in the 1870s and 1880s, when Charles Eliot served as an important spokesman. That belief gave way, at first gradually and then with increasing rapidity in the 1980s, to the view that multiculturalism is a tenet of liberal education. It is only one of the seven points enumerated in the consensus thesis, but the other six points likewise presuppose a long unfolding over time.[28]

III

The second thesis in the argument about "pragmatic liberal education" is what I am calling here the warrant thesis: the proposition that there is some philosophy or theory or metarationale that makes coherent and thereby legitimates the emergent consensus. In short, there is some rationale that warrants the consensus. Some commentators have asked why it is necessary or worthwhile to ask about the rationale for the emerging consensus.[29] My response is that of a philosopher in the liberal arts tradition who replies to orators' derogation of supposedly esoteric theorizing. Though a quotidian philosopher at best, I shall try.

One intrinsic reason for asking this question is simply to explain why the consensus is occurring, in a principled sense. Observers have noted that the American Association of State Colleges and Universities and the New American Colleges endorse most of the seven points enumerated above;[30] and knowing why these groups believe these points are right can help us to understand what is happening in liberal education today. But if we think again in terms of the consequences of the idea—about what difference it makes—then I would say that the primary reason for identifying a fitting rationale is that it is valuable to establish and understand the intellectual legitimacy of liberal education. After all, liberal education is expected to have some principled basis, notwithstanding the shaping influence exercised by the often discussed "social forces" of economy and demography.[31] When colleges and universities design a program of liberal education, we expect them to have some sense of conviction, even rightness, about it, which is not to say that eternal verities are required.

So, when colleges say that liberal education should integrate theory and practice, we expect them to have some justification for saying this beyond the latest announcement of downsizing at IBM. When colleges start responding to the state of the economy just as Wall Street stockbrokers respond to the nuances in Alan Greenspan's latest intimations about interest rates, then liberal education will start jumping around like the Dow Jones Average and the whole legitimacy of the enterprise will become suspect.[32] By the same token, the other frequently mentioned social force, changing demography, is also an important influence prompting change. But here, too, the often-heard arguments about changing birth rates or immigration patterns do not provide a principled warrant for the diversification of the curriculum and teaching methods. Surely, advocates of multiculturalism do not want to say that the reason to read Toni Morrison declines if demographic patterns reverse. Hence, we need to ask about the nature and source of the principled legitimacy for liberal education.

The warrant thesis proposes, then, that we should try to name "the ambient fluid" that surrounds liberal education—to use the insightful metaphor of Louis Menand in his original response to my essay.[33] And since the ambient fluid supports and sustains liberal education, we will inform ourselves about our situation if we understand the nature of that ambient fluid. To do this heuristic naming requires a method of assessing fit between the consensus and the philosophy, or metarationale, and a brief discussion of this method is required here because the doubts of a number of respondents to my argument derive from objections in this regard.[34]

One kind of objection stems from holding that only invocations of pragmatists in programs of liberal education can demonstrate the influence of a theory upon the consensus.[35] The problem with this criterion is that it is neither necessary nor sufficient. Direct knowledge of a theorist's ideas is not necessary for influence, because those ideas could be mediated by other thinkers and combined with elements of other doctrines. Surely no one would say that the intellectual influence of Darwin or Marx is limited to those who know—presumably could describe—Darwin's or Marx's position on a topic. Furthermore, knowledge of a theorist's ideas is not sufficient to demonstrate influence, because it leaves gaps between theory and practice and institutionalization. The countervailing currents in the historiography addressing the influence of progressive education demonstrate this point.[36] Given that intellectual influence is often indirect and complicated by extraneous doctrine, congruence between a theorist's ideas and the discussion and practice of liberal education is no less significant than direct citation of authors and texts.

A second kind of objection arises from disaggregating the putative consensus and showing that a given point might just as well fit a variety of metarationales or philosophies.[37] But the conceptual challenge is clearly to ask what foundational theory might warrant these points taken together, not considered individually. The associated task is to ask what historical metarationales would likely serve to rationalize and legitimate liberal education, given our situation. These conceptual and historical criteria lead to questions such as: which is most likely to name or warrant the ambient fluid surrounding liberal education in the United States in the 1990s: French existentialism, German idealism, or resurgent American pragmatism? Hence, the method of fitting is more complex than the disaggregating critique seems to appreciate.

IV

If one grants the first proposition, that a consensus is emerging around certain points in American liberal education, and the second proposition, that it is necessary and valuable to consider whether a meta-rationale warrants that consensus, then we arrive at the third proposition. This is the "pragmatism thesis," holding that pragmatism is now, for the first time, converging with liberal education. In other words, the legitimating rationale for the emerging consensus is the resurgent and now "ubiquitous" pragmatism, as James Kloppenberg has termed it.[38] Here again, rather than repeating what is said in the original essay, I wish to address the primary challenges to this pragmatism thesis, which have compelled me to rethink my views and try to explain myself more clearly.

On the one hand, there is the question of how well my general account of pragmatism actually fits the pragmatists. David Steiner and Eva Brann, for example, have each applied a philosopher's acuity (via a kind of Zeno's paradox) to suggest that the move from the texts of pragmatists to my general account of pragmatism is reductive. Their point is not so much to dispute the "pragmatism thesis" as to challenge the interpretation of pragmatism represented there.[39] Thus, Brann suggests that my general account of pragmatism "is an aggregate that is less than the original parts, and . . . exists in a mist in which all cats are grey."[40] As an alternative, Steiner calls for plumbing the sources of the movement to reach "depth pragmatism," and Brann requests the "intended meaning" of "individual authors."[41] My reply here is basically that of an orator in the liberal education tradition who responds to philosophical derogation of useful approximation.

The philosophers' objection would apply to virtually any account of any "ism," whether pragmatism, Marxism, Platonism, or Buddhism. One doubts whether any of the general accounts of the "characteristics," "themes," "maxims," "common features," "sloganistic characterizations," and "elements" of pragmatism would satisfy them.[42] As in Zeno's paradoxes, Achilles can never outrun the tortoise, because the act of generalization and abstraction, upon which an account of any "ism" must depend, never reaches the "depth" or "intended meaning." And in all of these cases, we need to be able to speak generally because there is something between the depth of intended meaning of the individual author and the institution or behavior to which it is said to correspond.

Conversely, the alternative of focusing on "depth pragmatism" or "the intended meaning" of "individual authors" leads to the abyss of figuring out what Dewey really said, or meant to say, in his 40-odd books and 800 articles, and what Peirce did mean, or intended to mean, in the collage of his collected works. Commentators have labored for decades to explain precisely what Peirce and Dewey meant either separately or taken together, yet the commentators still do not agree. Thus, the intended meaning of individual authors appears to be no less misty and grey than a general account of pragmatism. Conversely, the general account of pragmatism is at least a useful approximation or "a recognizable opinion scheme, a definable intellectual atmosphere," as Brann has termed it.[43]

Another primary challenge to the pragmatism thesis has come from a variety of commentators who have understood me to say that pragmatism *caused* the recent developments in liberal education.[44] In reflecting upon this interpretation, I have come to appreciate the statement of Edward Royce of Rollins College that I did "not examine explicitly or in much detail how . . . pragmatism . . . [came to] be connected to liberal education" at the present time.[45] I will try here to address this connection between the theory and the liberal arts by recalling once again the reformulation of liberal education that occurred in the high middle ages.

In the thirteenth century, Aristotle provided a powerful conceptual scheme for reorganizing both knowledge and the liberal arts curriculum; and Aristotle was quoted and cited repeatedly as "the master of them that know." Nevertheless, we would not say that Aristotle caused the Scholastic formulation of the liberal arts. For one thing, this formulation is not entirely Aristotelian; the Scholastics creatively modified and adapted his framework. For another, the Scholastics fought about it; they did not simply capitulate to the Aristotelians. After all, careers and reputations were at stake.

Finally, the thirteenth-century reformulation was preceded by the expansion of international trade that produced new wealth in Western Europe in the 1100s. This new wealth, as well as the subsiding of invasions and migrations, allowed for the incorporation of cities and the invention of a new kind of corporation, the guild or union of students and teaching masters. Meanwhile, an influx of new learning in fields such as mathematics and optics had led Dominicans in the mid-thirteenth century to the conclusion expressed by Thomas Aquinas in the 1250s: "the [traditional] liberal arts are no longer sufficient to categorize knowledge."[46]

Consequently, it was the economic renewal, the social conditions, the political arrangements, the professional interests, and the intellectual changes that provided the context within which it was not only possible, but necessary to reconceive liberal education. Given this, it would be no more justified to conclude that the Scholastics read Aristotle's *Metaphysics* and suddenly agreed to change their inherited liberal arts, than it would be to say that U.S. academics in the late twentieth century picked up John Dewey and suddenly saw the error of their liberal education. But what can be said is that Aristotle provided a sophisticated, philosophical rationale that—having been admired in Europe for centuries—was historically grounded in the culture. What Aristotle therefore provided was not so much a cause, as a way of coherently comprehending the old and the new in the liberal arts and making the reformulation legitimate—due both to the intellectual coherence of his philosophy and to the pedigree that his work carried.[47]

Without drawing any historical analogies, I am suggesting that the connection between a philosophy and the liberal arts is not a matter of simple causality. By proposing the emergence of pragmatic liberal education, I mean that a sophisticated philosophical rationale that is historically grounded in American culture "fits"—makes coherent—a set of points in liberal education that have arisen as a result of a variety of adventitious economic and social forces as well as intellectual imperatives.

V

Through these clarifications, I hope to have explained why I continue to believe that the general argument is persuasive. It may be the case, as some of the original respondents to the essay suggested, that Hegel or Sartre would do just as well as Dewey in making coherent the changes in liberal education in the United States at the end of the twentieth century.[48] But I think not. It seems to me that there is evidence and good reason to conclude that we have been and are participating in a fundamental shift in the meaning of liberal education that is deeply connected in some way to the resurgence and ubiquity of pragmatism.

At the very least, I think that this thesis is eminently plausible. Thus, to argue the matter a different way, I would like to conclude by suggesting some contextual reasons that this proposed connection between liberal education and pragmatism may strike some academics as implausible. This last inquiry is related to the question posed at the outset by Rollins College President Bornstein: why is it that many academics seem to like pragmatic ideas, but they will avoid endorsing pragmatism at all costs?[49] An explanation for this paradox may lie in two subliminal ironies, stemming from the professional aspirations of the professoriate, particularly those at research universities.

The emergence of pragmatic liberal education naturally requires that U.S. academics would find such merit in pragmatism that it would influence how they define liberal education. And finding merit in pragmatism presupposes that U.S. academics would be willing to see value in American intellectual traditions and resources. Consequently, the emergence of pragmatic liberal education requires the independence of U.S. academic culture from the historical dominance of the European. This independence of U.S. academics began to appear first in the natural sciences early in this century but developed much more slowly in the humanities and social sciences. Menand recently described the matter perfectly when he stated: "Mine was the first generation of American intellectuals who had no interest in European culture . . . . America was where culture was happening."[50] His statement expresses a precondition and stimulus for pragmatic liberal education.

Two ironies arise here, because this intellectual independence implies strengthening professional autonomy and boundaries, which contravenes pragmatism in two ways. On the one hand, the strengthened professional autonomy of the professoriate contravenes the pragmatic tendency to cross professional boundaries. Thus, increasing professional autonomy is required for U.S. academics to acknowledge and attend to this American intellectual tradition, but what they encounter in that tradition is a way of thinking that tends to weaken professional autonomy and boundaries. On the other hand, the increasing professional autonomy of the professoriate reinforces the historical distinction between schooling and higher education, and this distinction also contravenes pragmatism. Thus, the professionalization of the professoriate implies an invidious distinction between higher and lower education, whereas pragmatism implies pulling the universities and schools together.

In regard to this twofold irony, it is worth noting that William James and John Dewey were professional boundary crossers, while Charles Peirce was a professional failure. It should also be observed that both the boundary crossing and the association of higher and lower education appear most clearly in Deweyan pragmatism, so it is not surprising that Dewey appears to be the least palatable of the pragmatists to the U.S. professoriate.

My point that professional interest contributes to suspicion of pragmatism is consonant with Stanley Katz's recent observation that "disciplinary departments have functioned as intellectually conservative forces in the development of knowledge, and my question is how we can . . . find ways to clarify and dignify our roles if we are to flourish intellectually in America's persistent struggle between professionalism and democracy."[51] Katz here echoes the point made in the published report of the 1931 Rollins College Conference. Employing a charming metaphor, the conferees, chaired by Dewey, wrote as follows in 1931: "The present departmental organization of colleges . . . in[to] sterile compartments . . . is to be condemned. As in many long-cultivated agricultural areas of America, the most fertile soils are now found in the old fence-rows."[52]

The invidious isolation created by disciplinary and professional organization underlies the twofold irony that appears to explain the paradoxical relationship between pragmatism and the U.S. professoriate, as was identified by Bornstein. And it is worth noting that this invidious isolation is most pronounced at research universities.

In fine, I would say that the relationship between the professoriate and U.S. culture, on the one hand, and the relationship between higher and K–12 education, on the other, are deeply connected to the question of whether pragmatism and liberal education are now converging. My proposal about "pragmatic liberal education" entails the corollaries that these other two relationships are also being transformed: that the professoriate is becoming more closely connected to U.S. culture and that higher education is becoming linked with the schools or, at least, we are *recognizing* that it should be. The emergence of "pragmatic liberal education" is one philosophically sophisticated and historically grounded response to the widely voiced call to make academe connect to culture and to schooling in the United States. It seems to me that there is no better place to respond to this call than at Rollins College where John Dewey gave personal testimony of the relevance of his ideas for liberal education.[53]

Notes

1. "Toward Pragmatic Liberal Education," in Robert Orrill, editor, *The Condition of American Liberal Education* (New York: College Entrance Examination Board, 1995), xxi–122, hereafter referred to as *Condition*.
2. Thomas F. Green, "Needed: A Pedagogy Please!" in *Condition*, 238.
3. This is discussed in "Toward Pragmatic Liberal Education," 11–15. See *Orators and Philosophers: A History of the Idea of Liberal Education* (New York: College Entrance Examination Board, 1995).
4. William James, *Pragmatism: A New Name for Some Old Ways of Thinking* (1907; New York: Longmans, Green, 1925), 46–47.

5. Edmund W. Gordon, "Response to Bruce Kimball's 'Toward Pragmatic Liberal Education,'" 190; Robert B. Westbrook, "Wishful Thinking: On the Convergence of Pragmatism and Liberal Education," 229, *Condition.*
6. Julie Thompson Klein, "Knowledge, America, and Liberal Education," 145–50; Louis Menand, "Marketing Postmodernism," 142, *Condition;* George W. Shields, "Pragmatism, Interdisciplinarity, and Liberal Education . . . [review essay]," *Association for Integrative Studies Newsletter* 18 (October 1996), 8. Interdisciplinarity was included as a separate point in a draft of my list of points in the consensus, but I removed it, thinking that I could not yet say that there was a consensus around the virtue of interdisciplinarity, for it seemed that most academics are still securely entrenched within their disciplines.
7. In essays in *The Condition of American Liberal Education,* Francis Oakley is judiciously "agnostic" ("Historical Perspective and Our Current Educational Discontents," 136), Stanley N. Katz is "less sure" ("Possibilities for Remaking Liberal Education at the Century's End," 129), and Alan Ryan finds it outright "implausible" ("No Consensus in Sight," 245). The response to the consensus thesis also seems to vary with the perspective and context of the observer. Most of the original respondents who were doubtful of the consensus thesis work at institutions in the "top" 10 percent of the more than 3,000 postsecondary institutions in the country. Those tending to be persuaded by the consensus thesis come from the other 90 percent or from national associations or programs whose membership includes many from this sector. The correlation is not perfect, but still significant. While noting "that there are few contributors to this volume from the public sector," June K. Phillips of Weber State University insightfully points to this correlation: "Faculty and administrators who have spent significant amounts of their professional lives in the public sector of higher education, especially at the institutions that are not included in the research classification, might have been startled by Kimball's characterization of pragmatic liberal education as a destination not yet reached. Educators at public colleges and universities find themselves already well 'within' the pragmatic paradigm, whether or not they have consciously placed themselves in that philosophical context . . . . Several of the developments identified by Kimball as reflective of pragmatic liberal education constitute the core of initiatives underway at many of the nation's public four-year colleges and universities." ("Pragmatic Missions and the Struggle for Liberal Education in State Colleges and Universities," *Condition,* 151–54.) Phillips's putative surprise at the prospective character of the emergent consensus is the kind of reservation that I had anticipated about the thesis. Other commentators noting this correlation are Susan L. Forman and Lynn Arthur Steen, who observe that "Harvard and Brown and many other universities separate departments of pure and applied mathematics" and thereby run counter to the reform movement in mathematics education toward the "reunification of mathematics, pure and applied" arising from the fact that "more than half the students who study college mathematics today do so in two-year or community colleges." ("Reckoning versus Reasoning: A Struggle for the Soul of Mathematics," *Condition,* 262–63.) In sum, the consensus thesis proposes that, in about 90 percent of the almost 3,300 colleges and universities in the country, discussion and practice of

what is called "liberal education" in the mid-1990s reveals an emerging commitment to the seven points listed above.

8. John H. Morrow, Jr., "Pragmatism: Plausible or Panacean?" 198; Ellen T. Harris, "Prognostication and Doubt," *Condition,* 254.

9. Arturo Madrid, "Because I Like the Questions," *Condition,* 252. Perhaps "consensus" is the wrong word. Julie Thompson Klein proposes "emergent agreement" instead ("Knowledge, America, and Liberal Education," 150). I would have thought that "agreement" is a stronger word than "consensus," and I note that the qualifying adjective "emergent," used throughout my essay, appears here whereas it is dropped by a number of those denying the consensus thesis.

10. Morrow, "Pragmatism: Plausible or Panacean?" 198–99; Ryan, "No Consensus in Sight," 244–49.

11. Green, "Needed: A Pedagogy Please!" 239–43. The quotation is from W.B. Carnochan, who cites Oakeshott approvingly. "On the Purposes of Liberal Education," *Condition,* 182. See Timothy Fuller, ed., *The Voice of Liberal Learning: Michael Oakeshott on Education* (New Haven: Yale University Press, 1989).

12. The latter approach, admired by Westbrook ("Wishful Thinking," 230), of beginning with the texts of the pragmatists and envisioning a program of liberal education, has a contribution to make. But it tempts one to remain safe within the ivy-covered walls of the academy and invites a cynical lament that experience falls miserably short of elegance. The deductive approach also has the problem of defending its *a priori* principles, and this point constitutes my response to Sandra B. Rosenthal's instructive reservations about the "reduction of 'meaning' to 'use'" in my historical method. ("Pragmatism, Scientific Method, and Liberal Education," *Condition,* 218.) To avoid this reduction, Rosenthal acknowledges that she "must go out on a limb, so to speak, and offer a definition of liberal education" as a starting point for her discussion (219). But in this step she appears to lose all warrant for what follows, because there is no reason to subscribe to her starting-point definition of liberal education rather than any other. The same problem is encountered by Alan Ryan, I believe, when he relies on a presumptive definition of liberal education in order to set aside Dewey: "Problem solving . . . is not the essence of liberal education. The disinterested exploration of cultural traditions is" ("No Consensus in Sight," *Condition,* 248). Here, too, the warrant for this stimulating definition of liberal education is not clear.

13. Richard M. Freeland, "Pragmatism Won't Save Us But It Can Help," 158. Shirley Hune makes a similar point. ("Pragmatism, Liberal Education, and Multiculturalism: Utilizing the 'Master's Tools' to Restructure the 'Master's House' for Diversity," *Condition,* 167.)

14. Robert Orrill has written to me that a helpful distinction regarding the degree of commitment to the consensus would involve accounting for the difference between the views of administrators and those of faculty within various institutions. This accounting would be related in a complex way to the distinction posited above between elite institutions and the "other" 90 percent, inasmuch as the "elite" institutions have shaped the values of the faculties at many of the "other" institutions.

15. The prohibitions applied particularly to the metaphysics, ethics, and natural philosophy of Aristotle, while his treatises on logic were being taught. The statutes

are translated in Lynn Thorndike, ed. and trans., *University Records and Life in the Middle Ages* (New York: Columbia University Press, 1944), 26–28, 64.

16. Charles W. Eliot, "What is a Liberal Education?" (1884), reprinted in C.W. Eliot, *Educational Reform* (New York: Arno Press, 1969), 97. Indeed, in his account of the contentious process whereby "new" sciences have cyclically displaced established disciplines within the liberal arts, Eliot mentions in passing the debate over Aristotelian philosophy within the medieval universities, although the Unitarian Eliot deprecates Scholastic philosophy and theology as being the only curricular development in the history of liberal education that was apparently not an intellectual advance over anything that preceded it.

17. To be sure, the step is paradoxical inasmuch as Eliot virtually replaces Greco-Roman preeminence with English preeminence. Nevertheless, Eliot's suggestion of an alternative opens the door for studying a multiplicity of cultures based upon their relevance to the contemporary era.

18. This point is confirmed by John Dewey's recollection, in an address delivered in 1939 at the University of Vermont, that during his undergraduate education at Vermont in the late 1870s "we had not electives of any kind. We went through a list of courses one after the other, without its ever occurring to us that they were prescribed, so much were they a matter of course." Jo Ann Boydston, editor, *John Dewey: The Later Works*, Volume 14, 1939–41 (Carbondale: Southern Illinois University Press), 266–72. I am grateful to Robert Orrill for this reference.

19. Timothy J. Brosnahan, "The Relative Merit of Courses in Catholic and Non-Catholic Colleges for the Baccalaureate," 22–44, and James Burns, "The Elective System of Studies," 48–60, in *Report of the Second Annual Conference of the Association of Catholic Colleges of the United States* (Washington, DC, 1900).

20. W.E.B. du Bois and Augustus Granville Dill, *The College-Bred Negro American* (Atlanta: Atlanta University Press, 1910), 7–16.

21. James McCosh, *The New Departure in College Education, Being a Reply to President Eliot's Defense of It* (New York, 1885), reprinted in Richard Hofstadter and Wilson Smith, editors, *American Higher Education: A Documentary History* (Chicago: University of Chicago Press, 1961), v. 2, 715–16, 728–29.

22. The disjunction between what Eliot stated in the essay and the local context of Harvard can be seen in Eliot's annual report for the academic year 1883–84. Eliot devoted part of it to each unit in the university: the Law School, the Divinity School, and so forth; and his discussion of undergraduate education was devoted exclusively to the following topic: "Some of the inter-collegiate athletic contests last year gave grave offense to many persons. . . . In particular the game of foot-ball was played in such a brutal and dishonorable way that the Faculty, after waiting two seasons to see if the players could not reform the game themselves, have been obliged to prohibit inter-collegiate games of foot-ball altogether. It is very improbable that a game which involves violent personal collision between opposing players can ever be made a good inter-collegiate game." Charles W. Eliot, "President's Report for 1883–84," in *Annual Reports of the President and Treasurer of Harvard College, 1883–84* (Cambridge, MA: Harvard University, 1885), 32.

23. James McCosh, *The New Departure in College Education,* 722–24.

24. Robert Orrill, "An End to Mourning: Liberal Education in Contemporary America," *Condition*, xiv.
25. Robert H. Bork, *Slouching Towards Gomorrah: Modern Liberalism and American Decline* (New York: HarperCollins, 1996).
26. Richard H. Brodhead, "On the Debate over Multiculturalism," *On Common Ground*, Fall 1996, 18–19.
27. Francis Oakley, *Community of Learning: The American College and the Liberal Arts Tradition* (New York: Oxford University Press, 1992), 147–48. Even advocates of reading a canon of great books have expanded the canon in view of multiculturalism, as William Casement has recently discussed in *The Battle of the Books in Higher Education: The Great Canon Controversy* (New Brunswick, NJ: Transaction Publishers, 1996).
28. Dewey was also disposed to take a long view in assessing patterns of educational change. See his retrospective address delivered in 1939 at the University of Vermont in *John Dewey: The Later Works*, 266–72.
29. Suggesting that it "seems an indulgence," Freeland asks with good-natured impatience, "What use is the idea of 'pragmatic liberal education'?" ("Pragmatism Won't Save Us," 158.) W.B. Carnochan playfully likens positing a philosophy or metarationale for the liberal arts to "trying to blow wind into one's own sails" ("On the 'Purposes' of Liberal Education," 183). Eva Brann observes, "What is the good of all this fancy theorizing in the face of such a critical condition, one might ask" ("Four Appreciative Queries," *Condition*, 175). And Green suggests that the value of fitting or naming the consensus—of pointing out that "certain paths of reflection offer a recognizable interpretation of [educators'] practice"—is "a matter of slight importance, a mere curiosity" ("Needed: A Pedagogy Please!" 239).
30. See Phillips, "Pragmatic Missions and the Struggle," 153, on state institutions; Jerry Berberet and Frank F. Wang, "The New American College: A Model for Liberal Learning," *Liberal Education* (1985), 48–52.
31. One of the best discussions of these "social forces" is to be found in Oakley, *Community of Learning,* 159ff.
32. This is the real problem, it seems to me, that vocationalism presents to liberal education, pragmatic or not. It is not that the two are practiced or situated differently, for I rather think that there is much liberal learning that could be gathered from working and vice versa. But if liberal education is conceived as working, i.e., becomes vocational, then it loses its principled basis and intellectual warrant. The difference lies in the purpose, and the purpose transforms the experience. Wall Street is a terribly interesting place (and cultural tradition, *pace* Alan Ryan) in which to learn and get a liberal education, but the moment one studies there in order to earn a dime, or to prepare oneself to earn a dime, then that learning loses its liberal character. This is what Aristotle says, as I conceive it, in *Politics* 1337a–b, to which Brann refers ("Four Appreciative Queries," 171) in making the distinction between "free pursuits" and "useful arts." The effect of this position is that, although no one goes to Wall Street to get a liberal education, one could. Dewey agrees, as I read him.

33. Menand's full metaphor is as follows: "My picture of the situation Kimball is addressing looks like this: there are these things called the disciplines—English, philosophy, sociology, biology, and so forth—that operate as more or less autonomous, self-regulating departments of knowledge, but that all float in a kind of fluid. This fluid is 'the philosophy of liberal education'; it is the foundational ideology, the metarationale, of the whole enterprise, an account of what higher education 'does for you,' or what higher education 'is all about,' that is subscribed to by English professors, sociology professors, philosophy professors, and biology professors alike. . . . This ambient fluid is the stuff Kimball is attempting . . . to describe." "Marketing Postmodernism," *Condition,* 140–41.

34. A special case is Oakley's agnosticism, which follows from the cogent judgment that "we are almost certainly too close to the debates and disagreements of the recent past to be able to discern, in anything but the most tentative and provisional of fashions, the direction in which the intellectual and political currents of the day are sweeping us," "Historical Perspective," 136. To this, I can only reply, "and yet we must try."

35. Hence, Westbrook seems to assume that nothing short of invocations of pragmatists in programs of liberal education would count as evidence ("Wishful Thinking," 228), though I do present some of these. Similarly, Green states, "I have yet to discover a teacher or school administrator with more than the most rudimentary knowledge of what Dewey had to say on any matter vital to the conduct of education. I am tempted to conclude that the extraordinary reach of his influence . . . is the stuff of mythology" ("Needed: A Pedagogy Please!" 239). In this way, "influence" appears to mean "knowledge of what [a philosopher] had to say" on the topic under consideration.

36. For example, Arthur Zilversmit would appear to disagree with Green in maintaining that "the educational and philosophical writings of John Dewey . . . formed the essential core of progressive education." Yet, Zilversmit would agree that Dewey had little influence due to "the failure of progressive education to transform the schools." Arthur Zilversmit, *Changing Schools: Progressive Education Theory and Practice, 1930–1960* (Chicago: University of Chicago Press, 1993), 3, 168.

37. Edmund Gordon cites Sartre ("Response to Bruce Kimball's 'Toward Pragmatic Liberal Education,'" *Condition,* 190). Westbrook cites Hegel ("Wishful Thinking," 229). Green shows that one point could come from a variety of philosophers "none of whom could conceivably be described as pragmatists" ("Needed: A Pedagogy Please!" 240).

38. James T. Kloppenberg, "Pragmatism: An Old Name for Some New Ways of Thinking?" *Journal of American History,* June 1996, 101.

39. David Steiner regrets "the gray pragmatism on offer to the American academy . . . a flexible, rather mushy, but very American theory of pragmatism, which offers so much justification for the practices of so many" ("Funeral Rites," *Condition,* 235). Brann asks "whether a contextless and an authorless thought is more than an intellectual ghost" and whether "pragmatism-in-general . . . is a somewhat flaccid collage, which no particular pragmatist might wish to acknowledge" ("Four Appreciative Queries," 172). Similarly, philosopher George Shields has observed that the general account of pragmatism "does less well in . . . giving the

reader the full sense of the strong divergence of views [especially that of Charles Peirce] within the conventionally circumscribed 'pragmatist' tradition." George W. Shields, "Pragmatism, Interdisciplinarity, and Liberal Education," *Association for Integrative Studies Newsletter,* October 1996, 3. In the 1983 Rollins College Conference commemorating the 1931 conference, Gerald Grant also made the point that the pragmatic and progressive tradition in education is "so diverse in its manifestations, so diffuse in its perception of itself." This summation of Grant's paper is made by Robert Marcus, "The Rollins College Conferences in Progressive Education, 1931 and 1983," *Liberal Education* 70 (1984): 293–95.

40. Brann, "Four Appreciative Queries," 172.

41. Steiner, "Funeral Rites," 236; Brann, "Four Appreciative Queries," 172.

42. See Ernest Gellner, "Pragmatism and the Importance of Being Earnest," in Robert J. Mulvaney and Philip M. Zeltner, editors, *Pragmatism: Its Sources and Prospects* (Columbia: University of South Carolina Press, 1981), 60; H.S. Thayer, *Meaning and Action: A Critical History of Pragmatism,* 2nd ed. (Indianapolis, IN: Hackett, 1981), 4, 431, and Pt.4; John J. Stuhr, ed., *Classical American Philosophy: Essential Readings and Interpretive Essays* (New York: Oxford University Press, 1987), 5–11; Philip P. Wiener, *Evolution and the Founders of Pragmatism* (1949; Philadelphia: University of Pennsylvania Press, 1972), 190–91; Richard Rorty, "Pragmatism, Relativism, and Irrationalism," in *Consequences of Pragmatism (Essays 1972–1980)* (Minneapolis: University of Minnesota Press, 1982), 162ff; David A. Hollinger, "The Problem of Pragmatism in American History," *Journal of American History* 67 (1980), 93; Israel Scheffler, *Four Pragmatists: A Critical Introduction to Peirce, James, Mead, and Dewey* (New York: Humanities Press, 1974), 8.

43. Brann, "Four Appreciative Queries," 172.

44. Gordon, "Response," 190; Nicholas H. Farnham, "After Pragmatism, What?" *Condition,* 195; Westbrook, "Wishful Thinking," 229; David Shih, "The Emerging Liberal Arts Curriculum," *Planning for Higher Education* (Spring 1996), 36–38.

45. Edward C. Royce, [unpublished memorandum] "To Pragmatic Liberal Education Study Group," (Rollins College: Winter 1996), 1.

46. This is my paraphrase from the Latin. A literal rendering is: "the seven liberal arts are not sufficient to divide theoretical philosophy." Thomas Aquinas, *Expositio super librum Boethii DE TRINITATE* (Leiden: E.J. Brill, 1955), q. 5, art. 1, resp. 3.

47. One might say that Aristotelian philosophy provided, in Aristotle's terms, the "formal cause" of the Scholastic liberal arts, but the challenge to which I reply has attributed to me the mechanical view that pragmatism was, in Aristotle's terms, the "efficient cause."

48. Gordon, "Response," 190; Westbrook, "Wishful Thinking," 229.

49. This question was posed in different words by W.B. Carnochan of Stanford University, who asked: "Why is pragmatism both so pervasive and so regularly taken for granted?" "On the 'Purposes' of Liberal Education," 188. An example of this stance may be found in Edmund Gordon's embracing all but the name "pragmatism," for he states: "I prefer to read this history of higher education as indicative of continuing human efforts at the preservation of knowledge even as new knowledge is produced; at sense making and transformation of things in the interest of problem solving; at the interpretation and transfer of knowledge,

understanding, and technique; and fundamentally at the development and refinement of human intellective capacities. . . . I see this movement as purposeful, but directed at paradoxical purposes, i.e., both conservation and transformation" ("Response," 190). This position seems so consonant in spirit and content with the pragmatic method of inquiry that I can find virtually no substantive disagreement between myself and Gordon, who dissociates his views from pragmatism.

50. Menand is quoted in Robin Wilson, "Professor, Critic, Professional Gadfly," *Chronicle of Higher Education,* March 22, 1996, A16, A19.

51. Stanley Katz, Beyond the Disciplines. Presented at "The Role of the New American College in the Past, Present and Future of American Higher Education," sponsored by the Associated New American Colleges and the Woodrow Wilson National Fellowship Foundation, June 1996, St. Mary's College of California, Moraga, California, 2, 6.

52. John Dewey, et al., *The Curriculum for the Liberal Arts College, Being the Report of the Curriculum Conference Held at Rollins College, January 19–24, 1931* (Winter Park, FL: Rollins College, 1931), 13.

53. Alan Ryan exemplifies those who deny the fit of liberal education with pragmatism, or Dewey, on the grounds that "he had no great interest in higher education, nor even in the higher reaches of secondary education. . . . The process in which Dewey was interested was that of getting the child's mind to work as a self-propelled, problem-formulating, and problem-solving entity. In that area, he was a genius. . . . Problem solving, however, is not the essence of liberal education. The disinterested exploration of cultural traditions is" ("No Consensus in Sight," *Condition,* 248). This argument is reminiscent of the historical disjunction between Dewey and the academy that is discussed in my original essay. The move, made with all generosity, is not to deny the virtue of Dewey's thought, but to relegate it to children, while liberal education is said to be something higher.

But I would suggest that Ryan's rejection of the fit with pragmatism rests more on his own estimation of the inadequacy of pragmatism than on Dewey's actual intent or ultimate influence. In fact, there is much in Dewey suggesting that he viewed problem solving as the universal method of thought and education. What Ryan calls Dewey's "masterpiece" revealing Dewey's "genius" at understanding "the child's mind" was entitled *How We Think,* not *How Children Think,* and with good reason, for it is not confined to children. Further, it is difficult to believe that Dewey, the consummate public academic who wrote so much on education, really had little interest in higher education. Notwithstanding the relative *lacuna* in his writings, there are good reasons, mentioned in my essay, for thinking that it was impolitic for him to address higher education. Ryan's dismissal of Dewey's relevance on conceptual grounds serves as another datum to confirm this. Finally, there is little in Dewey suggesting that he would agree with Ryan's presumptive definition of liberal education. To the contrary, what Dewey did write on liberal education suggests that he viewed it as very much an extension of the educational approach he recommended for schools. Particularly instructive in this regard are the report and proceedings of the conference on the liberal arts held at Rollins College in 1931, which Dewey chaired and which constituted his most extensive involvement in this topic.

In my judgment, it is misleading even to say that until the 1931 Rollins College conference "Dewey had directed his thought and talent toward elementary and secondary education" while giving little attention to "the issue of progressive education in the liberal arts," as does Jack C. Lane, "The Rollins College Conference, 1931 and the Search for a Progressive Liberal Education: Mirror or Prism?" *Liberal Education* 70 (1984): 298–99. In support of this view, Lane quotes (305n) from a statement by Dewey from the proceedings of the 1931 conference; however, the statement is misquoted and does not quite confirm the idea that Dewey believed he had neglected liberal education. What Dewey says is: "while many conferences have been held to discuss problems of elementary and secondary education and some groups have taken up special problems of college teaching and curricula, this Conference is, so far as I know, unique in devoting itself exclusively to the fundamental principles of college education as distinguished from both that of lower schools and the university." John Dewey, Proceedings [of the Rollins College] Curriculum Conference, (19–24 January 1931). Typescript reposited in the Rollins College Library, Winter Park, FL, v. 3: 789–90.

Cosmopolitan Pragmatism: Deliberative Democracy and Higher Education

JAMES T. KLOPPENBERG

PROFESSOR OF HISTORY, BRANDEIS UNIVERSITY

Americans pride themselves on their pragmatism. Most mean, however, merely that they are realistic rather than naive; too few know that pragmatism is among the richest traditions of twentieth-century American philosophy. Even fewer understand the links that connect the philosophy of pragmatism with democratic culture and also with the goals of liberal education. For that reason, in my courses on American thought, I almost always include sustained study of the pragmatic tradition. When I teach the ideas of William James, I assign more or less standard selections from his psychology, his philosophical writings, and his studies of religious experience. But I also assign two wonderful essays less often read these days, perhaps because they don't fit neatly into historians' or philosophers' accounts of what James's pragmatism was and why it matters today. I will begin this paper by discussing these two of James's essays, which he first published at the end of a volume bearing the odd title *Talks to Teachers on Psychology, and to Students on Some of Life's Ideals.* James's ideas will help us understand why pragmatism should be central to our contemporary American ideal of democracy and our practice of liberal education.

In the first of these essays, "On a Certain Blindness in Human Beings," James probes our inability to understand the sources of delight for individuals other than ourselves. Missing the joy that others find in their own experience robs us of the most enriching dimension of life, the broadening and deepening of our understanding of

69

what it is to be human. We often miss that depth because we look only at the externals of the world and do not bother to probe beneath the surface of those people we know, even those we know well. Our challenge, James insists, is to see beyond that certain blindness, to see the profound human significance in the everyday, as Wordsworth and Whitman and Tolstoy did, to make ourselves receptive to grasping what James calls the "unfathomable significance and importance" of every human life.

The most highly educated, James observes, and that includes every contributor to this volume and every reader of this text, find recognition of this significance especially difficult, because we are especially inclined to see only the banality of another life's surface and thus to miss the tingling richness beneath. Instead, James urges his listeners in his concluding remarks, we should steadfastly resist "pronouncing on the meaninglessness of forms of existence other than our own." We should instead "tolerate, respect, and indulge those whom we see harmlessly interested and happy in their own ways, however unintelligible these may be to us. Hands off: neither the whole of truth nor the whole of good is revealed to any single observer, although each observer gains a partial superiority of insight from the peculiar positions in which he stands."[1]

Before attempting to link that insight with James's cosmopolitan pragmatism, and then to connect both with liberal education, I want to say a few words about the companion essay, "What Makes a Life Significant?"—an essay every bit as arresting as its title suggests. I remember the mixture of satisfaction and uneasiness I felt when a reader of an early draft of my dissertation wrote in his comments that the principal value of one chapter had been that it sent him scurrying off to read this essay by James. I had, of course, rather hoped the value might lie in my brilliant and penetrating argument, but I could understand what he meant. I feel much the same now. If this essay serves only to entice a few readers to study James's "What Makes a Life Significant?" I'll be content.

James begins with a simple observation. "Every Jack," James writes, "sees in his own particular Jill charms and perfections to the enchantment of which we stolid onlookers are stone-cold." Sophisticated, highly educated observers are especially quick to judge Jack deluded, James notes, and even quicker to see in Jack's exaggerations of Jill's virtues evidence of a quaint but unfortunate folly. Instead it is we ourselves who are victims of "a pathological anaesthesia as regards Jill's magical importance." The "profounder truths," James insists, reveal themselves to Jack, and not to us. Surely

> poor Jill's palpitating little life-throbs *are* among the wonders of creation, *are* worthy of this sympathetic interest; and it is to our shame that the rest of us cannot feel like Jack. For Jack . . . struggles toward a union with [Jill's] inner life, divining her feelings, anticipating her desires, understanding her limits as manfully as he can, and yet inadequately, too; for he is also afflicted with some blindness, even here. Whilst we, dead clods that we are, do not even seek after these things, but are contented that that portion of eternal fact named Jill should be for us as if it were not. Jill, who knows her inner life, knows that Jack's way of taking it—so importantly—is the true and serious way; and she responds to the truth in him by taking him truly and seriously, too (170–71).

At first glance this judgment seems no more than intellectual and emotional slumming, further evidence of James's credulous willingness to attribute profound human value to the most unimportant sentimental nonsense, just the sort of flabby thinking that drives his tough-minded critics crazy. But when James directs his attention to the unsentimental cynics in his audience, he likewise engages us, his even more unsentimental, and even more cynical, readers a century later. In fact, he stops us in our tracks: "Where would any of *us* be," he asks, "were there no one willing to know us as we really are or ready to repay us for *our* insight by making recognizant return? We ought, all of us," he urges, "to realize each other" in this way. We should learn not to exclude those who are not part of our own charmed circles, nor poison such sympathetic understanding with the petty jealousies that too often sour the sensibilities of what he calls "ordinary Jack and Jill affection" (171). Precisely the effort to understand every other person from within, from the perspective of his or her own precious aspirations, James offers as the goal for which we should strive. But how should we go about it, and more to the point, what does this elaborate detour have to do with liberal education?

As the essay unfolds, James dismisses several strategies that might promise to help us reach the broader goal of making our lives significant. He first describes the pleasant but sanitized experience of middle-class refinement, education, and contentment he observed at Chautauqua, New York, which was perhaps the closest thing in his experience to a combined visit in our day to Disney's Epcot Center, the Florida town of Celebration (the eerily charming Disney-planned community outside Disney World), and a colloquy on liberal education at bucolic Rollins College. After admitting the obvious appeal of Chautauqua, James abruptly dismisses the community as evidence for his fear that "an irremediable flatness is coming over the world," which threatens to extinguish the "element of precipitousness" that makes possible human greatness. Visitors to central Florida, including academic conference goers, likewise find such precipitousness in short supply today (unless they deliberately seek out the plentiful artificial inducements of the sensation).

James then reflects on another possible source of human significance, the spectacle of hard human labor, in which "the demand for courage is incessant," whether on freight trains or in factories, in cattle yards or mines, in fighting fires or building bridges. But as a general proposition, this, too, fails to satisfy James, because we cannot take for granted that such challenging, even apparently heroic work brings to those who do it the same ennobling significance attributed to it by writers and poets who view it from a distance.

Instead James concludes that intense experience can have such a significance "only when the inner joy, courage, and endurance are joined with an ideal." Moreover, such ideals must exist not only as objects of contemplation. To have meaning and power, their "sentimental surface" must be multiplied "by the dimension of active will, if we are to have depth, if we are to have anything cubical and solid in the way of character." So the mere entertaining of high ideals, the sort of activity that college professors and administrators typically engage in when they gather in conferences to think about liberal education, is, by itself, James warns, not terribly important. For "the ideals taken by themselves give no reality, the virtues by themselves no novelty." What matters instead is "that strange union of reality with ideal novelty," and recognizing such new forms of the ideal is, James argues, "the task of what we call intelligence." So "culture and refinement all alone are not enough. . . . Ideal aspirations are not enough, when uncombined with pluck and will. But neither are pluck and will, dogged endurance and insensibility to danger enough, when taken all alone. There must be some sort of fusion, some chemical combination among these principles, for a life objectively and thoroughly significant to result."[2]

Some readers will no doubt have already figured out where this ramble leads; others may be wondering why James's musings on a certain blindness and the significance of life have any significance in this collection of essays. The pragmatic dimensions of these two lectures can be stated simply, in terms that resonate with other contributions to this volume. Louis Menand argued persuasively that the goals of liberal education include sympathy, curiosity, a sense of principle, and independence of mind. The point of James's pragmatism was much the same: because knowledge derives from experience, truths cannot be considered absolute, and diversity of experience will yield diversity of beliefs. But that awareness need not make us either blind to each other or intolerant of such diversity. Instead, the pragmatic sensibility James describes is unusually alert to the internal significance of the alternate perceptions and valuations of other people unlike ourselves, and unusually sympathetic to various attempts to realize different ideals. James's pragmatism, then, celebrates diversity and condemns intolerance, condemns idle speculation and celebrates the attempt to realize the ideals of sympathy and experimentation in the practice of everyday life. It is that conscious, strenuous effort that makes a life significant.

For those of us who live our lives in colleges and universities devoted to the practice of the liberal arts, these are potentially instructive insights. They point us away from an exclusive emphasis on "the classics" or "the canon" as a fixed body of texts that does not change as cultures develop. They also point us away from exclusive emphasis on teaching "skills," crucial as those skills are, without exposing stu-

dents also to the wide range of substantive ideas about human experience and human excellence that will expand their horizons beyond
those they bring with them to college. James's ideas about "blindness"
and "significance" indicate the importance of helping our students
become human beings capable of thinking creatively and sympa-
thizing imaginatively with others. His ideas suggest the importance
of tying the texts, or the cases, or the problems we teach our students
about to the lives they are envisioning for themselves after they leave
us, lives we want to help them learn how to make significant.

By cosmopolitan pragmatism I mean precisely this emphasis on
fostering a broad perspective that undertakes to understand and
respect the perspectives of others, that prizes the ideal of reciprocity, and that recognizes the desirability of carrying that pragmatic sensibility from the realm of abstraction to the realm of daily life by engaging in the practice of deliberation as a means of truth testing and
problem solving. This cosmopolitan pragmatism is a sensibility I associate not with *savoir faire,* the ability to differentiate among the book-
shops on Charing Cross Road or the vintages of Bordeaux, or even
among the baseball fields where one can watch spring training in central Florida, valuable as all those kinds of knowledge are. It is instead
a way of thinking and acting in the world.

In contemporary American academic life, the meaning of pragmatism is the subject of heated debates that have obscured the arguments of early pragmatists such as William James and John Dewey.
Nevertheless, it is possible to uncover their principal arguments concerning the relation between democratic culture and liberal education. The early pragmatists emphasized the importance of experience, whereas some contemporary philosophers and critics who have
taken the linguistic turn are uneasy with that concept for reasons that
reflect crucial differences between competing versions of pragmatism. The early pragmatists believed their philosophical ideas had particular ethical and political consequences, whereas some contemporary thinkers who call themselves pragmatists consider it merely a
method enabling us to get along without any philosophical foundations whatsoever. Two rival camps are currently struggling over the
legacy of pragmatism. Early twentieth-century pragmatists envisioned

a modernist discourse of democratic deliberation in which communities of inquiry would test hypotheses in order to solve social as well as philosophical problems; contemporary pragmatists such as Richard J. Bernstein and Hilary Putnam sustain that tradition. To other contemporaries such as Richard Rorty and Stanley Fish, however, pragmatism is a postmodernist discourse of critical commentary in which textualists deny that we can escape the conventions and contingencies of language in order to connect with a world of experience outside texts.[3]

The early pragmatists sought to reorient philosophy from interminable and fruitless debates by insisting that ideas should be tested in practice. As part of their overall commitment to problem solving, their conception of experience was one of several themes that linked the philosophies of James and Dewey, the pragmatists who most powerfully influenced American culture during the first half of the twentieth century, and on whose work I will focus here.[4] What did James and Dewey mean by experience? Both rejected the dualisms—the separation of the mind from the body, and of the subject and the object—that had divided idealists from empiricists since Descartes and Locke. They were equally scornful of the nineteenth-century idealists' infatuation with introspection and the positivists' reduction of all philosophical questions to matter and motion. Instead they preferred other metaphors such as "field" or "stream" or "circuit" to suggest the continuity and meaningfulness of consciousness that had eluded both empiricists and rationalists; their "radical empiricism" rested on their revised concept of consciousness. Immediate experience as James and Dewey conceived of it is always relational (it never exists in the abstract or in isolation from a world containing both other persons and concrete realities, as did Descartes's rationalist *cogito*), creative (it never merely registers sense data passively, as did Locke's empiricist *tabula rasa*), and imbued with historically specific cultural values (it is never "human" or universal but always personal and particular). Rather than grounding values in the bedrock of timeless absolutes, they urged us to evaluate all of our beliefs—philosophical, scientific, religious, ethical, and political—before the test they considered the most demanding of all: our experience as social and historical beings.[5]

The early pragmatists' conception of testing the truth of ideas in experience ignited a firestorm of controversy that continues to rage. Philosophers such as Bertrand Russell, George Santayana, Josiah Royce, and Arthur Lovejoy immediately targeted James. Cultural critics such as Randolph Bourne, Van Wyck Brooks, and Lewis Mumford, and partisans of natural law such as (erstwhile pragmatist) Walter Lippmann and Mortimer Adler later went after Dewey, as did Marxists such as Theodor Adorno and Max Horkheimer. All these critics charged pragmatists with elevating expedient, novel, narrowly individualistic, instrumental, and technocratic considerations above truth and goodness revealed by philosophy, art, or theology.[6]

Much as such criticism stung, it sharpened James's and Dewey's formulations of their ideas. Some of their best writing, notably James's *The Meaning of Truth* (1909) and Dewey's *Experience and Nature* (1925), came in response to their critics. Certain clarifications require discussion here, because they reveal why some contemporary postmodernists' enthusiasm and some contemporary traditionalists' scorn are misdirected at James and Dewey. In *Pragmatism* (1907) James had already tried to head off some misunderstandings in advance. Looking back at his argument, it is difficult to see how anyone could accuse him of identifying truth with whatever it is expedient to believe. He specified "our duty to agree with reality" and expressed exasperation at his critics' "favorite formula for describing" pragmatists as "persons who think that by saying whatever you find it pleasant to say and calling it truth you fulfil every pragmatistic requirement." To the contrary, James protested: "Pent in, as the pragmatist more than anyone else sees himself to be, between the whole body of funded truths squeezed from the past and the coercions of the world of sense about him, who so well as he feels the immense pressure of objective control under which our minds perform their operations?"[7]

Such clarifications proved unavailing. When his critics continued to accuse him of counseling his readers to believe any fiction they might find it expedient to accept, James responded by writing *The Meaning of Truth*. There he specified in greater detail the circumstances in which one might invoke the pragmatic test of truth and clarified the conditions necessary for verifying any proposition pragmatically. First, and fundamentally, it must correspond to what is known from experience about the natural world. The following, apparently unambiguous sentence has escaped the attention of James's critics and some of his contemporary champions as well: "The notion of a reality independent of . . . us, taken from ordinary social experience, lies at the base of the pragmatist definition of truth." Calling himself an "epistemological realist," James explained that he simply took for granted the existence of that independent reality and did not consider it philosophically interesting or important. Second, to be judged pragmatically true, a proposition must be consistent with the individual's stock of existing beliefs, beliefs that had withstood the severe test of experience. That, James felt sure, would rule out simpleminded wishful thinking. Finally, a statement may be considered pragmatically true *if* it fulfills those two conditions *and* yields satisfaction. Religious faith represented to James a perfect illustration of the appropriate terrain for testing truth claims pragmatically: in the absence of irrefutable evidence, James judged relevant the consequences of faith for believers.[8] Dewey, whose prodding had helped spur James to refine his position, likewise argued throughout his long career that we should conceive of all our knowledge as hypotheses to be tested in experience.

The concept of experience formed the core of James's and Dewey's pragmatism. They conceived of knowing subjects as embodiments of reason, emotion, and values, and they emphasized the inadequacy of philosophers' various attempts to freeze, split apart, and compartmentalize the dynamic continuities and multiple dimensions of life as we live it. They conceived of individuals as always enmeshed in social conditions, yet selecting what to attend to from the multiplicity of conscious experience, and making history by making choices. They conceived of experience as intrinsically and irreducibly meaningful, and they insisted that its meanings were not predetermined or deducible from any all-encompassing pattern. They argued that meanings emerge as cultures test their values in practice, and that we encounter expressions of those meanings in the historical record.

Language was thus crucial for understanding the experience of others, but for James and Dewey language was only one important part of a richer, broader range that included interpersonal, aesthetic, spiritual, religious, and other forms of prelinguistic or nonlinguistic experience. Moreover, they realized that language not only feeds the imagination, it also places constraints on understanding by specifying a particular range of meanings. In a passage from *Pragmatism* important for arguments concerning language, reading, and historical understanding, James wrote, "All truth thus gets verbally built out, stored up, and made available for everyone. Hence, we must *talk* consistently, just as we must *think* consistently." Although James appreciated what is now characterized as the arbitrariness of signifiers, he drew the following noteworthy conclusion: "Names are arbitrary, but once understood they must be kept to. We mustn't now call Abel 'Cain' or Cain 'Abel.' If we do, we ungear ourselves from the whole book of Genesis, and from all its connexions with the universe of speech and fact down to the present time." We cannot test every proposition ourselves or enter the immediate experience of others. Yet we nevertheless have access to verifiable historical knowledge, even if only indirectly and through language. *"As true as past time itself was,* so true was Julius Caesar, so true were antediluvian monsters, all in their proper dates and settings. That past time itself was, is guaranteed by its coherence with everything that's present. True as the present *is* the past *was* also."[9] When dealing with verifiable data, whether about Caesars or about Ceratopsians, we place each datum in the web of evidence we humans have been spinning for centuries. Even when considering unverifiable narratives such as Genesis, we risk losing the coherence that makes communication possible unless we preserve meanings within our web of cultural memory. In neither case are our personal understandings "ungeared" from the conventions in which we find ourselves and through negotiations with which we constitute ourselves; in both cases we participate in and perpetuate our cultural tradition.

Dewey shared that appreciation of the importance of symbols and the indispensability of common understandings. "All discourse, oral or written," he conceded in *Experience and Nature,* "says things that surprise the one that says them." But that makes communication difficult, not impossible. Conversation understood as a quest for mutual understanding, with all its imprecision, provides the appropriate model.[10] In *The Public and Its Problems* Dewey wrote of *"communication* as a prerequisite" to undertaking social action. Through language "the results of conjoint experience are considered and transmitted. Events cannot be passed from one to another, but meanings may be shared by means of signs," eventually "converting a conjoining activity into a community of interest and endeavor." Dewey acknowledged the challenge of such communication: "mutual interest in shared meanings" does not emerge "all at once or completely." As was true of James, however, Dewey emphasized that such communication can yield provisional understandings of the past, its meanings for the present, and its role in the formulation of shared social aspirations. Such a cultural consciousness, for Dewey as for James, emerges ultimately from shared experience transmitted through language; experience remained an indispensable part of the process for both of them. For Dewey, dialogue between individuals in community, with its "direct give and take," provided the model for such communication: "the winged words of conversation in immediate intercourse have a vital import lacking in the fixed and frozen words of written speech."[11]

Listing some of the thinkers who aligned themselves with James and Dewey suggests their enormous impact. Sociologists such as George Herbert Mead; legal theorists such as Oliver Wendell Holmes, Jr., and Louis D. Brandeis; economists such as Richard T. Ely; political theorists such as Herbert Croly; theologians such as Walter Rauschenbusch and Reinhold Niebuhr; founders of the NAACP such as W. E. B. du Bois and William English Walling; and feminists such as Jane Addams and Jessie Taft all derived from pragmatism a conception of experience and a way of thinking about abstract and concrete problems that oriented them to historical analysis and away from inherited dogmas. Those who looked to philosophy and social science for solid, permanent principles found pragmatism disappointing and unattractive. But many of those who shared James's and Dewey's belief that the shift from absolutes to the test of experience might encourage independent thinking and democratic decision making endorsed pragmatism because it unsettled traditional ways of thinking without sinking into the morass of subjectivism that swallowed some turn-of-the-century rebels such as Nietzsche. The steadying lifeline of experience prevented pragmatists from sliding into fantasy, cynicism, or self-indulgence.

As the ripples pragmatism sent across American thought extended wider and wider during the early twentieth century, they met—and eventually were submerged by—more powerful waves coming from other directions. Among the most important of these was enthusiasm for the certainty widely attributed to the natural sciences, which stood in sharp contrast to the pragmatists' forthright admission of uncertainty. Behaviorists in psychology, sociology, and political science adopted Dewey's enthusiasm for testing hypotheses but jettisoned his concern with the qualitative dimensions of experience and inquiry in the human sciences. Philosophers turned increasingly toward the models provided by mathematics and physical science, a trend already underway before European émigrés began arriving in the United States in the 1930s. Their quest for precision and their impatience with pragmatism combined to transform American philosophy departments by elevating the study of language and logic and marginalizing James's and Dewey's concerns with epistemology, ethics, and political philosophy. A discipline scurrying to master the methods of Rudolf Carnap, who along with other logical positivists wanted to rid philosophy of all questions that could not be answered through scientific verification, had little interest in the early pragmatists' views of immediate experience and their democratic reformist sensibilities. Dewey had described the earlier work of British philosophers Bertrand Russell and G. E. Moore, the heroes of the movement known as analytic philosophy which sought to reduce philosophy to propositional logic, as "an affront to the commonsense world of action, appreciation, and affection" which threatened to "land philosophy in a formalism like unto scholasticism." James had urged Russell to "say good-bye to mathematical logic if you wish to preserve your relations with concrete realities!" But many midcentury American philosophers preferred Carnap and Russell to "common sense" and "concrete realities"; they shared Russell's long-standing contempt for pragmatism. The new breed of analytic philosophers shunned history, shifted toward technical discourse, and judged meaningless all propositions that could not be verified through strict scientific procedures. James's writings about religious experience, for example, and Dewey's about aesthetics, ethics, and politics, could hardly be said to meet such standards—indeed, they were designed to help philosophy escape such a narrowly restricted conception of its role.[12]

Developments within the pragmatist camp also made it increasingly vulnerable to such attacks. In the 1930s and 1940s some champions of pragmatism tried to popularize James's and Dewey's ideas by simplifying them for mass consumption. Whereas James and Dewey had urged their readers to undertake the task of thinking critically about their own experience and taking responsibility for shaping their culture, such writers as William James Durant, Irwin Edman, Horace Kallen, Max Otto, Harry Overstreet, John Herman Randall, and Thomas Vernor Smith made available versions of pragmatism compatible with the rough-and-ready democratic sentiments of most middle-class Americans. Such efforts did little to bolster the prestige of pragmatism among professional philosophers or other American intellectuals aspiring to scientific precision rather than democratic deliberation.[13]

After Dewey died in 1952, his ideas faded quickly into the background. Even though one of the most prominent thinkers of the post–World War II period, Reinhold Niebuhr, shared many of Dewey's and especially James's ideas, his critique of Dewey's optimism helped discredit pragmatism as too sunny-minded for serious intellectuals.[14] As Richard Rorty has put it, pragmatism was crushed between "upper and nether millstones": a revived interest in theology or existentialism for some, the "hard-edged empiricism" of Carnap for others.[15] For reasons reflecting changes within philosophy and in the broader culture, then, American intellectuals during the 1950s and 1960s either forgot about pragmatism or, as David Hollinger has argued, learned to get along without it.[16] That is no longer true. Explaining the resurgence of pragmatism requires at least sketching the complex cultural changes that cleared the ground and made possible its return.

First the claims to objectivity of the natural sciences, which had intimidated humanists and inspired philosophers and social scientists, and whose hold on solid knowledge had seemed so secure, were rocked by the historicist analysis of Thomas Kuhn, whose significance in this transformation is difficult to overestimate.[17] Many of the schemes for social engineering hatched by enthusiasts of science led to results that ranged from disappointing (the War on Poverty) to disastrous (the war in Vietnam), as both the findings of researchers and their application to social problems were shown to be grounded in questionable assumptions and susceptible to appropriation for ideological purposes antithetical to the scientists' notion of value neutrality.[18] Then social scientists began to admit what pragmatists and practitioners of the *Geisteswissenschaften* (human sciences), such as Wilhelm Dilthey, had known since the nineteenth century: Because human experience is meaningful, understanding both behavior and expression requires interpreting the complex and shifting systems of symbols through which individuals encounter the world and with which they try to cope with it. Meanings and intentions change over time and across cultures; as that realization spread, hopes of finding a universal logic or a general science of social organization faded. In its place emerged hermeneutics, the method of analysis that relies instead on methods of interpretation to achieve understanding of historical experience rather than trying to generate rules of transhistorical human behavior.

Marching behind the banner of hermeneutics came an influential band of scholars who challenged the ideal of scientific objectivity in the human sciences: Peter Winch, Clifford Geertz, Charles Taylor, Anthony Giddens, Paul Ricoeur, Michel Foucault, Jacques Derrida, Hans-Georg Gadamer, and Jürgen Habermas—this was a new litany of saints proclaiming variations on a revolutionary gospel of interpretation. They spoke a different language from those natural scientists, philosophers, and social scientists who sought to escape the clutter of history. Instead of timeless principles and truth, they referred to revolutionary paradigm shifts, incommensurable forms of life, the complexities of thick description, competing communities of discourse, archaeologies of knowledge, the universal undecidability of texts, the inescapability of prejudices, and the colonization of lifeworlds by an omnivorous technostructure.[19]

Although among these thinkers only Habermas explicitly placed himself within the pragmatic tradition, Americans familiar with James and Dewey noted the similarities between recent historicist critiques of the sciences and social sciences and those of the early pragmatists. As the work of these thinkers, many of whom were often grouped together (unhelpfully and even misleadingly) under the rubric "post-modernist," became increasingly influential, many scholars began to move away from the model of the natural sciences and toward various forms of analysis more congenial to hermeneutics and history, most notably toward pragmatism.[20]

Despite the undeniable importance of those broad changes in American thought, the resurgence of pragmatism is due in large measure to the remarkable work done by the Trojan horse of analytic philosophy, Richard Rorty. Rorty's historicism has had such explosive force because he attacked the citadel of philosophy from within. Troubling as was his insistence that philosophy could never attain the scientific status analytic philosophers yearned for, even more unnerving was Rorty's equally blunt judgment that the grail of objective knowledge would likewise continue to elude the natural sciences and the social sciences as well. Echoing arguments made by James and Dewey but presenting them in the discourse of analytic philosophy, he insisted in *Philosophy and the Mirror of Nature* (1979) that problems such as mind-body dualism, the correspondence theory of truth, theories of knowledge and theories of language, and ultimately the entire conception of a systematic philosophy devoted to finding foundations for objective knowledge all rested on misconceptions.[21]

In *The Consequences of Pragmatism* (1982), Rorty insisted that "there is nothing deep down inside us except what we have put there ourselves"; our most cherished standards and practices are merely conventions. Science, Rorty concluded with the provocative bluntness that has become his trademark, is only "one genre of literature"; all efforts to find solid, unchanging knowledge are futile.[22] Rorty himself realized that there was little in these claims that was completely new. Anglo-American philosophers in particular had marched down a road marked "truth" only to find James and Dewey waiting there for them. But because enthusiasm for science had overshadowed the historicism of earlier pragmatists, Rorty's revival of pragmatism seemed revolutionary.

Against critics who assailed him as a relativist, Rorty responded that the notion of relativism itself becomes incoherent when we appreciate the contingent status of all our knowledge. From his perspective, there is nothing for "truth" to be relative to except our tradition, our purposes, and our linguistic conventions. When we have come to that realization, a calm acceptance of our condition becomes possible. While pragmatism cannot offer objectivity, neither does it threaten the survival of civilization. Revolutionary as his message was, Rorty's mood was downright upbeat. He proclaimed pragmatism "the chief glory of our country's intellectual tradition" and noted that James and Dewey, although asking us to surrender "the neurotic Cartesian quest for certainty," nevertheless wrote, as Nietzsche and Heidegger did not, "in a spirit of social hope."[23]

Surprisingly, given the ardent anti-dualism that Rorty shares with James and Dewey, on the concept of experience he has substituted a new dichotomy for those James and Dewey attacked. Demonstrating the distance between his view and theirs has become considerably easier thanks to the appearance of Rorty's essay "Dewey Between Hegel and Darwin" (1994), in which Rorty acknowledges the difference between the historical Dewey and his "hypothetical Dewey," a philosopher who would have been "a pragmatist without being a radical empiricist," without, in other words, Dewey's crucial commitment to the importance of the reconceived idea of experience. The central distinction, Rorty now concedes, lies in Dewey's (and James's) continuing emphasis on experience, which Rorty finds quaint but unhelpful. "My alternative Dewey," he concludes wistfully, "would have said, we can construe 'thinking' as simply the use of sentences."[24] As a philosopher who sees the linguistic turn as a step forward rather than a dead end, Rorty dogmatically refuses to accept any version of philosophy in which something other than language, namely experience as James and Dewey conceived of it—*not* as introspection but as the intersection of the conscious self with the world—plays an important part. As Rorty now admits, James and Dewey had a very different conception of philosophy, and that difference continues to manifest itself in the contrasting versions of pragmatism in contemporary scholarship.

Rorty's move away from James's and Dewey's view of experience and toward a new cultural ideal in which poets and novelists would replace philosophers first became clear in his elegant, widely read *Contingency, Irony, and Solidarity* (1989). His shift has coincided with the shift of a number of different literary critics to self-characterizations as pragmatists.[25] Just as dissatisfaction with prevailing orthodoxies has sparked novel approaches in philosophy and the social sciences, so many students of literature have deserted the new criticism and structuralism and turned instead toward pragmatism. Reversing the common tendency, stemming from the writings of Randolph Bourne and Van Wyck Brooks and reaching fruition in Lewis Mumford's *The Golden Day* (1925), to contrast the pragmatists' supposedly arid fetish with technique against the Transcendentalists' celebration of imagination, some critics now invoke a refashioned pragmatism in their constructions of a rich, home-grown literary heritage. For example Richard Poirier argues in *Poetry and Pragmatism* (1992) for a continuous tradition of "linguistic skepticism" running from Emerson through James to the modernist poets Robert Frost, Gertrude Stein, Wallace Stevens, and T. S. Eliot. These poets share, according to Poirier, "a liberating and creative suspicion as to the dependability of words and syntax, especially as it relates to matters of belief."[26]

Poirier enlists James to provide an American alternative to varieties of post-structuralism imported from France and fashionable among contemporary critics. He quotes a phrase from James's *The Principles of Psychology* on "the reinstatement of the vague to its proper place in our mental life"—a phrase consistent with James's portrait of the depth and richness of immediate experience discussed above—then draws an etymological line from "vague" to "extravagance" and then to "superfluity." This tenuous link prompts him to assert that for James, as for Emerson, thinking involves punning, so that "gains and losses of meaning are in a continuous and generative interaction." Poirier compares the writings of Emerson and James with those of Frost, Stein, Stevens, and Eliot, whom they resemble in their use of metaphor and their "allusiveness and elusiveness of phrasing." Poirier characterizes James's language as "no less 'superfluous'" than the language of modernist poets, "subject to the same degree of metaphorical proliferation, slippage, and excess." James's language slides "out of bounds, toward the margin, until it becomes loose and vague." [27] Although James conceded the limits imposed on clarity by the ineffable in experience and the unstable in language, as his classic *Varieties of Religious Experience* makes abundantly clear, in his writings he sought to move beyond the vague rather than revel in it.

In a letter to his former student, Gertrude Stein, written shortly before his death, James explained why he had not yet finished reading a novel she had sent him: "As a rule reading fiction is as hard for me as trying to hit a target by hurling feathers at it. I need *resistance* to cerebrate!" [28] James's pragmatism likewise reflects his awareness of resistance in the world beyond his own fertile imagination. In the absence of any "resistance" in "external reality," writing can become an exercise in creativity, or an excuse for unrestrained self-indulgence. James also insisted on respecting the conventional meanings of words lest we become "ungeared" from our cultural tradition and thus unable to communicate with each other. When critics align his pragmatism with forms of "linguistic skepticism" that encourage creative (mis)readings by "strong poets"—a phrase of the critic Harold Bloom's, by which he meant to endorse the creative independence of critics to interpret texts unconstrained by conventional understandings—they depart from James's world. Without the resistance provided by "external reality," and by a range of meanings independent of the reader's imagination, interpreting texts becomes as challenging, and rewarding, as tennis played without a net. [29]

Two of the most prominent late-twentieth-century pragmatists, Richard J. Bernstein and Hilary Putnam, have challenged versions of pragmatism such as Rorty's and Poirier's that emphasize language and dismiss the concept of experience. Their work, less well known outside philosophy than Rorty's, is of particular interest because it extends the arguments of James and Dewey about experience and democracy into contemporary American discourse. For three decades, since the appearance of his first book, *John Dewey* (1966), Bernstein has worked to forge links between recent continental European philosophy and the American tradition of pragmatism. In *Praxis and Action: Contemporary Philosophies of Human Activity* (1971), he traced the pragmatist philosophy of activity to Aristotle's idea of *praxis* and contrasted the promise of that orientation with the danger that analytic philosophy might sink into Scholasticism under the weight of "its own demand for ever-increasing technical mastery." Dewey, by contrast, was alert to "the moral and social consequences" of his ideas, which demanded a community of inquiry devoted to the "shared values of openness and fairness." From the beginning, Bernstein's pragmatism was grounded in a Deweyan conception of experience and its consequences for social organization: "it is only by mutual criticism that we can advance our knowledge and reconstruction of human experience."[30]

The twin pillars of Bernstein's pragmatism have been a community of inquiry and social action. In *The Restructuring of Social and Political Theory* (1976), Bernstein exposed the reductionism of mainstream social science and looked for alternatives in hermeneutics, phenomenology, and Habermas's critical theory. In *Beyond Objectivism and Relativism: Science, Hermeneutics, and Praxis* (1983), he identified the "Cartesian anxiety" that had dominated and debilitated modern Western thought: *"Either* there is some support for our being, a fixed foundation for our knowledge, *or* we cannot escape the forces of darkness that envelop us with madness, with intellectual and moral chaos." As an alternative, Bernstein invoked the ideas of Hans-Georg Gadamer and Hannah Arendt as well as Habermas and Rorty, arguing that these thinkers pointed toward "the central themes of dialogue, conversation, undistorted communication, [and] communal judgment" that become possible "when individuals confront each other as equals and participants." Bernstein advanced a characteristically Deweyan conclusion on the consequences of these ideas: we must aim "toward the goal of cultivating the types of dialogical communities" in which practical judgment and practical discourse "become concretely embodied in our everyday practices,"[31] whether those practices involve organizing a neighborhood to build a playground or organizing a group of students to investigate a historical controversy and test alternative interpretations against the available evidence. Pragmatism, for Bernstein, originates in reflection on experience and culminates in altered experience. For contemporary instructors in the liberal arts, its attractiveness should be apparent.

Putnam established his scholarly credentials by contributing to debates in mathematical logic and philosophy of mind, but as did Rorty, he has become increasingly disenchanted during the last two decades with much of what passes for professional philosophy in America. Without denying the importance of logic, formal studies, or semantics, Putnam has nevertheless described such work as "peripheral" and a reflection of the "scientistic character of logical positivism" that likewise infects much analytic philosophy.[32] "Contemporary analytic metaphysics," he writes acidly, "has no connection with anything but the 'intuitions' of a handful of philosophers." He is equally scornful of the nihilism he sees in Derrida's deconstruction. "Analytic philosophers basically see philosophy as a science, only less developed, vaguer and newer, while Derrida basically sees philosophy as literature, as art. I don't think either is correct."[33]

In *Realism with a Human Face* (1990), Putnam sought to clarify his differences from Rorty; he listed five principles he, along with the early pragmatists, would endorse, but which he expected Rorty to reject. First, our standards of warranted assertibility are historical; second, they reflect our interests and values; and third, they are always subject to reform, as are all our standards. Rorty accepted those but challenged two of Putnam's claims: first, that "In ordinary circumstances, there is usually a fact of the matter as to whether the statements people make are warranted or not"; and second, "Whether a statement is warranted or not is independent of whether the majority of one's cultural peers would *say* it is warranted or unwarranted."[34] For Putnam, as for Bernstein, all inquiry presupposes values such as mutual understanding and cooperation, which, in turn, require free and open exchanges of ideas among equals who are committed to the value of the practice. All of these are deeply, irreducibly normative notions, and they require a conception of human thinking and agency that cannot be naturalized as Rorty seeks to do. At the conclusion of *Reason, Truth and History*, Putnam stated this crucial argument clearly and forcefully: "The notion of truth itself depends for its content on our standards of rational acceptability, and these in turn rest on and presuppose our values."[35]

Tempting as it is to describe the ideas of cosmopolitan pragmatism in greater detail, I will not elaborate further the ideas of Bernstein and Putnam, or the related ideas of others such as Randolph Bourne or Jane Addams or W.E.B. du Bois, who were, along with James, Dewey, and George Herbert Mead, among the leading theorists of this kind of pragmatism. Instead I want to focus on the relation between this cosmopolitan pragmatism, the ideas of deliberative democracy, and the practice of liberal education at the end of the twentieth century.

James and Dewey considered their pragmatism inseparable from their commitment to democracy as an ethical ideal. Both believed that their challenge to inherited philosophical dualisms and absolutes, their conception of truth as fluid and culturally created, and their belief that all experience is meaningful were consistent only with democracy, specifically with the principles of social equality and individual autonomy, which provided the standards of judgment for pragmatism. The ideals of equality and autonomy appealed to James and Dewey precisely because of their open-endedness and flexibility. They did not entail particular conceptions of the good life for all people at all times, although they did rule out fixed and hierarchical social systems sustained by appeals to allegedly universal truths that all members of the society must embrace. To the early pragmatists, such static and inegalitarian systems were not only uncongenial to their philosophy but inimical to democracy.

Both James and Dewey shared the conviction that experience itself necessarily involves valuing. The qualitative and social dimensions of all experience make pure "objectivity" or "neutrality" impossible for human beings. Dewey's enthusiasm for science is often misinterpreted as a narrow concern with technique to the exclusion of ethical considerations; to the contrary, Dewey valued the scientific method because it embodied an ethical commitment to open-ended inquiry wherein human values shaped the selection of questions, the formulation of hypotheses, and the evaluation of results. Dewey conceived of the ideal scientific community as a democratically organized, truth-seeking group of independent thinkers who tested their results against pragmatic standards, but those standards always reflected moral rather than narrowly technical considerations.

This unifying thread connects all of Dewey's writings. In *The Study of Ethics: A Syllabus* (1894), he insisted that knowing cannot be separated from valuing. In *The Public and Its Problems* he cautioned that "the glorification of 'pure' science" is but "a rationalization of an escape" because knowledge "is wholly a moral matter." In *Experience and Nature* he stressed the moral and aesthetic dimension of experience, its qualitative as well as cognitive aspect. In the lectures published as *Art and Experience* (1934), Dewey tried once more to clarify the position he defended throughout his career: Although many champions as well as critics have interpreted naturalism as "disregard of all values that cannot be reduced to the physical and animal," for Dewey "nature signifies nothing less than the whole complex of the results of the interaction of man, with his memories and hopes, understanding and desire, with that world to which one-sided philosophy confines 'nature.' "[36] Dewey judged the notion of "value-free" inquiry abhorrent as well as incoherent.

An address Dewey wrote for a banquet celebrating his eightieth birthday in 1939 states clearly and concisely the connection between his devotion to democracy and his philosophical conceptions of experience and ethics. Democracy, Dewey proclaimed, is "a way of life" that requires "faith in the capacity of human beings for intelligent judgment and action if proper [i.e., democratic] conditions are furnished" (227). To those who judged this faith naive or utopian, Dewey insisted that it derives neither from metaphysics nor wishful thinking but from the everyday experience of neighbors and friends gathering "to converse freely with one another. Intolerance, abuse, calling of names because of differences of opinion about religion or politics or business, as well as because of differences of race, color, wealth or degree of culture are treason to the democratic way of life" (227). Anything that blocks communication engenders "antagonistic sects and factions" and undermines democracy. Legal guarantees, which provide the focus of late-twentieth-century efforts to ensure the right to free expression, are inadequate when "the give and take of ideas, facts, experiences, is choked by mutual suspicion, by abuse, by fear and hatred" (228). For Dewey, democracy required more than securing individual rights. It required faith in the possibility of resolving disputes through uncoerced deliberation, "as cooperative undertakings" (228), instead of having one party suppress the other overtly through violence or more subtly through ridicule or intimidation. If such cooperation is impossible, then deliberative democracy as Dewey conceived of it is impossible.

The emphasis on difference in contemporary America does not discredit Dewey's pragmatism, as some writers unfamiliar with his ideas assume; instead, it echoes Dewey's own view of diversity. Achieving the degree of cooperation necessary for social life requires "giving differences a chance to show themselves," he insisted. "The expression of difference is not only a right of the other persons but is a means of enriching one's own life-experience" (228). Dewey urged us to stop "thinking of democracy as something institutional and external" and to see it as "a way of personal life," to realize that "democracy is a moral ideal and so far as it becomes a fact is a moral fact" (228). Dewey's conception of democracy involved enriching the range of choices, and expanding the possibilities of finding different kinds of fulfillment, for all persons. Democracy does not impose authority from above but relies instead on "the process of experience as end and as means" (229), as the source of authority and the means of choosing among and testing alternative directions. This process is continuous because its terminus cannot be designated or even imagined in advance of democratic social experimentation to create "a freer and more humane experience in which all share and to which all contribute" (230).[37] Dewey harbored no secret desire to bring all diversity to an end under the shelter of a snug but stifling consensus: to the contrary, a democracy without difference was a contradiction in terms, because he believed passionately that all individuals, in their uniqueness, make different contributions to democratic life. The richer the mix, the richer the culture that results from the interaction.

Dewey's commitment to pluralism and diversity, to the recognition and cultivation of difference, and to the potential of communication to engender cooperation and clarify if not resolve disputes,

illustrates how wrong-headed is the familiar claim that Dewey's emphasis on a community of inquiry reveals the latent elitism of pragmatism. Dewey explicitly and repeatedly denied this charge. Throughout the 1920s, against behaviorists and empirical social scientists who
invoked his pragmatism on behalf of their efforts at social engineering, he insisted on expanding the "community of cooperative effort
and truth." In *Individualism Old and New* (1929) he elaborated the
argument advanced in *The Public and Its Problems* concerning not merely the undesirability but the folly of relying on elites. He admitted that
some communities of scientists, "small groups having a somewhat
technical ability," did indeed illustrate how the process of inquiry
might work, yet he insisted that such groups reveal only "a possibility in the present—one of many possibilities that are a challenge to
expansion, and not a ground for retreat and contraction" from democracy.[38] Unfortunately, interpreters of Dewey's ideas sometimes ignore
such explicit arguments and assert that there must be something anti-
democratic about all communities of inquiry, even those that are
open, expanding, and democratically constituted.[39]

Although it has long been common to contrast James's individualism to Dewey's commitment to social action, their differences are
more subtle. They reflect in part the simple fact of James's death in
1910 and Dewey's growing involvement in the quite different political controversies of the following four decades, rather than any fundamental inconsistency in their political orientations. Both shared
the conception of lived experience as irreducibly social and meaning laden; both frequently invoked democracy as the social ideal consistent with their pragmatism. In response to the charge that democracy means mediocrity, James wrote, "democracy is a kind of religion,"
and for pragmatic reasons "we are bound not to admit its failure."
Such "faiths and utopias are the noblest exercise of human reason,"
and we must not surrender them to cynicism.[40]

For James, as for Dewey, the philosophical commitments of pragmatism corresponded with the ethical and cultural commitments of
democracy as he understood it. James attributed the "unhealthiness"
of labor relations, for example, to "the fact that one-half of our fel-
low-countrymen remain entirely blind to the internal significance of

the lives of the other half." Instead of entering imaginatively into their ways of life—to say nothing of entering into constructive, democratic dialogue with them—"everybody remains outside of everybody else's sight." In addition to endorsing what would now be characterized as deliberative or discursive democracy, in which the creative potential of egalitarian dialogue, not merely the provision of democratic institutions or the insistence on universal rights to participation in political activity, is considered essential to democratic culture, James also announced himself a champion of what would now be designated multiculturalism. As I noted at the outset, James's ideal of a democratic culture, grounded on his conception of immediate experience and his commitment to pragmatism, "commands us to tolerate, respect, and indulge" those "harmlessly interested and happy in their own ways, however unintelligible these may be to us." The political consequence of James's pragmatism was "the well-known democratic respect for the sacredness of individuality," the "tolerance of whatever is not itself intolerant."[41]

If we take seriously the ideals and strategies of these cosmopolitan pragmatists, we should redouble our efforts in higher education to balance the goals of individualization and socialization, as Dewey argued in his discussion of primary and secondary school in *Democracy and Education,* and as Thomas Erlich has urged us to do in his essay in this volume. Jack Lane, who in his essay "The Rollins Conference of 1931 and the Search for a Progressive Liberal Education" points out that in the last 65 years some self-styled progressive colleges have emphasized offering students lots of options, makes it clear that merely letting internships and independent studies and self-directed programs proliferate in order to satisfy perceived student "interests" stands at a considerable distance from what Dewey had in mind.[42]

Dewey always emphasized, by contrast, that interests must not be treated as brute but must be developed, nurtured, and helped to mature through discipline and through rigorous education. Instead, student affairs bureaucracies have mushroomed, and student services have grown almost to match (if not sometimes to exceed) the academic programs available at many of our most selective colleges. At the initial gathering of first-year students at some first-rate colleges in the United States, most of the speakers addressing the new students come from offices of student affairs rather than from the faculty. They describe in loving detail the wealth of nonacademic, extracurricular programs that can enrich students' lives while at college. Faculty are sometimes surprised by this focus, which some consider detrimental, or even antithetical, to the students' understanding of the purposes of a liberal arts education.

I share the belief that our current emphasis on each student's quality of life is a serious mistake. As a Jamesian and Deweyan pragmatist, I believe we must emphasize instead the importance of what goes on in the classroom and the library and the laboratory. As Troy Duster and Lee Shulman make clear in their essays in this volume, that is where we can make sure our students have the experience of engaged deliberation with others unlike themselves. Dewey considered the social experience of *learning together* a crucial feature of education, as Jack Lane makes clear, and that dimension of shared rigorous inquiry can get lost when we turn colleges into consumer-driven service centers oriented toward satisfying students' interests in clubs and movies and travel.[43] The proliferation of internship opportunities can have the same effect unless they are designed with great care and tied to students' academic programs. Although I share Louis Menand's worry that our current practice can isolate students from the world they will enter after they graduate, we can also err in the opposite direction: if the years of college education provide no opportunities for critical reflection on, or careful examination of, the world encountered off campus, such internship programs can prepare students for their worlds of work without providing them with the cognitive, ethical, and political tools that will enable them to make their lives more significant, in James's sense, rather than merely more successful. More fundamental than the provision of such services is the responsibility universities have to educate students in the cultural and intellectual resources available to them. As Charles Anderson points out in his essay, the pragmatists urged us to help students learn how to interrogate interests critically, not just to act on them or aggregate them. Students must, of course, acquire the tools necessary to accomplish their life goals, and various requirements for distribution, writing, and quantitative reasoning are quite properly designed to do just that.

But in addition to these tools—these life skills, as they are sometimes called—we must provide our college graduates with the broader and deeper cognitive, ethical, and, as Elizabeth Minnich emphasizes in her essay, political resources that should come with a liberal education. I believe that we *should* conceive of those resources pragmatically, in terms of the difference they can make in helping students become the "agents of social change" to which Alexander Astin's paper refers. As Dewey put it in a passage Robert Orrill quotes in his preface to *The Condition of American Liberal Education,* we must connect American higher education with the "dominant interests and activities of the great body of the American people."[44] Now, a cynic might argue that by hitching undergraduates to the student-affairs bandwagon, we are indeed connecting our universities with the dominant interests and activities of the great body of the American people: we are preparing them to be comfortable consumers of the goods and services that will satisfy their every desire.

Making that the "pragmatic" dimension of American higher education, however, would merely extend the worst caricature of pragmatism as a philosophy of commercialism and crass utilitarianism, the distortion that initially greeted James's remark about the "cash value" of ideas and that has since assumed a life of its own, a Frankenstein monster that first came to life thanks to early misreadings of James and persists in recent, equally undiscerning horror stories concerning the lost promise of pragmatism. It is clear that the scramble to compete for market share among shrewd student consumers may drive admission offices and student affairs bureaucracies to lobby for pouring money into ever grander athletic facilities that rival the most elegant health clubs, but that is clearly not what Dewey had in mind when he invoked "the dominant interests and activities of the great body of the American people."

To update Dewey's language somewhat without altering his meaning unduly, we could say that Dewey believed our students should learn not only the skills but the sensibility required for participating in a deliberative democracy. To echo Astin's challenge and append it to Menand's argument, if we do not teach them those habits of mind, who will?

It would be a mistake to exaggerate earlier cosmopolitan pragmatists' suspicion of reason or their commitment to the decentered self prized by postmodernists. Yet they did understand that encounters with different points of view can teach the virtue as well as the necessity of dialogical thinking. As recent pragmatists such as Putnam and Bernstein have pointed out in their responses to postmodernists and their refinements of the ideas of Habermas, encounters with diversity can help foster a commitment to communication and problem solving, as well as illuminating the instability of the individual subject, the complexity of judgment, and the difficulty of reaching agreement through interaction among selves constituted discursively. A commitment to cosmopolitan pragmatism in liberal education would lead us to help our students encounter "the other" in their academic work as well as in their daily lives, so that they confront regularly the need to acknowledge and accommodate difference. As Troy Duster argues in his essay in this volume, liberal education is a practice that enables students to learn how to confront difference, how to grow and change and learn from such confrontation, and how to experiment with moving beyond confrontation by taking differences seriously, even—perhaps especially—those differences that cannot be resolved. The experience of deliberation does not always yield the broadened perspective the early pragmatists sought. But occasionally, as in the academic experiences of students at the University of California described in that essay, deliberation inside the classroom can have that effect. Even though the facts of demographic diversity and cultural upheaval, more so than the ideals of cosmopolitan pragmatism, have altered the populations and curricula of American colleges and universities, such changes are more than just compatible with pragmatic ideals. These demographic and cultural transformations make far more likely the widespread development of a pragmatic sensibility than was the case prior to the changes of the last 30 years.

The ideal as well as the practice of deliberation is deeply rooted in the American experience with democracy. It can be traced back through the practices Tocqueville ascribed to the Puritans and Quakers. But we now enjoy an especially propitious moment for advancing that practice and explaining why pragmatism can provide its philosophical rationale. We live in an era lacking the confidence in natural law and revealed religion that marked the eighteenth-century Enlightenment in America and underlay the commitments to popular sovereignty and natural rights that gave us our political institutions.[45] Using pragmatism to undergird deliberative democracy is not and cannot be the strategy of serious postmodernists, as Louis Menand points out in *The Condition of American Liberal Education,* because from the perspectives of postmodernism, difference and diversity lead nowhere but toward a culture of irony and the cultivation of cynicism. But pragmatism can help those of us who remain committed to liberal education.[46]

Bruce Kimball argues in *The Condition of American Liberal Education,* as in *Orators and Philosophers,* that the educational tradition emphasizing "rhetoric" or "speech" and "persuasion" has traditionally been opposed to that of "philosophy" and "reason" or "knowledge." But whereas Kimball ties pragmatism to the latter rationalist or philosophical tradition, because of its concern with testing hypotheses, and ties Rorty to the oratorical tradition,[47] I would argue instead that in the cosmopolitan pragmatism of James and Dewey, and in the deliberative democracy of more recent pragmatists such as Putnam and Bernstein, those categories break down. Both James and Dewey considered persuasion through effective use of language a crucial part of deliberation, even though they realized, as I noted above, that language is fuzzy and that persuasion, although necessary, is not everything. They sought to combine the techniques of oratory and reason in service of their democratic and cosmopolitan ideals, and they valued pragmatism as the most appropriate means to those ends.

If we take seriously the pragmatism of James and Dewey, we should not treat the cultural resources of liberal education as a fixed, unchanging canon. But neither should we throw up our hands and dismiss all efforts at canon formation as an elitist, Eurocentric plot, because the canon has been changing for as long as there has been a canon. All the historical studies of liberal education, to underscore a point well made by Charles Eliot and more recently by Francis Oakley and Bruce Kimball, have demonstrated that cultural conflict begins the day after the canon is formed.[48]

As someone who volunteered in the late 1980s to serve as an ambulance driver in the culture wars and ended up serving a tour of active duty on the front, I can testify that it is possible to survive such an experience with one's commitments to pragmatism and to liberal education more or less intact. I spent the first five years of this decade working with Richard Wightman Fox editing *A Companion to American Thought,* a volume containing more than 600 original essays contributed by more than 220 contemporary scholars writing on everything from the Puritans to postmodernism, from Abigail Adams to Jane Addams, from Tecumseh to Toni Morrison. It includes, for example, an instructive essay on education by Ellen Condliffe Lagemann, a wonderfully complex essay on simplicity by David Shi, and an equable essay on evangelicalism by Mark Noll. Reviewers have noted that the book will stand as a record of the state of thinking about America in the last decade of the twentieth century; strikingly, the themes of democracy and pragmatism are central to the book.[49]

The experience of editing this volume left me simultaneously encouraged and troubled by the process of and prospects for rethinking liberal education. I am as impressed by the richness of the knowledge about American culture now available to students interested in dead white males such as Jonathan Edwards and Henry Adams as I am inspired by the recent blossoming of scholarship on Latino and Latina culture and feminist jurisprudence, to cite just two examples among many in the *Companion.* It is clear that we need not choose between an earlier generation's list of "the classics" and contemporary multiculturalism in our teaching or our research. But I am also sobered by the skepticism voiced by some critics about our belief that the contributors to our *Companion* could themselves represent, and could do justice to, different sides of contemporary scholarly debates. We asked our contributors not only to provide reliable information, but also to survey the controversies surrounding a topic and finally to explain why it matters to us today, to make clear what difference it makes that we know something about an idea or a problem or an individual. Most reviewers in newspapers and most talk show hosts and their audiences have welcomed this effort to incorporate diverse perspectives as a sensible alternative to increasingly strident culture wars. By contrast, some academic reviewers, at both ends of the political spectrum, have been more suspicious of the project. E.J. Dionne explained in *Why Americans Hate Politics* how those who keep alive false polarities in political debate can eventually marginalize themselves from the deeper concerns of most Americans.[50] I believe our experience confirms Dionne's analysis in the realm of cultural debate: most Americans seem eager to embrace what is valuable in the new and yet cherish what remains valuable from the old. Yet, even if all readers of *A Companion to American Thought* are not persuaded that it is possible to have deep convictions as a scholar while still trying to understand and respect the views of those with whom one disagrees, I believe that should be the goal of a pragmatically inspired liberal education.

One of our challenges as educators is to help our students understand the ways in which today's cultures have developed, or as Thomas Erlich puts it in his essay, to show students the sources of our problems, using the range of perspectives available from the past and from the present, from the United States and elsewhere. This strategy emphatically does not mean discarding the principal texts from European and American cultural history, or sacrificing depth for fashionable but unscholarly breadth in our courses. But it just as emphatically does not mean excluding new voices from outside those received traditions. In liberal education we should be aiming, as James and Dewey were aiming, to increase our awareness of the historicity of ideas and the diversity of cultures, not for their own sake but because that awareness makes possible the participation of educated individuals in the construction of a democratic culture, and because it contributes to our students' realization that the process of constructing a democratic culture is endless. This is education conceived not in the terms of Robert Maynard Hutchins's or Allan Bloom's timeless truths, but in terms of the pragmatists' ideas of interactive experience, instrumental knowledge, and their ideals of reciprocity and deliberative democracy.

The ideas that have supplanted older versions of gender dominance and racial supremacy in America are not unlike those that underlie expanded conceptions of liberal education. Such ideas require acceptance of something like W.E.B. du Bois's notion of "double consciousness," the effort to keep in balance, because it is not possible fully to reconcile, the competing demands of the self and the other. Such a cosmopolitan and pragmatic self is constituted by the tension between one's own awareness of membership in a particular community, whether racial or otherwise, and one's aspiration to membership in the larger, more cosmopolitan and transracial human community, a tension further deepened by the awareness that the "other" is multiple rather than singular. Those contradictory demands alert individuals—especially but not exclusively members of racial minorities, du Bois argued—to the necessity of working to legitimate a cultural ideal beyond the summing of purely individual preferences.[51] Only when the preferences of members of a majority are formed through interaction with and recognition of the different desires of members of minorities can the latter hope to escape oppression. Only by persuading all members of democratic cultures that their ideal must incorporate the "double consciousness" to which some members of racial minorities come naturally (albeit painfully), and to which other people come by embracing ethical imperatives such as the categorical imperative or the Christian law of love or political ideas such as the ethic of reciprocity, can we move beyond Horace Kallen's cultural pluralism toward the ideal of an American "transnationalism" that Michael Walzer has described or the "postethnic America" that the historian David Hollinger so persuasively laid out in his essay on cosmopolitanism in the *Companion to American Thought* and in his wonderful book entitled *Postethnic America.*[52] If we remain partisans of an enlarged liberal education, our aim need not be an uncritical universalism nor a cynical and undiscriminating skepticism, neither the unchastened confidence of Enlightenment rationalists nor a universal hermeneutics of suspicion. We can instead aim toward the flexible, constructive, and cosmopolitan pragmatism of James, Dewey, and du Bois.

In concluding this essay, I want to shift gears. After discussing cosmopolitan pragmatism in some detail, I want to present an ethnography, a case study—call it what you will—a brief autobiographical narrative that suggests at least a few possible combinations of pragmatism and liberal education. In his contribution to *The Condition of American Liberal Education,* Menand suggests that the interdisciplinary programs now developing at the graduate level at American universities might eventually filter into undergraduate education; he develops that idea further in his contribution to this volume. My own experience has been that such filtering has been going on for quite some time, and that it has led to at least some conscious attempts to advance the ideas of pragmatism and liberal education together. As a Dartmouth undergraduate, I wrote an interdisciplinary senior essay on pragmatism and modernism in Europe and America. As a Stanford graduate student, I studied the great books in an interdisciplinary liberal arts program along with my disciplinary focus on American history. There I first read Eliot and Hutchins and John Henry Newman under the guidance of William Clebsch, a scholar of American religious thought who championed the old-fashioned but vital maxim that any book worth reading is worth reading twice. At Stanford I also deepened my interest in pragmatism, which I shared with the first graduate student I met there, Robert Westbrook, a fellow native of Colorado who went on to write *John Dewey and American Democracy,* the most comprehensive historical study of Dewey's political philosophy.[53]

I did not consider these two enterprises, the study of the great books and the study of pragmatism, incompatible. To me, the books in which James and Dewey advanced the philosophy of pragmatism ranked among the greatest of the great books, and I continue preaching that gospel to my students at Brandeis in the university's distinguished program in the History of Ideas and in its interdisciplinary graduate program in American Civilization. I served on the Brandeis faculty committee that designed an interdisciplinary program of clusters, groups of courses on common themes or topics that build bridges across departments and even across the supposedly unbridgeable divides between the cultures of the natural sciences and the human sciences. Each Brandeis student now completes, in addition to a field of concentration, a supplementary cluster of courses designed to identify and clarify thematic coherences that emerge from different disciplines and traditions of inquiry, including several that focus on the areas of law, business, and health that Menand correctly identified as especially important in our current cultural moment. Many of these clusters have experiential or service-oriented components, and some link course work with the world of work outside the university in just the way Menand and Lee Shulman recommend in their contributions to this volume.

I currently serve as chair of the Brandeis program of first-year seminars in humanistic inquiry, which draws its faculty from across the university, from physics and biology, music and theater, as well as literature and social science. This program, as the others I have described at Stanford and at Brandeis, takes for granted that different scholars and students have different kinds of expertise, different interests, and different convictions, and stipulates only that the courses be interdisciplinary and broad-based historically, and that they acquaint students with major texts from Western and non-Western civilizations. This program is quite self-consciously an updated version of an older ideal of liberal education. It is also pragmatic—although rather less self-consciously so for some of the faculty involved than it is for me—in that it reflects our awareness that there are no fixed, unchanging answers to the questions of what constitutes a "discipline," a "broad historical focus," or texts "central" to various civilizations. The program depends on the community of scholars, in this case constituted by the committee that oversees the program, to evaluate the courses. We depend even more on individual instructors to learn, from their own experience and that of others who have taught in the program, what works, what yields results in terms of getting students to read carefully, write coherently and effectively, and think critically about central issues of the human experience. The student evaluations of these courses are the most detailed and extensive I have ever seen, and we review them very carefully. In sum, my academic life for 25 years has orbited around a constellation of ideas that connects pragmatism and liberal education with the ideals of tolerance and reciprocity.

I would not go quite so far as Bruce Kimball does in asserting that a consensus is emerging on the close relation between pragmatism and liberal education. Such a consensus was not required to create any of the programs I have described at Stanford and Brandeis. Yet neither would I go so far as my friend Robert Westbrook, who complains in *The Condition of American Liberal Education* that Kimball is engaging in "wishful thinking."[54] I would argue instead that a connection between pragmatism and liberal education is not only possible but that it makes sense. It is conceptually coherent. I propose for further deliberation the proposition that such a combination, even if it is not yet recognized by many in American higher education for various reasons, *should* undergird a renewed commitment to liberal education for the twenty-first century.

Conceding to Kimball's critics that pragmatism has not caused the diverse developments that culminated in the kinds of liberal education now prevailing in many American colleges and universities, I advance instead the prescriptive case that such a commitment to cosmopolitan pragmatism not only can but *ought to* inform our continuing efforts to bring coherence to liberal education, a set of practices that is otherwise vulnerable to the cultural left's charges of political naiveté and the cultural right's charges of nihilism. In addition to advancing that argument on its own merits, I would point to my own local knowledge, my own lived experience, as evidence that a commitment to the ideals of liberal education and a commitment to pragmatism, at least as practiced at Stanford and Brandeis, can shape a life in higher education, and that the combination need not be dangerous to one's health.

I will close by returning to the conclusion of James's essay "What Makes a Life Significant?" because there he connects his musings directly with the vocation of teaching. If "a stock of ideals were all alone by itself enough to render a life significant," James suggests, then "your college professor, with a starched shirt and spectacles," would "be the most absolutely and deeply significant of men." But his listeners sense "instinctively," James concedes, that such a conclusion is "erroneous. The more ideals a man has, the more contemptible, on the whole, do you continue to deem him, if the matter ends there for him, and if none of the laboring man's virtues are called into action on his part—no courage shown, no privations undergone, no dirt or scars contracted in the attempt to get them realized." It is necessary to back one's ideals with virtuous activity, "multiply their sentimental surface by the dimension of the active will, if we are to have *depth*, if we are to have anything cubical and solid in the way of character." For the "meaning of life," James wrote, "is always the same eternal thing—the marriage, namely, of some unhabitual ideal, however special, with some fidelity, courage, and endurance, with some man's or woman's pains. And whatever or wherever life may be, there will always be the chance for that marriage to take place."[55]

It is in our everyday activity as teachers, as we interact with our students and our colleagues, that we have the best opportunity to practice our ideals of reciprocity and critical inquiry. In our practice as teachers, in the mundane tasks of leading seminars, reading and commenting on students' essays and exams, and counseling students as their advisers, we have the chance to nurture the virtues necessary for a democratic culture. That practice is hardly heroic; it inflicts no visible scars. Yet sustained commitment to the pragmatic ideals of critical inquiry, deliberation, and reciprocity, if embodied in the practice of teaching the liberal arts, can make a difference in our students' experience.

Commitments to cosmopolitan pragmatism and liberal education might make a life significant only from within, by giving meaning to what James termed one's own "palpitating little life-throbs" that might easily escape others' attention. Such commitments, though, can help us know why we do what we do as scholars, as teachers, and as faculty members at liberal arts institutions. While that is surely not all we want from the union of pragmatism and liberal education, it is not insignificant.

Notes

1. William James, "On a Certain Blindness in Human Beings," *Talks to Teachers on Psychology, and to Students on Some of Life's Ideals* (New York: W. W. Norton, 1958) 149–69.

2. William James, "What Makes a Life Significant?" *Talks to Teachers*, 170–91.
3. Parts of what follows are adapted from James T. Kloppenberg, "Pragmatism: An Old Name for Some New Ways of Thinking?" *Journal of American History* (June 1996), 100–38. Readers seeking further clarification of these debates in contemporary American discourse, particularly on the issues of race, gender, law, and historical scholarship, should see this article.
4. In this essay I will concentrate on James and Dewey instead of Charles Sanders Peirce for two reasons. First, Peirce explained in 1904 that he "invented" pragmatism "to express a certain maxim of logic . . . for the analysis of concepts" rather than "sensation" and grounded it on "an elaborate study of the nature of signs." For the precise reason that Peirce's ideas have influenced analytic philosophers and semioticians, his work is less pertinent here. On these differences see H.S. Thayer, *Meaning and Action: A Critical History of Pragmatism*, 2nd ed. (Indianapolis, IN: Bobbs-Merrill, 1981), 493ff. Second, discussing the recent torrent of work on Peirce—more than 40 books in the past seven years alone— is beyond the scope of this essay. A fine introduction is James Hoopes, editor, *Peirce on Signs: Writings on Semiotics by Charles Sanders Peirce* (Chapel Hill: University of North Carolina Press, 1991); on Peirce's tortured life see also Joseph Brent, *Charles Sanders Peirce: A Life* (Bloomington: Indiana University Press, 1993); and on his philosophy of science see C.F. Delaney, *Science, Knowledge, and Mind: A Study in the Philosophy of C. S. Peirce* (Notre Dame: University of Notre Dame Press, 1993).
5. Because assessing the continuities and differences between James's and Dewey's ideas and those of contemporary pragmatists necessitates understanding these early pragmatists' ideas, I will discuss their work in some detail, but it is obviously impossible to convey the depth and richness of their writings here. The most thorough account of James's concept of immediate experience is James M. Edie, *William James and Phenomenology* (Bloomington: Indiana University Press, 1987); more comprehensive are Ralph Barton Perry, *The Thought and Character of William James* (Boston: Little, Brown, 1935), which remains indispensable; and the magisterial work by Gerald E. Myers, *William James: His Life and Thought* (New Haven, CT: Yale University Press, 1986). The best account of Dewey's life and thought is Robert B. Westbrook, *John Dewey and American Democracy* (Ithaca, NY: Cornell University Press, 1991); on qualitative issues in Dewey's philosophy, see James Gouinlock, *John Dewey's Philosophy of Value* (New York: Humanities Press, 1972).
6. A handy compilation of these criticisms is available in John Patrick Diggins, *The Promise of Pragmatism: Modernism and the Crisis of Knowledge and Authority* (Chicago: University of Chicago Press, 1994). James Hoopes, Robert Westbrook, and I explain why we are unpersuaded by Diggins's interpretation of pragmatism, and he responds to our criticism, in *Intellectual History Newsletter*, 17 (1995), 3–30. On Bourne, Brooks, and Mumford, who valued the capacities of creative individuals above pragmatists' more mundane concerns with communities of discourse and social justice, see Casey Nelson Blake, *Beloved Community: The Cultural Criticism of Randolph Bourne, Van Wyck Brooks, Waldo Frank, and Lewis Mumford* (Chapel Hill: University of North Carolina Press, 1990). On Lippmann and Adler, see

Edward A. Purcell, Jr., *The Crisis of Democratic Theory: Scientific Naturalism and the Problem of Value* (Lexington: University Press of Kentucky, 1973). On Adorno and Horkheimer, see Martin Jay, *The Dialectical Imagination: A History of the Frankfurt School and the Institute of Social Research, 1923–1950* (Boston: Little, Brown, 1973).

7. William James, *Pragmatism: A New Name for Some Old Ways of Thinking* (Cambridge, MA: Harvard University Press, 1975), 111–12.

8. William James, *The Meaning of Truth* (Cambridge, MA: Harvard University Press, 1975), 106, 117, 126–28.

9. James, *Pragmatism*, 102–103.

10. John Dewey, *Experience and Nature*, in Jo Ann Boydston, editor, *John Dewey: The Later Works*, Volume 1, 1925–1953 (Carbondale: University of Southern Illinois Press, 1981–1990), 152.

11. John Dewey, *The Public and Its Problems*, in *Later Works*, Volume 2, 330–31.

12. On the triumph of scientism in American social science, see Dorothy Ross, *The Origins of American Social Science* (Cambridge: Cambridge University Press, 1991), 390–470; on the relation between scientism and the transformation of philosophy, see Daniel J. Wilson, *Science, Community, and the Transformation of American Philosophy, 1860–1930* (Chicago: University of Chicago Press, 1990); and Laurence C. Smith, *Behaviorism and Logical Positivism: A Reassessment of the Alliance* (Stanford, CA: Stanford University Press, 1986). For Dewey's judgment of Russell and Moore, see John Dewey, *Essays in Experimental Logic*, in Jo Ann Boydston, editor, *The Middle Works, 1899–1924*, Volume 10 (Carbondale: University of Southern Illinois Press, 1976–1983), 357–58; James's letter to Bertrand Russell, Oct. 4, 1908, is reprinted in *The Meaning of Truth*, appendix IV, 299–300. Russell's jibe appeared in a volume containing numerous critiques of Dewey from unsympathetic philosophers, Paul P. Schilpp, editor, *The Philosophy of John Dewey*, 2nd ed. (New York: Tudor, 1951); see Westbrook's discussion of this volume in *John Dewey and American Democracy*, 496–500.

13. George Cotkin, "Middle-Ground Pragmatists: The Popularization of Philosophy in American Culture," *Journal of the History of Ideas* (April 1994), 283–302. On Durant, see Joan Shelley Rubin, *The Making of Middlebrow Culture* (Chapel Hill: University of North Carolina Press, 1992).

14. On Niebuhr see Richard Wightman Fox, *Reinhold Niebuhr: A Biography* (New York: Pantheon, 1985); and Daniel F. Rice, *Reinhold Niebuhr and John Dewey: An American Odyssey* (Albany: State University of New York Press, 1993).

15. Richard Rorty, "Pragmatism without Method," in *Philosophical Papers*, vol. I: *Objectivity, Relativism, and Truth* (New York: Cambridge University Press, 1991), 64. For similar accounts of the transformation of American philosophy departments away from pragmatism and toward analytic philosophy and logical positivism, see Hilary Putnam, *Reason, Truth and History* (New York: Cambridge University Press, 1981), 103–26; Bernstein, "The Resurgence of Pragmatism," 815–17; and the fine synthetic overview in David Depew, "Philosophy," in Stanley Kutler, editor, *Encyclopedia of the United States in the Twentieth Century* (New York: Scribners, 1996), IV, 1635–63.

16. David A. Hollinger, "The Problem of Pragmatism in American History," *Journal of American History* 67 (1980): 88–107. On these developments see also the fine

overview by Thomas Bender, "Politics, Intellect, and the American University, 1945–1995," *Daedalus* (Winter 1997), 1–38.

17. Paul Hoyningen-Huene, *Reconstructing Scientific Revolutions: Thomas S. Kuhn's Philosophy of Science,* trans. Alexander T. Levine (Chicago: University of Chicago Press, 1993).

18. On the uses of social science in public policy, see Ellen Herman, *The Romance of American Psychology: Political Culture in the Age of Experts* (Berkeley: University of California Press, 1995).

19. On these developments, see Richard J. Bernstein, *The Restructuring of Social and Political Theory* (New York: Harcourt, Brace, Jovanovich, 1976); Fred R. Dallmayr and Thomas A. McCarthy, editors, *Understanding and Social Inquiry* (Notre Dame, IN: University of Notre Dame Press, 1977); and Quentin Skinner, editor, *The Return of Grand Theory in the Human Sciences* (Cambridge: Cambridge University Press, 1985).

20. Overviews of these changes in philosophy and political theory include John Rajchman and Cornel West, editors, *Post-Analytic Philosophy* (New York: Columbia University Press, 1985); and David Held, editor, *Political Theory Today* (Stanford, CA: Stanford University Press, 1991).

21. Richard Rorty, editor, *The Linguistic Turn: Recent Essays in Philosophical Method* (Chicago: University of Chicago Press, 1967); Rorty, *Philosophy and the Mirror of Nature* (Princeton, NJ: Princeton University Press, 1979). Among the many discussions of Rorty's work, see Alan Malachowski, editor, *Reading Rorty: Critical Responses to Philosophy and the Mirror of Nature* (Cambridge: Blackwell, 1990); and Herman J. Saatkamp, editor, *Rorty and Pragmatism* (Nashville, IN: Vanderbilt University Press, 1995).

22. Rorty, *Philosophy and the Mirror of Nature,* 392; Richard Rorty, *The Consequences of Pragmatism: Essays, 1972–1980* (Minneapolis: University of Minnesota Press, 1982), xl, xliii.

23. Rorty, *Consequences of Pragmatism,* xviii, 160, 161.

24. Richard Rorty, "Dewey Between Darwin and Hegel," in Dorothy Ross, editor, *Modernist Impulses in the Human Sciences, 1870–1930* (Baltimore: Johns Hopkins University Press, 1994), 46–68. In this essay Rorty acknowledges his debt to intellectual historians for demonstrating the difference between the historical Dewey and his "hypothetical version," then contends that the ideas of Dewey's generation no longer make sense.

25. For a treatment of pragmatism as the antithesis of literary theory and a rationale for critics to focus on recovering authors' intentions, see Steven Knapp and Walter Benn Michaels, "Against Theory," *Critical Inquiry* (Summer 1982), 723–42. For the claim that we must supplement pragmatism with other value orientations (such as Marxism) because the pragmatic method "cannot help us do the social work of transformation," see Frank Lentriccia, *Criticism and Social Change* (Chicago: University of Chicago Press, 1983), 4. Stanley Fish argues that we create the meaning of texts when we interpret them; trying to catch the meaning of pragmatism for Fish is thus like trying to catch a fly with a fish net. See, for example, Fish's diverse essays collected in *Doing What Comes Naturally* (Durham, NC: Duke University Press, 1989).

26. Richard Poirier, *Poetry and Pragmatism* (Cambridge, MA: Harvard University Press, 1992), 5.

27. Ibid., 44, 46, 92, 131. Compare Poirier's provocative characterization with James's own cautionary words about language, which might initially seem to confirm Poirier's view: "Good and evil reconciled in a laugh! Don't you see the difference, don't you see the identity?" James asked. "By George, nothing but *o*thing! That sounds like nonsense, but it is pure *on*sense!" James published these epigrams, however, to show how words that struck him as brilliant when he wrote them—under the influence of nitrous oxide—dissolved into meaninglessness when the nitrous oxide wore off. As James characterized the experience himself, in such extravagant language "reason and silliness united." See William James, *The Will to Believe and Other Essays in Popular Philosophy* (Cambridge, MA: Harvard University Press, 1979), 219–20; see also William James, *The Principles of Psychology* (Cambridge, MA: Harvard University Press, 1981), I: 254–55. For another imaginative and rewarding interpretation of James, which also stresses the instability of James's writings but emphasizes what James hoped to accomplish thereby as a pragmatist, see William Joseph Gavin, *William James and the Reinstatement of the Vague* (Philadelphia: Temple University Press, 1992).

28. James's letter to Gertrude Stein, May 25, 1910, is in the Houghton Library, Harvard University. On William James's letters to his brother Henry contrasting the writing of fiction with his own struggles against the "resistance" of "facts" and the ideas of "other philosophers," see R.W.B. Lewis, *The Jameses: A Family Narrative* (New York: Farrar, Straus, and Giroux, 1991), 409–10.

29. Poirier, *Poetry and Pragmatism*, 166–67. For an alternative view, see David Bromwich, in "Recent Work in Literary Criticism," *Social Research* (Autumn 1986), 447. Too often, Bromwich writes (with Fredric Jameson and Terry Eagleton in mind rather than Poirier, to be sure), critics who indulge their own impulses as readers obliterate the past, thereby minimizing "the differentness of the past," a consciousness of which "performs a critical function." Historical materials "are not altogether tractable: they will not do everything we want them to." When recounting changes in American literary criticism in the final chapter of *Poetry and Pragmatism,* Poirier underscores Bromwich's point by shifting from "linguistic skepticism" to a commonsense reliance on shared meanings of words. Poirier's practice is often at odds with the "linguistic skepticism" he endorses in theory.

30. Richard J. Bernstein, *John Dewey* (New York: Twayne, 1966); Richard J. Bernstein, *Praxis and Action: Contemporary Philosophies of Human Activity* (Philadelphia: University of Pennsylvania Press, 1971), 319, 314.

31. Bernstein, *Restructuring of Social and Political Theory;* Richard J. Bernstein, *Beyond Objectivism and Relativism: Science, Hermeneutics, and Praxis* (Philadelphia: University of Pennsylvania Press, 1983), 18, 223.

32. Putnam, *Reason, Truth and History,* 126.

33. Hilary Putnam, *Renewing Philosophy* (Cambridge, MA: Harvard University Press, 1992), 197; and the interview with Putnam in Giovanna Borradori, *The American Philosopher,* trans. Rosanna Crocitto (Chicago: University of Chicago Press, 1994), 60–61, 66.

34. Putnam, *Realism with a Human Face* (Cambridge, MA: Harvard University Press, 1990), 21.

35. Putnam, *Reason, Truth and History*, 215. For a recent restatement of this argument, see Putnam, "Pragmatism and Moral Objectivity," in James Conant, editor, Putnam, *Words and Life* (Cambridge, MA: Harvard University Press, 1994), 151–81.

36. John Dewey, *The Study of Ethics: A Syllabus*, in Jo Ann Boydston, editor, *The Early Works, 1882–1898*, Volume 4 (Carbondale: University of Southern Illinois Press, 1967–1972), 339; Dewey, *Public and Its Problems*, 344–45; Dewey, *Experience and Nature*, 74–76; and John Dewey, *Art as Experience*, in Boydston, editor, *Later Works*, Volume 10, 156.

37. Dewey, "Creative Democracy—The Task Before Us," in *Later Works*, Volume 14, 224–30. On this dimension of Dewey's pragmatism see also Putnam, "A Reconsideration of Deweyan Democracy," in Putnam, *Renewing Philosophy*, 199–200; and on the importance of pluralism to pragmatism, see also Putnam, *Words and Life*, 194–95.

38. Dewey, *Individualism Old and New*, in *Later Works*, Volume 5, 115.

39. The assumption that knowledge inevitably masks and imposes power often underlies such charges of elitism, but from a Deweyan perspective one might at once concede the point and ask what alternative is preferable to stipulating that democratic principles should shape the process of inquiry and the formation of those communities that evaluate knowledge claims. Particularly for scholars, the refusal to admit that there are better and worse—more and less democratic—ways to generate knowledge is self-defeating. On this issue, see also the judicious review essay by Thomas Bender, "Social Science, Objectivity, and Pragmatism," *Annals of Scholarship* (Winter-Spring 1992), 183–97.

40. William James, "The Social Value of the College Bred," in Bruce Kuklick, editor, *William James, Writings, 1902–1910* (New York: Library of America, 1987), 1245.

41. James, *Talks to Teachers*, 188–89; 169; 19–20. Although I recognize the differences between James's tragic sensibility and Dewey's indomitable faith in human capacity, their similarities also deserve emphasis, as I have argued in *Uncertain Victory: Social Democracy and Progressivism in European and American Thought, 1870–1920* (New York: Oxford University Press, 1986). On James's politics, cf. the contrasting emphases of Deborah J. Coon, "'One Moment in the World's Salvation': Anarchism and the Radicalization of William James," *Journal of American History* (June 1996), 70–99; and George Cotkin, *William James: Public Philosopher* (Baltimore: Johns Hopkins University Press, 1990); and, for an interpretation closer to my own, Joshua I. Miller, *Democratic Temperament: The Legacy of William James* (Lawrence: University Press of Kansas, 1997). On Dewey's democratic ideas, compare Westbrook, *John Dewey and American Democracy*, and Alan Ryan, *John Dewey and the High Tide of American Liberalism* (New York: Norton, 1995). An account restating the long-standard view of the differences between James's and Dewey's outlooks is James Campbell, *The Community Reconstructs: The Meaning of Pragmatic Social Thought* (Urbana: University of Illinois Press, 1992). For an interpretation critical of the Chicago pragmatists Dewey, Mead, and James Tufts for trying to moderate class conflict and translate their Protestantism and republicanism into

a reformism that he considers ill-suited to the industrial era, see Andrew Feffer, *The Chicago Pragmatists and American Progressivism* (Ithaca, NY: Cornell University Press, 1993). An imaginative analysis that credits Dewey and especially James with realizing that the new age of corporate capitalism ushered in new possibilities for a "postmodern subjectivity" is James Livingston, *Pragmatism and the Political Economy of Cultural Revolution, 1850–1940* (Chapel Hill: University of North Carolina Press, 1994).

42. Jack C. Lane, "The Rollins Conference, 1931 and the Search for a Progressive Liberal Education: Mirror or Prism?" *Liberal Education* 70:4 (1984).

43. Lane, "The Rollins Conference of 1931," 303.

44. Dewey, *The Way Out of Educational Confusion* (Cambridge, MA: Harvard University Press, 1931); quoted by Robert Orrill, "An End to Mourning: Liberal Education in Contemporary America," *The Condition of American Liberal Education* (New York: College Entrance Examination Board, 1995), xvii.

45. I trace these developments in greater detail in Kloppenberg, *The Virtues of Liberalism* (New York: Oxford University Press, forthcoming in 1998).

46. Louis Menand, "Marketing Postmodernism," in *Condition of American Liberal Education,* 140–44.

47. Bruce Kimball, "Toward Pragmatic Liberal Education," in *Condition of American Liberal Education,* 98f.; and more generally, Kimball, *Orators and Philosophers: A History of the Idea of Liberal Education,* expanded edition (New York: College Entrance Examination Board, 1995).

48. Francis Oakley, *Community of Learning: The American College and the Liberal Arts Tradition* (New York: Oxford University Press, 1992); Kimball, *Orators and Philosophers.*

49. Richard Wightman Fox and James T. Kloppenberg, editors, *A Companion to American Thought* (Oxford and Cambridge: Blackwell, 1995); see especially the Introduction, x–xv.

50. E. J. Dionne, *Why Americans Hate Politics* (New York: Touchstone, 1992).

51. W.E.B. du Bois, *The Souls of Black Folk* (New York: New American Library, 1969).

52. Michael Walzer, "What Does It Mean to Be an American?" *Social Research* (Fall 1990), 591–614; David A. Hollinger, "Cultural Pluralism and Multiculturalism," in *Companion to American Thought,* 162–66; Hollinger, *Postethnic America: Beyond Multiculturalism* (New York: Basic Books, 1995).

53. On the study of pragmatism and democratic social criticism at Stanford in the 1970s, see Robert Westbrook, "Doing Dewey: An Autobiographical Fragment," *Transactions of the Charles S. Peirce Society* (Fall 1993), 493–511.

54. Kimball, "Toward Pragmatic Liberal Education," 3–122; Robert B. Westbrook, "Wishful Thinking: On the Convergence of Pragmatism and Liberal Education," in *Condition of American Liberal Education,* 226–32.

55. James, *Talks to Teachers,* 186–90.

Pragmatism, Idealism, and the Aims of Liberal Education

CHARLES W. ANDERSON

PROFESSOR EMERITUS OF POLITICAL SCIENCE AND INTEGRATED LIBERAL STUDIES, UNIVERSITY OF WISCONSIN–MADISON

We are looking for a binding theme for liberal education, one that might guide American institutions of higher education into the new century. We are asking whether we can find such a theme in the legacy of philosophic pragmatism, that tradition that so much influenced all our habits of thought through much of this century.

It is well that we proceed warily and cautiously in this matter. To raise the question of educational philosophy is to open the door to great controversy. It is not at all clear that we of the academy are ready for this. To be sure, we cannot go on as before. The public today is asking hard questions about the university. (I will speak of "the university" as the more general term, implying thereby the colleges as well as all of our institutions of higher education.) It expects us to do better. It has asked us to justify our ways. But the university is proving to be a peculiarly unreflective institution, unusually sensitive to criticism and highly resistant to change. It is odd that the institution whose very task is to be critically self-conscious about all human projects and practices is itself so unself-conscious about its own ways.

There are reasons why the universities have been so vague about their educational purposes. To endorse an educational philosophy is to set priorities. It enables us to "economize" in the moral sense. It provides us with reasons for preferring this program to that, for putting resources here rather than there. An educational philosophy would enable us to compare the *worth* of various subjects. This runs strongly counter to the dominant temper of the academy, in which all existing disciplines are thought to be equally worthy and thus entitled to a share of the pie. The university as it exists today is the outcome of a very long truce.

Scholars find it hard to discuss their common educational purposes. The university exists as a loose assembly of disciplines. Most scholars assess the meaning of the whole from the vantage point of their specialized calling. They see the collective effort with their own habits of mind at the center. For the mathematician, the essence of thought lies in form and measure. For the social scientist, the basic aim of education is to understand the human situation. For the humanist, it is to seek and express meaning through all the instruments of human imagination. Scholars are awkward and halting in trying to press beyond these established lines, to ask what common sense of purpose could conceivably unite them, what transformations of the mind and heart they intend to effect in students, and the community, through their collective efforts.

Still, change is in the air. Fundamental battles over the concept of the university, over curriculum and epistemology, are being waged. Thus it is well that we proceed deliberately, cautiously, craftily, as though we might be taken seriously, as though some universities might actually pick up on the ideas discussed here and try to put them into effect.

In what is to come, I shall argue for a conception of liberal education based on what I shall call pragmatic idealism. I do not choose this path because I think it is the most convenient or the most consensual. Rather, I think many will find this approach to the integration of the liberal arts curriculum startling, far too radical, for it is based on an idea of the capabilities of the human mind and spirit that is provocative and controversial, and, in a way, daunting.

Nonetheless, I think that, for many, this is where reason will take us when we have examined the evident alternatives, when we have pondered them critically and carefully, when we have asked of each in turn: Is this the best we can do?

The Case for the Going Concern

The lineaments of the American university have been in place for a long time. The curriculum is organized around strong departments, representing the structure of knowledge as it has been created by the great academic professions and taught in the major graduate schools. The idea of teaching is to pass on these steadily accumulating, steadily improving bodies of knowledge, the product of collective, organized inquiry. A liberal education then includes "breadth," a sampling from the main branches of structured knowledge, and "depth," the major. Over time, this pattern has become standard for the system. The liberal arts colleges, community colleges, and the denominational schools, with but very few exceptions, try to recreate the program of a research university on a more intimate scale. Perceived quality comes from how closely and carefully they do this, how many of their teachers are drawn from the major research institutions, how close they are to the "cutting edge."

This program has been frozen in place for almost a century. It must have something going for it. This is what we have come to expect from our institutions of higher education. But what on earth is the educational rationale for this system? Why is this supposed an appropriate and an efficient way of nurturing the powers of mind?

Let me then begin by making the case for the going concern, for a liberal education *without* integrating theme or purpose, one that is essentially an idiosyncratic selection from the broad array of specialized courses offered by the university.

Epistemologically, the existing structure would seem to reflect our contemporary belief in the pluralism of knowledge. Academics today do not customarily believe that knowledge is one. There are diverse roads to truth, if it is in order to speak of truth at all. Rather, it is perhaps better to speak of human understanding, the patterns of meaning that seem agreeable to mind, and such understanding is located in the diverse analytic structures we have created. These constructions of reality, these schemes of reason, are independent of one another. The criteria of validity and soundness of argument and evidence are internal to the discipline. There is no privileged master theory, no vantage point from which the merits, the truth, the value of any of these distinct schemes of reason can be judged. Each then is an independent mode of understanding. The professionals in the field are masters of their house. The university simply represents the existing array of such systems of knowledge. It cannot judge among them; it has no authority to discriminate, assigning a greater priority to some, specifying an integrating relationship among them. Were it to prescribe an integrating ideal for liberal education it would, in effect, be presuming to possess a higher, unitary mode of understanding, by which the relative contribution of the specific disciplines could be judged. And this, contemporary relativism and constructionism avers, it simply cannot do.

In this elective, free-form conception of liberal education, integration, if it occurs at all, occurs in the mind of the individual student. And is this not as it should be? Students bring diverse interests, aptitudes, and needs to the university. Each will be assimilating what is taught to an evolving pattern of understanding that is unique and one's own. She has a flair for history and for the big picture, thrills to see the interrelationship of philosophy, science, the arts, politics, in each epoch. He is tough-minded and quantitative, wants to find a core of demonstrable certainty in each subject he studies. She is a storyteller, fascinated by how the mind can weave worlds of its own, in love with analogy, metaphor, literature. He is critical and much aware of the phenomenology of power, looking for who benefits, and who loses, from any form of human organization, any form of human understanding.

All of these perspectives and many more are available, open options, in the contemporary free-form university. As is true of the economic marketplace it so closely mimics, in a university, teachers offer what they wish, students study more or less what they desire, and the system, ultimately, is responsive to consumer demand. Is this not true academic freedom and precisely what a liberal education is intended to achieve?

Indeed it is, unless we believe that some patterns of integration and significance that students develop in the course of their education are better than others. Indeed it is, unless we believe that not every combination of electives is as good as any other, that there are some patterns, some schemes of thought, that are more worthy, more durable, more faithful to the highest qualities of the mind.

Now we can see precisely where our quest for an integrating theme for liberal education must take us. This is not a congenial, easygoing search for new ways of "packaging" the curriculum. The perils are epistemological and, in that sense, moral. We are going to have to assert that some ways of understanding are *better* than others; that some tell more truth, more reliably inform us about the world; that some are more seemly, or civil, or more effective as guides to action. To say this is to break the tacit truce of skepticism on which the contemporary curriculum rests. It is to say that the colleges and universities are responsible for distinguishing between the reasonable and the unreasonable, the warranted and the unwarranted, the better and the worse, that it is their calling to distinguish among the possibilities of belief and comprehension, and to teach, to prescribe, the better habits of mind.

A Survey of Evident Alternatives

Again, in recommending an idealist version of pragmatism as an integrating philosophy of liberal education, my case is not that this is an expedient position, a set of common assumptions that we all can agree to, but rather that this is what we would come to were we to ask, in dead seriousness, how we can best go on from here, how we can perfect the powers we acknowledge we possess to enhance and enlarge the capabilities of the mind.

So far, I have argued that the present free elective system will not serve, that appealing to a market-like model of responsiveness to individual interest and taste is not quite good enough, that in the end we will acknowledge that the university cannot be neutral about its teachings but must decide, explicitly, what is worthy of being taught and what is not.

Now I must go on to consider other evident possibilities. There are other dominant ideas of how one thinks and what thought is all about that are prevalent in the contemporary university. These ideas are familiar. They define the schools of thought about the foundations of knowledge that are in contention today. Any one could serve as an integrating ideal for education. Indeed, for many scholars, these visions do define their ideas of appropriate method, their sense for what is known and knowable. My object is to show, even to those who endorse such philosophies, that they would not want to adopt them as integrating doctrines for liberal education. I think this is so not because these ideas are contentious, or because they expect too much of us, but rather, and oddly, because I think we will recognize that they expect, and permit, less of us than we know we can achieve.

Positivism

We should begin by acknowledging that, at least since midcentury, the liberal arts curriculum has in fact been integrated by an implicit ideal of knowledge. Gradually, since early in the century, the social sciences and humanities sought to transform themselves by adopting the methods, the approaches to inquiry, that were characteristic of the natural and physical sciences. By the 1950s and 1960s, the results were striking. Students in that period found it clearly intimated, across the curriculum, that there was one proper way to proceed intellectually in every field.

The positivist approach to science taught some very firm doctrines about the proper work of the mind. The privileged position for inquiry was that of the detached observer. The phenomenon, whether natural event, social institution, or literary text, was understood as an object apart, an element of the external world, and the point of inquiry was to explain the behavior of the phenomenon as the product of lawlike regularities. One could place trust in careful observation but not in the meanderings of the subjective mind. Thus, one had to check out all suppositions against the facts of the matter, hard facts, facts we all could see. Thinking thus, thinking scientifically, was the proper approach to all subjects and it exhausted the domain of inquiry. Questions of "value" could not be treated this way. Therefore, they were not fit subjects for intellectual analysis.

More than perhaps we realize, this was the message of liberal education for a long generation. In many fields, in many courses, this understanding of the proper work of the mind persists, though by now it has been challenged, softened, qualified, and recast in a variety of ways. But there are many in the academy today who would still affirm that this is the only legitimate mode of intellectual analysis. This remains the orthodoxy of research and teaching in many disciplines. But I doubt that many would want to prescribe this as an integrating ideal for liberal education today. Time has passed. We have become more sophisticated about the ways in which the mind can work in disciplined inquiry. Our philosophy of science has become broader, more reflective of the diverse ways of actual scientific investigation. We know that the raw positivist conception of truth and method was artificial, too limited, that it excluded arbitrarily a large part of what we desperately needed to study and understand.

Postmodernism

Just as in the positivist moment it was thought that the method of science should become the method of the university, so today some feel that approaches to analysis born in literary criticism tell the truth about the products of thought and all the constructs of mind should be appraised by these methods.

Hence, scientific theories, as social philosophies or psychological investigations, can all be read and should be read as if they were stories, as if they were texts. All of these are works of human creation, hence they are contingent, they could not be otherwise. As is done with a novel, the critic can take apart the doctrines of biology, or a church, and establish the principle of their construction. Thus, "deconstructing" a story, one establishes how an effect is achieved, in literature, in science, in politics, and in a certain sense, one can *explain* a work as the product of certain cultural, or historical, conventions. In this way, postmodernism acts as a metascience; its task is to account for the phenomena of thought themselves.

Many scholars today might intimate that postmodernism ought to define the mission of liberal education. The point of education is to achieve self-consciousness, autonomy of thought. This is only possible when one is liberated from taking received ideas as necessary and inevitable. The great danger lies in thinking that any intellectual structure reflects the order of nature, of the world. Today, for many who teach in this fashion, the task of criticism is not complete until one has shown the political quality of dominant systems of thought, the ways in which law or science serves to justify the domination of some and the subordination of others.

So the question arises: should that self-consciousness that post-modernism seeks, that capacity to free the individual from inherited or customary understandings and expectations, be taken as the essential aim of liberal education?

Many will deplore the Nietzschean excess of postmodernism, its tendency to explain all ideas through political reduction, as artifacts of power. Many will respond that our science, and many other of our products of mind, are not *just* constructions, that they, in fact, do reflect the order of the world and the architecture of mind as we have come to understand them so far. At this point, the argument becomes one squarely and truly of metaphysics.

It is worthy of note that postmodernism, as positivism, takes the point of view of the detached observer. The appropriate position of the self-conscious mind is *outside* any enterprise of thought, any tradition, school, method, creed, or doctrine. Here the liberal intellectual might uneasily concur. Is not the object of liberal education to teach people to "think for themselves"? And at this point, we reach a crucial juncture in the argument. For pragmatism, in any of its forms, must take the view that we think best not alone, but as participants, as parties to an ongoing project of inquiry.

How many would in fact concur that the liberation of mind in the Nietzschean sense should be the unifying goal for liberal education? There are indeed many of us who do continue to believe—and today this is not a commonplace but a defiant proposition—that we do have reliable knowledge to teach and methods that we can fairly show will enable us to learn more. We do believe that some modes of analysis can be shown to be better than others in helping us reach an understanding both of the starry universe above and the moral law within. In all these senses, there is a clear difference between the rationalist and pragmatic view of the progressive nature of inquiry and the postmodern conviction that all the constructions of thought are supposition, whimsy, and conjecture.

And yet, it would seem essential to any pragmatic theory of liberal education that we teach students to see philosophy, systems of thought, and literature as human work, that they learn to "deconstruct" these works, analyzing them, discovering their principle of design, improving on them if they can. After all, ever since Socrates, it has been a central principle of liberal education that we, the people, deliberately examining the beliefs we have been taught, can do better, can transcend culture and established learning, can find closer approximations to the vague but nagging ideal that motivates our criticism. And further, it is an axiom of all classical learning, as of modern pragmatism, that our best efforts to penetrate to underlying reality will be but approximations, that they will yield but another human construction that must be the subject of further criticism and dissection in the light of that elusive ideal, as we seek the answer that as Peirce said we are all "fated" to find, but perhaps only at the end of time.

Thus, the postmodern critical theorist and the pragmatic idealist share the view that it is essential that students learn to understand the structures of science, philosophy, religion, law as artifacts of thought that should be dissected, criticized, and improved upon if we can. The difference is that the pragmatist would teach students to view these systems as participants in the project of mind they embrace, not merely as observers. And it is also true that the pragmatist assumes that there is an underlying order that we are trying to grasp while the postmodernist seems to assume that there is no order to be discovered. Apart from this small difference concerning the nature of the cosmos, these two philosophies of education have some significant common features.

Intellectual Pluralism and Cultural Conservatism

Because they share a common epistemology, I want to discuss together a series of approaches to liberal education that are highly antagonistic, and seem to occupy quite different places in the political and intellectual spectrum of the contemporary academy. First in this category are some, but not all, of those who see the core of the curriculum in the teaching of Western civilization and the "great books," and perhaps a particular moral code. Second are those who believe that students of diverse ethnic or gender groups should be taught a conception of culture of their own. Third are those who would teach that there are a great variety of cultural understandings in the world, that none is superior, and that it is best if we proceed each in our own ways with tolerance for those who are different. What these seemingly hostile approaches to liberal education share, of course, is a conservative epistemology, the belief that understanding is fundamentally a cultural artifact, that the aim is not to "think for oneself" about established conventions and institutions, but to internalize them, to make them one's own, with deep appreciation and reverence.

We can now begin to appreciate the complexity of our contemporary epistemological quarrels. Postmodernists and multiculturalists share the view that understanding is a social construction. But the aim of deconstruction, to free the individual from cultural constructs, is far different from that of those who would teach that there are modes of understanding that are special and distinctive for African Americans, Hispanics, or women. And this deeply conservative relativism is, oddly, shared by many who seem to proclaim the most absolute values and the purest conception of truth, as that is revealed in the great texts of Western civilization. (The deep pessimistic relativism of such thinkers as Leo Strauss and Allan Bloom is seldom recognized. But closely examined, their idea is that we must teach the great works of our civilization *as though they were true,* else we will fall into barbarism.) And the aims of all of these are different from those in the social sciences and area studies who would expose students to the dazzling differences in understanding, manners, and mores, in the name of multicultural toleration. It is no wonder that these groups are among the most hostile of adversaries in the contemporary university. At base, they have a great deal in common. Implicitly, theirs is a battle over the implications of shared assumptions.

What would a pragmatic conception of liberal education have to say about all of this? Pragmatism must begin by teaching a great appreciation for intellectual pluralism and diverse perspective, and an absolute tolerance for differences of understanding and opinion. However, pragmatism's reasons for toleration are strikingly different from those of the cultural relativist. Here we reach a clear epistemological divide. For the cultural relativist, there is no appeal from cultural understanding. There is no philosophy, no way of knowing, that can be used to demonstrate that one conventional system of understanding, or one moral code, is superior to another. All cultures must be regarded as equally valid, for there is no way to adjudicate among them. However, for the pragmatist, the reason for absolute tolerance of diverse viewpoints is different. It follows from pragmatism's categoric opposition to *a priori* metaphysics, best expressed in Peirce's famous dictum that one must never "block the path to further inquiry." For pragmatism, the greatest intellectual mistake is to prefigure the form that an answer to a problem must take. Thus, we cannot exclude certain views or perspectives from deliberation for we have no way of knowing, *in advance of inquiry,* whether or not they are true.

The reactions of the cultural relativist and the pragmatist to intellectual pluralism are totally distinct. For the cultural relativist, the response to diversity must be one of acceptance, for we have absolutely no way of knowing which perspective, which set of ways of knowing or doing is better. But for the pragmatist, diversity of perspective creates the occasion for practical reason, for inquiry. In the face of diverse counsel we are puzzled, perplexed. The question necessarily arises: Which way is best? How shall we now proceed?

It is no accident that philosophy is created in the harbor towns, the university towns, the trade centers, the places where cultures meet and ideas clash and collide. Where everything is settled and sure, centuries on end, there is no need for inquiry. It is only when we are met, every day, with different views, manners, mores, that we have to ask fundamental questions about truth, justice, and the good, that we have to decide such questions. It is only when we realize that it is possible to think otherwise that we come to question culture and convention, that out of puzzle and perplexity we try to transcend established wisdom, that we seek a better, truer way.

That is why pragmatists like diversity, the tumult of argument, the exercise of dialogue. And that is why pragmatists seek tolerance, not because they believe there is no difference between views, that all are of equivalent worth and merit, but precisely because they want to know which of these views yields a more reliable understanding of reality or a sounder guide to action.

I have now surveyed certain alternatives to our current free-elective approach to liberal education. I have tried to show that these approaches rest on deep epistemological differences, greatly divergent views of what is known and knowable. I have argued that neither the positivist contention that all we can know are observed material regularities, nor the postmodern view that the aim is to disabuse students of the possibility of knowing by showing them the artifice behind all systems of understanding, nor thc conscrvative relativist view that all we can know are the traditions and practices of a culture, will satisfy our real beliefs in what can be done with the powers of mind. It is in that spirit that I will make the case for a pragmatic conception of liberal education. I believe it demands more and opens the greater possibilities, that it comes closer to our best expectations of what the human mind can accomplish, of what we can come to understand.

Pragmatism and Idealism

I suspect that many may be attracted to pragmatism as an integrating theme for liberal education because it seems to fit well with the dominant skeptical temper of the academy. Either in its philosophical or its popular usage, the term pragmatism seems to connote an open and flexible way of thinking—adaptive, situational, "practical." Pragmatism seems the alternative to rigidity or dogma in any form. As Bruce Kimball suggests, pragmatism stands for a hypothetical and revisable notion of truth, for a method of experimental inquiry that aims at resolving doubt and solving problems, and that takes both questions of fact and value as proper subjects for collaborative inquiry.[1]

Pragmatism seems to underwrite a flexible and open curriculum. It ought to be open to diverse perspectives, a pluralism of approaches to knowledge. Kimball believes that pragmatism goes well with such ideas as multiculturalism, community service and citizenship, general education, and a pedagogy of active inquiry.[2] Pragmatism has always been congenial to science. But, in recent formulations (particularly those of Richard Rorty) pragmatism also seems compatible with current trends of critical theory in the humanities.[3] And, of course, the social sciences, and law, were strongly influenced by pragmatism in their formative years.

All of this may seem to argue for pragmatism as a relatively uncontentious way of bringing coherence and a sense of common purpose to the university and the teaching of the liberal arts. However, I do not speak for pragmatism on these grounds. Rather, I believe that pragmatism is the strongest philosophy we have for countering the dominant skepticism, iconoclasm, and pessimism of the contemporary university. I believe that pragmatism is our proximate link to the classic tradition of rationalism that runs from Plato and Aristotle to Hegel and Kant and beyond. I believe that pragmatism offers the best opportunity to reopen the basic questions of truth, excellence, and the good.

I realize that there are many versions of pragmatic philosophy and that pragmatism means different things to different people. However, I think that any understanding of this philosophy will have to account for what Hilary Putnam calls pragmatism's "realism" and its "holism."[4] Pragmatism, in any of its classic forms, presumes that systematic, organized inquiry will pay off, that we can learn more about how the world works and how best to lead our lives. This implies that there *is* an order to the world that is, at least in part, accessible to human understanding. Further, it must be assumed that this order is both material and mental—or moral. The last is a clear implication of pragmatism's "holism," its sense that questions of fact and value cannot be separated.

This idealist conception of pragmatism is closest to Peirce, though it can certainly be found in James and Dewey, as well. After all, the aim of pragmatic inquiry is the discovery of reliable knowledge, knowledge we can count on, knowledge that works well in practice, and reliable knowledge must be that which corresponds to the actual order of things. Objectivity is real: the world hits back when our subjective ideas do not match its essential patterns, its meaning in itself. And when our ideas do not fit reality (including the reality of the moral law within) and thus do not work well in practice, we face puzzlement and perplexity, and we inquire, we explore and correct, until we find a pattern of beliefs that enables us to go on, predictably and rightfully, at least until we face perplexity again.

Pragmatism entails a very specific view of human nature. It is, I believe, the only twentieth-century philosophy that takes the mind seriously. Most other theories of our time try to explain it away. They try to reduce mind to something else: economics to the calculation of pleasure and pain, sociobiology to the adaptive needs of the species, Freudianism to the repression of libidinal energy, psychology to stimulus and response, and so on. But pragmatism defines the human being as essentially an inquirer. Trying to figure out who we arc, whcrc we are, and what we are intended to do is the most natural activity of our species. Pragmatism, as I said before, is our last great link to the classic tradition, the tradition that took philosophy seriously.

Pragmatism teaches that inquiry is properly cooperative and collaborative and thus pragmatism might be regarded as a "communitarian" doctrine. But pragmatism also implies a very strong sense of the individual and the value of individual freedom. It is the individual who faces puzzles and predicaments. It is the individual who questions the workability and the rightfulness of established customs and conventions. It is the individual who tries to find a better way. In other words, pragmatism assumes not that the individual is created by culture but that the individual has the capacity to transcend culture. This view of the sacredness of the individual, of the individual soul as the ultimate immanent bearer of truth, is, of course, one that pragmatism shares with Socrates, Aristotle, Stoicism, Christianity, and liberalism—with all the great individualist traditions of thought.

The pragmatic theory of inquiry insists that we *confirm* our individual judgments together, intersubjectively, for the individual mind is subject to fantasy, illusion, error, distorted perspective. But simple agreement is not the pragmatic test of truth. While Rorty and others seem to say, at times, that pragmatic truth is just about any system of ideas that people agree on, for Peirce and James and Dewey agreement is wrought grudgingly. It is the idea that has been put to all the tests, exposed to all the doubts, and that still works well in practice that is tentatively and cautiously accepted as our best approximation, for the moment at least, of the way things actually are. And again, it is the individual, not the group, who must give assent, willing, uncoerced assent, assent after consideration of all the facts and all the options: assent as in the Socratic dialogue, assent as in science, assent as in liberal democratic deliberation.

Pragmatism is a suggestive theme for the reconstruction of liberal education not because it is at home with skepticism, relativism, and contemporary intellectual nihilism. Quite the contrary. In terms of Kimball's distinction between two great traditions of liberal education, that of the philosophers and that of the orators, pragmatism is squarely on the side of the philosophers.[5] Pragmatism would want liberal education to lead people to inquire further, probe deeper, to seek greater understanding, not simply to "speak well" according to the established doctrines of the day. Pragmatism does not encourage the mind to leap boundlessly, recklessly, as in the tradition of Nietzsche. Rather, it invites us to think carefully, responsibly, creatively, as in the best traditions of science and philosophy.

Pragmatic Liberal Education

The distinguishing features of a pragmatic liberal education follow directly from this image of human nature, of the powers of the individual, of the aims of inquiry. No scheme of education is impartial among human capabilities. Each tries to draw forth specific powers of the mind and spirit, powers that it takes as exemplary, as crucial, philosophically, to the human venture of thought. Other conceptions of liberal education might try to nurture detached, precise observation or intellectual autonomy, a skeptical wariness of all organized beliefs and practices. Pragmatism would encourage an idea of the work of the mind that is at once personal and social, that takes the point of view of the participant rather than the onlooker.

Elsewhere I have argued that the qualities of mind that liberal education should foster are those of practical reason, thereby suggesting a lineage that runs to Aristotle as much as Dewey.[6] I have outlined a scheme of education that would summon and strengthen these qualities. Here let me just give a brief sketch of the nature of that program and its rationale.

Practical reason is a human capacity as mysterious as it is commonplace. It arises whenever we realize that a performance is not as good as it could be, though we can evoke no specific model, no explicit set of criteria by which to specify just how the activity we are considering fails to meet the mark. Rather, we are measuring a performance against an ideal that exists nowhere in tangible reality but only in the mind. The ideal may be a dim conception of essential end or purpose, an Aristotelian conception of *telos*. (This is, you say, following all the possible binding themes surveyed in this paper, not quite all that a liberal education should be about, though you can give no clear picture, no precise operational definition, of what liberal education should aim at, what it ought to do.) Or our uneasiness may seem, eerily, like the Platonic conception of ideal form. (I have been sitting half an hour trying to write this paragraph. Something is not quite right. I don't know what it is, but my dissatisfaction suggests an image of inherent shape, and I am trying to make the words conform to that unconscious image, that strange, blurred sense of form.)

We do this every day, all the time. We say that we do not live in a perfect community, though we have never seen such a community. It does not exist in our experience. So where does this image come from?

This is the idealist element in pragmatic thought. Pragmatic puzzlement, the awareness of a problematic situation, does not arise only because a pattern of beliefs fails to predict results. Pragmatic puzzlement also occurs when we realize that our present beliefs are guiding us to actions that we sense are not quite right: we are working on assumptions that lead us to do things that we think are unjust, unfitting, or unlovely.

To take the cultivation of practical reason, which is to say, to take the nurture of the dispositions of mind that link Aristotle to pragmatism as the aim of liberal education is to advocate a distinctive conception of both research and teaching. But, as we shall see, this view of the work of the university is hardly radical or unfamiliar. We recognize it instantly. It is what we expected the university to do all along.

It has been the task of the university, through all the ages, to scrutinize the practices of society, the disciplines of thought, art, and action, to see if they could be made more efficient, more consistent with their own inherent point and purpose. Practical reason must see practice not as blind tradition but as technique, corrigible through critical analysis in the light of an understanding of essential purpose. This was the aim of the Scholastic university as it was of the universities of the Enlightenment. And it has been the aim of the American universities in the age of pragmatism, though here we see a revolutionary extension of the aim. For what truly distinguishes the American university is its assumption that practical reason is to be applied to the most humble subjects as well as the exalted ones. Thus, if reasoned analysis, the self-conscious scrutiny of practice, could make for better philosophy, medicine, or art, so could it make for better agriculture, commerce, and home management. The truly astonishing premise of the pragmatic American university has been that the ways of scholarship should become the ways of democracy.

It is the task of the university to teach the better habits of mind. The university should not be a place where we just toss ideas around, trade viewpoints without examining those viewpoints and asking how sound they are. Its pedagogy should be to teach best practice. Thus, the overall aim in teaching any subject is to show students how to correct and perfect their work in light of an exemplar, a model, and finally, when they are ready, an image of the intrinsic point of the study at issue.

We can think of the cultivation of practical reason as a teaching that must proceed through a series of distinct stages. The first step in learning is to do a thing at all. Later, you correct and improve. Then you do things your own way. Finally, if you are lucky, you become self-conscious about the standards you have been taught. You look for a better way. You become creative.

To play the piano, you must first find out where the notes are, how the scale works, what makes for harmony. Then you play a simple tune. Then you imitate your teacher. Later you interpret. You cannot reverse the process.

It is the same in every subject. The first aim of education after the students know the parts and how the system of ideas works, is to present them with exemplars, models, rules of good practice, standards. Then you create a situation: an essay, an experiment, a problem, and you let them try to reach the standard, correct and refine their performance, in light of the model. This is how you teach, or *should* teach, skiing, physics, large animal veterinary practice, creative writing, political philosophy, or dance.

But this cannot be the end of liberal education. It may be enough for the technician to imitate best practice. It is not enough for the true professional. The professional is a full citizen in a practice, a calling. The true professional does not simply follow doctrine but *examines* doctrine, critically, aware of it as an imperfect, flawed structure that always begs for improvement. Such a professional must be liberally educated. This person must come to see the discipline as a human construct, a rough approximation of an ideal form. To be liberally educated is to pass through the relativizing experience taught by the skeptic, the debunker, the postmodern critical theorist, the pragmatic idealist. But the aim of this teaching is not estrangement from a discipline but an enticement to creativity within it.

The final aim of liberal education is to evoke creativity, and creativity does not mean doing things differently but doing them better. Creativity may be an act of defiance but it is also an act of loyal participation in a genre, a science, a profession, an art. Creativity means breaking the rules. But it also means being guided by that dim idea of essential purpose that gives meaning to the life of any human activity. So it is the engineer who asks "What is good design?" the doctor who asks "What is health?" the attorney who asks "What is justice?" who stands the best chance, pragmatically, of being creative.

Practical reason is a general disposition of mind that applies to every art and activity, every craft and calling. In liberal education this is the work of all the disciplines, a coordinated effort, in which each has its own part to play. In fact, to take the cultivation of practical reason as the goal of liberal education requires that scholars *transcend* discipline in quest of a common purpose.

Elsewhere, I have described my own model of a liberal arts curriculum.[7] In it, I have a special place for the history of ideas, for the great books, for through such study students can learn the uncertain development, the contingency of thought. They can get a picture of the brief moment they occupy in the ongoing adventure of the mind.

I think liberal education should be strong on science. The liberally educated person should know the current scientific worldview and how we contrived it, all the breathtaking things about the age of the earth, the intimate structures of life, the size of the cosmos, that we have learned so recently, as well as all the ways in which our scientific theory has become more baffling and confounded, all the ways in which we now, more humbly, realize that we do not quite understand.

We inquire to reach understanding, to find shared meaning, and those huge realms of experience and thought that escape scientific analysis are still, properly, the domain of the humanities. Pragmatic idealism means that we keep trying to catch a vision that lies always beyond our reach and that is, of course, also the aim of poetry, of literature.

The social sciences tried, in our century, to imitate the physical sciences, and they failed, massively, to render human nature lawlike. What they achieved instead, perhaps more valuable, through patient and often daring inquiry into all our ways, our peculiarities and idiosyncracies, is a remarkable and recognizably unfinished picture of how complex and contradictory we are, and how diverse. And practically, the social sciences have taught us something about how to systematize sympathy and compassion, how to fit our practices a little better to our nature.

Finally, I would want students to have a deep understanding of scientific inquiry in the fullest, most philosophical sense, and of liberal political thought. These are our two fundamental instruments of practical reason, of drawing together, finding community and common purpose. Scientific method represents the optimistic side of our nature, the remarkable thought that if we investigate systematically, check things out, take nothing for granted, we might conceivably come to understand things in the same way. Liberal political theory stands for the tougher, more realistic and pessimistic side of our nature. It teaches us how to live together when we know we will not agree, when we know we will understand things differently, seek different conceptions of the good. It teaches us how to get along when inquiry fails, or before it succeeds, in tolerance, in mutual respect.

The pragmatic idea of practical reason can provide a unifying ideal for liberal education. It is the habit of thought that must guide us in meeting our everyday needs and that can take us as well to the edge of the mountains, to the regions of our most sublime visions and our highest aspirations. The effort to match practical action to ideal purpose applies to all our everyday activities. It is what we must do in making a tool, raising a child, managing a firm. Practical reason in this broad, essential sense, is what guides our science and our art, all our efforts to embody our intelligence and sensitivity in a shared cumulative system. But the habit of asking about essential purpose and how we can best approximate it in our actions can take us also close to the heart of our wonder. For those who have developed the habit of thinking this way will eventually come to ask why mind exists in the world and how we, the thinkers, are supposed to use this inexplicable power. At this point, all barriers and pretensions have to crumble, and science and religion have to meet. If we can bring our students all this way, bring them to know a way of thinking that starts in the most mundane tasks and leads to the absolute edge of awe and understanding, then we, the educators, will have done our job.

Notes

1. Bruce A. Kimball, "Toward Pragmatic Liberal Education," in Robert Orrill, editor, *The Condition of American Liberal Education* (New York: College Entrance Examination Board, 1995), 83.
2. Ibid., 97.
3. Richard Rorty, *Contingency, Irony, and Solidarity* (New York: Cambridge University Press, 1989).
4. Hilary Putnam, *Pragmatism* (New York: Blackwell, 1995), 5–7.
5. Bruce A. Kimball, *Orators and Philosophers* (New York: College Entrance Examination Board, 1995).
6. Charles W. Anderson, *Prescribing the Life of the Mind* (Madison: University of Wisconsin Press, 1993).
7. Ibid., chaps. 6–7.

Innovation in the Liberal Arts and Sciences

Douglas C. Bennett
President, Earlham College

W hat is the shape of innovation today in the liberal arts and sciences? How is the curriculum of the liberal arts college changing in the United States? We are not now in an era of dramatic transformation. The last such major change came toward the end of the nineteenth century. In contrast, at the present time, we can see many smaller, but vital changes being implemented at colleges and universities across the country. These bend, extend, and question the framework of the modern liberal arts curriculum, the one we have been working within for about a century. But despite considerable exploration and impulse to innovate, I do not believe it is yet possible to see the shape, even dimly, of a completely transformed curriculum of the liberal arts and sciences.

From this starting point I want to make some observations about how the liberal arts curriculum is changing today, and I want to make them against the backdrop of the last major transformation—which took the nineteenth-century college largely by surprise. The focus of

These reflections are based on two sources. One is a project of the American Council of Learned Societies on Innovation and Vitality in Liberal Education, which is funded by the John D. and Catherine T. MacArthur Foundation. With these funds ACLS has been sponsoring a grant competition for innovative projects at relatively less well-endowed liberal arts colleges, and studying broader patterns of innovation in the liberal arts and sciences. The other source is research I have been conducting on the transformation of the structures and purposes of education in the liberal arts and sciences between 1880 and 1920. In working on this project, I have drawn on resources in the archives of Haverford, Reed, and Swarthmore Colleges, and in the extensive collection of college catalogs at the Center for Research Libraries in Chicago. I am grateful for assistance from staff members at all of these institutions.

this discussion is on four-year liberal arts colleges, but a great deal of what I have to say pertains to liberal arts colleges within universities, as well. At the end I want to suggest some contexts that will shape the possibilities for innovation over the next decade and also raise a question about the purposes of innovation.

The Curriculum of the Nineteenth-Century Liberal Arts College

When Reed College opened in 1911 as a bold initiative in the liberal arts and sciences, it offered courses and majors organized around the following subjects: biology, chemistry, economics, education, English, German, Greek, history, Latin, mathematics, philosophy, physics, politics, psychology, romance languages (French, Italian, Spanish), and sociology.

This list of offerings is familiar: it is a menu of the disciplines that continue to comprise the liberal arts and sciences. Missing from the current, common list of liberal arts and disciplines are only anthropology and the fine and performing arts (creative writing, dance, music, and theater). All would be added at Reed, and only education would subsequently disappear, cast out for being a professional field.

The list of fields in the Reed curriculum is remarkable only if we turn and look at it from the other direction, from the standpoint of the nineteenth century. Only a few decades before, no liberal arts college would have organized its curriculum around these two dozen or so fields of knowledge. Nor would any college have provided students with such a degree of choice among fields of study. But between (approximately) 1870 and 1910, in a revolution whose consequences have continuing force today, the curriculum of liberal arts colleges was reorganized around these disciplines.

Before 1870, the undergraduate curriculum at virtually every college and university in the United States was composed of a series of studies prescribed by year. Latin, Greek, and mathematics figured prominently in these prescribed studies. Significant attention was also given to elocution and rhetoric, to natural philosophy (particularly, early on, astronomy and geology; later chemistry and physics), to men-

tal and moral philosophy, and (though on the decline over the course
of the century) to religious instruction.

Thus, for most of the nineteenth century, the major characteristics of the curriculum were:

- Single preparation for all purposes. It was conceived with the
  view that a single course of study was the best preparation for all
  that might follow. Over the first three-quarters of the nineteenth
  century, just one fissure appeared in this single preparation: most
  institutions came to offer a "scientific course" as an alternative
  to the "classical course," thereby placing less emphasis on Greek
  and more on modern languages, and including a few more scientific subjects, both prescribed and elective.
- Undivided faculty. The prescribed curriculum was conceived to
  be taught by a single, undivided faculty. While professors had
  titles identifying their areas of special competence, they were not
  differentiated into separate schools or departments. Although
  individual members of the faculty conducted recitations in particular subjects or gave lectures in their area of special competence, all shared responsibility for the whole curriculum.
- Unity of knowledge. The curriculum was rooted in a distinct, if
  only occasionally articulated, conception of the unity of knowledge. It was a synthesis rooted in the medieval harmonizing of
  reason and revelation, of Athens and Jerusalem. While the curriculum had made a place for empirical science by the early nineteenth century, it found increasing difficulty in accommodating
  some of the fruits of that science, particularly after the publication of *On the Origin of Species* in 1859.
- Explicit pedagogy. There was an explicitly stated conception of
  how the course of study, conceived as a whole, was intended to
  educate and improve those who followed it from beginning to
  end. There was a justification of the role of each part in the whole.
  The Haverford catalog statement of 1860, for example, justified
  the study of Greek and Latin as intending "to improve and cultivate the taste by the study of the great masterpieces of antiqui-
  ty, and to train and strengthen the reasoning powers, by the analy-

sis of words and thoughts required in translation, and particularly by the investigation of the syntax of the Greek and Latin—the best practical logic."

This was a curriculum little touched by the Enlightenment.

Over the course of the nineteenth century, the major innovation was to increase the amount of attention given to natural philosophy—the sciences. Nearly everywhere, even in the new public institutions, there were courses showing that the new science and the old revealed truths were not in conflict. *(Evidences of Christianity* and *Analogy of Natural and Revealed Religion* were the titles of widely used textbooks.) The emphasis remained on the presentation of a core of established knowledge. For most of the century, it did little good to insist that this curriculum did not include the most modern discoveries and advances in knowledge. This was not the point. An influential report of the Yale faculty in 1828 argued for a pedagogy of mental discipline:

> The two great points to be gained in intellectual culture are the discipline and furniture of the mind; expanding its powers, and storing it with knowledge. The former of these is, perhaps, the more important of the two. A commanding object, therefore, in a collegiate course of study, should be to call into daily and vigorous exercise the faculties of the student.[1]

Indeed, this education did have some of the characteristics of sessions at the gym. It was composed of a sort of mental calisthenics. There

The Old Curriculum and the New in the Liberal Arts and Sciences

	19th century	*20th century*
curriculum	nondisciplinary	disciplinary
	fixed course of study	elective-choice/majors
faculty	lay generalists	specialized professionals
mode of instruction	recitation and disputation	lecture/discussion
		lecture/lab
	lectures for new advances	seminars for advanced work
specialized facilities	display cabinets	libraries
and settings		laboratories

were recitations in the morning during which students repeated lessons memorized the evening before, and disputations in the afternoon, in which students engaged in a stylized form of oral argumentation.

The Disciplining of the Curriculum

The great change in the American curriculum, which began to gain momentum in the last quarter of the nineteenth century, is generally described as "the triumph of the elective system," or the "opening up of the curriculum" to new subjects. Charles William Eliot, president of Harvard, is rightly seen as the leader, the champion of the new curriculum. It is largely his description we use when we see this as an "opening up." But I believe it is more revealing, and more accurate, to see this change as the coming of the disciplines: as *the disciplining of the curriculum.*

Eliot saw that the received, time-honored curriculum was unexciting, boring. It awoke no passion, no interest in the students. Around him he saw a range of subjects, new fields of learning, that he felt would energize the curriculum and make it more effective. He waged a long campaign (joined by others, of course) to include these new fields. He urged, for example:

> To the list of studies which the sixteenth century called liberal, I would therefore add, as studies of equal rank, English, French, German, history, political economy and natural science, not one of which can be said to have existed when the definition of liberal education which is still in force was laid down.[2]

Several things are worth noting about Eliot's statement. First is that all of these fields did come to be securely included in the liberal arts curriculum within 20 years, and as fields of equal rank. Some of these fields came to be organized, as disciplines, along somewhat different lines than he suggested. Natural science would be (already was, for the practitioners) clearly partitioned into physics, chemistry, and biology. (In some institutions, astronomy and geology would also be included in separate disciplines within the arts and sciences.) Political economy would come to be included as separate disciplines of economics and political science. And there are fields whose case he did not press, but which would also be added over the next two decades, such as anthropology, sociology, and psychology. Finally, Eliot referred to these as "studies" rather than "disciplines." In 1884, we are still somewhat in advance of the firm crystallization of knowledge into discrete disciplines.

In the transformation, the sciences led the way: they were the first fields to form themselves into disciplines. They constituted what a discipline is, and younger fields in the humanities and social sciences were compelled either to fit this conception or establish a new one.

In the transformation, each of the key features of the old, prescribed curriculum was altered. No longer would there be a single invariant course of study for all students. The faculty came to be divided into departments, though it took some time for the modern array of departments to emerge. Learned societies in each of the new disciplines were founded during this period, and through them faculty sought professional identity and recognition in their field. With the formation of separate disciplines and an array of departments, all semblance of the unity of knowledge was broken. Finally, as each field explored how best to educate its students, the idea of a single, explicit pedagogy passed from view.

Problems in the New Curriculum

Between approximately 1875 and 1910, the change that Eliot and others had set in motion worked a grand transformation in the undergraduate curriculum. Many new subjects/disciplines were added, and students found themselves with an expanding array of choices in meeting the requirements of a B.A. or B.S. degree. Of course, the progress was uneven and each of the institutions that went through this change has its own unique story. Nonetheless, any institution founded before the Civil War, and most founded before 1900, went through some form of transition from the unified, prescribed curriculum to the new disciplinary one.

Everywhere, the new disciplinary curriculum replaced the old single course of study rooted in mathematics, Greek and Roman classics, and the Bible. Why are we not more aware of this great transformation? Because our attention has been focused (now as well as then) on a number of other major changes in the world of higher education: the formation of universities in the true sense, the formation of graduate programs, the professionalization of the faculty, public institutions supplanting private ones in terms of numbers of students, and a greater emphasis on research and education directly serving the economy. These changes created a context that shaped the transformation of the undergraduate curriculum, but they also obscured from view the dramatic transformation of a centuries-old strategy of liberal arts education.

By the first decade of the twentieth century, the new, elective curriculum, or rather the new curriculum organized in terms of disciplines, was so firmly entrenched that Thermidor had begun to set in. Faculties were so concerned about what they viewed as chaotic student choices that most colleges instituted *majors* to ensure some structure in student programs. In view of the conservative impulse behind the introduction of majors, it is ironic that this served further to strengthen the place of the disciplines as the organizing fabric of the curriculum.

By 1910, the new curriculum was organized around 20 to 25 disciplines, each with its own department, its own introductory and advanced courses, and its own major. The word "course" was no longer used to describe the overall program of study, but rather to describe each of the dozens, then hundreds, and perhaps thousands of distinct offerings from among which students could choose in assembling a program.

This new curriculum gave rise to two enduring problems, enduring because they are problems given in the very structure of the curriculum: (1) What learning should be common for all students? and (2) what fields or disciplines will be included in the liberal arts and sciences (and which excluded)? Let us call these the problem of common learning and the problem of inclusion. Each deserves a much longer discussion, but let me say a few words about each.

The Problem of Common Learning As additional fields of study (disciplines) were added to the curriculum, it quickly became clear that students could not be asked to study them all. The elective principle came to dominate the curriculum, but still there was the question of what should be the common learning. Broadly speaking, there are only three possible answers. Each has been tried frequently; each has severe drawbacks. Almost every institution has rotated through these various possibilities. Almost no institution has found a stable solution.

- Denial. An institution can deny the problem by asserting that a college education should be a specialized one. With this view, general education should be completed by the end of high school. This has been the least common of the three answers. The difficulty with this solution is that it merely relegates the problem to a different setting. If common learning is a problem for the high schools, how should it be organized in that setting?
- Core. A second answer has been to construct an introductory "core" course of study distinct from the disciplines in which students can major. The most successful of these core curricula have been spacious intellectual constructions of confident individuals or groups at particular universities. The recurring problem of such core curricula arises from their lack of foundation in the disciplines that constitute professionalism for faculty. Rarely have these great "cores" survived the transition from one generation of faculty at an institution to the next. Rarely have they been successfully transplanted from one institution to another.
- Distribution. The third and by far most frequent solution to the problem of providing common learning has been to require that students gain a modest acquaintance with a variety of disciplines by requiring students to take one or a few courses in several different disciplinary groups. This approach accepts that knowledge cannot be successfully organized or conveyed outside disciplinary boundaries. Because of the sheer number of disciplines that have been accepted into the canon of the liberal arts and sciences, this strategy requires some accepted grouping of the many disciplines into a few areas that either provide menus of choice for students or areas for construction of common courses. While this has been the most practical strategy, from the standpoint of drawing and

holding faculty support, it has been least satisfactory intellectually because it is not common learning at all. The groupings can
be more political than intellectual constructions. There need not
be any regular contact among the fields or faculty in a group.
There may be nothing genuinely common in what students learn.

The Problem of Inclusion As the curriculum was reorganized around disciplines, difficult decisions had to be made about which fields would
be included within the "new" liberal arts and sciences, and which would
be left outside. Many of the early disputes over this problem of inclusion have been forgotten. Let me quickly outline a few of the implicit lines of inclusion, and note a few of the fields that were left out.

■ Mental/not physical. Physical education (or gymnastics) was an
integral part of the traditional curriculum, but it did not survive
the transition to the new, disciplinary, elective curriculum, nor
did instruction in drawing, both free-hand and mechanical. These
had also commonly been part of the traditional curriculum, and
not as creative endeavors but as practical arts. The new, accepted disciplines were primarily those of the mind.
■ Speculative/not practical. Many liberal arts colleges added an
engineering course soon after they added a scientific course,
and engineering has persisted as a department within some liberal arts colleges. Some liberal arts colleges also organized departments of education at the turn of the century. A few even added
law. On the whole, however, practical fields such as education,
engineering, law, business, and journalism came to be organized
as separate colleges within universities, not as disciplines within the liberal arts. The disciplines accepted into the liberal arts
tended to be theoretical and speculative domains of inquiry.
■ Written/not oral. Rhetoric, elocution, and forensics had been
common subjects in the prescribed curriculum, and students were
often examined orally both through daily recitations and periodic
formal presentations. Rhetoric survived, if at all, not as a separate
discipline but as part of English language and literature. Freshman composition courses became its most common venue. The

oral arts, once a particular focus of instruction, were largely excluded. Why this exclusion of the oral arts? Perhaps because the authoritative form of communication in the new academic disciplines
was written (research papers, scholarly journals) rather than oral.

■ Secular/not sacred. The prescribed curriculum was elaborated
within an overarching religious frame, and within it were some
religious subjects. Scriptural readings were often included through
all four years, even in public institutions. "Evidences of Christianity," which squared the Bible with the progress of knowledge
in other fields, was a subject often included in the third or fourth
year. Neither survived the transition to the new order. Only after
some decades had passed did religion begin to be added as a
secular academic discipline.

The problem of common learning and the problem of inclusion are
endemic given the construction of the modern, twentieth-century curriculum of the liberal arts and sciences. They continue to dominate faculty attention to the shape and substance of the curriculum.

The Frontiers of Innovation Today

Broadly speaking, we have had two major waves of innovation subsequent to the dramatic transformation of the curriculum in the late
nineteenth century—the transformation that brought the "disciplining" of the curriculum. The first was in the 1920s when (for example) Bennington College (1925) and Sarah Lawrence College (1926)
were founded. The second was in the 1960s when (for example)
Hampshire College (1965) and Evergreen State University (1967)
were founded. In the 1920s, the arts began to be introduced into the
curriculum; the 1960s were marked by a greater emphasis on interdisciplinary studies; both waves of innovation saw a greater emphasis
on independent student projects.

The 1990s are not another major era of innovation, but we are
in a time of exploration, a time of pressing against many of the limits and given features of the curriculum of the liberal arts and sciences
in this century. We are seeing many efforts to broaden the curricu-

lum to include new kinds of courses, to broaden the strategies of instruction, and to broaden the appeal to new kinds of students. There are efforts to integrate fields of study in new interdisciplinary and multidisciplinary courses and programs, and to integrate different skills and technologies within them. A curriculum that has been kept largely separate from the world is now being more closely connected to it via workplace internships, service opportunities, and collaborations with schools. And there are many explorations of ways to assess more fully and precisely what students are learning.

These, I believe, are the major frontiers of innovation in the curriculum of the liberal arts and sciences today.

Internationalization

For most of this century, the curriculum of the liberal arts and sciences has been bounded by the ancient civilizations of the Near East, Greece, and Rome, and by the history, languages, and cultures of Western Europe. For the past three decades, many colleges and universities have been broadening their curriculum to embrace a much wider range of cultures in Africa, Asia, and Latin America, and also to embrace a fuller array of racial and ethnic groups and social classes within the United States. This has involved the introduction of additional languages (Chinese, Japanese, Arabic), and also stretched the resources of these institutions to encompass this greater reach. At many colleges and universities, the interest in a more international curriculum has been accompanied by increased opportunities for foreign study in a wider array of countries and in a manner more easily integrated with majors other than those in the foreign languages.

Interdisciplinary Fields

By 1940, the liberal arts and sciences had come to include about two dozen disciplinary fields in the arts, humanities, social sciences, and sciences; and the curriculum had come to be organized around courses and majors offered by faculty appointed in departments organized around these fields. With quickening pace since the 1960s, there have been efforts to break this disciplinary segmentation via the creation of integrated, interdisciplinary fields of study. Area studies have been important for integrating across the humanities and social sciences, for example. The natural sciences have also been swept up in this interdisciplinary impulse through such new fields as environmental studies and cognitive science.

Also included in this surge of interdisciplinary studies have been renewed efforts to construct interdisciplinary core curricula for general education purposes, and efforts to distribute the learning of basic capabilities such as writing, speaking, quantitative reasoning, and ethical judgment broadly across the curriculum.

Collaborative Learning

For most of this century, students engaged in college and university study have worked alone on projects on which they are evaluated: exams, papers, laboratory exercises, creative projects. There is now a noticeable interest in strategies of collaborative learning. Across the curriculum, teachers ask students to work together, to assist one another in their learning, to do projects and even examinations together. In teaching writing, for example, many programs are asking students to read and critique one another's drafts. In the sciences, group projects are becoming more common. While collaborative strategies appear to improve student learning, they seem to do this in a way that does not require a smaller faculty:student ratio.

Experiential and Service Learning

The liberal arts curriculum of the twentieth century has largely approached learning in a speculative rather than a practical mode. Classrooms have been places apart; students have studied their subjects in settings separated from the actual sites and daily activities of the subject in question. Another frontier of innovation is bringing more experiential and hands-on learning activity into the classroom. Science education has always involved a degree of hands-on work in the laboratory, but today there is a new stress on getting students involved earlier and more often in hands-on, discovery-oriented problem solving in the laboratory, in the classroom, and out of doors.

Other disciplines are exploring the efficacy of hands-on, experiential learning as well through laboratory-like exercises, simulations, and off-campus activities. A closely related development is the dramatic increase of interest in service-learning programs that involve students in a wide variety of service activities and ask them to reflect in a structured way on what they experience.

Information Technology

The technologies of digital networks promise dramatic change in the ways students and faculty communicate with one another, and in the kinds of library/information environments available for teaching and learning. We are only beginning to explore this promise, but already it is clear that we can provide new and varied kinds of opportunities for carrying discussion beyond the classroom, and that we can break down the traditional boundaries between library and classroom or laboratory. We may not yet know how vital face-to-face interaction is to a liberal arts education, and thus not yet know the possibilities and limitations of the liberal arts and sciences via distance education. Nevertheless, we do know that digital networks are allowing students to explore resources and cultures at a considerable distance.

Wider Access

A last kind of innovation is different from the others. Liberal arts education has predominantly served students from more affluent families. African-American and Hispanic students have been less likely to enroll in such programs. Consequently, many colleges and universities are exploring ways to widen access to liberal arts programs and to increase the diversity of their student bodies. Finding additional resources for financial aid (both need- and merit-based) is one strategy for accomplishing this. But colleges are also trying to find ways to ease the transition to such a program by offering the first year closer to home (in the high school or in a nearby church) or by increasing the opportunities for peer or professional advising and counseling.

How do these changes alter or question the basic framework of the liberal arts and sciences curriculum in this century? In these ways, I believe:

- The exploration of interdisciplinary subjects presses against the disciplinary framing of the curriculum. A greater openness to interdisciplinarity may also ease, somewhat, the search for a solution to the problem of the first two years. But there is nothing to suggest we are close to abandoning disciplines as the basic way we organize knowledge and the curriculum.

- In a number of ways, we are reopening the battles over inclusion and exclusion of fields. With experiential, hands-on learning becoming more common, we are moving beyond the mental to the physical, as well. With service learning and a greater interest in the professions, we are opening a door to the practical as well as the speculative. An almost exclusive focus on the written word is now being challenged by greater attention to oral performance, and to audio and visual materials. New technology is making these more accessible for teaching and learning. And the exclusion of the sacred? This is least clearly under threat, but I believe there is a kind of sacred edge in the development of multidisciplinary "identity studies" fields such as women's studies, African-American studies, ethnic studies, and the like.

- The modern curriculum of the liberal arts and sciences has been bounded by the edge of the campus and by the Western world. These limits are being dismantled in a thoroughgoing way, but will this fundamentally alter the basic framework of the modern curriculum? I believe it is too early to tell.

- Finally, we are seeing not so much a questioning of faculty expertise as a critical element in teaching/learning, as a gathering consensus that students can also learn powerfully from one another by engaging together in inquiry and exploration. The experiments with collaborative learning point in this direction, but the commitment to greater ethnic and racial diversity within the student body also has this as a basic premise. (Diversity is good because students learn even more from one another when they come from a variety of backgrounds.) And digital networks will make this kind of collaborative activity much easier to encourage and sustain.

Forces for Change in the Future

What will change the curriculum of the liberal arts and sciences in the future? Each of the six frontiers of innovation outlined above is likely to entail further significant change. So far, innovation along these lines has pressed against the framework of the modern curriculum, but without constituting or precipitating a fundamental transformation. Will innovation continue along these lines? It is not possible to say, just as (I believe) it was impossible to foresee the restructuring of the liberal arts and sciences along disciplinary lines until the change was very much upon us. Instead, let me identify a few contexts that, I believe, will be decisive in shaping how the liberal arts and sciences will change over the next decade or two.

Changes in Knowledge

The last dramatic restructuring of the curriculum took place at a time when the structure of knowledge was itself changing. The disciplines were crystallizing into a kind of archipelago: a linked series of discrete fields with limited contact with one another. At the same time, learned societies were formed to care for each of the newly independent fields of study, and the terms of preparation (graduate education) of a now-professionalized professoriate were worked out. It is reasonable to suppose that the next major transformation of the curriculum will be conditioned by a significant restructuring of knowledge. Perhaps the emergence of interdisciplinary and multidisciplinary study has this potential, but only if it becomes much more thoroughgoing—a change that would redefine the structure of knowledge, not just make links within an existing disciplinary structure.[3]

The Redesign of Higher Education

Driven especially by a withdrawal of public financing, the shrinkage of both state support for public universities and federal support for financial aid, colleges and universities are being forced to refocus their activities and adhere to much stronger insistences for accountability. Students and parents are being forced to shoulder a much larger share of the cost of an education. Will the liberal arts and sciences survive this withdrawal of support? Will their purposes be redirected? The space for innovation could shrink dramatically, but at the same time there could be fresh impulse to bring about change—to make the liberal arts and sciences as vital and relevant as possible.

The Reform of K–12 Education

During and following the late-nineteenth-century transformation of the liberal arts curriculum, the divide between schools and colleges deepened considerably. At the same time, many of the features of the newly emergent curriculum in the colleges were replicated in the schools, particularly disciplinary organization and discrete courses (elective choice not nearly so much).

Quite a different situation pertains today. Much more than in higher education, K–12 schools are currently a focus of intense public scrutiny; a comprehensive reform agenda is being worked through. Its elements include developing state or national standards for assessing student learning, insisting on greater accountability for individual schools to achieve or exceed these norms, and placing a greater emphasis on facilitating transitions from school to work.

Facilitating transitions from school to college is much less a current focus of concern, but, without doubt, the changes that do transpire in K–12 education (intended or not) will have significant impact on the shape of higher education. If students are taught differently in schools than they have been in the past, will this not alter their expectations for how they will be taught in college? If education standards are broadly implemented in a number of areas, is there not likely to be a call for more advanced standards to be adopted in the same subject areas by higher education institutions? Might this not put a brake on the development of interdisciplinary courses and programs? For several decades, innovations have tended to pass down the educational ladder from college to school. Today it is more likely that innovations (or lack thereof) will pass from the schools to the colleges.

The Purposes of Innovation

I want to close by posing a question about the *purposes* of innovation. What are we trying to accomplish with any change? Innovations should serve the basic purposes of an education in the liberal arts and sciences, making such an education even more effective, or adjusting it to fit changed circumstances. Consequently, we need to ask what will be improved, what purposes will be served, by making an education in the liberal arts and sciences more interdisciplinary, or more international, or more experiential?

I raise this question because I believe we have drifted away from clarity about what a liberal arts education is intended to accomplish and because we are in an era when students, parents, public officials, and others will ask searching questions about the value of such an education—and about whether it is worth the cost.

Again, the backdrop of the last major transformation is valuable. In the nineteenth century, there was broad agreement about the purposes of such an education: the purpose was "the shaping of character." The supporters of the old curriculum believed that a liberal education would develop certain intellectual and moral capabilities. They believed that development of these intellectual and moral capabilities would improve not only how one thought, but how one acted in the world. The idea of "character" was the most accepted way of talking about how knowledge informed or guided action in the world. It had governed the idea of the liberal arts and sciences for centuries.

The change from the old to the new curriculum was very much seen as a change in *means,* not in ends. The disciplining of the curriculum in terms of new fields of study (the opening up of the curriculum) was meant to make it more effective with regard to the same purposes, not to make a change in this purpose. "There is a vast difference in intellectual content between the old college and the new," asserted Alexander Meiklejohn in 1915. He was president of Amherst College and one of the most visionary education leaders at the beginning of the twentieth century. He added, "but the new institutions are at one in the belief in the value of knowledge as the guide of human life."⁴ Meiklejohn was affirming that something dramatic had taken place in the curriculum, but he was also insisting that the purpose had not changed: the reformed institutions would continue to adhere to a view that knowledge should be the guide of human life.

Over the course of this century we have retreated from this conception. We are very unlikely today to speak at all of "shaping character." And though we are unlikely to spcak of "virtues," we are much more likely to think in terms of developing intellectual virtues (critical thinking, creativity, and tolerance of ambiguity) than of developing moral ones (honesty, integrity, generosity, and the ability to make aesthetic and moral judgments). Another indication of the drift away from clarity about purpose is this: we usually juxtapose a liberal arts education with a vocational one, but in an odd reversal we have come to talk about the goals of a liberal arts education in terms of developing certain "skills," such as writing, speaking, critical thinking, and the like. Does this not suggest ambivalence or discomfort in thinking in terms of more exalted purposes?

Speaking of "character" has an old-fashioned ring for many who today care passionately about the liberal arts and sciences, and for some even suggests a particular political agenda. Consequently, let me pose this question instead: do we expect an education in the liberal arts and sciences to be *additive* or *transformative?* Do we expect it simply to add some skills to our capabilities and improve others? Or do we expect it to transform students in some more fundamental way? (Do we expect it to "turn the soul?") I believe we will find it difficult to justify the considerable personal and financial investment required for a liberal arts education if we are not prepared to defend a transformative purpose.

Oddly enough, I expect the purposes of "shaping character" have been better served by the twentieth-century curriculum than by the nineteenth-century one. The curriculum of the twentieth century has engaged students more forcefully, and what we know about "how college affects students" suggests (for example) that the strengthening of moral reasoning is one of the most significant consequences of a college education.⁵ The innovations of the present are probably working even further in this direction. But in an era when greater account-ability is being insisted upon, there is considerable danger in being vague about our goals. There is perhaps even greater danger in speaking of our goals in a more diminished way than we mean. If people believe our goals are only to develop skills, we are vulnerable to even further erosion in public support for the liberal arts and sciences as the best kind of education. Perhaps, therefore, the most meaningful innovation to come is a renewal of our purposes.

Notes

1. Yale Report of 1828 (a report of the Yale faculty), in Richard Hofstadter and Wilson Smith, editors, *American Higher Education: A Documentary History* (Chicago: University of Chicago Press, 1962).
2. Charles William Eliot, "What Is a Liberal Education?" in *Educational Reform: Essays and Addresses* (New York: The Century Company, 1898), 113. The essay was first published in 1884.
3. On changes in the disciplines, see the Winter 1997 issue of *Daedalus:* "American Academic Culture in Transformation: Fifty Years, Four Disciplines." For a provocative account of what is happening to one discipline (English), see Louis Menand, "The Demise of Disciplinary Authority," in Alvin Kernan, editor, *What's Happened to the Humanities?* (Princeton, NJ: Princeton University Press, 1997), 201–19.
4. Alexander Meiklejohn, "What the Liberal College Is Not," in *The Liberal College* (Boston: Marshall Jones Company, 1920), 24.
5. See Ernest T. Pascarella and Frank T. Terenzini, *How College Affects Students: Findings and Insights from Twenty Years of Research* (San Francisco: Jossey Bass, 1991), 335–68. For a thoughtful, contemporary account of "shaping character" as the goal of a liberal arts education, see Rudolph Weingartner, *Undergraduate Education: Goals and Means* (New York: American Council on Education and Macmillan, 1992), 68–82.

Professing the Liberal Arts

LEE S. SHULMAN

CHARLES E. DUCOMMUN PROFESSOR OF EDUCATION,
STANFORD UNIVERSITY, AND PRESIDENT, THE CARNEGIE FOUNDATION
FOR THE ADVANCEMENT OF TEACHING

Introduction

One of the prevailing themes of this volume is the presumed tension between the *liberal* and the *pragmatic*. These strains are often associated with a distrust of "the vocational" or "the professional" among liberal arts faculty and administrators, who view these orientations as slippery slopes down which unsuspecting educators might slide into a horrific purgatory. Liberal learning, we are warned, is pursued for its own sake, and cannot be subordinated to the aims of application or vocation. I come to offer a shocking alternative view. I wish to argue that the problem with the liberal arts is not that they are endangered by the corruption of professionalism. Indeed, their problem is that they are not professional enough. If we are to preserve and sustain liberal education, we must make it more professional; we must learn to *profess the liberal arts*.

I offer this heresy as a peculiar hybrid of two ostensibly incompatible traditions. I am a graduate of the College of the University of Chicago which ought to identify me as a devotee of the purest form of liberal education, the Hutchins orientation toward the great books, the traditional canon itself. And I view my education in the Hutchins College as the most precious gift I have ever received. However, I am also a student of Joseph Schwab, the Chicago biologist and philosopher who was one of John Dewey's strongest advocates and spokespersons in higher education, even though he was also seen as a protégé of Hutchins. Many educators whom I respect deeply, such as Tom Ehrlich, point out that the Hutchins and Dewey views of liberal education are inherently incompatible. Yet I would claim, without embarrassment, that I define myself as a legitimate offspring of that liaison between Dewey and Hutchins and I feel unusually blessed to be progeny of that unlikely coupling.

I am reminded of David Hume's clever characterization of abstract ideas such as "cause" or "external existence," which he claimed were illegitimate logical constructs because they lacked direct empirical sources. How was it possible that the human knower could be so confident that he could use concepts such as "cause" even though they were not adequately connected to experience? Hume dubbed such concepts "bastards of imagination impregnated by experience." These abstract ideas were the illegitimate offspring of a liaison between imagination and experience, but could claim no legitimate epistemological standing. In that spirit, I come to you as a bastard of Deweyan progressivism impregnated by the Hutchins College. I am the illegitimate issue of an illicit liaison between two incompatible philosophies. As with most other bastards, I not only insist that I can live my life without being crippled by my ancestry, I claim that this merger of perspectives offers an unusually fruitful perspective.

I am also, I must confess, someone who, unlike most contributors to this volume, does not spend most of his time engaged with the liberal education of undergraduates. I've actually spent most of my career of more than 30 years actively engaged in the education of two distinct groups of professionals called school teachers and physicians. I have designed new programs for the education of these professionals. I have taught in these programs. I have conducted empirical research on the processes and outcomes of such professional education. I have attempted to develop theories of learning and of action that explain how such professionals learn and how they organize and use their knowledge and skill. I am, in both senses of that ambiguous phrase, a "professional educator." Education is my profession and the education of professionals is my area of inquiry.

I come to challenge you, therefore, with these questions. What if all those who fear the corruption of liberal education by professionalism and vocationalization have got it wrong? What if the problem of liberal education is that it isn't professional or vocational enough?

If, indeed, we were to professionalize liberal education, might we not only give it an end, a purpose in practice and in application and in human service, and instead of thereby diluting and corrupting it, might we even make it more liberal? I hope you will find that a provocative conjecture.

The Challenges of Professional Learning

Features of a Profession

I am prepared to argue that the idea of a "profession" describes a special and unique set of circumstances for deep understanding, complex practice, ethical conduct, and higher-order learning, circumstances that define the complexity of the enterprise and explain the difficulties of prescribing both policies and curriculum in this area. What do we mean by a *profession* and what is so hard about preparing people for professions? Let us begin with a recent definition:

> As an ideology, professionalism had both a technical and a moral aspect. Technically, it promised competent performance of skilled work involving the application of broad and complex knowledge, the acquisition of which required formal academic study. Morally, it promised to be guided by an appreciation of the important social ends it served. In demanding high levels of self-governance, professionals claimed not only that others were not technically *equipped* to judge them, but that they also could not be *trusted* to judge them. The idea was expressed in classic form by R. H. Tawney: "[Professionals] may, as in the case of the successful doctor, grow rich; but the meaning of their profession, both for themselves and for the public, is not that they make money, but that they make health or safety or knowledge or good government or good law. . . . [Professions uphold] as the criterion of success the end for which the profession, whatever it may be, is carried on, and [subordinate] the inclination, appetites, and ambition of individuals to the rules of an organization which has as its object to promote performance of function." These functions for Tawney and for many other advocates of the professions, were activities that embodied and expressed the idea of larger social purposes.[1]

Steven Brint's characterization of professions is consistent with many others. From this account, I will claim that there are, at the very least, six characteristics of professional learning that set the terms for the challenge of preparing people to "profess." These characteristics are 1) service, 2) understanding, 3) practice, 4) judgment, 5) learning, and 6) community.

- First, the goal of a profession is *service;* the pursuit of important social ends. Professionals are those who are educated to serve others using bodies of knowledge and skill not readily available to the man or woman in the street. This means that, fundamentally, a mature professional or someone learning a profession must develop *moral understanding* to aim and guide their practice. The ultimate rationale for their work is, in Tawney's words, "that they make health or safety or knowledge or good government or good law." They must develop both technical and moral understanding.
- Second, a profession is a practice rooted in bodies of knowledge that are created, tested, elaborated, refuted, transformed, and reconstituted in colleges, universities, laboratories, libraries, and museums. To call something a profession is to claim that it has a knowledge base in the academy broadly construed. It has research and *theories.* Therefore, professions change not only because rules of practice change, or circumstances change, or policies change, but because the process of knowledge growth, criticism, and development in the academy leads to the achievement of new understandings, new perspectives, or new ways of interpreting the world.
- Third, although a significant portion of the knowledge base of a profession is generated by scholars in the academy, it is not professional knowledge unless and until it is enacted in the crucible of "the field." The field of *practice* is the place where professions do their work, and claims for knowledge must pass the ultimate test of value in practice. Thus, the arenas for theory and practice in a profession are quite disparate, and this constitutes one of the defining problems for professional education. There is always a wide and troublesome gap between theory and practice.

■ Fourth, professions are nevertheless not simply conduits for taking knowledge from the academy and applying it to the field. If that were all that were necessary, professions would not be as complex, interesting, and respected as they are. What intervenes between knowledge and application is the process of *judgment*. The challenge of understanding the complexities of judgment defines another of the essential puzzles of professional education. Human judgment bridges the universal terms of theory and the gritty particularities of situated practice. And human judgment always incorporates both technical and moral elements.

■ Fifth, up to this point my analysis has implied that all of the movement of knowledge is, as it were, from left to right, from the academy to the field. But the most formidable challenge for anyone in a profession is *learning from experience*. While an academic knowledge base is necessary for professional work, it is far from sufficient. Therefore, members of professions have to develop the capacity to learn not only from the academy but, even more importantly, from the experience and contemplation of their own practice. This is true not only for individual professionals, but equally for the entire community of practice. Lessons of practice must have a way of getting back to inform and to render problematic knowledge development in the academy itself.

■ Sixth and finally, professions are inherently public and communal. We speak of someone not only *being a professional,* but also being a *member of a profession.* Professional knowledge is somehow held by a community of professionals who not only know collectively more than any individual member of the community ("distributed expertise" is a distinctive feature of a professional community, even though each member is thought to possess a substantial common core of skill and knowledge), but also have certain public responsibilities and accountabilities with respect to individual practice. Thus, professionals operate within their particular communities under privileges granted by virtue of their recognition by the broader society. Such autonomy and privilege is granted when the profession is viewed as holding specialized knowledge whose warrant only its own members can evaluate, and when its members are trusted to take responsibility for such evaluation.

Elaborating on the Principles: Educating for Profession

What can we say about the challenges of professional education in light of these six principles?

Profession as Service As Brint observed, the starting point for professional preparation is that the aims of professionalism involve social purposes and responsibilities that are grounded both technically and morally. The core meaning of a profession is the organized practice of complex knowledge and skills in the service of others. The professional educator's challenge is to help future professors develop and shape a robust moral vision that will guide their practice and provide a prism of justice and virtue through which to reflect on their actions.

Theory for Practice Second, the notion that formal professional knowledge is rooted in academic knowledge bases creates the essential pedagogical problem of professional education. That is, the recurrent challenge of all professional learning is the unavoidable gap between theory and practice. There are at least two versions of the problem. Theory achieves its power through simplification and narrowing of the field of study. In that sense, theories deal with the world in general and for the most part, making rough places smooth and messy settings neat. A second characteristic of theories is that they generally operate within identifiable disciplines while practical problems cross disciplinary boundaries with the abandon of rum-runners and meandering streams. Theories are extraordinarily powerful, which is why they are the treasure of the academy and valued by the professions; they are also frequently so remote from the particular conditions of professional practice that the novice professional-in-training rarely appreciates their contributions.

Any reader who has been educated for one of the professions, say in the two with which I am most familiar, medical education or teacher preparation, will immediately recognize the problem. My teacher,

Joseph Schwab, devoted most of the last 20 years of his life and career to the problems of practical knowledge and its relations to theory. One need only try to connect the Krebs cycle with the intricacies of a particular clinical diagnosis, or the Loop of Henley with some specific aspect of kidney failure, to appreciate the problem. As a teacher educator, I have tried to help students see how one traverses the gap between Piaget's developmental theory and what to teach on Monday morning, or between Vygotsky's zones of proximal development and the pedagogical potential of group work. We who have tried to educate future professionals understand the challenge that is created when your starting point for a learned profession is bodies of academic knowledge. We prepare professionals in universities because we make the strong claim that these are *learned* professions and that academic knowledge is absolutely essential to their performance.

Now, this may be a false claim. It may well be that academic knowledge is essential only as an *entitlement* to practice and is not functionally necessary for practice. My point is that the claim of rootedness in a theoretical, empirical, and/or normative knowledge base is central to all of the professions. This is a crucial issue for the liberal arts, both conceptually and fiscally. The uniquely American view that a liberal education of some sort is a prerequisite for the study of medicine, law, teaching (foundations), and the like sets an interesting problem for the liberal arts at two levels: defining the foundation for understanding and practicing a profession on the one hand, and stipulating the liberal arts and sciences *per se* whose grasp would identify an individual as "educated" or "learned" and therefore entitled to pursue a learned profession. Only the second of these concerns is uniquely American, because the United States is nearly unique in treating most professions as graduate rather than undergraduate domains.

Third, while the theoretical is the foundation, practice is the end to which all the knowledge is directed. Student teaching, medical residencies, architects' apprenticeships, student nursing, all are examples of carefully designed pedagogies to afford eased entry into practice accompanied by intensive supervision. This is why in all professional preparation we find some conception of a supervised clinical experience. In medicine it seems to go on forever. One of the things that makes law so interesting is that legal educators have somehow managed to avoid the responsibility for introducing a serious clinical component into legal education, expecting the employing law firm to assume that burden.

The apprenticeship, the practice, the application that goes on in the field is not only a nearly universal element of professional learning, but typically, once a professional reaches the field of practice, he or she looks back on the theoretical preparation and begins to devalue it. There are always interesting tensions between the clinical and the theoretical.[2]

One of the sources of those tensions is that theoretical preparation, in spite of the conservatism of the academy, tends to be more radical and reform-oriented than is practice itself. Indeed, academicians often see themselves as the critical conscience of professional practice, taking upon themselves the responsibility for criticizing current practice and developing a vision for the future. And it is, again, almost universally the case in professional preparation that the students arrive at their clinical experiences only to hear the nursing supervisor, or the veteran teacher in the fifth grade where they're student teaching, or the chief of clinical services in the hospital admonish them to forget all the b.s. they were taught at the university because now they will learn the way it is really done. So, interestingly, the academy is the source of radical ideas. The field is where you encounter the bungee cord that pulls things back to the conservation of habits of practice. This kind of tension is, as I say, generally characteristic of professional education.

The Role of Judgment Another complication of professional learning is that the academy, to the extent that it addresses problems of practice at all, presents them as *prototypes*—simplified and schematized theoretical representations of the much messier and variable particularities of everyday life. When student-professionals move out to the fields of practice, they find inevitably that nothing quite fits the prototypes. The responsibility of the developing professional is not simply to apply what he or she has learned to practice, but to transform, to adapt, to merge and synthesize, to criticize and to invent in order to move from the theoretical knowledge of the academy to the kind of practical clinical knowledge needed to engage in the professional work. One of the reasons judgment is such an essential component of clinical work is that theoretical knowledge is generally knowledge of what is true universally. It is true in general and for the most part. It is knowledge of regularities and of patterns. It is an invaluable simplification of a world whose many variations would be far too burdensome to store in memory with all their detail and individuality. Yet the world of practice is beset by just those particularities, born of the workings of chance. To put it in Aristotelian terms, theories are about *essence,* practice is about *accident,* and the only way to get from there to here is via the exercise of *judgment.*

Experience As Dewey observed in his classic essay on the influence of Darwinism on philosophy, chance, error, and accidents present both the sciences and the fields of practice with their most fascinating puzzles.[3] The great challenge for professional learning is that *experience* occurs where design and intention collide with chance. Without the violation of expectations, it is impossible to learn from experience. Learning from experience, therefore, requires both the systematic, prototype-centered, theoretical knowledge characteristic of the academy and the more fluid, reactive, prudential reasoning characteristic of practice. The professional must learn how to cope with those unpredictable matters, and how to reflect on his or her own actions. Professionals incorporate the consequences of those actions into their own growing knowledge base, which ultimately includes unique combinations of theoretical and moral principles, practical maxims, and a growing collection of narratives of experience.

In comparing John Dewey and George Herbert Mead with Jane Addams, all of whom were good friends in Chicago in the first five years of this century, Ellen Lagemann observed that for Dewey and Mead, the tools of their trade were the scientific hypothesis and the investigation; for Jane Addams it was the anecdote and the biography. In professional practice, the hypothesis rapidly gives way to the narrative. Jane Addams's Hull House was the setting in which the academic perspectives of Dewey and Mead were brought into collaborative contact with the truly professional practice embodied by Addams and the settlement movement.[4] The ideals of service clearly dominated the thinking of those who were inventing the professions of social work and community development, but the desire to ground those practices in the academic disciplines of social philosophy, sociology, and a professional school of social service administration were already a serious challenge.[5]

In Jerome Bruner's terms, in these situations the paradigmatic way of knowing shares space with the narrative. To foreshadow the concluding section of this essay, when we seek a pedagogy that can reside between the universal principles of theory and the narratives of lived practice, we invent something called a *case method* that employs cases as ways of capturing experience for subsequent analysis and review, and then creating a pedagogy of theoretically grounded experience. We render individual experiential learning into community property when we transform those lessons from personal experience into a literature of shared narratives. Connections between theoretical principles and case narratives are established when we not only ask, "what's the case?" but more critically, "what is this a case of?" In developing those connections between the universal and the particular, between the universal and the accidental, we forge professional knowledge. Such knowledge cannot be developed and sustained adequately by individuals experiencing and reflecting in isolation.

Community The sixth and final term is the notion of a community of practice. Although individual professionals carry the responsibility for practice, the assumption is that they are members of a community that defines and regulates the standards for that practice and that, as a community, knows more than does any individual practitioner. The public can turn to the professional community when questions of the quality of practice are at stake. From the perspective of professional pedagogy, the community of practice plays a critical role. The academic discipline serves the academy as a learning community whose invisible colleges ensure that knowledge gained is vetted for its warrant through peer review and then distributed among members of the community through journals and other forms of scholarly communication. The community of practice for a profession plays a similar role with regard to learning from experience, accumulating and critiquing the lessons gained and subsequently codified, and, in general, helping practitioners overcome the limitations of individual practice and individual experience. Without a community of practice, individual professionals would be trapped in a solipsistic universe in which only their own experiences were potentially educative. When the work of communities of practice is created and fostered, individual experience becomes communal, distributed expertise can be shared, and standards of practice can evolve.[6]

Professing and Liberal Learning

I began by asking what liberal learning would look like if we treated it as a profession. If we said, that is, that liberal learning has as its end professional practice, doing something of service to the community in a manner that is both technically defensible and morally desirable. If we, therefore, saw the theory/practice problem as an inherent problem, as an inherent challenge in all liberal learning. If we recognized that taking theory and moving it into practice may not only be the challenge for theoretical understanding, but also the crucible in which merely theoretical understanding becomes meaningful, memorable, and internalizable. Indeed, what if we argued that theoretical understanding is inherently incomplete, even unrequited, until it is "practiced"? To address those questions I will begin by asking what are the major impediments in liberal learning now? That is, what challenges do liberal educators currently confront that define some of the perennial problems of that endeavor?

The Challenges of Liberal Learning

What are the challenges of liberal learning? I will rather dogmatically suggest that liberal learning, as all learning for understanding (that endangered species of cognition), confronts three central challenges: the loss of learning, or *amnesia;* the illusion of learning, or *illusory understanding;* and the uselessness of learning, or *inert ideas.* These states can be exemplified by three student exclamations: "I forgot it,"

"I thought I understood it," and "I understand it but I can't use it." If we were ever to conduct proper evaluations of the long-term benefits of liberal education, I suspect we would encounter all three of these with painful frequency.

The first challenge of liberal learning is the problem of *amnesia*. It is a problem exemplified by the fact that, after having participated in a wide variety of courses and programs in colleges and universities, it is very sobering to discover that students rapidly forget much of what we have taught them or that they have ostensibly learned. Let me suggest a depressing exercise: conduct an exit interview with students at the end of their senior year (or a couple of years beyond) in which you sit them down with the transcript of the four years they have spent with you in the institution and say: "Treat the transcript as a kind of itinerary that you have followed for the last four or five years. Why don't you simply go course by course and just tell me what you remember doing and learning." This is not a test of deep understanding, but if students don't even remember the experience, it's quite hard for them to learn from it. This is one of the reasons that nearly every one of the professions, with the stunning exception of teaching, spends an incredible amount of time and energy teaching future professionals to develop habits of documentation and recording their practice. In medicine, in law, in nursing, in social work, in architecture, there are incredible archives of practice because amnesia is the great enemy of learning from experience. Yet in liberal learning, one of the ubiquitous problems we face is the fragility of what is learned. It's like dry ice. It just evaporates at room temperature and is gone. Students seldom remember much of what they've read or heard beyond their last high-stakes exam on the material. The first problem, therefore, is how do we address the problem of amnesia?

A second enemy of liberal learning is *illusory understanding*. It's far more dangerous and insidious than amnesia, because it is the kind of understanding where you think you do remember and understand, but you don't. A great problem of liberal learning is the confidence with which our graduates imagine that they understand many things with which they have only superficial acquaintance and glib verbal familiarity. They thus can throw around phrases like "supply and demand" or "survival of the fittest" with marvelous agility, albeit without substantial comprehension. There is a wonderful video that begins with graduating students at a Harvard commencement being asked two questions by faculty: Why do we have seasons and what accounts for the phases of the moon? In every case the respondent replied with great confidence. With little hesitation, and very few exceptions, respondents offered a similar theory of the seasons. They explained that we had summer when the elliptical orbit of the earth brought it closer to the sun, and winter when we were further away. When asked to explain the phases of the moon, similarly mistaken accounts were put forward. Here were well-educated students, many of whom had taken courses in the sciences, including astronomy and astrophysics, who were confidently expounding quite misconceived theories of how the solar system functioned. The illusion of understanding is as frequently encountered as it is infrequently detected by educators. The study and documentation of these kinds of misconceptions before and after formal education has beome one of the most fascinating aspects of research in science and mathematics learning.

Some of the most interesting work in the history of philosophy deals with the philosophers' concern with illusory understanding. Nearly every one of the Socratic dialogues is an example. The Socratic dialogue is a form of pedagogy designed to confront the knower with what he was sure he knew but indeed doesn't understand. Socratic wisdom is said, therefore, to begin with the unveiling of Socratic ignorance. The whole metaphor of the cave in Plato's *Republic* is a metaphor about illusory understanding. And it is no accident that the way Socrates attempts to diagnose and treat illusory understanding is through an active, interactive process of dialogue in a social setting. Similarly, one of Francis Bacon's most memorable essays is about "the idols of the mind," all the ways in which we, as human intelligences, come to believe we know things that, in fact, we just don't understand.

Alfred North Whitehead warned us that "above all we must beware" of *"inert ideas,"* thus punning on Plato's reverence for the innate variety. Such ideas, he said, "are merely received into the mind without being utilized, or tested, or thrown into fresh combinations." Ideas escape inertness by being used, tested, or thrown into fresh combinations. Application is not only the ultimate test, it is the crucible within which ideas come alive and grow. Whitehead observes, "Pedants sneer at an education which is useful. But if education is not useful, what is it? Is it a talent, to be hidden away in a napkin?"[7]

Principles of Professional Learning

If the three horsemen of the liberal learning apocalypse are amnesia, illusion, and inertness, what kinds of pedagogical strategies can we invoke to fend them off? The salvation of understanding is in our grasp. *The key to preserving the liberal arts is to profess the liberal arts.*

The principles through which we overcome amnesia, illusory understanding, and inertness are the same as those that enumerate the conditions of profession: activity, reflection, collaboration, passion, and community. These principles not only derive from current research in cognitive science and social learning, they also map very nicely onto the wisdom of practice in professional education. At the risk that an overly dogmatic rhetoric may give the lie to the very points I am making, I shall briefly explain these principles.

The first is *activity*. Students who are learning in professional settings are remarkably active most of the time in that they are engaged in clinical or practical work. They are designing, diagnosing, and arguing. They are writing; they are investigating; they are in the library or at the computer getting information. They are talking to one another, sharing information, and challenging one another's ideas. At every opportunity, the level of activity of the students is higher than in the average college classroom. The outcome should not surprise anyone. We all know from our practice as well as from theory that active learning results in more enduring learning than does passive learning. It is one of the key principles of all human learning, equally relevant for young adults as for children.

As a first principle, authentic and enduring learning occurs when the learner is an *active* agent in the process. Student learning becomes more active through experimentation and inquiry, as well as through writing, dialogue, and questioning. Thus, the college settings in which the students work must provide them with the opportunities and support for becoming active agents in the process of their own learning.

The second thing we know about effective learners is that they are not merely active, because activity alone is insufficient for learning. As Dewey observed many years ago, we do not learn by doing; we learn by thinking about what we are doing. Successful students spend considerable time, as Bruner calls it, "going meta," that is, thinking about what they are doing and why. Their teachers give them plenty of opportunities to talk about how they are learning, why they are learning in these ways, why they are getting things wrong when they get them wrong and right when they get them right. A very high level of carefully guided *reflection* is blended with activity.

Activity and reflection are hard work. If you are a typical learner, you often find yourself working alone, intending to read an article or a book. You sit down after dinner with a good reading light on, with good music playing softly in the background, and with no distractions in the room. Ten minutes later, you find yourself in the middle of a chapter with absolutely no recollection of what you have read up to that point. It can be very hard for anyone to engage in active and reflective learning alone. For college students, it is even harder.

One of the most important inventions of Ann Brown (with Annemarie Palinscar) was called "reciprocal teaching"—a process of enhancing young students' reading comprehension as they work with one another, scaffolding each others' learning; helping each other focus, attend, and question, actively, critically, and reflectively as they jointly read complicated text.[8] Active, reflective learning thus proceeds best in the presence of a third principle, which is *collaboration.*

College students can work together in ways that scaffold and support each others' learning, and in ways that supplement each others' knowledge. Collaboration is a *marriage of insufficiencies,* not exclusively "cooperation" in a particular form of social interaction. There are difficult intellectual and professional challenges that are nearly impossible to accomplish alone, but are readily addressed in the company of others.

Elsewhere in this volume, Sandy Astin discusses the educative functions of collaboration—the educational advantages enjoyed through the juxtaposition and confrontation of perspectives for people to rethink, to reflect on what they thought they already knew, and through collaborative exchange *eventually to deepen their under-standing of an idea.* So when we say that reflection is important, that collaboration is important, these aren't just pieties. These are essential elements of a pedagogical theory, a theory of learning and teaching that explains why it is that even if your goal is liberal learning, per se, and if what you want is people to learn ideas and concepts and principles that will be robust, that will be deep, that will be not merely inert ideas, shadows on the wall of the cave—the way you temper those ideas is through reflection and through interaction and collaboration. Otherwise it may well be just the illusion of under-standing. These are some of the things we're learning about liberal learning.

This kind of learning is not exclusively cognitive or intellectual. Indeed, there is a significant emotional and affective component that inheres in such work. Authentic and enduring learning occurs when students share a *passion* for the material, are emotionally committed to the ideas, processes, and activities, and see the work as connected to present and future goals. Although the language of liberal learning is heavily intellectual, the importance of emotion, enthusiasm, and passion is central to these efforts, for both students and for their teachers. And there is a special quality to those affective responses that develop within individuals who have become interdependent members of well-functioning, cohesive groups. Simply observe the spirit that develops among the members of an athletic team, or the cast of a play, or residents of a cabin at camp, and you can begin to discern the special emotional qualities associated with working collaboratives that function as learning communities.

In that same vein, authentic and enduring learning works best when the processes of activity, reflection, emotion, and collaboration are supported, legitimated, and nurtured within a *community* or *culture* that values such experiences and creates many opportunities for them to occur and to be accomplished with success and pleasure. Such communities create "participant structures" that reduce the labor intensity of the activities needed to engage in the most daunting practices that lead to teaching and learning. Put another way, this kind of learning can rarely succeed one course at a time. The entire institution must be oriented toward these principles, and the principles must be consistently and regularly employed throughout each course and experience in a program. One of the "secrets" of the remarkable impact of the Hutchins College was probably the persistent and all-encompassing effect—course after course—of critical dialogue within small seminars as *the* pedagogical practice of the college.

Consistent with the centrality of teaching and learning, professional education programs that are characterized by activity, reflection, and collaboration in learning communities are inherently uncertain, complex, and demanding places. Both learning and teaching in such settings entails high levels of risk and unpredictability for the participants. Students and faculty both require a school and a community that support and reward those levels of risk taking and invention characteristic of such approaches to learning for understanding and commitment.

If we take these principles seriously as instruments for overcoming the major challenges to liberal learning, then, with Whitehead, I would assert that the kind of pedagogy that we associate with, say, service learning, is not simply a cocurricular extravagance. It may actually be central to the kind of pedagogy that would make a liberal education more professional, in the case of service learning, a pedagogy that would give the liberal arts a clinical component or the equivalent of an internship experience. Moreover, it may well be one of the ways in which we overcome the triple pathologies of amnesia, illusory understanding, and inert ideas. How might that sort of thing go on?

A Pedagogy for Professing

Cases as Conduits Between Theory and Practice

I shall now discuss a pedagogy of cases as an example of the kind of teaching and learning that begins to address the central problems of academic learning, in general, and professional learning, in particular. I am *not* arguing that all liberal and professional learning should immediately become case based!

For me, what is so alluring about a case is that it resides in that never-never land between theory and practice, between idea and experience, between the normative ideal and achievable real. One of the interesting things about cases is that they capture pieces of experience that initially existed solely within the life of a single individual and transform that solitary experience into text. You can do all kinds of things when you've rendered something into a text that can be shared by members of a group, all of whom are trying to make sense of the text. The function of the case as a means for preserving and communicating experience is clear given the persistent problems of amnesia.[9]

The great challenge for professionals who wish to learn from experience is the difficulty of holding experiences in memory in forms that can become the objects of disciplined analysis and reflection. Consider the possibility that cases are ways of parsing experience so that practitioners can examine and learn from it. Professionals are typically confronted with a seamless continuum of experience from which they can think about individual episodes or readings as cases, but rarely coordinate the different dimensions into meaningful experiential chunks. Case methods thus become strategies for helping professionals to "chunk" their experience into units that can become the focus for reflective practice. They therefore can become the basis for individual professional learning as well as a forum within which communities of professionals, both local and extended, as members of visible and invisible colleges, can store, exchange, and organize their experiences. How is case learning related to the principles we reviewed above? I will describe a situation—not infrequent in professional education—where the learners not only study and discuss cases written by others, but are actively participating in some sort of field experience around which they also write cases that document and analyze their own practice.

First, whether as case analyst or as case writer, the case learner becomes an active agent in his or her own understanding. When a student is wrestling with a case, whether as an occasion for analysis or a stimulus to reflect on his or her own experience as a prelude to writing, active agency is engaged. Second, cases are inherently reflective. They begin with an act of cognition, of turning around one's own lived experiences and examining them to find events and episodes worthy of transformation into telling cases. Even when the goal of case learning is not case writing, the discussion of cases eventually stimulates reflection on one's own experiences and reactions. Third, case methods nearly always emphasize the primacy of group discussion, deliberation, and debate. The thought process of cases is dialogic, as members of a group explore different perspectives, the available elective actions, or the import of the consequences. In case-based teaching, the interaction of activity, reflection, and collaboration is apparent. But what of community or culture?

Teaching and learning with cases is not an easy pedagogy. Active learners are much more outspoken and assertive than are passive learners. They are less predictable than their more passive counterparts, as they investigate their options, explore alternative interpretations, and challenge prevailing views. Because cases encourage connections between personal experiences and those vicariously experienced through narratives, the directions in which discussions might develop are rather difficult to anticipate, further complicating the pedagogy. Finally, the collaborative mode of instruction once again reduces the authority of the teacher and vests a growing proportion in the initiatives of students. Taken together, the enhancement of agency, reflection, and collaboration makes teaching more complex and unpredictable, albeit by reducing the authority of teachers and their ability to plan for contingencies. When uncertainty increases and power is distributed, the need for a supportive culture or community becomes paramount for teachers and students alike. A supportive culture helps manage the risk of contemplating one's failures and reduces the vulnerability created when one candidly discusses a path not taken. A supportive culture engages each member of the community in parallel risks. It celebrates the interdependence of learners who rely on one another for both insights and reassurance. A learning environment built on activity, reflection, and collaboration—which is an apt characterization of a well-functioning case-learning and case-writing community—proceeds smoothly only in the presence of a sustaining culture and community.

An Example

How might we envision a clinical component to a liberal education? Consider the possibility that there are forms of service learning that could perform the function. One of the most frequently encountered forms of service learning is tutoring. Although only one among many activities that are quite appropriately classified as legitimate service learning, I want to offer the hypothesis that the tutoring of young children, of adults, or of peers has some uniquely powerful characteristics with regard both to the objectives of offering service and the objectives of making liberal learning more meaningful, more memorable, and more useful, that is, less inert.

In this regard I share the values of the medieval university, which viewed the ability to teach something to someone else as the highest, most rigorous, and final test of whether a scholar understood his discipline or profession deeply. It based this view on Aristotle's observation in the *Metaphysics* that it is the distinctive sign of a man who knows deeply that he can teach what he knows to another. Aristotle recognized that, in order to teach something to someone else, you have to engage in an act of reflection on and transformation of what you know, and then connect those insights to the mind, experience, and motives of somebody else. Teaching is a dual act of intelligence and empathy. It entails both technical and moral reason. By the same token, in order to make your own learning more meaningful and memorable, you have to somehow interconnect the many things you know in an intrapersonal network of associations and implications. Each time you can make a connection, whether in your own mind or with the minds of others, amnesia becomes less likely. Each connection serves as both anchor and springboard. Every time you can figure out a new way to take what you know and apply it, connect it, teach it to someone else, you've not only rendered a service, but you have deepened and enriched your own understanding.

I propose that one of the ways in which we can combine the notion of service and the notion of liberal learning is with the expectation that every one of our undergraduates who is engaged in liberal learning undertake the service of teaching something they know to somebody else. They also undertake writing about the experience as a case, describing both teaching and student learning. For me this isn't hypothetical. It's the way I prepare people to teach. They write cases of their own practice. But they don't write them for me. They write them for the other members of their community, because our argument is that experience is too precious to be limited in its benefits solely to the person who experienced it. We need to move from individual experiential learning to learning in a scholarly community of practice.

Then we form small case conferences where groups of students come together and exchange their cases. Case discussions are very interesting. When the discussions are well managed, participants can move the case discussion in two directions. One is exploring the facts of the case. Here, participants are pressed to describe the context more richly and in greater detail. They are urged to elaborate on their accounts of what actually happened, what was said and done, how all that occurred made them feel. They are pressed to dig deeply into the particularity of the context, because it is in the devilish details that practice dramatically differs from theory.

Yet, at the same time that the participants are being sucked into depths of the particular, the skillful pedagogue (and eventually the students themselves) begins to build in a second-order genre of question which is, "what is the case an exemplar of?" What are some other principles, concepts, or ideas that link these two or three cases together or that make you think about your case in relation to some more general principle?[10]

Sitting astride theory and practice, the case both enriches the grasp of practice and at the same time links back to the world of theory and the world of principle. I already do that kind of work with prospective and veteran teachers, and can readily imagine being able to do something similar with undergraduates. Such a strategy would be an example of professing the liberal arts, in having students teach others what they know, in providing service in conjunction with our academic learning which was then captured in written cases. Those cases would then become the curriculum for seminars whose purpose was to link the experiences of application back to the theoretical understanding.

There is a powerful strategic value in writing and analyzing cases that have been written by the members of a case forum, and in systematically exploring the tough question "what this is a case of?" When I write a case describing my own practice, I am the protagonist in the plot. This means that I'm writing not only *what* I did, but I am writing about *why* I did it. I am writing not just about my strategies and actions, but about my intentions, goals, and values. I write, in Martin Buber's terms, not only about "I" and "thou," but reflexively about "I." In that sense, by injecting the self as protagonist into the deliberations around one's academic learning, we bring the moral dimensions of liberal learning back to center stage. This is only proper; the ultimate rationale for treating liberal learning as a worthy end in itself is a moral argument, not an instrumental one.

If we were to professionalize in these terms, if we were actively to connect learning with service, with practice, with application, and were further to capture that practice in a kind of pedagogy that uses cases and case methods in ways analogous to some of the ways we use them for professional preparation, we would not only achieve the moral ends of service, we would very likely do better at overcoming the challenges to liberal understanding. Through service, through application, through rendering their learning far more active, reflective, and collaborative, students would actually learn more liberally, understand what they have learned more deeply, and develop the capacity to use what they have learned in the service of their communities.

Notes

1. Steven Brint, *In an Age of Experts: The Changing Role of Professionals in Politics and Public Life* (Princeton, NJ: Princeton University Press, 1994), 7.
2. It is also quite interesting when the supervised clinical experience affords such opportunities in only part of a future role, as when the future university professor is heavily mentored in the scholarship of discovery but receives little or no supervised clinical experience in the scholarship of teaching.
3. John Dewey, "The Influence of Darwinism on Philosophy," in Martin Gardner, editor, *Great Essays in Science* (Buffalo: Prometheus, 1994).
4. Ellen Condliffe Lagemann, "The Plural Worlds of Educational Research," *History of Education Quarterly* 29 (1988), 184–214.
5. William Rainey Harper, first president of the University of Chicago, wrestled with questions of how the professional school could fit into the new research university. Chicago had schools of theology, pedagogy, and social service. Dewey wrote a short paper on the topic of how the university-based school of pedagogy must be distinct from the traditional normal school, most particularly in its relationships with academic disciplines and research.
6. At least that's the theory. Professions are not equally successful in creating communities of practice that effectively play this role. Thus, medicine and engi-

neering probably do it rather well. Law does it well for court cases but badly for the daily practice of law. Teaching, both K–12 and postsecondary, has barely scratched the surface of transforming the experiences of pedagogy into scholarship and community property.

7. Alfred North Whitehead, *The Aims of Education and Other Essays* (New York: Macmillan, 1929).
8. A.S. Palinscar and A.L. Brown, "Reciprocal Teaching of Comprehension–Fostering and Monitoring Activities," *Cognition and Instruction* 1 (1984), 117–75.
9. Sibling to amnesia is the challenge of *nostalgia,* in which forgetting is replaced by mis-remembering, usually in the service of reinforcing the mnemonist's interests, needs, or preferences. Nostalgia is not identical to illusory understanding, but it is likely to be a significant contributing condition.
10. Although I am using the example of tutoring, it should be apparent that this strategy for case-based liberal learning could be applied to a variety of other clinical experiences as well, both those that entail service and others that are more traditional—applied research and the like.

The American Tradition of Aspirational Democracy

ELIZABETH KAMARCK MINNICH

PROFESSOR OF PHILOSOPHY AND WOMEN'S STUDIES,
UNION INSTITUTE, OHIO

The Alchemy of Democracy and Education:

Our Times and Theirs, an Opening Collage

Moral ideals:

[T]o get rid of the habit of thinking of democracy as something institutional and external and to acquire the habit of treating it as a way of personal life is to realize that democracy is a moral ideal and so far as it becomes a fact is a moral fact. It is to realize that democracy is a reality only as it is indeed a commonplace of living.

John Dewey, "Creative Democracy—The Task Before Us," in Debra Morris and Ian Shapiro, editors, *John Dewey: The Political Writings* (Indianapolis/Cambridge: Hackett, 1993), 244.

Cultural criticism:

The pragmatists' preoccupation with power, provocation, and personality—in contrast, say, to grounding knowledge, regulating instruction, and promoting tradition—signifies an intellectual calling to administer to a confused populace caught in the whirlwinds of societal crisis, the cross fires of ideological polemics, and the storms of class, racial, and gender conflicts. [It is grounded in] a conception of philosophy as a form of cultural criticism in which the meaning of America is put forward by intellectuals in response to distinct social and cultural crises.

Cornel West, *The American Evasion of Philosophy: A Genealogy of Pragmatism* (Madison: University of Wisconsin Press, 1989), 5.

Progressive education:

What We Believe: A Credo for Bank Street School for Children

What potentialities in human beings—children, teachers, and ourselves—do we want to see develop?

175

- A zest for living that comes from taking in the world with all five senses alert.
- Lively intellectual curiosities that turn the world into an exciting laboratory and keep one ever a learner.
- Flexibility when confronted with change and ability to relinquish patterns that no longer fit the present.
- The courage to work, unafraid and efficiently, in a world of new needs, new problems, and new ideas.
- Gentleness combined with justice in passing judgments on other human beings.
- Sensitivity, not only to the external formal rights of the "other fellow," but to him as another human being seeking a good life through his own standards.
- A striving to live democratically, in and out of schools, as the best way to advance our concept of democracy.

Our credo demands ethical standards as well as scientific attitudes. Our work is based on the faith that human beings can improve the society they have created.

> Lucy Sprague Mitchell [The Bank Street School was granted a provisional charter in 1931 by the Regents of the State of New York, but had been evolving slowly for many years before that.]

Epistemologies:

> In the consciousness of our failures, we risk lapsing into boundless difference and giving up on the confusing task of making a partial, real connection. Some differences are playful; some are poles of world historical systems of domination. Epistemology is about knowing the difference.
>
> Kathleen Lennon and Margaret Whitford, editors, *Knowing the Difference, Feminist Perspectives in Epistemology* (London and New York: Routledge, 1994), frontispiece.

Equality:

> Higher education's goal, we believe, should be to deepen public and campus knowledge of United States diversity histories, to reengage with democratic aspirations as a moral compass for intersecting communities, and to recommit ourselves—as educators and as citizens— to the still-elusive goal of meaningful equality for every American.
>
> The Drama of Diversity and Democracy: Higher Education and American Commitments (Washington, DC: Association of American Colleges and Universities, 1995).

Why Would Anybody Want to Read the Pragmatists Anyway?

Personal/Political Contexts

I speak about pragmatism far less as a scholar than as someone who, if you'll forgive my putting it this way, falls in love again every time I return to it. Despite years in which "Oh, do be more pragmatic!" meant, in popular speech, something like calm down, get sensible! and when, in academic circles, "the pragmatists" referred to a small group of generally agreed to be rather sloppy American thinkers who might better be taught (if taught at all) in U.S. cultural or intellectual history courses, I have retained that passionate response. I read the works of pragmatists with intellectual excitement, political and moral relief, and the particular emotional pleasure that tells me I am in the company of friends. I confess that I also read them as an equal, not because I have inflated notions of myself (reading them always fills me with awe, in fact), but because I come to them now as one among the many who have been called into philosophizing because of our deep commitment to making democracy, and the education upon which it so essentially depends, surpass its own failures in a renewed attempt to realize its aspirations.

Thinking today about pragmatism, progressive education, and feminism, then, I am particularly aware that I draw on a mixture of knowledge, moral and political values, and, of course, my own experiences that are informed by and inform knowledge, values, and politics. Most particularly, I draw on my experiences as a philosopher and educator working during the past 30-some years of what I have come to call an *age of movements* that has affected us as a nation in two large waves. The first was for *equal rights* for those long denied them—for black people, women of all groups, Native Americans, poor people, people with disabilities, farmers, migrant workers, lesbians and gays, racially ethnicized groups, old people, rank-and-file union members, students, welfare recipients, tenants, people who are by current prescriptions "fat," and others. Discrimination on the basis of ascribed membership in a devalued group was challenged, in this equality-seeking wave, particularly insofar as it publicly disadvantaged people.

To seek equality was, in a sense, to seek to be de-privatized, to be fully free and empowered to speak and act effectively among equalized others in public life.

More recently, we have entered a second wave of the age of movements, characterized by agitation for full *recognition* that goes beyond the granting of rights to claim public, cultural, and personal acknowledgment, respect, and value. "Identity politics," academic research and teaching in "special" programs, curriculum transformation projects, "diversity initiatives," multiculturalism, floods of memoirs and autobiographies, these and more have emerged to say, "Here I am; here we are: see us, hear us, take us fully into account, *recognize* us." These are calls that depend on recognition of public rights, but they also ask us to recognize the implication of public rights and life for personal and community contexts. They remind us that the rights-bearing individual is a powerful abstraction that, as lived, has never actually been empty of particular gendered, racialized, culturally formed content. To stand a chance of meaning what we say when we speak of wishing to be able to see, and treat, each person as a unique individual, we need to be able to recognize and value who that person actually is, which, for the creatures of shared meanings that humans are, includes, without ever being reducible to, "where she is coming from." In a sense, the wave of movements for recognition comprises claims on a dominant culture to recognize personal, private lives among those who, lacking the protections of the public realm, also lacked them in the private.

Obviously, this age of movements has by now challenged many long-established boundaries on which personal as well as political lives have been premised and, in so doing, has raised anew profound moral and intellectual questions as well. In such times, education cannot simply conserve past knowledge and support the creation of new learning that fits smoothly into traditional and/or professionalized fields. It is called on to help us all make sense of our worlds in ways that help a massive set of institutions, intellectual as well as other kinds, shift so that they can work with the resurgence of democratic values.

Swimming through these waves, sometimes lifted up by them, sometimes swamped and gasping, I earned my B.A. at the highly individualistic and embarrassedly privileged but still progressive Sarah Lawrence College, which was, during my time there, also one of the homes of the northern students' movement in support of the southern civil rights movement. I was, then, fortunate to have been studying at a place in a time in which individual creativity was nurtured in the context of politics that called people into action for moral reasons, in the name of an aspirational democracy. Later, during my work for the Ph.D., first at the University of California: Berkeley in political science and then in philosophy at the Graduate Faculty for Political and Social Science of the New School in the anti–Vietnam War days, I studied, among other things, pragmatism. I was advised to write my dissertation on John Dewey by my mentor, Hannah Arendt (whose advice it was always in many senses wise to take). She suggested Dewey to me because "Americans should know their own philosophical tradition," but also, and more important to her, because, "Dewey is one of the few philosophers who ever understood and valued action." This had particular appeal to me because, studying with and being teaching assistant for Arendt, whose lifework I would characterize as trying to find a grounding for ethical action in thinking and judgment rather than in universalized principles or creeds or ideologies, I was increasingly troubled by a radical disconnection between prevailing ways of knowing and constructions of knowledge and the messy, confusing, changeable, yet always morally fraught and compelling realm of action.

One might think that what was troubling me was an obvious impetus to study John Dewey, and that, in times such as the sixties and seventies in this country, Dewey and the pragmatists would have been taken very seriously. But when I went to defend my dissertation, the first question I was asked was, "Tell me: Why would anyone want to study Dewey anyway?" Being a philosopher of and for American democracy who focused on experience and education, he was in the view of many philosophers at that highly analytical, language-centered, logical positivist time not a candidate for Serious Philosophical Study. Had I not had on my (anxious graduate student) side the very weighty Hannah Arendt as well as Richard Bernstein, to whom she sent me for his deep knowledge of Dewey and his own focus on the concepts of *praxis* and *action,* I rather doubt that my dissertation would have been accepted, regardless of how good it was or was not, or how well or poorly I defended it.

Today I work in more compatible settings (and my old settings have, through this age of movements, become more compatible as well, I am pleased to note). My present employer, the Graduate School for Interdisciplinary Studies of the Union Institute, was founded, among like-minded others, by the Dewey scholar and education practitioner Goodwin Watson. Union, for which I left a deanship at Barnard College (a school I admire but could not manage to find educationally interesting except as it struggled to find ways to justify its existence as a small women's college) requires consideration of "social relevance" in relation to the interdisciplinary doctoral programs it offers under the aegis of its mission to serve "underserved populations."

After my undergraduate work, I spent a year in India on a Fulbright to study post-colonial education (and Bharat Natyam, classical Indian dance, which I managed to convince my funders was related to the purpose that took me there); and a year trying to organize grove workers in central Florida (fortunately with the guidance and restraint of many people far wiser than I). Among these and other projects with which I am deeply grateful to have been involved, I have worked with and participated in developing feminism as it has reemerged in our times. My own work has particularly focused on feminism's philosophical, moral, and politically significant challenge to education to critique its intellectual scope, the significance of its subject matters, the reach and adequacy of its methods and pedagogies, its systems and structures, and its grounds for selecting and ways of treating its participants in all roles.

Rather to my amazement, I find now that I have been consistent in my choices of schools to study and work with, philosophers and theorists to converse with, critiques to accept as positive challenges, and political/ethical ideals to which to aspire even as they remain open to critique and change. What has impelled me in my own limited way to philosophize, to work in education, and to be involved with feminism and diversity work is the belief that democracy is a crucial moral ideal still compromised at its roots in ways that raise the most important of philosophical as well as political and educational questions. Or, to put it the other way around, that the most important philosophical, political, and educational questions concern what it has meant and can, might, and should mean to be humans living democratically.

I refer to my work now, in conceptual shorthand, as an effort to discern how the *given* of human differences was turned into the *problem* of diversity, informing—deforming—virtually all the systems within and through which we struggle to live together. It is clear to me, as it has by no means always been to my colleagues, that this is philosophical work. But then, I have continued to feel that Hannah Arendt and John Dewey, Jane Addams and W.E.B. du Bois knew very well what philosophy should be, and that it should be intimately related to, rather than severed from, issues of moral action, of politics/public life, and that has helped. My passion for pragmatism has always contained a large dose of gratitude.

Imagine, for example, how grateful one can be at finding this in John Dewey when one's colleagues today are once again angry about the "politicizing" of academia, the "disuniting" of America, the "obsession" of "those people" with "victimization," and are calling on us to return to the safety of an only supposedly disinterested academic quest that holds itself aloof from questioning what "human being" has actually been construed and constructed to mean through the millennia, centuries, years, and daily moments of all-pervasive invidious prejudices.

> Systematic hatred and suspicion of any human group, "racial," sectarian, political, denotes deep-seated scepticism about the qualities of human nature. From the standpoint of a faith in the possibilities of human nature possessing religious quality it is blasphemous. It may start by being directed at a particular group, and be supported in name by assigning special reasons why that group is not worthy of confidence, respect, and decent human treatment. But the underlying attitude is one of fundamental distrust of human nature. Hence, it spreads from distrust and hatred of a particular group until it may undermine the conviction that any group of persons has any intrinsic right for esteem or recognition—which, then, if it be given, is for some special and external grounds, such as usefulness to our particular interests and

ambitions. There is no physical acid which has the corrosive power
possessed by intolerance directed against persons because they belong
to a group that bears a certain name . . . An anti-humanist attitude is
the essence of every form of intolerance.[1]

Dewey and other progressives clearly never made the mistake of
holding that how we philosophize and the beliefs we hold and act on
concerning others are separable. What human being means is at the
questioning center of politics as it is of morals and philosophy, and
any liberal education worthy of the name refuses to forget that.

An American Tradition: Aspirational Democracy

This journey and its work I share, of course, with many other contemporary educators with and from whom I am deeply grateful to
learn, but we also join a long American radical tradition, which I am
calling the tradition of aspirational democracy, reaching back to the
painfully contradictory founding of this nation. The nation began,
after all, with a revolution justified by the invocation of basic human
rights deriving from a principle of equality even as Native Americans
were being "removed," betrayed, slaughtered; Africans were being
enslaved; and all women remained privatized by being denied here,
too, the rights and protections of public life and citizenship. The radical tradition that ensued, inspired by American-adopted and created principles and driven by their blatant failures in practice, includes
but is not limited to the pragmatists.[2]

Still, it is the pragmatists who speak to many of us most directly
particularly because, I think, we are today deeply worried by situations very like those they faced at the turn of the last century. They,
too, were worried about an influx of people, and peoples, that some
were not sure could or even should become fully a part of the nation.
They, too, were searingly aware of dangerously vast gulfs between the
rich and the poor, and were deeply concerned about the desperation
of lives being led in the tenements of our supposedly great cities. And
they, as we have learned to be, were leery of Utopia-promising programs even as we are desperately aware that we must have a vision
powerful enough to keep today's problems from worsening until we
collapse into either chaos or tyranny. Facing all this, we, as did the

pragmatists, are turning back to the ideals of democracy not as warrants of our success and righteousness but as challenges to engage close-in with meliorative change that recognizes the centrality of education to the crucial task of opening minds, informing hearts and imaginations more generously, and thereby contributing to the ongoing effort to keep social, cultural, economic, and political hierarchies from locking only a few in, the majority out.

More Partners for Our Conversation

If we are today to consult the wisdom of the pragmatists as it engages democratic aspirations, public philosophizing, and education in relation to these, I believe we should do so with the roiling, engaged, passionate, contentious lot of them. "The Pragmatists" included white women and women and men of color who philosophized in the name of aspirational democracy through action as well as writing, and more white men than most of us have heard of who concurred. John Dewey, William James, Charles Sanders Peirce, Josiah Royce, and (on some lists) George Herbert Mead do not constitute a quorum. The shrinking of the group of pragmatists to this or some slightly varied short list, and subsequent scholars' focus on the less overtly socially/politically engaged writings even of that group, could suggest that "the best" of the group and "the best" of their works have "emerged over time." It could also, and I think does, suggest that pragmatism and "the pragmatists" have been tamed, made more properly academic and respectable—depoliticized. In fact, I think this process has, until very recently, not only cut our lists of people and of their works in order to depoliticize them but, in doing so, has philosophically decentered what is most basic to pragmatism.

The pragmatists collectively offer strong medicine for ills they considered very serious, and this, as Jane Addams once put it, violates rules of good social behavior. Making the best use of their work for our times requires us to take the risk of reencountering them as the specifically American, not always polite kind of radicals they were. Another way of putting that is to maintain, as I do, that the philosophical problems that animate and characterize pragmatism were and remain moral political problems, problems of justice—of the *ad/just/ment* of humans to themselves, each other, to nature, to religion in ways that require adjustment of some powerful institutions and systems.

John Dewey called on his compatriots to undo invidious hierarchies and divisions of all kinds among humans in order to release our full intelligence, which indicates how radical in several senses his understanding of *intelligence* was. Perhaps his most well-known definition of democracy is that it is "organized intelligence," and by that he meant nothing like, say, a Platonic state devised by philosophers who have seen Justice-Itself but, rather, an ongoing process involving as many as possible that is constantly re-ad/justing itself. He writes:

> Wherever social divisions and barriers exist, practices and ideas that correspond to them fix metes and bounds, so that liberal action is placed under restraint. Creative intelligence is looked upon with distrust; the innovations that are the essence of individuality are feared, and generous impulse is put under bonds not to disturb the peace . . . . Morals are assigned a special compartment in theory and practice *because* they reflect the divisions embodied in economic and political institutions.[3] (emphasis added)

To undo some of the effects of the "social divisions and barriers" that reasserted themselves and were imposed on "the pragmatists" as a large group such that we ended up with so few, and the related decentering of pragmatism from its political passions, I have culled a (woefully inadequate but, I hope, tantalizing) group of quotes from some of them.

John Dewey *on the primacy of political/social/economic experiences for philosophizing and hence for education:* The origin of these divisions [in theories of knowing] we have found in the hard and fast walls which mark off social groups and classes within a group: like those between rich and poor, men and women, noble and baseborn, ruler and ruled. These barriers mean absence of fluent and free intercourse . . . . [T]hey end in a division between things of this world as mere appearances and an inaccessible essence of reality. So far as these divisions persist and others are added to them, each leaves its mark upon the educational system.[4]

Carter G. Woodson, *on the need for education to liberate people from distortions created by political/social/economic systems:* It may be of no importance to the race to be able to boast today of many times as many "educated" members as it had in 1865. If they are of the wrong kind the increase in numbers will be a disadvantage rather than an advantage. The only question which concerns us here is whether these "educated" persons are actually equipped to face the ordeal before them or unconsciously contribute to their own undoing by perpetuating the regime of the oppressor.[5]

William James, *on the moral and political implications of recognizing differing people's "subjective" knowledge:* The subject knows a part of the world of reality which the judging spectator fails to see, knows more whilst the spectator knows less; and wherever there is a conflict of opinion and difference of vision, we are bound to believe that the truer side is the side that feels the more and not the side that feels the less. . . . [W]hat is the result of all these considerations . . . ? [They forbid us, he says,] to be forward in pronouncing on the meaninglessness of forms of existence other than our own . . . . Hands off: neither the whole of truth, nor the whole of good, is revealed to any single observer, although each observer gains a partial superiority of insight from the peculiar position in which he stands. It is enough to ask of each of us that he should be faithful to his own opportunities and make the most of his own blessings, without presuming to regulate the rest of the field.[6]

Anna Julia Cooper, *on the importance of including all women if we want adequate knowledge of/as human beings:* It is not the intelligent woman versus the ignorant woman; nor the white woman versus the black, the brown, and the red—it is not even the cause of woman versus man. Nay, 'tis woman's strongest vindication for speaking that *the world needs to hear her voice.* It would be subversive of every human interest that the cry of one-half the human family be stifled . . . . The world has had to limp along with the wobbling gait and the one-sided hesitancy of a man with one eye. Suddenly the bandage is removed from the other eye and the whole body is filled with light. It sees a circle where before it saw a segment. The darkened eye restored, every member rejoices with it.[7]

Jane Addams, *on the relation of U.S. black/white racism to the ignorance of ethnic prejudice:* It is difficult to write of the relation of the older and most foreign-looking immigrants to the children of other people—the Italians whose fruit carts are upset simply because they are "dagoes" or the Russian peddlers who are stoned and sometimes badly injured because it has become a code of honor in a gang of boys thus to express their derision. The members of a Protective Association of Jewish Peddlers organized at Hull House related daily experiences in which old age had been treated with such irreverence. . . . The Greeks are filled with amazed rage when their very name is flung at them as an opprobrious epithet. Doubtless these difficulties would be much minimized in America, if we faced our own race problems with courage and intelligence, and these very Mediterranean immigrants might give us valuable help . . . . They listened with respect and enthusiasm to a scholarly address delivered by Professor du Bois at Hull House on a Lincoln's birthday, with apparently no consciousness of that race difference which color seems to accentuate so absurdly.[8]

W. E.B. du Bois, *on the necessity of liberal education for all:* Consider our so-called educational "problems." "How may we keep pupils in high school?" Feed and clothe them. "Shall we teach Latin, Greek, and mathematics to the 'masses'?" If they are worth teaching to anybody, the masses need them most. "Who shall go to college?" Everybody. "When shall culture training give place to technical education for work?" Never. These are not "problems." They are simply "excuses" for spending less time and money on the next generation. . . . The result is grotesque! We bury genius; we send it to jail; we ridicule and mock it, while we send mediocrity and idiocy to college, gilded and crowned. For 300 years we have denied black Americans an education and now we exploit them before a gaping world. . . . To this there is but one patent way, proved and inescapable, Education. . . . All children are the children of all and not of individuals and families and races. The whole generation must be trained and guided and out of it as out of a huge reservoir must be lifted all genius, talent, and intelligence to serve all the world.[9]

Fred Newton Scott, *in response to reports from a Harvard study condemning the teaching of rhetoric and composition between 1892 and 1897:*

Should we not—at least those of us who are pragmatic philosophers—apply to the young offenders the crucial test of pragmatism? . . . Back of this mess and confusion were genuine individuals with likes and dislikes, with budding ambitions, with tingling senses, with impulses toward right and wrong. Where did these individuals come in when judgement was passed on their faulty English? What were they trying to do? What motives lay behind these queer antics of the pen? If one could only tear away the swathings, set the imprisoned spirits free, and interrogate them, a strange new light might be thrown upon the causes of bad English.[10]

Mary Parker Follett, *on unifying without homogenizing differences:* The test of the vitality of any experience is its power to unite into a living, generating activity its self-yielding differences. We seek a richly diversified experience where every difference strengthens and reinforces the other through the interpenetrating of spirit and spirit, differences are conserved, accentuated, and reconciled in the greater life which is the issue. Each remains forever himself that thereby the larger activity may be enriched and in its refluence, reinforce him.[11]

(Re)Defining

Consider, with those voices still sounding, John Dewey's (in)famous definition of philosophy as "the theory of education as a deliberately conducted practice."[12] In the company of his peers, the definition is harder to read as an expression of his supposed "instrumentalism," or of his still hopeful (in a way we can barely imagine) faith in modern science as a model for democratic thinking. For Dewey, philosophy in America must be radically changed so that finally it can stop subverting democratic aspirations and start doing its proper work of providing just, moral democratic practices with an epistemological grounding. That purpose, I submit, shaped what he and the other pragmatists took to be philosophically tenable rather than the other way around. And it is that purpose that seems to me to answer the question, "Why would anyone want to study Dewey [let alone the whole large group of academic *and* activist pragmatists] anyway?"

I want to say, then, that progressive education, pragmatism, feminism, and multicultural/diversity critiques all have at their animating core a conviction, inspired by democratic ideals and agitated by consistent failures of those ideals, that old, deeply entrenched, hierarchically ranked divisions among human "kinds," lives, and abilities must be critiqued and dismantled. That is a task that moves us into all spheres, from the philosophical through the educational to the political and into the moral. In all these areas—and perhaps especially in epistemology, which in some senses provides a pivot point for or a common thread among them—such critique aims to reveal the mutual implications of legitimated knowledge and ways of knowing and of injustices systemically as well as interpersonally inflicted on categorically defined and devalued groups. It does so because, as many progressives have said, it is unjust divisions of humans that subvert not "only" democracy's aspirational ideals but also the possibility of the unbiased, open inquiry that human betterment and the education upon which it depends requires.

Hierarchical views of humankind produced and reproduce hierarchical philosophies that divide mind (= some few privileged males) from body (= females and large groups of men defined by their physical type and/or labor). It is such philosophies (the kinds that inform cultures) that deform education such that it serves the "vicious intellectualism" against which James so passionately railed, making education compatible with vicious social/economic systems. "Vicious intellectualism," as Stephen Rowe puts it, "is a retreat from the complexities of real life into intellectual formulations that have become sealed off from any new insight or energy from lived experience."[13] This is philosophically wrong; it is also very dangerous in ways pragmatists care about. As James further suggested, using an innocuous example to make a point whose sharpness is evident when it is read in the context of what we know about all prejudices: "[A] person whom you have once called an 'equestrian' is thereby forever made unable to walk on his own feet."[14]

On the positive side, through such critique, progressive, pragmatic, feminist/diversity commitments work for an affirming, empowering release of the full capacities of all our minds, hearts, spirits, and bodies. They offer a different model of fruitful human interrelatedness and interdependency—within ourselves; to each other; across cultural, historical, and regional groupings; to the earth and the worlds humans create on it; and to a less alienating and divisive understanding of the divine than is often found in the actual histories of established religions. This model has at its heart a picture of egalitarian, face-to-face, creative, engaged discussion among respectfully differing people that is throughout open-minded, exploratory, fallibilistic. It is carried on in the context of mutually communicative, educative action in a world compatibly understood to be inherently transactional rather than composed of discrete entities that can only be more or less forcefully related by external means. We should thus, by this model of what is both desirable and most basically given, hold ourselves in conversation with ongoing experience that checks the meanings of abstractions turned into unchanging absolutes, or into the settled terms of professionalized academic expertise. Mary Parker Follett said, pithily, "I think it better when practicable to keep to verbs; the value of nouns is chiefly for post mortems."[15]

Translating this recentering of philosophy into a democratizing educational vision for today that is strikingly compatible with the visions we can discern through the voices I quoted above, Maxine Greene writes:

> Democracy, Dewey wrote, is a community always in the making. If educators hold this in mind, they will remember that democracy is forever incomplete: it is founded in possibilities. Even in the small, the local spaces in which teaching is done, educators may begin creating the kinds of situations where, at the very least, students will begin telling the stories of what they are seeking, what they know and might not yet know, exchanging stories with others grounded in other landscapes, at once bringing something into being that is in between . . . . It is at moments like these that persons begin to recognize each other and, in the experience of recognition, feel the need to take responsibility for each other.[16]

The Urge to Depoliticize Recurs Pragmatists are interested people moved by the promise of democracy and incited to philosophize as they are to act in the world by its problems and failures. There are many things to hear in their committed passionate voices, but not, it might be said—it has been said—the *gravitas,* the high level of abstraction, the conceptual precision of philosophers, or the disinterested calm of specialized expertise suitable for educators. What, then, are we to do with them? Well, we could join most professional academic philosophers and educators from their times to ours in ignoring them, perhaps muttering regretfully that they were impressive people but sadly they are just too sloppy in their thinking, too caught up in eloquence to be precise, and in general too politically impassioned to be trusted. Or we could return to a small group of them (Dewey, James, Peirce, perhaps Royce, perhaps George Herbert Mead), and from this small group make a careful selection of their writings, and see what they have to offer when read from the perspective of today's academic intellectual quandaries—particularly for what they might suggest to help philosophers and those who work with them undo the sterility of analytic philosophy, the collapse of all realities and meanings into linguistic issues. They have a lot to offer that effort.

But when we read them for purposes that were not central to them, it turns out that they remain rather easy to criticize and discredit. Those few pragmatists, and the short list of their works that have continued to be studied a bit, do indeed deal with what are still recognized as philosophical problems, but they do not do so with other academic philosophers as their primary audience nor are academic discussions their primary context or originating impetus. Of course they then appear to stumble, to be a bit inept, compared to those who are engaged in quite a different game.

Put the pragmatists, all of them, back into conversation with progressive educators, with feminists and those working for diversity in an aspirational democracy that knows its own failures with regard to the mutuality of equality, and they do not stumble at all. Listen, for example, to Dewey's good friend and colleague, Jane Addams, with whom he learned about relations of theory to practice, the experimental attitude, fallibilism, the importance of ends-in-view as means for action.

Jane Addams describes Hull House as "an experimental effort to aid in the solution of the social and industrial problems which are engendered by the modern conditions of life in a great city," and continues to make it clear that she intended with her work no application of preformulated principles to an alien or recalcitrant reality but, rather, an open engagement with instructive actual conditions as they are experienced. She wrote of "the Settlement" that, "From its very nature it can stand for no political or social propaganda . . . . The one thing to be dreaded in the Settlement is that it lose its flexibility, its power of quick adaptation, its readiness to change its methods as its environment may demand. It must be open to conviction and must have a deep and abiding sense of tolerance." Such openness, she makes it clear, does not reflect a renunciation of values (which would be a very unpragmatic position). She writes of "the Settlement" that it "is an attempt to relieve, at the same time, the overaccumulation at one end of society and the destitution at the other."[17]

Similarly, Carter Woodson wrote that in designing an education, the actual historical situation of people and of peoples must be taken into account: "It is merely a matter of exercising common sense in approaching people through their environment in order to deal with conditions as they are rather than as you would like to see them or imagine that they are."[18]

These are sensible, if not conventionally approved, positions true to a pragmatic epistemology, and it is in such statements, and projects, that the pragmatic test of truth is by its own warrants to be found as they are worked out in practice, not in their "soundness" by professionalized philosophical standards that are, after all, not those of the pragmatists. For such thinkers, we might say that justice is a necessary propaedeutic for inquiry even as it is also an object, or end-in-view of inquiry itself. And that is why we need, and turn to, them today: if there is one way of characterizing the issues that are most agitating this nation right now, it is, I repeat, that they are issues of social, political, and economic justice.

Other Progressive Pragmatists' Projects

Today, the work of those who continue the regularly interrupted but stubbornly persistent tradition of aspirational democrats who challenge various establishments also includes that of educator/theorists/activists such as Maxine Greene and Cornel West. Both of these widely read educators (in the full sense) draw explicitly on pragmatism not as authority, and not, either, as a merely academic philosophical discourse, but as an intellectual/political/moral resource for our times. Charlene Haddock Seigfried has also written a crucial book, *Pragmatism and Feminism: Reweaving the Social Fabric.*[19] Seigfried not only retrieves the women who have been erased from pragmatism's academic history, but also discusses as compatible with pragmatism contemporary feminist theorists such as Nancy Fraser, Susan Bordo, bell hooks, and Patricia Hill Collins. She thus challenges the more narrowly defined meanings as well as exemplars of pragmatism, making it possible to read the important nouveau pragmatism works of Richard Rorty and Richard Bernstein, among others, in ways that hold open the challenge not to repeat past erasures and perpetuate their errors.

Bruce A. Kimball has also been influential in resurfacing the pragmatists. He concludes his essay, "Toward Pragmatic Liberal Education," "I am proposing here that Peirce, James, and Dewey are waiting at the end of the road on which American liberal education has been traveling during the twentieth century. After a long disjunction, pragmatism and liberal education now appear to be converging. U.S. colleges and universities at the end of the century are thus yielding a view of liberal education that is both new and traditional and that, being rooted in or rationalized by pragmatic conceptions, may be termed 'pragmatic.' "[20]

I am in agreement with Kimball, although I am not sure that the "view of liberal education" of the academy today (still centered in the professionalized academic disciplines even as it is also increasingly infused and decentered by the new academy) is "rooted in or rationalized by pragmatic conceptions." It could be, although I doubt if it has been, on the one hand, and on the other, "pragmatic conceptions" still need to be retrieved from what I have called their political decentering (or sanitizing). They also need to be brought into fruitful interaction with many useful new conceptualizations, theories, languages, and bodies of knowledge developed largely by people drawing on other resources, such as the distinction between sex and gender; the human-agency-retrieving concept of *racialization* rather than the static, essentializing *race* that haunted the United States in the pragmatists' times (cf. works by Omi and Winant, David Theo Goldberg); dramatic shifts in meanings of *culture* as a result of various fields of critical cultural theorizing; the illuminating metaphors of relationality as well as knowledge of the new field of ecology; analyses of "ways of knowing" (Belenky, Clinchy, et al.) and studies of "multiple intelligences" (Gardener); discussion of an "ethics of care" (Gilligan, Ruddick, Nodding, Tronto); creation of "post-colonial" and ethnic studies that have given us many new ways of thinking about and with people in the United States and also around the globe (Mohanty, McLaughlin); feminist epistemologies that engage with many philosophical and political positions other than pragmatism (Bordo, Harraway, Nelson, Scheman).

Such work does not need to be "rooted" or "rationalized" by an older version of pragmatism, even as it can of course be enriched by engaging that rich tradition as it provides points of contact very hard (albeit observably possible) to find in some other traditions that are still dominant. It has its own integrity, sets its own terms, and it is by bringing those fully into conversation with pragmatism as well as other friendly traditions on equal grounds that its proponents will help us all learn the most, not by submitting to the authority of what perhaps (politically sanitized as it has been) still seems the greater safety and respectability of U.S. pragmatism's short list of authors and works. The longer list of pragmatists whose works have actually been retrieved, so far as I can tell, primarily by those animated not by a particular interest in what has been defined as pragmatism but by the age of movements and the new academy is actually already, but still not in a widespread way, in such fruitful conversations.

Kimball might concur with much of what I have been saying, although he does not seem to put political passions for justice at the core of what pragmatism is all about as I do. He lists as "seven developments" of our times that are "compatible with pragmatism":

- multiculturalism,
- values and service,
- community and citizenship,
- general education,

- commonality and cooperation between college and other levels of the education system,
- teaching interpreted as learning and inquiry,
- assessment.[21]

This is a good and useful list, but I cannot help feeling that it represents Kimball's sense of the generosity of short-list pragmatism, its friendly desire to cross boundaries creatively, rather than capturing the passionate justice-seeking heart of the matter. Hence, issues such as multiculturalism and community and citizenship become no more than additives.

In his essay, "Pragmatism: An Old Name for Some New Ways of Thinking?" James T. Kloppenberg also considers Cornel West and some feminists who know themselves to be doing work compatible with pragmatism.[22] Unfortunately, he encapsulates his discussion of this work in a brief section under the subhead, "Varieties of Contemporary Pragmatism," as he does not encapsulate the work of mainstream philosophers such as Rorty who came to the short list of pragmatists from professionalized analytic philosophy rather than from the work of the new academy. Kloppenberg, as Kimball does also, gives us some recognition that feminist and antiracist concerns were compatible with, but not in his view central to, pragmatism proper. He writes, "Such early pragmatists as James, Dewey, and George Herbert Mead considered pragmatism a weapon in the campaign against restrictive gender roles for the same reason they considered it a weapon in the campaigns against imperialism and racism and for democracy. They allied with feminist activists and championed feminist scholars such as Jessie Taft *because their conception of pragmatism extended beyond language* to an awareness of the experience of people who were denied choices, or unnecessarily restricted in their choices, by prevailing assumptions and patterns of social relations" (emphasis added).[23] It will be no surprise if I say that I would reverse the order here to suggest that "their conception of pragmatism extended beyond language" *because* of their driving awareness that democracy was not working as it should and that all our minds are seriously limited and our quests for knowledge distorted when humankind divides itself from itself.

Kloppenberg rather dismisses Cornel West's *The American Evasion of Philosophy: A Genealogy of Pragmatism,* albeit respectfully: "Although lack of precision and inattention to detail," he writes, "make West's [book] problematic as a history of philosophy, it is a spirited and provocative piece of pragmatic cultural criticism."[24] He rather implies that "cultural criticism" and philosophy are more separable than I think the long list of pragmatists would want to say. I also cannot help remembering that the usually-taken-to-be exemplary pragmatists have themselves been dismissed from academic philosophy for quite similar reasons. Although, of course, it is in contemporary language— and perhaps troublingly so to some academic readers because West speaks to audiences far outside of and long excluded from the ivory tower—West's passionate cultural critique sounds a lot more like the talk of the larger group of pragmatists than does the work of most of today's scholars of pragmatism. He, too (I think here of charges still made, for example, against William James), is more eloquent, evocative, and stirring than "properly" precise.

West, in fact, also writes about the short-list version and exemplars of pragmatism, but he does so to tell a story of American development that he thinks more adequate, closer to truly dealing with the searing problems the pragmatists (all of them) so notably tried in their times and ways to face. He writes,

> American pragmatism emerges with profound insights and myopic blindnesses . . . resulting from distinctive features of American civilization: its revolutionary beginning combined with a slave-based economy; its elastic liberal rule of law combined with an entrenched business-dominated status quo; its hybrid culture in combination with a collective self-definition as homogeneously Anglo-American; its obsession with mobility, contingency, and pecuniary liquidity combined with a deep moralistic impulse; and its impatience with theories and philosophies alongside ingenious technological innovation, political strategies of compromise, and personal devices for comfort and convenience.[25]

To recognize such tangles and contradictions as a step toward engaging with them to sort them out for the better, by our lights in our times, is to speak from the animating center of the pragmatic tradition rather than from what there is of an established academic discourse about it. That is, West is right to call our attention to the "rebelliousness" of American pragmatism which is cognizant of the exclusion of peoples of color, certain immigrants, and women, and he is right, too, to be on the lookout for where older pragmatism also betrays a fearfulness "of the subversive demands these excluded peoples might make and enact." [26] These were fearful issues; they still are. Very few of us can face up to and think with them consistently.

But more among the larger group of pragmatists did so than we have been helped to remember. Seigfried thus reminds us that,

> The pragmatist belief that theory unrelated to practice is moribund inspired some of their more radical students to abandon purely conceptual analysis. West points out that C. Wright Mills, a student of Dewey's, gave up philosophy after earning his M.A. and turned to social theory, declaring war on Talcott Parsons's sociology because it supported the corporate liberal establishment. W.E.B. du Bois "also gave up philosophy after studying under William James at Harvard, turning to the study of history and society". . . . If the pragmatists had succeeded in stopping philosophers from turning their backs on active engagement in solving society's most pressing problems, then feminists of our generation would not have had to endure the continuing struggle both to break into academia and to deinstitutionalize and open up academic deliberations to the wider community.[27]

None of this implies that more narrowly philosophical analyses of what the short list of pragmatists were trying to do are unimportant or basically wrong, of course. They are simply, as I have said, off center insofar as they do not take account of the political/moral passions that led the pragmatists to philosophize as they did.

Characterizing Pragmatic Philosophizing

Seigfried quotes a useful effort to define pragmatism thematically and historically by John J. Stuhr ("who prefers the label *Classical American Philosophy* to *pragmatism*"):

> (1) the rejection of the central problems of modern philosophy, which presuppose such dichotomies as percept/concept, reason/will, thought/purpose, intellect/emotion, appearance/reality, experi-

ence/nature, belief/action, theory/practice, facts/values, and self/others; (2) fallibilism, or the impossibility of attaining unrevisable, certain empirical knowledge as an irreducible dimension of the human condition; (3) pluralism of experiences, values, and meanings; (4) radical empiricism, according to which experiencing subject and experienced object constitute a primal, integral, relational unity; (5) treatment of the results of experimental inquiry as the measure of theory; (6) meliorism, the view that human action can improve the human condition; and (7) the centrality of community and the social, such that the individual is intrinsically constituted by and in her or his social relations, thus linking the attainment of individuality with the creation of community.[28]

Kimball, too, has a helpful list of characteristic pragmatist positions:

(1) that belief and meaning, even truth itself, are fallible and revisable; (2) that an experimental method of inquiry obtains in all science and reflective thought; (3) that belief, meaning, and truth depend on the context and the intersubjective judgment of the community in which they are formed; (4) that experience is the dynamic interaction of organism and environment, resulting in a close interrelationship between thought and action; (5) that the purpose of resolving doubts or solving problems is intrinsic to all thought and inquiry; and (6) that all inquiry and thought are evaluative, and judgments about fact are no different from judgments about value.[29]

Seigfried notes that "These theoretically necessary but artificial definitions and distinctions . . . can also function to obscure important dimensions."[30] I agree: the problems and contradictions of democracy are captured here only indirectly, in their (yes, related) formulations as "problems of modern philosophy" in its struggles over epistemological issues. We do not hear, for example, of "such dichotomies" as those so passionately noted by Dewey and others between classes, races, ethnicities, sex/genders, but of what they saw as the effects of those dichotomies when those who live by them turn to philosophizing, such as theory/practice, politics/ethics, knowledge/experience, percept/concept, reason/will, etc. Nor do we hear of James's warning that we should keep "hands off" claims to have complete knowledge because it leads us to shut off learning from others, or Addams's firm commitment to an experimental openness at Hull House so that it can respond effectively to real situations. Instead, we are told of "fallibilism" in pragmatism as it concerns "the impossibility of attaining unrevisable, certain empirical knowledge," without explicit recognition of the dangers to our living together posed by lust for such impossible knowledge.

And, while "pluralism of experiences, values, and meanings" is listed, it is not connected with the need Addams, Cooper, du Bois, Woodson, and others saw to work for political, social, economic, and educational change to make such pluralism something other than an invocation of old pieties in a hierarchical world. In fact, every one of the pragmatists' characteristic philosophical moves can, and should, be translated also into its moral, political meanings or we lose the reasons for those moves just as we find ourselves directed to something other than their "real-world" consequences for their proper pragmatic test.

But, you might say, what about Charles Sanders Peirce, whose work on logic has been retrieved recently, too? Surely it is not right to say that *all* the pragmatists were animated by political, moral, economic passions.

Peirce, in fact, wrote passionately about what he called "evolutionary love," and was a defender of the democratic passions of the French Revolution. In an 1893 essay for *The Monist,* Peirce writes:

> What I say, then, is that the great attention paid to economical questions during our century has induced an exaggeration of the beneficial effects of greed and of the unfortunate results of sentiment, until there has resulted a philosophy which comes unwittingly to this, that greed is the great agent in the elevation of the human race and in the evolution of the universe. . . . The twentieth century, in its latter half, shall surely see the deluge-tempest burst upon the social order—to clear upon a world as deep in ruin as that greed-philosophy has long plunged it into guilt.[31]

Further, to undercut one of the defenses of "that greed-philosophy," Peirce asks his readers to refuse to be intimidated by its attacking of *"sentimentalists"* as "persons incapable of logical thought and unwilling to look facts in the eyes," and as dangerous proponents of a way of thinking that led to the horrors that followed upon the French Revolution. Admitting that "ever since the French Revolution brought this leaning of thought into ill-repute, and not altogether undeservedly, I must admit, true, beautiful, and good as that great movement was," Peirce claims proudly to have "some tincture of sentimentalism." And he proceeds to discuss various theories of evolution to make his case for "the doctrine that great respect should be paid to the natural judgments of the sensible heart," and that "progress comes from every individual merging his individuality in sympathy with his neighbors," following "the movement of love," which is "circular, at one and the same impulse projecting creations into independency and drawing them into harmony."[32]

It is hard to avoid the conclusion that to do no more than tack on consideration of what we have today from the age of movements and its new academy to our efforts to retrieve and renew pragmatism as a philosophy for liberal education as if those demands were not from the very heart of what democracy and truth both ask of us would be once again to fail what pragmatism in the tradition of aspirational democracy asks of us.

Claiming Our Own Progressive, Feminist/Diversity Pragmatism

A contemporary reconfiguration of the tradition has resurfaced with the new academy as epitomized in the reports from the national panel of the Association of American Colleges and Universities' (AAC&U) project on "Diversity, Democracy, and Liberal Learning." In the reports that have issued from this national panel, we encounter an example of today's reinvigoration of an alternative U.S. tradition in education as in politics. I have been calling this a tradition of aspirational democracy. This morally centered tradition embraces the generative tensions of this always diverse, always multicultural nation as necessary for an egalitarian, relational pluralism in which humankind practices what Dewey called the arts of associative living. It was present in those founders of the nation who chose in principle and for moral and educational as much as political reasons to entrust the people with their own governance, and who knew that "the people" could not without dangerous self-contradiction be an exclusive concept. It was most fully present in those who were appalled by the cheating and killing of Native Americans, those who instead tried to live with and learn from them, as it was present among those who opposed slavery and who argued for woman suffrage and the equal rights of working people in all groups, no matter from what country or racialized/ethnicized group they came.

The panel's reports thus recognize that we are still aspiring to democracy, still trying to see whether heterogeneity welcomed rather than suppressed and too often oppressed can achieve its promise in the realization of all human capacities working together across even the most difficult divisions. The panel, as did the pragmatists and others in the tradition of aspirational democracy, believes that education is crucial to this ongoing effort, this continuing experiment.

Summarizing "the broad themes addressed in [the] separate . . . reports," the panel called on liberal learning to:

1. Recognize American campuses as meeting grounds for American pluralism. . . .
2. Engage the centrality of diversity in higher education's responsibilities to democracy. . . .
3. Continue and extend our commitment to help students find their own sources and expressions of self and voice. . . .
4. Transform the curriculum so that it acknowledges and prepares students for the multiplicity of contemporary society. . . .
5. Learn how to foster human capacities supportive of a diverse democracy. . . .

And, to quote the final charge to liberal learning in full:

6. Confront contradictions and discover their possibilities. We must not be afraid to help our students and our communities confront the contradictions of their own histories and the history of the American republic. Only through the realization of our historical and present tensions can we hope to nurture the development of individuals who will become active participants in the American narrative without the false hope of easy resolution, but with the sustained

commitment to work toward a society in which democratic aspirations become democratic justice, and diversity becomes a means of forging a deeper unity.[33]

In its second report, *Liberal Learning and the Arts of Connection for the New Academy,* the national panel turned to conceptual reframings suggested by the new academy.[34] That is, the panel realized, as all those in the tradition of aspirational democracy have, that cultural ways of thinking and of construing and constructing knowledge can work with or can subvert possibilities of mutual, respectful, egalitarian associative living. In its own ways, but hardly alone—the pragmatists were certainly among the resources upon which they drew—the panel turned to philosophizing. Under a general call for the liberal arts to include as central to its mission in today's ever-more-interdependent world the art of translation in its fullest sense, the panel called for conceptual reframings to support the possibility of the kinds of democracy-enhancing commitments of the first report.

The second report then considers ways to rethink concepts that the panel found to be particularly potent in either forwarding or, when stuck in oppositional framings, skewing, even paralyzing, national discussions of liberal learning, diversity, and democracy—concepts such as universal/particular, timeless/historical, central/marginal, human/kind of human, and individual/community.

Finally, in the panel's third report, *American Pluralism and the College Curriculum,* there is a picture of a possible set of effects—a good pragmatist test—of U.S. liberal learning regrounding itself in the new academy and its too-long-submerged, aspirationally democratic tradition. That picture, which I will quote, follows recommendations for "education for citizenship in a diverse democracy" related to "four kinds of courses and experiences." Those courses/experiences are:

1. **Experience, identity, and aspiration:** The study of one's own particular inherited and constructed traditions, identity communities, and significant questions, in their complexity.
2. **United States pluralism and the pursuits of justice:** An extended and comparative exploration of diverse peoples in this society, with

significant attention to their differing experiences of United States
democracy and the pursuits—sometimes successful, sometimes frus-
trated—of equal opportunity.

3. **Experiences in justice seeking:** Encounters with systemic constraints
   on the development of human potential in the United States and
   experiences in community-based efforts to articulate principles of
   justice, expand opportunity, and redress inequities.

4. **Multiplicity and relational pluralism in majors, concentrations, and
   programs:** Extensive participation in forms of learning that foster
   sustained exploration of and deliberation about contested issues
   important in particular communities of inquiry and practice.[35]

These are startling proposals when one reads them from within
an academy still centered on the professionalized disciplines in which
selections and judgments of many kinds are made with an eye on the
standing of departments and whole schools in relation to their contributions to those professionalized disciplines. They are far less startling when read in the light of many schools' mission statements, in
which citizenship and a lively, engaged life both publicly and privately
informed by continuing learning are almost always invoked as goals.
And they are still less so when we think of education trying to live up
to its mission-claimed goals in our present world, with its particular
needs for an educated citizenry prepared to join an increasingly interdependent world.

In the light of our claimed educational missions in today's world,
the pragmatic test for the proposals made in these reports is telling:

> Envision a group of Americans, different in background and economic
> resources. They are vigorously debating a contentious societal issue,
> perhaps the justice of limiting welfare support to three years as a life-
> time maximum. Each is listening carefully, without interrupting, to
> what the other is saying. Each is able to explain why other members
> of the group see the issues as they do. Each can describe how differ-
> ent histories and affiliations have shaped participants' different under-
> standings. Each spends a great deal of time considering the effects of
> particular policies on different cases: the hard-working legal immi-
> grant parent whose efforts to be self-sufficient are hindered by a poor
> labor market and employment preference for United States citizens;
> the drug addict who is not really available to work; the teenage moth-

er with a sickly child. No one attacks the motives, intelligence, or worth of anyone else in the conversation. No one applies a principle without considering its implications. Several people in the group have had family experiences or field studies that involved them in welfare issues; they bring a base of experience to the discussion.

By the time the discussion ends, every participant in the dialogue has recast at least part of his or her original position in light of insights and opposing views offered in the conversation. The group has decided on the points where agreement has to be reached and spent the most time on those points. They have also acknowledged issues where continued disagreement must be accepted. Every participant can readily explain how the several histories and perspectives reflected in the group improved the quality of their own and others' thinking.

How is this different from traditional aspirations for liberal and general education? In principle, not very. What is different is the practice. Participants in this imaginary dialogue . . . know the topic experientially as well as analytically. . . . [T]hey have had extensive experience in confronting multiplicity and negotiating deep-rooted difference. . . . [E]very one of them believes, on the basis of experience, that the diverse backgrounds and perspectives represented in the group add to the quality of their insight and understanding. . . . No one of them would think excellence enhanced if the group could become less diverse—and less complex.[36]

It seems to me evident that the panel and all those who participated in its work over several years and across this nation express an American dream that has inspired, haunted, and driven this country through its tumultuous history—an aspirational dream invoked even by those it has most failed in practice when they stood up to claim their rightful places. The pragmatists and their sisters and brothers in the progressive educational and political movements of their times are being "rediscovered" today because they, as the many voices emerging from the new academy, believed too deeply in aspirational democracy to accept injustices and ways of thinking and knowing that serve them.

Dewey, toward the end of his long life, said in response to another occasion recognizing his work, "I *know* . . . that such a manifestation of friendliness as I have experienced is a demonstration of sympathy for the things that make for the freedom and justice and for the kind of cooperative friendship that can flourish only where there is a freedom which untold multitudes possess in common," in which "communication is progressively liberated from bondage to prejudice and ignorance . . . [and we are all] emancipated from oppressions and suppressions."[37]

I trust that we will try, at least, to live up to his faith in those who continue to manifest friendliness to his work—that we are really willing to risk joining the aspirational democratic tradition, that feisty, distinctly U.S. activist tradition that has been reinvigorated through this age of movements.

Notes

1. Debra Morris and Ian Shapiro, editors, *John Dewey: The Political Writings* (Indianapolis/Cambridge: Hackett, 1993), 227.
2. See Rick Tilman, *C. Wright Mills: A Native Radical and His American Intellectual Roots* (University Park and London: Pennsylvania State University Press, 1984).
3. John Dewey, *Art As Experience* (New York: Putnam, 1980), 348–49.
4. John Dewey, *Democracy and Education* (Toronto: Free Press, 1966), 333–34.
5. Carter G. Woodson, *The Mis-Education of the Negro* (Trenton, NJ: Africa World Press, 1990), xi.
6. William James, "On a Certain Blindness in Human Beings," in Stephen C. Rowe, editor, *The Vision of James* (Rockport, MA: Element Books, 1996), 53, 75.
7. Anna Julia Cooper, *A Voice from the South* (New York: Oxford University Press, 1988), 121.
8. Jane Addams, *Twenty Years at Hull House* (New York: Signet Classic, 1981), 183.
9. W.E.B. du Bois, *Darkwater: Voices from Within the Veil* (New York: Schocken Books, 1972), 216–17.
10. "What the West Wants in Preparatory English," quoted in Jean Donovan Sanborn, "The Essay Dies in the Academy, Circa 1900," in Patricia A. Sullivan and Donna J. Qualley, editors, *Pedagogy in the Age of Politics: Writing and Reading (in) the Academy* (Urbana, IL: National Council of Teachers of English, 1994), 121–38.
11. Mary Parker Follett, *Creative Experience* (New York: Longmans, Green & Co., 1930), 302.
12. Dewey, *Democracy and Education,* 332.
13. Rowe, *Vision of James,* 31.
14. Quoted in ibid., 31.
15. Mary Parker Follett, *The New State* (New York: Longmans, Green & Co., 1926), 7.
16. Maxine Greene, "Diversity and Inclusion: Toward a Curriculum for Human Beings," *Teachers College Record* (1995: 2): 211–21.
17. Addams, *Twenty Years at Hull House,* 98.
18. Woodson, *Mis-Education,* xi.

19. Charlene Haddock Seigfried, *Pragmatism and Feminism: Reweaving the Social Fabric* (Chicago: University of Chicago Press, 1996).
20. Bruce Kimball, "Toward Pragmatic Liberal Education," in Robert Orrill, editor, *The Condition of American Liberal Education: Pragmatism and a Changing Tradition* (New York: College Entrance Examination Board, 1995), 99.
21. Op. cit., 97.
22. James T. Kloppenberg, "Pragmatism: An Old Name for Some New Ways of Thinking?" *Journal of American History* (June 1996).
23. Op. cit., 127.
24. Cornel West, *The American Evasion of Philosophy: A Genealogy of Pragmatism* (Madison: University of Wisconsin Press, 1989); op. cit., 126.
25. West, *American Evasion*, 5.
26. Op. cit. 5.
27. Seigfried, *Pragmatism and Feminism*, 21–22.
28. Ibid., 7–8.
29. Kimball, "Toward Pragmatic Liberal Education," 83.
30. Seigfried, *Pragmatism and Feminism*, 8.
31. Charles Sanders Peirce, "Evolutionary Love," in Nathan Houser and Christian Kloefel, editors, *The Essential Peirce: Selected Philosophical Writings*, vol. 1 (1867–1893) (Bloomington: Indiana University Press, 1992), 354–56.
32. Ibid., 356, 365, 357, 353.
33. *The Drama of Diversity and Democracy: Higher Education and American Commitments* (Washington, DC: Association of American Colleges and Universities, 1995).
34. *Liberal Learning and the Arts of Connection for the New Academy* (Washington, DC: Association of American Colleges and Universities, 1995).
35. *American Pluralism and the College Curriculum: Higher Education in a Diverse Democracy* (Washington, DC: Association of American Colleges and Universities, 1995).
36. Ibid.
37. "John Dewey Responds," in *Political Writings*, 248.

Liberal Education and Democracy: The Case for Pragmatism

ALEXANDER W. ASTIN

ALLAN MURRAY CARTTER PROFESSOR OF HIGHER EDUCATION AND WORK,
DIRECTOR, HIGHER EDUCATION RESEARCH INSTITUTE,
UNIVERSITY OF CALIFORNIA, LOS ANGELES

Some defenders of the status quo in liberal education will argue that our quest for a more pragmatic liberal education is little more than a revival of the Philistine call for "relevance" that caused folks in the humanities so much distress during the late 60s and early 70s. Whether or not there is any truth in such a claim, I believe that there is a completely different—and more constructive—way to look at the issue. Instead of advocating that we start tinkering with liberal education with the aim of making it "more relevant" to the "real world," I'd propose that we first consider three questions:

First, what's wrong with contemporary U.S. democracy and society? Where have we gone astray? What needs fixing?

Second, what part, if any, has our education system played in helping to create and perpetuate these problems? In particular, what part has our *higher* education system played?

And finally, what role, if any, can higher education play in helping to alleviate these problems? More specifically, are there ways in which our colleges and universities can begin to deal more constructively with contemporary social problems and—at the same time—preserve what is most vital and fundamental to effective liberal education? More optimistically: are there reforms that we can undertake which will increase our capacity to serve U.S. society and U.S. democracy while simultaneously strengthening our liberal education programs?

207

When it comes to the first question, there is no need here to belabor the obvious: contemporary U.S. society is replete with myriad social problems that need fixing. Many of these problems—shaky race relations, growing economic disparities and inequities, excessive materialism, decaying inner cities, a deteriorating infrastructure, an irresponsible mass media, declining civic engagement, and the increasing ineffectiveness of government, to name just a few—seem to be getting worse by the day. In a democracy, of course, citizen disengagement from politics and governmental ineffectiveness not only go hand in hand, but also cripple our capacity to deal constructively with most of the other problems.

With respect to the second question I can be even more brief: our education system—and higher education in particular—has played a significant role in helping to create these problems. But rather than simply playing the "blame game," I'd like to move next to consider in some depth the third question: What can be done? Before discussing specific reforms, let's first take a closer look at *how* our higher education system helps to perpetuate the problem.

The Central Role of Beliefs

The more I reflect on the problems confronting higher education and the larger society, the more I become convinced that at the heart of our problems in trying to effect positive social change are issues of *beliefs*. By this I mean not only our beliefs about the meaning and purpose of a liberal education, but also our notions about educational *excellence* and especially our view of the role that higher education should play in the larger society. The problem is not so much that we might differ in our beliefs about these matters, but rather that these beliefs remain unexposed and unexamined while we discuss and debate the education policies and practices that emanate from them.

As a starting point, let's take the issue of the relationship between liberal education and society. Different people can hold very different beliefs about this relationship. An extreme view, which would probably be endorsed by only a small number of hard-core purists such as Robert Maynard Hutchins, is that the university should remain walled off from the external world of practical affairs so that the students can study and learn and faculty can pursue truth undisturbed by worldly distractions. While this "Ivory Tower" concept of higher education has a certain appeal for scholars, it never could, and never will, represent a viable conception of higher education in modern U.S. society. Like it or not, U.S. higher education is a *creature* of society, is sanctioned and supported by that society, and has in turn pledged itself to serve that society in its mission statements, catalogs, and other public pronouncements.

An alternate belief system, which seems to dominate in discussions of education "policy" these days, is what I like to call the "pegboard" view. With this view, the outside world is like a giant board containing an array of differently shaped job slots, and the role of higher education is to produce the right-shaped people—the "pegs"—to fill these slots. This is the dominant belief system not only of our captains of industry, but also of most politicians and policymakers, not to mention many students, teachers, and parents. The pegboard view is also what drives the advocates of the "competitiveness" argument, namely, that higher education must deliver more people with expertise in science, technology, and modern management techniques so that America's economy can remain competitive with the economies of Western Europe and especially the burgeoning economies of countries on the Pacific Rim.

My main problem with the pegboard view is that it represents an extremely limited conception not only of the role of higher education, but also of the larger society. When we consider the major problems plaguing contemporary U.S. society, it is ludicrous to argue that they can all be summed up in the issue of economic competitiveness. Competitiveness in the international marketplace bears only a marginal connection to the domestic issues of racial polarization, poverty, joblessness, crime, a deteriorating infrastructure, environmental degradation, political apathy, and distrust of our social institutions. There is nothing inherently wrong with higher education's attempting to produce graduates who possess more of the job skills required by modern business and industry, but it is naive to think that this will make much of a dent in our myriad social problems. Indeed, becoming more "competitive" economically may well be antithetical to any effort to deal constructively with problems such as the infrastructure, crime, and especially the environment.

Still another conception of the role of higher education in society is what I call the "private economic benefit" viewpoint, which, simply stated, maintains that the role of higher education is to provide opportunities for individuals to obtain higher-level and higher-paying jobs and, in general, to live a more comfortable and affluent lifestyle. This is obviously a close cousin of the pegboard view, in that it focuses on employment, upward economic mobility, and the development of "human capital." One might also call this the "consumer" viewpoint, in the sense that it sees individual students as consumers who invest time and money in higher education in order to receive greater economic benefits later on. This idea of a trade-off, an investment for a later return, is what economists do when they calculate the rate of return to higher education. Proponents of higher education who tout the increased earnings associated with higher education are also operating from this same belief system. Even if one accepts the argument that private economic benefits provide the main justification for higher education, this particular belief system is extremely limited because it has little to say about how the society as a whole is served by such an approach. In other words, while it may be a laudable goal to contribute to the economic comfort and well-being of those citizens who are fortunate enough to enter and complete higher education, this viewpoint has little to say about what is going to happen to people who are *not* able to complete higher education, nor does it say anything about how, if at all, the many other social and economic problems of our society will be addressed by such an approach.

An entirely different kind of belief system is implied in the various public pronouncements that U.S. colleges and universities make in their catalogs and mission statements. In many ways, these sometimes lofty statements come as close as anything to Dewey's conception of the proper role of education in society. If we were to study the mission statements of a randomly selected group of U.S. higher education institutions, we would seldom, if ever, find any mention of private economic benefits, international competitiveness, or filling slots in the labor market. On the contrary, when it comes to describing its educational mission, the typical college or university will use language such as "preparing students for responsible citizenship," "developing character," "developing future leaders," "preparing students to serve society," and so forth. In other words, if we are to believe our own rhetoric, those of us who work in the academy see ourselves as *serving* the society and promoting and strengthening our particular form of democratic self-government. While such a belief system does not preclude individual economic benefits or the preparation of people to serve the needs of employers, the central focus is on responsible citizenship and service.

Clearly, the manner in which we approach the social or "pragmatic" implications of liberal education will depend heavily on which belief system or worldview we embrace. "Pragmatism" implies one thing if we see ourselves simply as helping young people to lead more comfortable and affluent lives, but quite another thing if we see ourselves as working together to strengthen our society and our democracy. I would argue that we really have no choice but to embrace the latter view.

The problem, of course, is that if you look at the typical U.S. college or university—its curriculum and cocurriculum, its teaching and personnel practices, and the values that govern its administrative policies—it's very difficult to find evidence of a core commitment to preparing students for responsible citizenship. Most institutions, in short, have simply not put their "citizenship" and "service" commitments into practice.

Perhaps the most pressing reason to begin taking our public pronouncements about our societal mission more seriously is the sorry shape of contemporary U.S. democracy. Most citizens don't vote, negative campaigning reigns, and public distrust, contempt, and hostility toward "government" have reached unprecedented heights. The most recent freshman surveys conducted by the Higher Education Research Institute indicate that student interest and engagement in politics is at an all-time low.[1] While academics frequently comment on this sorry state of affairs, they seldom suggest either that higher education may have played a part in creating these problems or that it can or should attempt to do anything about them.

Leadership and Citizenship

Most of us probably think of democracy primarily as an *external* process, where people *do* things such as discussing issues and politics, campaigning for candidates, or voting. While these activities are indeed important elements of a healthy democracy, none of these external behaviors is likely to occur in the absence of appropriate internal conditions: an understanding of how democratic government is supposed to function, an appreciation of the individual's responsibilities under such a form of government, and a willingness, if not a determination, to be an active participant. In other words, democratic behavior is most likely to occur when the person has acquired certain knowledge, understanding, beliefs, and values. These internal qualities are precisely the kinds of qualities that educational institutions are in an ideal position to foster.

The problems that plague U.S. democracy and civic life are in many respects problems of leadership. By "leadership" I mean not only what elected and appointed public officials do, but also the large and small civic acts performed by countless individual citizens who are actively engaged in making a positive difference in the society. A leader, in other words, is anyone—regardless of formal position—who serves as an effective social change agent, so in this sense every student—and every faculty and staff member—is a potential leader.

Discussions about the frail state of U.S. democracy typically make reference to such problems as lack of citizen engagement, distrust of government, racial divisions, unethical politicians, the excessive influence of money, and an irresponsible mass media. While each of these problems needs more of our attention, the biggest problem with contemporary civic life in the United States may be that too few of our citizens are actively engaged in efforts to effect positive social change. Viewed in this context, the "leadership development" challenge for higher education is to empower students, to help them develop those special talents and attitudes that will enable them to become effective social change agents. While the list of relevant leadership talents is a long one, it would almost certainly have to include such qualities as communication skills (especially listening skills), empathy, generosity, commitment, self-understanding, honesty (i.e., the ability to develop trust), and the ability to work collaboratively with others. These are the same qualities, of course, that are needed for effective citizenship.

The problem for us in the higher education community, in a nutshell, is that we have not done a very good job of developing these qualities in our students because we have been preoccupied with other things. While many of my faculty colleagues may argue that the failure or success of our system of representative democracy is not higher education's responsibility or concern, they forget that promoting "good citizenship" and "developing future leaders" are two of the most commonly stated values in the mission statements of colleges and universities. Like it or not, we are publicly on record as committing ourselves and our institutions to promoting leadership and citizenship.

What Can Be Done?

Although I may well be accused of oversimplification, I would submit that there is currently available to all of us who teach the liberal arts a simple but extremely powerful tool that not only promises to make liberal learning more "pragmatic" in addressing our myriad social problems, but that also provides us with an opportunity to strengthen the most important features of a classical liberal education. I am speaking here of "experiential learning," and the special form of it that has come to be known as "service learning." The basic idea behind service learning is to use a community or public service experience to enhance the meaning and impact of traditional course content. Service learning can not only enrich traditional course content by giving the student an opportunity to "test" or "demonstrate" abstract theory in the real world, but can also improve the quality of the service being performed by giving it an intellectual underpinning. Although increasing numbers of institutions are giving serious consideration to the idea of expanding their service learning opportunities for students, this particular pedagogical innovation is still a relatively infrequent, if not marginal, activity on most college campuses. The obstacles to more widespread use of service learning are many, including lack of faculty experience and expertise, the belief that it may incur additional costs, faculty resistance, and the question of efficacy: Does it really work?

Recently at the Higher Education Research Institute, we completed a series of empirical studies of how students are affected by participation in community service, and the findings are nothing short of remarkable. In one national longitudinal study, we attempted to assess the impact of President Clinton's small grant program for promoting volunteer service on college campuses, known as Learn and Serve America, Higher Education.[2] In this study we compared service participants with nonparticipants using 35 different outcome measures covering three broad areas: academic development, civic values, and life skills. What was especially remarkable about the findings was that *every one* of the 35 student outcomes was positively influenced by service participation. While the magnitude of the positive effects on academic development—such things as grades, retention, hours spent studying, interaction with faculty, and interest in postgraduate study—was quite modest, the most important finding was that there were *no negative effects*. In other words, the argument that academic work suffers because of the additional time and energy required by the service experience is simply not supported by the evidence. Indeed, participation in community service during the undergraduate years appears to *enhance* academic development. Recent research also indicates that these favorable outcomes are enhanced if this service is not merely volunteer work, but rather is performed as part of a course.[3]

In another longitudinal study, we sought to determine whether there are any lasting effects of the undergraduate service experience that extend into the first five years after college.[4] Once again we found uniformly positive effects on a range of postcollege outcomes, including enrollment in postgraduate study, commitment to community values, participation in community service after college, and satisfaction with the extent to which the undergraduate experience prepared the student for postcollege employment. Also—of special interest to college presidents and directors of development—is the finding that undergraduate participation in community service increases the likelihood that an alumnus will contribute money to the alma mater!

Turning now to costs, there is no question that service learning—properly done—involves significant additional costs. Our site visits to campuses that received Learn and Serve America grants convinced us that any significant program of service learning requires a staff of experienced professionals who can develop field placement opportunities in the community and who can work directly with faculty to assist in the development of service learning components in courses. This is no work for amateurs. Moreover, if the faculty has to do this on its own, it will be very difficult to expand service learning significantly. Even with such professional help, however, service learning tends to require more faculty time and effort than does traditional classroom instruction. It also, of course, requires much more engagement from the student. One obvious and simple way to deal with these "cost" issues is to award more credit for courses that incorporate service learning. Such an approach would certainly seem to be justified, given the additional faculty and student effort involved.

One of the most attractive features of service learning is that it affords us an opportunity to incorporate, in one learning experience, some of our most powerful but currently underutilized pedagogical techniques. One of these is cooperative or collaborative learning. Service learning readily lends itself to collaboration, where small groups of students work together, teaching and learning from each other. According to a large and growing body of research, collaborative learning is more effective than traditional individual or competitive learning.[5] This form of learning capitalizes on the power of the peer group, which recent research has shown to be the most potent source of influence on the undergraduate.[6] Students are more likely to invest time and energy in the learning experience if they know that their efforts will be scrutinized by peers, or if they know that they are part of a larger effort in which fellow students must depend on each other.

Service learning also incorporates a good deal of another powerful pedagogical device: reflection. This typically involves students reflecting on the service experience, not only in terms of its significance for the theoretical course content, but also in terms of what it means to them personally.

For me, the process of considered reflection on one's experience—whether it takes the form of quiet meditation, introspective writing, or group "processing"—comes closer than almost anything else we can do in the liberal arts to promoting a real understanding of oneself and others. While the ancient injunction to "know thyself" is at the core of almost all of our great philosophical and religious traditions, it typically receives very little attention in contemporary curriculum and pedagogy. I would certainly add it to the list of qualities provided by Louis Menand elsewhere in this volume; maybe even put it at the top!

Creating a True "Citizenship Curriculum"

If we really want to make good on our professed commitment to democracy and citizenship, we need to examine all aspects of our liberal education programs with the following questions in mind: Does this course, or this requirement, or this teaching technique, or this education policy contribute to the student's ability to become an informed, engaged, and responsible member of society? Are there alternative approaches that might be more effective in helping us realize these goals?

A real citizenship curriculum would no doubt include much of what we currently call the liberal arts, but the "packaging" and "delivery system" might be very different. The new curriculum would also include a number of new elements. Most important, it would be designed around a thoroughgoing conception of (1) what students need to know about contemporary U.S. democracy and how it actually works, and (2) what skills and attitudes students need to develop to become engaged and effective citizen/participants.

My own sense about such a curriculum is that it would enrich, rather than diminish or dilute, the traditional "liberal education" now being offered in most of our colleges and universities. In particular, the humanities and social science requirements that so many students now find to be "boring" or "irrelevant" could be given new life and meaning if the content and pedagogical approach were to be more directly connected to issues of citizenship and government. Contemporary U.S. democracy and society and their problems afford countless opportunities to explore concepts such as truth, honesty, self-knowledge, power, and the law, and to deliberate fundamental value issues such as competition versus collaboration, the individual versus the community, material versus spiritual values, freedom versus responsibility, equity versus excellence, and the distribution of wealth.

Pedagogy would also have to change, of course, in recognition of the fact that civic life and engagement are not just things one talks or thinks or writes about, but also things one *does* and *experiences*. Undergraduate instruction in the natural sciences has long been based on a recognition that abstract theory cannot be fully understood or appreciated in the absence of hands-on experience in the laboratory or in the field. Could not the humanities and the social sciences also introduce "lab" components, say, in the form of service learning? When properly designed and implemented, service learning can not only give greater meaning to and otherwise enrich the theoretical content of lectures and textbooks, but can also provide students with firsthand experience in civic responsibility, leadership, and collaboration.

Most of the contributors to this volume seem to agree with the notion that we need to abandon our near-exclusive preoccupation with content and talk more about pedagogy. While our research on college students would certainly support such a view,[7] I think we also need to take a fresh look at content.

If those of us who consider ourselves to be liberal arts educators want to get serious about revitalizing U.S. democracy, we also need to consider what the content of a "good citizenship" curriculum would really look like. We need to ask ourselves not just whether our students know about U.S. history, the Constitution, and the three branches of government, but how much they really know about contemporary U.S. government and the way it functions. The unpleasant reality is that there is an enormous difference between what our democracy is supposed to be and what it really is. Do students really understand how beholden politicians at all levels and in both major parties are to their big contributors? Do they really understand the critical role played by the mass media, not only in trivializing political discourse but also in narrowing the range of political discussion and debate? Do they understand why the corporately controlled mass media can no longer play the critical maverick role that has traditionally been the responsibility of the "fourth estate"? With the near-exclusive media focus on "who's ahead" in the competition for public office, do students really understand that democracy is at root a cooperative form of government, and that taxation is a process whereby we pool our resources so that we can receive services that we cannot obtain on our own? Do they really understand that the much-maligned "tax and spend" approach is the way that government *must* operate if it is to operate responsibly, and that the real issue is not tax and spend versus some other form of government but rather who pays how much of the taxes and how the money gets spent?

Students also need to understand that this widespread public ignorance about democratic self-government and the issues of taxes and spending has produced a virtual paralysis of government at all levels. While polls show that we as citizens clearly want more and improved government services in many critical areas—education, health care, inner cities, the infrastructure, and the environment—our elected leaders feel helpless to deliver anything significant in any of these areas because they believe we are broke (i.e., the massive deficit) and are afraid to ask us for more money (i.e., increase taxes).

The Role of Higher Education:
The Pursuit of "Excellence"

The relevance of all of these problems to what we do in higher education is clear: we educate a large proportion of the voting citizenry, not to mention most of the politicians, journalists, reporters, and news commentators. We also educate all of the school administrators and teachers who, in turn, educate the entire citizenry at the precollegiate level. And we also do much to shape that precollegiate curriculum through what we require of our applicants. In short, we in the higher education community not only have helped to create the problems that plague U.S. democracy, but we are also in a position to begin doing something about them. However, if we are to have any hope of implementing real reforms, we must begin to reexamine some of the time-honored practices that have so far prevented us from fulfilling our commitment to democracy.

The fact is that higher education is to a certain extent an expression of society, just as much as it is a servant of that society. If I could change just one thing about the way we academics approach our own work, it would be to develop a greater sense of self-awareness about the values and beliefs that drive our policies, and especially about the extent to which we have, perhaps unconsciously, embraced some of society's least noble and perhaps even self-destructive values and beliefs.

I've already discussed our various beliefs about our role in society. Let's now consider our beliefs about academic "excellence." For a number of years now I've been very critical of our traditional approaches to making ourselves academically excellent, which often seem to be reduced to acquiring as many resources as possible and building up our institution's reputation so we can move up as far as possible in the institutional pecking order. My concern about these approaches is that they fail to directly address our basic societal purposes of teaching and public service. Not that we don't need reputations or resources in order to teach and serve, but rather that a unidimensional focus on resource acquisition and reputation-building as ends in themselves can ultimately cause us to neglect our basic educational and service missions.[8] Paradoxically, it can also cause us to neglect our research mission, because we become focused more on acquiring top scholars and researchers than on developing the scholarly talents of the incumbent faculty.

The roots of many of our seemingly most intractable problems can be found in this preoccupation with resource acquisition and reputational enhancement: the valuing of research over teaching, the struggle between equity and excellence, and the lack of community that we find on many campuses. We value research more than teaching because we believe that outstanding scientists and scholars will add more to our reputation and resources than will outstanding teachers or mentors. And when we define our excellence in terms of the test scores of our entering freshmen—the high-scoring student being viewed here as a "resource" that enhances our reputation—we set our sense of excellence in direct conflict with our desire to promote educational opportunities for those groups in our society whose test scores put them at a competitive disadvantage. Finally, when we place the highest value on the individual scholarly accomplishments of our students and faculty, we reinforce their competitive and individualistic tendencies, making it very difficult for them to develop those qualities that help to promote a sense of community on the campus: good colleagueship, collaboration, community service, citizenship, and social responsibility. These latter qualities, of course, are the same ones that are needed to make any democracy work.

Our students are going to be influenced at least as much by what we academics do as by what we say in our mission statements and classroom lectures. In other words, we are modeling certain values in the way we conduct ourselves professionally: how we treat our students in and out of class, how we deal with each other as professional colleagues, and how we run our institutions. If we want our students to acquire the democratic virtues of honesty, tolerance, empathy, generosity, teamwork, cooperation, service, and social responsibility, then we have to model these qualities not only in our individual professional conduct but also in our curriculum, our teaching techniques, and our institutional policies.

The problem that plagues our contemporary democracy is in many respects the same problem that de Tocqueville identified more than one hundred fifty years ago: the tension between individualism and community. This tension is exacerbated by the mistaken belief that we are independent of and separate from each other. Even our most recent research on students highlights the importance of community: the single most important source of influence on the individual student turns out to be the peer group. We associate freedom with individualism, and democracy with community, but the two are really inseparable: we create our own democracy and our government through our individual beliefs and actions, while at the same time the condition and quality of our community and democracy define what kind of individual freedoms and what kind of life we enjoy. The real question is what kind of community and democracy we want to have.

In certain respects, our preoccupation with enhancing resources and reputations is simply a reflection of our changing society, which during the past few decades has increasingly come to celebrate the values of materialism, competitiveness, and individualism. But our continuing adherence to these values represents a major obstacle not only to our attempts to deal with our myriad social problems, but also to our attempts to realize a truly functioning democracy in the United States.

Revitalizing Democracy and Citizenship

At the risk of sounding like an alarmist, I'd like to suggest that our more arcane discussions of curriculum content sometimes make me wonder if we are just fiddling around while Rome burns. If higher education doesn't start giving citizenship and democracy much greater priority, then who will? Corporate business? The news media? The church? Politics? How can we ever expect the democratic dream to become more of a waking reality unless education changes its priorities? Some of my academic colleagues might respond that a "traditional liberal education" is the best thing we can do to prepare young people for the responsibilities of citizenship. While there may be some truth in that argument, the uncomfortable reality is that whatever we are currently doing—call it liberal learning, if you like—simply isn't getting the job done. Most of our citizenry, and that includes most of our college-educated citizenry, seem neither to understand what democracy is all about nor to accept individual responsibility to make it work. And judging from the choices that those relatively few who do bother to vote make when they go to the polls, it seems clear that we have not done an effective job of showing our students how to avoid being bamboozled by politicians and the major news media. What I am really suggesting here is that the future of U.S. democracy is to a certain extent in our hands, and if we want to do anything to improve the current state of democracy, we have to change some of our ways of doing business.

It would be a mistake, I think, to construe my argument simply as an appeal to our sense of altruism or social responsibility. To get really pragmatic about it, higher education has an enormous personal stake in producing graduates who understand the key roles that information and education play in our democracy. We continually need to remind ourselves that our students are the same people who will be voting on education bond issues and choosing among candidates who are either friendly or hostile toward education. The quality of their experience in our institutions will be a prime determinant of how they will view education later on.

What other societal institution has the resources, the understanding, or the will to undertake such a major rehabilitation and renewal of our faltering democracy? The point is simply this: we in the higher education community do not have to be content with simply griping about the conduct of the media and the ignorance of the electorate; we are actually in a position to do something about it.

In light of the reduced funding and other external pressures that many of us are experiencing today, it seems only fair to ask whether it's realistic to think that we have the wherewithal to undertake any new ventures such as I have been suggesting here. In our haste to man the barricades to defend ourselves against external threats, we are inclined to forget that the autonomy that we seek to protect may be the most powerful tool that we have for reshaping liberal education in the interests of promoting democracy and citizenship. There is no one standing in our way except ourselves. The fact remains that we still retain control over practically all of the decisions that really matter: whom to admit and how to admit them; what courses and what work to require of our students; what to teach, and how to teach it; how we assess and evaluate our students; how we structure our cocurricular programs; how we hire, reward, and tenure our colleagues; what policies and procedures we utilize to govern ourselves; and what subject matter we choose for our research and scholarship.

The implications here are clear: If we genuinely believe that it would be in our own best interests—not to mention those of our students and of the society that supports us—to introduce a central focus on democracy and citizenship into our curriculum and other campus activities, we have both the autonomy and the intellectual skill to do it.

Notes

1. A.W. Astin, S.A. Parrott, W.S. Korn, and L.J. Sax, *The American Freshman: Thirty-Year Trends, 1966–1996* (Los Angeles: Higher Education Research Institute, 1997).
2. A.W. Astin, L.J. Sax, and J. Avalos, *Long-Term Effects of Volunteerism During the Undergraduate Years* (Los Angeles: Higher Education Research Institute, 1996).
3. Scott Myers-Lipton, Effects of Service Learning on College Students' Attitudes toward International Understanding, *Journal of College Student Development* 37 (1996), 659–68.
4. A.W. Astin and L.J. Sax, *How Undergraduates Are Affected by Service Participation* (Los Angeles: Higher Education Research Institute, 1997).
5. D.W. Johnson, R.T. Johnson, and K.A. Smith, *Active Learning: Cooperation in the College Classroom* (Edina, MN: Interaction Book Company, 1991).
6. A.W. Astin, *What Matters in College? Four Critical Years Revisited* (San Francisco: Jossey-Bass, 1993).
7. Ibid.
8. A.W. Astin, *Achieving Educational Excellence: A Critical Assessment of Priorities and Practices in Higher Education* (San Francisco: Jossey-Bass, 1985).

Dewey versus Hutchins:
The Next Round

THOMAS EHRLICH

DISTINGUISHED UNIVERSITY SCHOLAR,
CALIFORNIA STATE UNIVERSITY

Several years ago I participated in a public forum at the American Academy of Arts and Sciences. The issue was whether community-service learning is a sound pedagogy for undergraduates. By community-service learning I mean linking academic study and community service through structured reflection so that each reinforces the other. Professor Charles Fried, former Solicitor General of the United States, was among the participants, and he objected to the concept. During the undergraduate years, he said, there should be a "moratorium" on student interactions with society. Young people in those years, he urged, should "be confronted with ideas, with truths, with reflection somewhat detached, perhaps even entirely detached, from the practical consequences of what they are learning." Undergraduates will be "submerged in practical consequences for the whole rest of their lives." College years are a time to learn "things that are to be understood for their own sake, understood for the truths they contain."[1]

I thought of these comments in reflecting on a sharp debate that took place in 1936 between John Dewey and Robert Maynard Hutchins, the young president of the University of Chicago, where Dewey had formerly taught. The key issue was the nature and purpose of a liberal education, including how undergraduates should acquire that education. Hutchins proposed answers that paralleled Fried's "moratorium" approach. The debate was joined when Dewey, in direct response, presented a contrary position.

In Dewey's view, education in our society should be about more than preparation for lives of personal fulfillment and professional accomplishment. In *Democracy and Education,* he argued that all aspects of the education systems in the United States ought to be designed to make democracy work. "A democracy," he wrote, "is more than a form of government; it is primarily a mode of associated living, of conjoint communicated experience." This mode of experience requires that "each has to refer his own action to that of others, and to consider the action of others to give point and direction to his own."[2] Educational institutions should be shaped to nurture communal values, abilities, and understandings. This can happen only if students are constantly collaborating and interacting with others both within and outside the institutions. Their teachers should establish, within the controlled environment of a school—but closely linked to the broader societal setting—the cooperative arrangements that enable students to learn from each other and to learn cooperatively. In the process, a democratic community of learning is created that provides education for a lifetime of civic engagement.

Hutchins had a much different view. He certainly believed that an educated citizenry was necessary to a democracy, but he rooted that requirement in what Dewey called "the superficial explanation that...a government resting upon popular suffrage cannot be successful unless those who elect and who obey their governors are educated."[3] To Hutchins, an education for citizenship meant a liberal education, and a liberal education meant reading and discussing the great books of the Western world, with particular emphasis on metaphysics.

To the contrary, Dewey wrote, students learn best not by sitting in a closed room and reading the works of Aristotle and other great Western minds in search of first principles, as Hutchins proposed, but by opening the doors and windows of experience to the problems that surround us. Learning starts with problems rooted in experiences, Dewey urged, and continues with the application of increasingly complex ideas and increasingly sophisticated skills to increasingly complicated problems. There must be both experiences that interest students and problems that emerge out of those experiences. To resolve the problems, students naturally need information and techniques. Aristotle can be a superb teacher in that process. But learning starts with experience and problems. The goal of education is not intellectual inquiry for its own sake, as Hutchins proclaimed, but the betterment of democratic practice across the whole of American society.

Although the exchange between Dewey and Hutchins has been characterized as a "brisk little spat" in Alan Ryan's splendid biography,[4] it continued in full force up to and through World War II, with each side attracting its own measure of adherence and criticism. In 1945, for example, Harvard's famous Red Book, *General Education in a Free Society,* presented its approach to liberal education in part as a commentary on the opposing positions taken by Dewey and Hutchins. More significant, the debate set the terms of engagement on the substance, the pedagogy, and the recipients of that education in colleges and universities throughout the country. These issues persist today and continue to underly our disagreements about the nature and purpose of undergraduate education, even though we may not readily associate them with the names of Dewey and Hutchins. It is worthwhile, then, to revisit this debate for the purpose of asking where matters now stand and where they are going.

The Purpose of Education

The catalyst for the debate was a little book by Hutchins, *The Higher Learning in America.* He began by deploring "the plight of higher learning" and by attributing most of the mess to a lust for money, a lust that had created "the service-station conception of a university,"[5] a conception that a university must hold itself out to perform all tasks that society asks of it. That debasement of John Henry Cardinal Newman's vision of a university, he argued, had turned that institution away from the cultivation of the intellect for its own sake and toward an anti-intellectual practicality. Hutchins complained that "empiricism, having taken the place of thought as the basis of research, took its place, too, as the basis of education. It led by easy stages to vocationalism."[6] In his view, the university had become a vast center of vocational training. It was past time, he pressed, "to stand firm and show our people what the higher learning is. As education it is the single-minded pursuit of the intellectual virtues. As scholarship it is the single-minded devotion to the advancement of knowledge."[7]

To meet the scourge of vocationalism, which leads to "triviality and isolation" and debases the course of study and the staff, Hutchins proposed "a course of study consisting of the greatest books of the western world and the arts of reading, writing, thinking, and speaking, together with mathematics, the best exemplar of the processes of human reason."[8] In an often-quoted paragraph he proposed this challenge: "Education implies teaching. Teaching implies knowledge. Knowledge is truth. The truth is everywhere the same. Hence education should be everywhere the same."[9]

It could hardly have surprised Hutchins, his protests notwithstanding, that Dewey picked up the challenge. Dewey wrote a series of review articles about the book in a monthly journal called *The Social Frontier,* for which he was an editor and regular contributor. He began by applauding the attack by Hutchins on "the aimlessness of our present educational scheme."[10] But readers should be aware of the Hutchins remedies, he urged, for they are as dangerous as the disease, perhaps worse. Hutchins really wanted to insulate higher learning from contemporary social life, Dewey argued. "This conception is explicitly seen in the constant divorce set up between intellect and practice, and between intellect and experience."[11] The concern of Hutchins for excessive "practicality" masked an effort to separate general education at the university level from the practical problems of the world around us. In the terms that Fried used, Hutchins wanted a "moratorium" on experiences in society at just the time when, Dewey urged, such experiences were the necessary catalysts to learning. Most important, education for democracy could not occur within an institution sealed off from society.

To Hutchins, wrote Dewey, general education began with a set of "ultimate first principles," found in writings by great Western thinkers, particularly Plato, Aristotle, and St. Thomas Aquinas. Perhaps Hutchins wouldn't like the label "authoritarian" applied to his scheme, wrote Dewey. But that is exactly what it was. And while "I would not intimate that the author has any sympathy with fascism, . . . his idea as to the proper course to be taken is akin to the distrust of freedom and the consequent appeal to some fixed authority that is now overrunning the world. There is implicit in every assertion of fixed and eternal first truths the necessity for some human authority to decide, in this world of conflicts, just what these truths are, and how they shall be taught."[12] Some may prefer Aristotle or St. Thomas Aquinas. Others may look to Hegel or Karl Marx or even Mussolini "as the seers of first truths; and there are those who prefer Nazism." Unfortunately, "Hutchins has completely evaded the problem of who is to determine the definite truths that constitute the hierarchy."[13]

Hutchins was not pleased. He rejected the charge that he wanted to divorce thinking from facts and experience. He said he would not apply the terms "fixed" or "eternal" to the principles or truths that he espoused. And he naturally did not take kindly to the "dexterous intimation that I am a fascist in result if not in intention (made the more dexterous by his [Dewey's] remark that he is making no such intimation)."[14]

Dewey responded that *The Higher Learning in America* is "a work of great significance" because it exposed the confused state of higher education, and particularly because it raised a basic issue about the nature of knowledge and learning. In essence, Dewey argued, the classic traditional view was the one Hutchins expounded: "there is a power or faculty of Reason or Intellect . . . which is capable of grasping first and ultimate truths that are the measure and criterion of all inferior forms of knowledge, namely, those which have to do with empirical matters, in which knowledge of both the physical world and practical affairs is included."[15] To the contrary, Dewey urged "the primary place of experience, experimental method, and integral connection with practice in determination of knowledge and the auxiliary role of what is termed Reason and Intellect in the classic tradition."[16] Above all, he saw democracy as a great experiment, one with no "first and ultimate truths." Rather, the policies of a vibrant democracy are constantly changing in response to new evidence, while it maintains a collaborative mode of inquiry and an openness of mind to new ideas and approaches.

Education and Democracy

Dewey's rejoinders to Hutchins are permeated with implicit links between education and the goal of democracy, though he neither makes those links explicit nor provides concrete examples. Indeed, when I perused *Democracy and Education* for the first time, I asked Bob Orrill where in the book Dewey focuses directly on the links. Bob's right answer was that Dewey doesn't do that, because in his vision all dimensions of a good educational institution—the substance and pedagogy of the curriculum, the extracurricular activities, and the social interactions—contribute to training in the practice of democracy. In this sense, the whole book is about the links.

Though Hutchins refused to accept the battleground as defined by Dewey, much of his work in subsequent years was devoted to securing and defending intellectual turf that reads remarkably like what Dewey was so sharply criticizing. As Harry Ashmore describes in his wonderful biography, Hutchins focused enormous energy on the Great Books Project, which included just those works that Hutchins urged were the core of a liberal education.[17] That education, he said in effect, involves going into a library lined with the Great Books, closing the door, and studying those books. When you have gained the learning they contain, you are an educated person. In the introductory volume to the project, Hutchins wrote an extended essay supporting his views and devoted an entire chapter to a critique of Dewey and his views.[18]

Dewey argued that this approach was dangerous nonsense. Dangerous because the notion of fixed truths requires a seal of authenticity from some human authority, which leads away from democracy and toward Fascism. Nonsense because purely intellectual study should not be separated from practical study or from the great social problems confronting society. Separation can only weaken the intellect and undercut the resolution of those problems. Study Aristotle, Plato, Aquinas, and the others, Dewey urged, but recognize that contemporary learning from their writings requires the application of their insights to contemporary issues. The interaction of knowledge and skills with experience, focused on a problem, is key to learning.

The debate continued long after 1936. For example, in 1944 Dewey had a sharp exchange on the substance of a liberal education with Alexander Meiklejohn, a friend of Hutchins and a strong defender of his approach. (Meiklejohn was head of the experimental college at the University of Wisconsin and a member of the editorial board for the Great Books Project.)

Dewey wrote an essay in the pages of *Fortune* magazine, in which he once more blasted the notion that the realm of morals involved a separate and higher level of inquiry than the sciences, that distinct approaches were appropriate to each, and that first principles could be gleaned from a few shelves of great works. "The idea that an adequate education of any kind can be obtained by means of a miscellaneous assortment of a hundred books, more or less, is laughable when viewed practically."[19] He particularly deplored primary reliance on the works of ancient Greek and medieval scholars. That "reactionary movement," as he called it, "ignores and in effect denies the principle of experimental inquiry and firsthand observation that is the lifeblood of the entire advances made in the sciences."[20] The method of inquiry for both morals and sciences should be that same experimental mode. The argument that morals were rooted in first and immutable principles was exactly the one made centuries before about the sciences—and proven false. In both realms, the approach must be the same: "working hypotheses that on the one hand condense the results of continued prior experience and inquiry, and on the other hand direct further fruitful inquiry whose conclusions in turn test and develop for further use the working principles used."[21]

Meiklejohn responded as one of Dewey's opponents.[22] He gave a spirited defense of St. John's College and its curriculum based on the Great Books. Dewey dismissed the response as missing his point, for he was attacking a philosophy much more important than a single institution.[23] Meiklejohn came back once again with the comment that just as he may have misunderstood Dewey, so Dewey misunderstood him.[24] But Dewey would have none of that. In a four-line rejoinder Dewey, the gentle philosopher, wrote that while Meiklejohn was "entitled to admit that he misconstrued" Dewey's views, "when he speaks of a 'joint failure' I find him over inclusive."[25] So much for collegiality when it came to the philosophy of education.

Implications for Today and the Future

Three great issues were at stake in the debate between Dewey and Hutchins on undergraduate education. What is the purpose of that education and who should be the students? What should be learned? What should be the learning process?

On the purpose of an undergraduate education, Hutchins urged that liberal learning should be learning for its own sake and for living the "good life" in the Aristotelian sense. Properly designed, a general education should inculcate students with "the intellectual virtues," which are "good in themselves and good as means to happiness. By the intellectual virtues I mean good intellectual habits."[26] Hutchins cited Aquinas as the primary definer of those habits. Even the professional education that might follow a general education should have little to do with practical issues of society, and even less with baser matters of what he termed "vocationalism."

Dewey took a much different view. Democracy should be the goal of education, and education for democracy requires a community of learning in which members learn together and from each other. Education is obviously necessary for personal fulfillment, he argued. And education for personal goals should not be separated from education for career objectives, for the same skills and substantive knowledge are often relevant to both. But an education system that aims solely at the personal and the professional is still inadequate; democracy should be the ultimate aim.

Dewey rejected the Hutchins attack on "vocationalism" in blunt terms. In a lecture at Harvard a few years before the Hutchins debate, Dewey had quoted with approval the president of Antioch College, Arthur E. Morgan,

> In so far as the liberal arts college stands for a perpetuation of the traditional conflict between vocation and culture, it seems doomed to play a constantly decreasing role in education . . . . It is rapidly becoming a fact that study within one's vocational preparation is an impor-

tant means of freeing and liberating the mind. This being true, the inevitable trend in education is toward the rapid thinning of the traditional educational wall between vocational and cultural. The liberal arts college will survive and render service in proportion as it recognizes this fact and brings its course of study and administrative set-up into effective conformity with it.[27]

Who Should Be the Students?

In contrast, Hutchins believed that his approach to liberal learning provided the best education for leadership. He was an elitist in his views about society and its functioning, and how education should support that functioning. He did hope to expose wide audiences to the Great Books, and his project included a number of guides to help average citizens through the Western wisdom of the ages. He wrote a chapter called "Education for All" for the introductory volume in the Great Books series. In this chapter, Hutchins argued that the democratic ideal requires that everyone should have an education in the Great Books—i.e., a liberal education. His elitism was expressed in terms of who should be the teachers and should control the teachings.

Hutchins also believed that higher education should be restricted to a relatively small segment of the population who could, by his standards, truly benefit from that education. Ideally, they should be chosen on the basis of intellectual potential, not wealth—an aristocracy of intellect, limited in number. He shared that view with most of the presidents of major private universities at the end of World War II, who resisted the GI Bill because it was designed to open higher education to masses of returning servicemen.

Lawrence Cremin put their differences this way: "For Dewey, education was a process of growth that had no end beyond itself, a process in which individuals were constantly extending their knowledge, informing their judgments, refining their sensibilities and illuminating their moral choices. For Hutchins, education was nothing more or less than the cultivation of the intellect, the training of the mind."[28] In Dewey's view, a democratic society is a collaborative, interactive one in which individuals continuously learn from each other in making the whole more than the sum of the parts. It is hardly surprising that, for Dewey, higher education should be open to expanding numbers, while to Hutchins it should be reserved for an elite. Viewed from today's perspective, on this issue, Dewey has won in the court of public opinion. When he crossed swords with Hutchins, fewer than one in five high school graduates went on to college. Today the figure is almost two-thirds.

The Purpose of Education

It is hard to know for certain what the undergraduates of the 1930s, or their parents, wanted from an undergraduate education, but it is clear that the primary concern today is employment. Over the past several years, Richard Hersh, president of Hobart and William Smith Colleges, and Daniel Yankelovich of DYG, Inc. surveyed prospective and current college students and their parents as part of a long-term effort to analyze the challenges facing liberal arts education in America. The results of their surveys are clear: College-bound youth and their parents believe "that the overarching purpose of higher education is help with getting a job and guiding a career and that acquiring 'career skills,' therefore, is the paramount goal."[29] One can bemoan the loss of learning for its own sake, as Hutchins did. Certainly the founding of Rollins College in 1926, rooted in liberal studies and the education of the whole person, would have cheered him. On the basis of anecdotal evidence, however, I am skeptical that most students in most colleges and universities during the years before World War II sought learning for its own sake with anything like the fervor that academics with nostalgia for that era would have us believe.

Can an undergraduate education be liberal if the primary purpose of most students in seeking that education is to find a job? Elsewhere in this volume, Bruce Kimball says "no." He writes that "much liberal learning . . . could be gathered from working and vice versa. But if liberal education . . . becomes vocational, then it loses its principled basis and intellectual warrant. The difference lies in the purpose, and the purpose transforms the experience." Kimball says that Dewey agreed with his position, but I can't square this with Dewey's stress on the necessary joinder of liberal and vocational education. I see no reason to define liberal education in terms of purpose rather than content and skills.

On today's campuses, Hutchins also lost the argument in terms of the substance of undergraduate education, though Dewey can hardly be said to have won it. Almost no one outside the walls of St. John's College urges a primary focus on the Great Books as the source of first principles to guide undergraduates. The issue is not whether those works should be read by undergraduates; they should be read. And it is not whether courses that focus on the texts of those works should be supplemented with works particularly by women and non-whites; almost all agree that this is also needed. But no undergraduate curriculum that I've read or heard about in recent years takes the Hutchins approach. The problem, of course, is that most of those curricula do not seem to adopt any other coherent approach, either. They certainly are not focused on democracy as a goal in the sense that Dewey proposed.

What should be the essential elements or goals of a baccalaureate degree? During my first year as president of Indiana University, I led an ambitious planning process designed to enhance that university's academic quality. We sought at the outset to answer the question, and concluded that there was broad agreement across all campuses on nine elements. Many would have added a tenth, though there was no consensus on which one should be included. Those nine were:

- writing and speaking English clearly, correctly, persuasively, and interestingly;
- reading carefully and critically, both for personal growth and enjoyment, and to acquire information and knowledge;
- computing and reasoning both quantitatively and analytically;
- understanding the physical world and its relationship to human activities;
- reading, writing, and understanding at least one foreign language;
- using concepts from the behavioral and biological sciences to comprehend human relationships and human communities;
- devising insights and pleasure from intellectual and artistic achievement in both contemporary and historical contexts;

- recognizing and appreciating the contributions of both Western and non-Western cultures in the modern world and throughout human history; and
- developing a consciousness of the ethical implications of human actions and the ability to define and articulate personal and cultural values.

We also found broad agreement that breadth of experience, "which marks the most exciting undergraduate adventure, should be complemented by a rigorous, in-depth exposure to a major discipline, field, or profession. The ideal undergraduate program thus registers the creative tension between the general and speculative curriculum, on the one hand, and the professional, practical, and specialized curriculum on the other."[30]

Similar statements are made in the catalogs of most of the country's 3,000-plus colleges and universities. But I readily acknowledge that they fail to tell much about the learning outcomes that students and others (including those who pay tuition bills) can or should expect from a baccalaureate, and even less about either how colleges and universities should achieve those outcomes or how the public can know whether the institutions succeed in doing so.

What Should Be the Learning Process?

In the realm of pedagogy, Hutchins clearly won. The dominant mode in liberal education is still a pile of books and a closed classroom. Modes of active learning—reaching outside the classroom to engage students in the problems of the world around them—are the exception. Dewey put primary emphasis on the need to link theory and practice, part of his broader view that experience is the catalyst for learning, and that experiential learning is essential for a democratic society. Although his views have helped shape professional education on the undergraduate as well as graduate level, liberal education has remained relatively immune. The Red Book approach of Harvard in 1945 has been generally followed throughout the country. It emphasizes a spectrum of learning in the humanities, social sciences, and sciences, and a range of techniques of inquiry to reflect those disciplines, but the approach was essentially a victory for Hutchins. It was also a rejection of Dewey's concept of students learning together, as a community, in interaction with the society around them.

The most obvious reason for Hutchins's victory is that the "moratorium" approach is easier for faculty members, for they need not be concerned that they may not know something that their students are learning. But my exchange with Charles Fried illustrates a deeper rationale of many faculty in the arts and sciences. They believe that the "moratorium" approach is sound, that the undergraduate academic experience should occur in an ivory tower surrounded by an invisible moat separating the college or university from the society it serves.

New Learning Strategies—Dewey May Yet Win

Fortunately, from my perspective, a number of "anti-moratorium" strategies, consistent with Dewey's approach and Kimball's analysis, are gaining momentum on many college and university campuses. They may even be reshaping undergraduate education, though I am skeptical of a transformation. They are certainly far removed from issues of political correctness that have so troubled Allan Bloom and other current heirs of Hutchins. These strategies are not focused on the substance of undergraduate learning as much as on the ways in which that learning can be enhanced.

Four strategies seem to me particularly interesting. They are community-service learning, as opposed to closed classroom learning; problem-based learning, as opposed to discipline-based learning; collaborative learning, as opposed to individual learning; and the use of interactive technology, as opposed to chalkboards. These are not the only emerging pedagogic strategies in undergraduate education. Increased attention to undergraduate research and expanded use of narratives generally (case studies particularly) could also be cited. But these four seem to me the most promising for realizing Dewey's ideas and ideals, and wholly consistent with the trends that Kimball cites. The strategies also underscore that how a subject is taught is as important as what is taught. Substance and pedagogy are closely intertwined.

Common to these strategies are two threads that spiral through them like a double helix. Education as a social and socializing function is the first—what Professor Jack Lane of Rollins terms the "communalization of education." This is the thread that most directly reflects Dewey's focus on democracy as the overarching goal of education. As Lane stresses,

> For Dewey, the two principles of individualization and communalization of education were interdependent. The one motivated students to learn, the other made that learning worthwhile. Individualization without community led to self-indulgence and to the privatization and atomization of learning; community without individualization tended toward conformity, coercion, and even stagnation.[31]

But, as Lane also notes, the concept of community never infused learning in American higher education, even in progressive colleges such as Sarah Lawrence and Antioch, but was left to extracurricular activities and living arrangements.

The second common thread is a shift from teaching to learning and a shift in the role of faculty member from teacher to coach. In this sense, the thread marks a return to Dewey's concept that student interest should be the starting point in education, as urged in the 1931 Rollins Conference Report. Of all elements comprising Dewey's views on education, this can be the most easily misunderstood, for it sounds suspiciously like a call to let students play in sandboxes or do whatever else they want to do. Instead, it was a call to shape learning experiences around the individual interests and needs of students.

It may be helpful to use Portland State University and its new programs in general education as an example of the four pedagogic shifts that are occurring nationally. The university is well along in revising its entire undergraduate curriculum, with a particular emphasis on general education. In the words of former President Judith Ramaley, the new general education curriculum "responds to our students' need to learn how to learn for a lifetime so that they can respond to continuous societal change. We will use real situations and problems as a means to achieve our educational goals, so that our students will learn, and at the same time, serve the community."[32] Dewey would have been delighted.

There is an extensive and growing literature that describes and discusses each of the four strategies, so I will do no more than touch on a few key points. Community-service learning has been my particular interest for some years, in my own courses and in helping to reshape undergraduate education at several institutions, so I begin with that strategy and comment on it at greater length than the others.

Community-Service Learning The substance of community-service-learning courses varies widely, but all include academic study, community service, and structured reflection to integrate that study and service. The community service may assume a variety of forms: direct aid to individuals in need, education and outreach activities, and policy analysis and research. Community-service learning—a subset of experiential learning, which, in turn, is a subset of active learning—has been around a long time, but as with the other movements described here, it has received strong support in recent years.

In the new Portland State undergraduate curriculum, all first-year students must enroll in a program called "Freshman Inquiry" in which they choose from a series of problem-based courses. While the problems in each course differ, common learning goals are specified. Teams of five faculty members plan and teach each course. One example is "Embracing Einstein's Universe: Language, Culture, and Relativity," led by faculty from the anthropology, computer science, English, physics, and sociology departments. The course examines both the life and thought of Einstein and "the shift from pre-Einstein to Einsteinian physics as a special case of a profound shift in twentieth-century thought about absolutes . . . (and its expression) in the arts, social theory, literature and the use of language, and other forms of communication."[33]

Students in the course not only learn about these subjects, but are also engaged in community service by teaching about them to high school students who, in turn, teach about them to elementary school students. In an essay in this volume, Lee Shulman recalls that Aristotle judged teaching to be the highest form of understanding, that "no test of human understanding was more demanding than the test of whether you could take something you thought you knew and teach it to someone else." Students in this course were doubly put to that test.

The most important rationale for community-service learning, and the other learning strategies I am discussing, is that it strengthens academic learning. I do not urge that academic learning can be enhanced by community-service learning in every course, any more than I suggest that all intellectual abilities can be developed only through application to community problems. But I am convinced that the academic learning of students in many courses covering most academic fields can be increased by integrating community service with readings, papers, lectures, class discussions, and other course work.

The conclusions of one study may help to illustrate the point. Three political science professors recently reported on a course they taught, "Contemporary Political Problems," at the University of Michigan.[34] From a large class, they randomly selected one group to be involved with community service, along with readings and written assignments, while the other sections did some added traditional assignments. On three scales, they found that the students in the community-service-learning sections succeeded more than did their classmates. Their grades were better (by blind grading), they reported higher satisfaction in course evaluations, and their awareness of societal problems was greater as measured by a questionnaire. The effort was repeated and the results were equally positive. The faculty members emphasized that a key factor in these results was time spent integrating community service into the curriculum through regular discussion sections.

In a broader study, two Vanderbilt professors have coordinated an analysis of data from more than 1,500 students in community-service-learning courses at 20 colleges and universities across the country.[35] Preliminary results indicate that students reported they learn more, are more intellectually stimulated, and work harder in community-service-learning courses than in their other classes. A RAND study of the Learn and Serve Program, sponsored by the Corporation on National Service, reached similar conclusions.[36] The preliminary results of the Vanderbilt and RAND studies also indicate that community-service learning has a significant impact on citizenship skills and attitudes of social responsibility.

Although different community-service-learning courses emphasize different outcomes, they share a stress on academic learning. Three other learning dimensions are also important. Recognizing that each instructor may have a somewhat different perspective and may use different terminology, I term these dimensions civic learning, moral learning, and social development/career learning. The first two are unique to community-service learning. The third is common to many forms of experiential learning, of which community-service learning is a subset.

Civic learning means coming to understand how a community functions, what problems it faces, the richness of its diversity, the need for individual commitments of time and energy to enhance community life, and, most of all, the importance of working as a community to resolve community concerns. Benjamin Barber of Rutgers, in *An Aristocracy of Everyone,* writes about the importance of education in increasing community involvement.[37] That this is important is attested to by Robert Putnam of Harvard, in a now-famous article titled "Bowling Alone." Putnam has chronicled the sharp decline in participation in community activities throughout the country, with a resulting decline in what he calls "social capital."[38]

Both of these writers, and many others, have stressed that community service is one of the most important ways, often the most important, to counter these trends among students. Civic learning—in the sense of how a community works and how to help it work better—and academic learning are mutually reinforcing, as Dewey stressed. This is also true of the moral learning that students gain through community-service learning. By moral learning I mean reinforcing the elements of character that lead to ethical actions. These elements include respect for the autonomy and dignity of others; compassion and kindness; honesty and integrity; and a commitment to equity and fairness.

The undergraduate years, particularly for those transiting from adolescence to adulthood, have a profound impact on moral character.[39] Robert Coles of Harvard has argued eloquently in *The Call of*

Service for the proposition that moral character is enhanced by community-service learning.[40] He has shown that community-service learning helps students think about themselves in relation to others—who are their neighbors and what are their obligations to their neighbors? Service connects thought and feeling in a deliberate way, creating a context in which students can explore how they feel about what they are thinking and what they think about how they feel. The interaction of academic study and community service, linked by guided reflection, offers students opportunities to consider what is important to them—and why—in ways they too rarely experience otherwise.

I link social development and career learning because interpersonal skills such as careful listening, sympathy for others, and abilities to lead, to compromise, to change one's mind, and so forth, as well as personal traits such as self-esteem, are all important to personal interaction in any setting and also vital to success in most careers. Time and again, employers complain that new workers do not "get along" in the workplace, particularly with those from backgrounds different from their own. No community-service-learning course can transform a student, but faculty members frequently report on the significant difference such a course can make in the understanding and insight students have about themselves and their relations with others.

The potential for community-service learning is particularly significant at the great majority of colleges and universities where most of the students commute. These students are usually familiar with their community and its problems, and expect to continue to live and work there. They become undergraduates to gain the knowledge and skills they think they need to lead productive lives in that community. All too often, however, they see little link between their intellectual learning and the issues they want to address personally or professionally. In the experience of faculty members across the country, community-service learning is an important means of providing that link.

Although I have suggested that Dewey would have been delighted by the increased interest in community-service learning, I do not claim that democracy is its goal in the sense that Dewey envisioned for education generally. Civic learning is an important impetus, but it is not the primary rationale in the minds of many—probably most—

faculty members who are teaching community-service-learning courses. And civic learning in the sense that Barber and others use such
terms is narrower than the learning that Dewey envisaged as preparation for democracy. But the purpose of civic engagement is similar,
and the process of community-service learning is itself a democratic
process in the sense that Dewey conceived.

Problem-Based Learning The second emerging strategy is increased attention to problem areas, as opposed to disciplines. Problem-based learning has been emphasized by some higher-education faculty for a long
time, but has received increased attention in recent years. The essential element is not simply that problem-based courses are interdisciplinary, but rather that a problem is the starting point in designing a
course. As students advance, they tackle increasingly difficult problems, using increasingly sophisticated techniques and increasingly
complex knowledge bases.

Among the Freshman Inquiry courses at Portland State, for example, are The Making of a Pluralistic Society: Who We Are and How
We Came To Be; The City: Vision and Realities; The Ways of Knowing Home; and Values in Conflict: Knowledge, Power, and Politics.
More important than the titles, the subject matter in each course is
explored as problems to be solved. Each involves bringing experiences to bear on those problems. Dewey would have been pleased.

General education courses designed around problems use the
multiple prisms through which different academic disciplines view a
problem to be analyzed. Taken together, those courses can aid students in examining problems, breaking them into component issues,
resolving each issue, then putting the pieces back together again.

Case studies have come to be seen, in a number of fields, as a particularly useful means to address problems. Professional schools in business, education, and law have been using various forms of case studies
for some time, but they are now becoming increasingly common in
liberal arts and science courses as well. The form, organization, and
use of case studies varies widely among different disciplines—in business, law, and education, for example. A comparative analysis of case
studies and their uses across disciplines would be particularly helpful.

Dewey put particular emphasis on the problem or "project" approach as "the way out of educational confusion" that permeated colleges and universities.[41] A central error of higher education, he charged, was the arbitrary categorization of academic study into disciplines divorced from the complex concerns of society and its citizenry. The failure to integrate disciplines, and to focus student inquiry on problems, made learning arid and abstract. Linking liberal and vocational education, which was so important to Dewey, was also tied to the problem approach, for it enabled students to develop skills and insights by training their attention on matters that seemed to them real and important, not remote and bloodless. "A reorganization of subject matter which takes account of out-leanings into the wide world of nature and man, of knowledge and of social interests and uses, cannot fail save in the most callous and intellectually obdurate to awaken some permanent interest and curiosity. Theoretical subjects will become more practical, because more related to the scope of life; practical subjects will become charged with theory and intelligent insight. Both will be vitally and not just formally unified."[42] Shaped in this way, higher education could enhance a lifelong process of growth in all dimensions of intellectual and emotional development.

The problem approach is also key in preparing students for active participation in the ongoing renewal of democracy. That renewal involves much more than attention to the minimum responsibilities of a citizen—to vote, to participate in various civic organizations, and the like—though these responsibilities are certainly both important and ignored by most citizens today. But democracy also calls for citizens to identify community problems and to work communally to resolve those problems. Again, I do not suggest that this benefit of the problem approach is a factor in the minds of most faculty members who use it in their classrooms, but it is another piece in a larger picture that may be moving higher education closer to Dewey's vision.

Collaborative Learning Cooperative or collaborative learning (I use the two terms interchangeably, though some commentators define them differently) is a third strategy that both has a long history and is increasingly part of undergraduate education. A recent volume states that "collaborative learning may well be the most significant pedagogical shift of the century for teaching and learning in higher education."[43] As with the problem-centered approach, collaborative learning is integral to Dewey's view of democracy as the goal of education, though not explicit in the minds of most faculty members who use it.

As president of Indiana University, the most common criticism of graduates I heard from employers was that they were ill-trained to work as members of a team. Although most of the tasks these graduates would be called upon to perform in the workplace would be done as team members, most of their undergraduate work was done alone. Collaborative learning is a pedagogy particularly targeted toward enhancing the skills and abilities required to be a productive team member.

The movement toward collaboration at every stage of undergraduate learning is accelerating in undergraduate education generally, particularly in preprofessional and professional fields such as business, but also in the liberal arts. Students in the Freshman Inquiry courses at Portland State, for example, work in teams on projects, whether papers, research, or field work. A relatively rich literature exists on collaborative learning, so I will not review it here.

Interactive Technology The use of interactive technology is a fourth strategy with potentially significant pedagogical impact on undergraduate learning.[44] Although no one has yet improved on the one-to-one, face-to-face tutorial approach to undergraduate learning in terms of outcomes, it is rarely possible because of cost. However, technology may provide some of the same interactive benefits. I doubt that a "virtual university," along the lines that the western governors are planning, can support student learning in most undergraduate fields without significant face-to-face contact.[45] But many courses can be taught primarily with interactive computer software, as long as opportunities exist for counseling and advising on an individual basis.

Computer conferencing is the best means to break the requirement that the time schedules of teacher and student be the same. As is not true with audio and video conferencing, students can learn from computer conferencing 24 hours a day. E-mail enables students and teachers to communicate with each other at any time. Separate bulletin boards for each course enable teachers to have continuing dialogues with students taking a specific class. Teachers can post a draft document and students can comment on and revise it together. Teachers can also, for example, check on student comprehension by asking each member of even a large class to send an e-mail explanation. Collaborative learning becomes much easier when the collaborating students need not be in the same place at the same time, but can cooperate through computer technology. Community-service-learning sites can also be linked to faculty offices through that technology. In this sense, use of interactive technology is less a separate pedagogy than a means to enhance the others.

Many colleges and universities are engaged in one, or even two, of the four strategies as the result of conscious, campuswide policies. (At every institution of higher education, individual faculty members are using particular strategies in their individual teaching.) A few campuses are leaders in all of them, though none of those campuses is on the list of major research universities or most prestigious liberal arts colleges. Further, they are not among the "wannabes" for inclusion on that list. Rather, they are campuses where wise leadership and faculty cohesion have supported rigorous rethinking and restructuring across the entire curriculum. Alverno College—a small, private institution—is a prime example. Led by President Joel Reed, its faculty members have done extraordinary work in analyzing the interactions of pedagogy and learning for several decades. Their findings, which have been well publicized, have profoundly important implications for all of higher education. Portland State University—a large, public university formerly under the leadership of President Ramaley—is another example of pedagogic change on an institutionwide basis, though its efforts have been less well publicized.

Education for Undergraduate Teaching

The four learning strategies can make a difference, of course, only to the extent that they are actually being incorporated into the undergraduate classroom. What is going on in terms of training teachers for that classroom? Until recently, unfortunately, the answer was "not much." But another cluster of steps that Dewey would applaud today concern the training of undergraduate teachers. From my perspective as a former administrator at three research universities, the single worst failing of those institutions is the lack of serious training in teaching for graduate students. At Stanford, at Pennsylvania, and at Indiana University, Bloomington, I watched our graduate students leave for teaching positions with little or no education in how to teach. Their faculty supervisors gave close review to scholarly abilities, through supervision of dissertations, but almost no attention to teaching abilities. Perhaps most troublesome, most of our faculty had little first-hand sense of what the professional life of those graduate students would be like when they began at one of the more than 3,000 colleges and universities in the country—usually not at one of the 75 or so research universities. On the regional campuses of Indiana University, teaching loads were at least double what they were at Bloomington. This is equally true at campuses of the California State University, where I now teach.

Disciplines in the arts and sciences are certainly not alone in their lack of attention to education for teaching. Professional schools are at least as guilty. I can use law schools as an example, both because I have taught in them for most of my professional life and because, of all professional school faculty, law professors traditionally pride themselves on being teachers who are also scholars, rather than the reverse. But new law teachers today, as when I began teaching at Stanford, have no formal or informal instruction in pedagogy. They are told to teach, and if lucky, they have a mentor or two who might offer advice from time to time. I recall asking a friend to videotape some of my classes in my first year of teaching and learning a great deal from the terrifying experience of watching. But that was my own idea, done because I had a friend with a video camera. Teaching is certainly considered along with scholarship in terms of promotion and tenure, and most law teachers I know spend considerable time preparing for class. But there are few opportunities for new law teachers to examine carefully what law students are expected to learn, how different students best learn, and what a caring teacher can do to promote the learning process.

Unfortunately, I see only faint signs of change in terms of the education of teachers in law and other professional disciplines. A few schools assign senior faculty members to mentor their new colleagues. Others encourage new faculty to attend workshops organized by one of the professional organizations. The teaching resource centers at some universities have special training sessions for those faculty. But these are modest steps to ameliorate a sad situation.

In the realm of the arts and sciences, I sense more attention to the problem. One important step has been a national initiative on "Preparing Future Faculty," jointly sponsored by the Association of American Colleges and Universities and the Council of Graduate Schools and funded by the Pew Charitable Trusts. This effort was designed to develop model programs for the preparation of college faculty, with a particular emphasis on teaching and service, in addition to scholarship. About one million dollars was awarded in 1994 to 17 doctoral universities. Each of these institutions was expected to create partnerships with a small group of diverse, primarily undergraduate institutions. This joinder was intended to enable graduate students to gain firsthand experience with different types of institutions and student bodies. In a report on the first year of the program, the initiative directors stated that: "A total of 85 institutions are part of the project—18 community colleges, 7 historically black colleges and universities, 6 women's colleges, and schools of liberal arts and comprehensive institutions, along with 11 land-grant universities and 9 members of the Association of American Colleges and Universities."[46]

In a survey of students, faculty, and administrators involved in the program, responses from all three groups were overwhelmingly positive at the end of the first year. As might have been expected, training future teachers takes time, energy, and effort, and an insufficient amount of each was sometimes allocated. But the overall picture gives reason for optimism that significant steps are possible with relatively modest funding.

Other universities have started their own teacher-preparation programs. At Indiana University, for example, graduate students at Bloomington now have opportunities to teach at the seven other university campuses in the system. Outstanding faculty from those campuses serve as mentors for the graduate students, who must also participate in a pedagogy program. Ten of the largest departments at Bloomington have developed their own programs, which include pedagogy courses within their disciplines, and the university has a general program, as well.

I do not know how quickly teacher-training efforts for graduate students will replicate along the lines of the Pew-sponsored program and the ones at Indiana and elsewhere. In an essay in this volume, Louis Menand expresses confidence that the move is underway. As he wrote in the *New York Times Magazine,* "Sooner or later, universities engaged in the production of new professors are likely to decide that if they want their graduates to get these jobs, they will have to train them appropriately. And when the way professors are trained changes, the whole picture will start to change. The dog will finally be big enough to wag the tail."[47] I hope he is right, though the tail has proved powerfully independent for a long time.

If colleges and universities hiring new faculty give increasing preference to those with serious and sustained training in teaching, the market will force this move. Because those responsible for hiring were themselves rarely trained as teachers, however, the move will be resisted. But the public pressures for increased attention to teaching may break down the resistance. Particularly within large public systems such as California State University, there is great potential to pressure research universities. In the next 10 years, half of the current CSU faculty will reach retirement age. Not all of those will retire, but many will leave before that age. The 22 campuses of the university plan to hire mainly new Ph.D.'s. A significant share will, in all likelihood, come from the University of California. CSU has great leverage, therefore, to press UC for an enhanced program of teacher training for its graduate students, and a major CSU planning effort now underway includes this step in its proposals.

Learning Assessment

I have described two clusters of change for college and university teachers that would have pleased Dewey. Both show significant promise for enhancing higher education generally and undergraduate education particularly. Although their primary purpose, in the minds of their practitioners, may not be Dewey's vision of democracy, the results can have important benefits in furthering that vision. But the full promise of each cluster will be realized only if they are linked together, only if teacher training for graduate students includes the four pedagogic strategies.

Both clusters of change are directed at enhancing student learning. Underlying the strategies is an assumption that student learning can be improved when students engage in community-service learning, in problem-based learning, in collaborative learning, and in technology-assisted interactive learning. That assumption underscores the need to assess what students learn, and assessment is one of the seven trends that Kimball highlights. When the primary focus is on learning inputs, as it has been in U.S. higher education, assessing learning outputs is not a priority. If the focus shifts to learning outputs, as these four strategies are designed to do, then assessing those outputs becomes critical. A sad reality of the higher education scene, however, is that until recently relatively little attention has been focused on learning assessment.

Higher education is generally judged by what goes in, not what comes out. The advantages to weaker faculty members of the input approach are obvious: What comes out is not their responsibility. Perhaps most striking, degrees are awarded on the basis of how long students sit in class. The currency of the realm is course credits, or "credit hours," of instruction. A student who completes a course that meets for three 50-minute hours per week generally earns three credit hours, without regard to what she or he has learned. Students are usually entitled to a baccalaureate degree on accumulating 120 semester credit hours (up to 150, depending on the institution and program). The amount of learning varies substantially among three-unit courses, but they are treated the same for degree purposes.

Similarly, faculty workloads are measured in terms of courses and credit hours. A faculty member at Berkeley, for example, will be expected to teach two three-credit courses, or perhaps only one, per semester. At California State, the expected load is generally four such courses.

But at both institutions, seat time is the currency of the realm. The advantages of this input approach to the least able faculty members are obvious and a primary reason for its great attraction. Work and workload are judged without regard to the amount of learning that occurs.

Accountability

Fortunately, not only are internal reforms of undergraduate education imposing pressures to assess learning, and to shift away from the input approach, but external forces are pressing in the same direction, as well. Legislators and their constituents are asking what is the "value added" from a college education and what are the outcomes that they can expect from a baccalaureate? The most obvious pressures are tightening public budgets. "What are we getting for our money?" is always a question that taxpayers and their representatives ask, but they ask it with a special edge when budgets are being cut. Substantial fiscal shortfalls are forcing all institutions and their funders to respond to issues of accountability far more directly and clearly in the 1990s than in preceding decades, and institutions of higher education are not exempt.

The demand for accountability leads directly to calls for measures of success in education—what are the desired learning outcomes and how does the public know whether they are achieved? Public colleges and universities are the primary targets, but public funding of private institutions is substantial, and those institutions are subject to essentially the same lines of inquiry, though not always from the same questioners or with the same intensity.

An even more powerful set of external pressures results from changing public perceptions of education generally and higher education particularly. Throughout our history, Americans have believed that opportunities for their children would be better than their own opportunities, that their children's standards of living would be higher, and that education would be the engine of this progress. In recent decades, increasing numbers of Americans have come to doubt this version of the American dream, to believe that children will not be as well off as their parents have been. Whether this perception will become reality makes less difference than does the fact that it now exists, and that its logical corollary is to blame the engine of progress for having stalled, if not slid back downhill. With that blame come demands for clear evidence that institutions of higher education are producing results. Results can be measured in various ways. "Are graduates getting jobs?" "Are they satisfied with their education?" "Are they good citizens of their communities?" But the most fundamental issue is, "Are they educated?" Answers to those questions require assessment.

In response to these twin pressures—internal pressures for reform of undergraduate education and external pressures for accountability—the assessment movement has gained substantial momentum over the past decade and a half. Some of this progress simply marks a return to techniques that were generally abandoned in the 1970s, such as capstone experiences for seniors and comprehensive examinations in fields of concentration. Other assessment efforts are more substantial.

Assessments of assessment in higher education have been published by numerous commentators.[48] It may be helpful in the context of liberal education, however, to provide a particular example. The Center for Reading and Language Studies at Indiana University, under the leadership of Professor Roger Farr, developed a set of performance-based assessments to determine whether undergraduates at the university were becoming critical readers and writers and in-depth problem solvers. This assessment effort was made because of concerns that there was too much reliance on multiple-choice and short-answer questions that gave too little attention to critical skills. Although performance assessment was widely used in the School of Music and in other arts programs, it was not part of general education assessment. The assessments devised by Farr and his colleagues provide students with realistic problems that call on them to read a variety of texts, develop and write thoughtful responses to problems, and direct those responses to particular audiences. Students are urged to take notes while reading the texts, to organize their notes, to prepare a first draft, and then to revise and edit their response as a final draft. Six assessments were prepared that covered the integration of reading and writing, while including science, social science, and literature, and covering an integration of mathematics knowledge and communications skills.

One of the analytic reasoning (mathematics) problems, for example, asked the students to write a memorandum on whether it was practical to tow icebergs from Antarctica into the waters off the coast of Los Angeles as a means of meeting the critical water shortage in southern California. A substantial amount of information is provided about icebergs, how quickly they melt, and so forth. The results are evaluated in terms of reasoning, understanding of mathematical concepts, use of procedures, and communications skills.

The program was tested with about 2,000 undergraduates in 1994. The aim is not to evaluate each student but to assess the institution. How well is it providing general education to its students? Where the assessments reveal gaps, how can the curriculum be revised to correct them? In considering many more traditional assessments, faculty members voice concerns that they will be forced to "teach to the test." This is a frequent fear in professional fields such as law and nursing, where standardized (often multiple-choice) tests are given on a statewide basis.

By contrast, the Indiana assessments are designed to help in curriculum revision. Faculty are encouraged to shape their courses to these assessments. The Indiana program provides solid evidence that performance-based testing can determine the extent to which undergraduates are able to demonstrate key abilities they need to complete in-depth academic work in a major and to function in the adult world after graduation. It also underscores that assessment and curriculum development should be closely linked.

Any revolution in undergraduate education, as opposed to tinkering, will require a shift away from seat time as the common academic currency. Credit for students and support for faculty must be linked to learning. This does not mean that time spent in performing a task is unimportant, but only that it is an element in the learning process rather than an end in itself. For students, this shift will certainly mean increased attention to self-paced learning, as well as to the four strategies that I discussed. For faculty members, it will mean more effective uses of time to promote learning. It will not be enough to announce that seat time is no longer the measure of academic credit; outcome measures will need to be devised in its place.

A number of innovative efforts to do just that are underway. Some, such as those at Alverno College, have been in operation for some years. Many more are recent developments. Two at California State University campuses may serve as examples. The faculty and administration of the new Monterey campus are committed to outcomes-based learning and to awarding degrees on the basis of demonstrated competencies. Under the leadership of President Peter Smith, they have developed seven broad learning goals. A set of 15 university learning requirements are used to measure achievement of those goals. A student's mastery of learning in each of the 15 can be assessed by an instructor in a course approved as providing the necessary experiences. If the instructor determines that a student has demonstrated proficiency, without regard to hours in class or other traditional standards, the student has met the requirement. In addition, students may design other means for completing each requirement, and then register for assessment in that requirement. It is too early to tell how successful this effort will be, but it holds great promise, not only for the Monterey campus, but for the whole California State University system.

Major efforts are also underway at Sonoma State University to reconceptualize teaching and learning. Over a three-year period, two faculty members are working in each of four disciplines to reformulate the introductory material in those disciplines, with the assistance of a full-time assessment expert, into one-unit modules, each of which has specific learning objectives, anticipated outcomes, and assessment tools. Each faculty member works to take each student as far along in the sequence of modules as the student can progress in a single semester. With the help of the assessment expert, each faculty member assesses the satisfactory completion of each unit of the module by students in the section taught by the other faculty member in the discipline. Students in the program all have computers, and extensive use is made of interactive technology, as well as collaborative learning.

The faculty and administration expect that most students will demonstrate the mastery of more than a single course's worth of concepts and content by the end of a semester and will be given credit accordingly. As a result, a section of 25 students might generate the equivalent of 40 enrollments. When this fact is joined with the reality that the failure-to-completion ratio in these courses usually ranges from 10 to 40 percent, it is entirely possible that faculty productivity may double.

What's Next—A Speculation

What the future will look like depends in great measure on resolution of a fundamental issue that divided Dewey and Hutchins, and still divides U.S. higher education a half century later. Will that education continue to be shaped primarily by a small group of universities dedicated to training an elite cadre of intellectual leaders, using the model if not the substance urged by Hutchins? Or will undergraduate education be increasingly formed by the needs of its consumers and by institutions that view their primary mission as responding to those needs?

Formidable forces favor the status quo. Almost all faculty members in higher education receive their credentials at one of about a hundred so-called research universities. Those credentials are almost exclusively related to research rather than teaching. The credentials are awarded by faculty who themselves were educated in the same system and know no other. The faculty at these institutions are an extraordinarily dedicated group of teachers, but what they learned about teaching and learning did not come from their doctoral programs or the universities that granted their doctoral degrees. Further, my experiences at four research universities—Harvard, Stanford, the University of Pennsylvania, and Indiana University at Bloomington—all suggest that most faculty members at those institutions see and feel no serious impetus to change. Particularly at the most prestigious research universities, demand among potential students is still virtually impervious to extraordinary price increases. The currency of the realm among faculty members at these institutions is not teaching, but rather released time from teaching. These are all elements that do not encourage a rosy view for those of us who think change is essential.

If this analysis is right—that the country's major research universities are not and will not be in the lead in promoting systemic change in undergraduate education—how will change occur and what will be the catalyst? These questions buttress my hesitation to agree with Kimball that the consensus he identifies is actually happening, much as I hope he is right. Arguing against this, though, is the fact that the elite universities that organized the Association of American Colleges and Universities have long been the engines of change in higher education. And these are the institutions most firmly embracing the status quo.

The desire on the part of other colleges and universities to follow the leadership—or lack of leadership—of research institutions is also a dominant force in higher education. Kimball finds evidence of a consensus in the fact that "most of . . . [those] respondents . . . doubtful of the consensus thesis work at institutions in the 'top' 10 percent. . . . Those tending to be persuaded by the consensus thesis come from the other 90 percent." I want to concur, but find no clear evidence now that the latter group really embraces the trends he identifies, or are prepared to do much to pressure change if they do. If systemic change will not be led by the research universities, how might it happen?

One catalyst for change could be money or the lack of it. If higher education continues to face sharp cuts in funding, pressures to change may accelerate, and some of the trends that I have described may be supported as sound means to enhance the value of limited resources. But every academic leader knows how much harder it is to make real change when resources are limited, and it is a tribute to those, such as President Ramaley at Portland State, who manage significant shifts while budgets are slashed.

The other role for money in this realm, of course, is as a positive incentive. I am continually amazed by how relatively small amounts of money lead to substantial changes in higher education. The funding of behavioralism in the social sciences by the Ford Foundation in the 1950s is an example. The entire discipline of political science was altered in a relatively brief period, as Peter J. Seybold has chronicled.[49] But major research universities were chosen by the Ford Foundation to lead the change. The only instance I know of when that was not true was in clinical legal education, also promoted by funding from an offshoot of the Ford Foundation. In that case, faculties at the law schools of most major research universities at least acquiesced in the movement, and Harvard Law School was the home of the major conceptual thinker, Professor Gary Bellow. Whether funds from Kellogg and other interested foundations can have a similar impact in this realm is not clear to me, even assuming that such funds are available. I hope an effort is made to find out. And if money is not the driving force for change, I no less hope that other forces will serve the same end. But I am uncertain what those forces might be.

In spite of the hurdles, I am cautiously optimistic that Dewey's answers will ultimately prevail in the struggle to shape the substance and pedagogy of undergraduate education. This optimism is rooted in a number of forces that should ultimately be unstoppable, though I do not predict how fast they will move.

First, and most obvious, Dewey has clearly won against those who wished, with Hutchins, to reserve higher education for an elite. The percentage of young people seeking a college education is growing at an accelerating rate, and there is ample reason to believe this trend will continue. These students are coming in increasing numbers because they accurately conclude that they cannot utilize their talents and energies in the workplace without a college education. One reason is that a college degree serves as a surrogate for qualities such as maturity and discipline that employers seek. But the more important rationale is the training college students receive in career-related abilities, particularly critical thinking and communications skills.

Second, the numbers of undergraduate students in elite research universities and liberal arts colleges are static, while those in other institutions of higher education are growing. When Dewey wrote, the majority of all undergraduates were attending private institutions. This is one reason he focused more attention on primary and secondary education, which was—and still is—overwhelmingly public. Today only about 20 percent of undergraduates are in private institutions and that share is continuing to decline. Community colleges have exploded; they are a major force in higher education, not holding pens for students waiting to learn in prime time at four-year institutions. The leverage of the elite institutions should erode as their market share shrinks, though the point at which they may lose critical mass is unclear.

Third, and more speculative, voices are increasingly being heard that colleges are doing an inadequate job of providing the career-related skills that are the primary rationale for attending college among undergraduates and their parents. This is hardly surprising because the curriculum that emerges from faculty trained to be research scholars is largely irrelevant to the working futures of most students. When undergraduate education was limited to those transiting from adolescence to adulthood, this disconnect was not as obvious to the consumers of higher education as it is today when many undergraduates are older, part-time, working students with families. These students are demanding that their education be geared to their needs. This does not mean to their next job, but rather to a lifetime of work that will likely involve numerous career shifts. Employers are urging the same changes. These are the forces that want undergraduate education to focus on solving problems in various modes of active learning, to have undergraduate teachers trained in these modes, and to have assessment techniques employed that will define and demonstrate learning outcomes.

Purpose Remains an Issue

There is a deeper level at which the debate between Dewey and Hutchins is again at center stage in U.S. higher education. It has become a commonplace to bemoan a loss of civic responsibility, particularly among young people, and to urge increased attention to civic education among students at every level. If the issue is viewed solely as one of information transfer—fifth-grade civics in a more advanced form—the role of higher education is inevitably a modest one. This is no less true if the issue is seen solely as proselytizing students to vote and pay attention to politics. But Dewey had much more in mind. He viewed U.S. democracy and education as inexorably intertwined. This is not simply because our citizenry must be educated to responsibly choose political leaders and hold them accountable. Much more important, a democratic society is one in which citizens interact with each other, learn from each other, grow with each other, and together make their communities more than the sum of their parts. Dewey urged that a community of learners is the primary mechanism through which this democratizing process can best occur. To be successful, the community needs both vision and skepticism. The vision is of an interactive, collaborative society in which the processes of decision are more important than the decisions themselves. It is balanced by skepticism, which serves as a constant reminder that uncertainty surrounds every decision and every fact on which a decision is based. There are no ultimate answers, as Hutchins had claimed, and tentative answers emerge only through empirical inquiry. What seems certain today, even in science and certainly in society, may prove false tomorrow.

Dewey had two radical insights about U.S. society. One was that most citizens, not just an elite, can have a life of the mind. The other was that a life that is only of the mind is inadequate to the challenges of U.S. democracy. Our society requires civic engagement to realize the potential of its citizens and its communities. These were important lessons that Hutchins failed to grasp.

One of the reasons more has not been done in higher education to promote civic responsibility is that we do not have much empirical knowledge on a range of important issues, and Dewey did not give us many concrete leads. He was never one to practice what he preached—a failing of most of us in the academy. These issues include: What are the essential elements of effective citizenship for an American in the next century? What specific knowledge, skills, and values contribute to those elements of good citizenship, recognizing that there may be a range of different ways to be a good citizen? What evidence is there about the contribution that higher education can make to developing these qualities in sustained and effective ways? What evidence is there about the types of civic education efforts that are most effective in preparing for responsible citizenship? What problems confront colleges and universities that attempt to engage in sustained civic education, and what are the best strategies to overcome these problems?

These are the kinds of issues that must be addressed if Dewey's vision of democracy and education is to be realized. The efforts that I have described are steps in that direction, but they are not yet part of a larger whole that has the sound functioning of a democratic society as its objective. The issues that I just raised are the subject of a multiyear project on civic responsibility and higher education that is being sponsored by the American Council on Education. Other projects in related arenas are underway as well. Together they hold some promise of providing operational insights into how to achieve the linkages between democracy and education that were so clear to Dewey in theory, though continue to be clouded in practice.

If U.S. higher education is to help realize Dewey's vision of democracy, new forms of learning and new forms of defining what we mean by knowledge must emerge. We must recognize that a learning community means one in which no one single member of the community knows everything, in which every member can contribute something, in which there is a clear vision of a better future combined with a healthy skepticism about the abilities of anyone to know all the answers—whatever the questions. This was the democratic society that Dewey wanted and for which he posited a powerful role for higher education. It is past time for us in colleges and universities to meet his challenge.

Notes

1. Roundtable on Service Learning in the Academic Curriculum, American Academy of Arts and Sciences, New York, March 13, 1995, 9–10.
2. John Dewey, *Democracy and Education* (New York: Macmillan, 1923), 101.
3. Ibid.
4. Alan Ryan, *John Dewey* (New York: W.W. Norton, 1995), 278.
5. Robert Maynard Hutchins, *The Higher Learning in America* (New Haven, CT: Yale University Press, 1936), 3, 4, 6.
6. Op. cit., 26.
7. Op. cit., 32.
8. Op. cit., 43, 85.
9. Op. cit., 66.
10. John Dewey, "President Hutchins' Proposals to Remake Higher Education," *The Social Frontier* (January 1937), 103. This is the second of two articles. The first was Dewey, "Rationality in Education," *The Social Frontier* (December 1936), 71.
11. Dewey, "President Hutchins' Proposals," 104.
12. Ibid.
13. Ibid.

14. Robert Maynard Hutchins, "Grammar, Rhetoric, and Mr. Dewey," *The Social Frontier* (February 1937), 137–38.
15. John Dewey, "The Higher Learning in America," *The Social Frontier* (March 1937), 167.
16. Ibid.
17. Harry S. Ashmore, *Unreasonable Truths* (Boston: Little, Brown, 1989), 98–103.
18. Robert Maynard Hutchins, "The Great Conversation," in *Great Books of the Western World: Volume I* (Chicago: Encyclopedia Britannica, 1952).
19. John Dewey, "Challenge to Liberal Thought," in Jo Ann Boydston, editor, *John Dewey: The Later Works,* Volume 15 (Carbondale: Southern Illinois University Press, 1989), 261, 266.
20. Op. cit., 267.
21. Op. cit., 272.
22. Alexander Meiklejohn, "A Reply to John Dewey," *Later Works,* 475.
23. "Dewey vs. Meiklejohn," *Later Works,* 333.
24. "Meiklejohn Replies to Dewey," *Later Works,* 486.
25. "Rejoinder to Meiklejohn," *Later Works,* 337.
26. Hutchins, *The Higher Learning in America,* 62.
27. John Dewey, "The Way Out of Educational Confusion," in *Later Works,* Volume 6, 84–85.
28. Lawrence A. Cremin, *Popular Education and Its Discontents* (New York: Harper & Row, 1990), 7.
29. Richard H. Hersh and Daniel Yankelovich, "Intentions and Perceptions: A National Survey of Public Attitudes Toward Liberal Arts Education," *Change* (March/April 1997), 16.
30. Indiana University, *Academic Planning Paper—Indiana at Its Best* (Fall 1988), 8–9.
31. Jack C. Lane, "The Rollins Conference, 1931, and the Search for a Progressive Liberal Education. Mirror or Prism," *Liberal Education* (70: 1984), 297, 303.
32. Portland State University, "you@psu.pdx.edu: Freshman Inquiry," (Fall 1994), 3.
33. Op. cit., 5.
34. Marcus, Howard, and King, "Integrating Service into a Course in Contemporary Political Issues," *Educational and Policy Analysis* (15: 1993), 410.
35. Janet Eyler and Dwight E. Giles, "The Impact of Service-Learning Program Characteristics on Student Outcomes: Summary of Selected Results for the FIPSE Comparing Models of Service-Learning Research Project," Presented at National Council for Experiential Education Conference, October 1996.
36. Alexander W. Astin, et al., *Evaluation of Learn and Serve America, Higher Education: First Year Report* (Los Angeles: RAND, 1996); see also Alexander W. Astin, Linda J. Sax, and Juan Avalos, *Long-Term Effects of Volunteerism During the Undergraduate Years* (Los Angeles: UCLA, 1997).
37. Benjamin R. Barber, *An Aristocracy of Everyone* (Dubuque, IA: Kendall/Hunt, 1993).
38. Robert D. Putnam, "Bowling Alone: America's Declining Social Capital," *Journal of Democracy* (1:1995), 65.

39. See Ernest T. Pascarella and Patrick T. Tezenzini, *How College Affects Students* (San Francisco: Jossey-Bass, 1991).
40. Robert Coles, *The Call of Service* (Boston: Houghton-Mifflin, 1993).
41. "The Way Out of Educational Confusion," in *The Later Works,* Volume 6, 74, 87.
42. Op. cit., 88.
43. Kris Bosworth and Sharon J. Hamilton, editors, *Collaborative Learning: Underlying Processes and Effective Techniques* (San Francisco: Jossey-Bass, 1994), 2.
44. See Diana Laurillard, *Rethinking University Teaching* (London: Routledge, 1993).
45. See "Western Governors' University: A Proposed Implementation Plan" (Denver: Western Governors' Association, June 24, 1996).
46. Jerry G. Gaff and Anne S. Pruitt, *Preparing Future Faculty: Experiences of Graduate Students, Faculty Members, and Administrators in Programs for Preparing Future Faculty—Year One* (Washington, DC: Association of American Colleges and Universities, November 1995), 1.
47. Louis Menand, "Everybody Else's College Education," *New York Times Magazine* (April 27, 1997), 49.
48. See Peter T. Ewell, "To Capture the Ineffable: New Forms of Assessment in Higher Education," *Review of Research in Education* (17: 1991), 75.
49. Peter J. Seybold, "The Ford Foundation and the Triumph of Behavioralism in American Political Science," in Robert I. Arnove, editor, *Philanthropy and Cultural Imperialism* (New York: Macmillan, 1980), 269.

The Stratification
of Cultures as the Barrier
to Democratic Pluralism

TROY DUSTER

*DIRECTOR, INSTITUTE FOR THE STUDY OF SOCIAL CHANGE,
UNIVERSITY OF CALIFORNIA, BERKELEY*

As many of my fellow contributors to this volume have also indicated, it is difficult, at times impossible, to discuss the future of higher education, liberal or otherwise, without reference to the larger societal context. However, as we proceed, the bearing of this analysis on our judgments of models of liberal education should become increasingly clear. A model informed by pragmatism is now much needed. It is with that in mind that we begin our analysis.

With the increased mobility of migrant labor across national boundaries, societies with a multicultural or plural cast are becoming more and more a normal feature of the global landscape. The long-term Turkish "guest-workers" in Germany, the growing Vietnamese communities of Australia, and the increasingly visible African (northern and sub-Saharan) presence in France are all indications of an international trend. Economic forces may be driving these developments, but nation-states are ill-prepared to deal with the political and social consequences, and are further constrained by very limited models of "success." Group relations in societies that strongly identify members by linguistic, religious, ethnic, or racial demarcation, and whose members so self-identify, tend toward an *iron law:* Because economic and political power are never evenly distributed in plural societies, "who says differentiation says stratification."[1] Especially on the matter of racial and ethnic differences, when there has been sustained contact among different groups, the major pattern around the globe has been to have one group dominate the other(s).[2] That might well be called *the iron law of pluralism.*

In response, subordinated groups often band together to assert or claim their rights. In the very act of coming together to confront a grievance or to make such claims against the dominant order, they send an alarm through the political system. Arthur Schlesinger, Jr., a liberal historian who was part of John F. Kennedy's "kitchen cabinet," has expressed a strong sense of impending trouble. Even while acknowledging the nation's history of racial injustice, he calls attention to what he sees as new separatist and nationalist tendencies in the United States centered around ethnic and racial politics:

> What happens when people of different ethnic origins, speaking different languages and professing different religions, settle in the same geographical locality and live under the same political sovereignty? Unless a common purpose binds them together, tribal hostilities will drive them apart. Ethnic and racial conflict, it seems evident, will now replace the conflict of ideologies as the explosive issue of our times.[3]

Indeed, it is notable that liberal, conservative, and even leftist writers have all tended, in recent years, to converge around a remarkably limited, binary conception of "the problem" of cultural group differences. Either a society moves toward the obliteration of differences, and thus proffers only a singular model of assimilation,[4] or, if assimilation does not happen, the only possibility is an Armageddon-style conflict over scarce resources and/or the persistence of ethnic and racial and religious enclaves. For example, Schlesinger is joined in this formulation by D'Souza on the right, and, more recently, Gitlin on the left.[5] The gloomy and almost apocalyptic portrait of "the problem" that can be garnered from the title of Schlesinger's book, *The Disuniting of America,* is matched by Gitlin's attack on "identity politics," *The Twilight of Common Dreams: Why America is Wracked by Culture Wars.* Gitlin laments the ascendancy of a politics of group interests around a variety of identities (over and above social class) that he sees as fracturing and fragmenting more totalizing conceptions of cross-group politics.

Philosopher John Rawls takes up a position somewhere in the center of this debate in *Political Liberalism.* Rawls's earlier classic treatise, *A Theory of Justice,* was admittedly based upon the presumption of cultural homogeneity, and to this he openly confesses.[6] In his more recent work, Rawls tries to come to terms with the reality of a democratic pluralism and is very much in continuity with the concerns expressed by Schlesinger and Gitlin when he asks: "how is it possible for there to exist over time a just and stable society of free and equal citizens, who remain profoundly divided by reasonable religious, philosophical, and moral doctrines?"[7]

To address this question, Rawls draws heavily from Joshua Cohen's essay entitled "Moral Pluralism and Political Consensus."[8] Cohen distinguishes between "pluralism" and "reasonable pluralism," reasonable pluralism being the kind in which various segments in a plural society agree upon the rules of engagement, but not on the content of values, morals, religion, etc. Rawls makes much of this distinction, although how one gets at "overlapping consensus" is both formalistic and idealistic—with the idea of "the good" generated from each set of doctrines, not from lived experience.[9]

Once again, it is important to note that even for the centrist, societies are presumed to have only two choices: that different groups either shed their religious, philosophical, and cultural differences, or there will be ethnic, racial, and religious enclaves with a perpetual danger of tribal war. If these are the delimited terms, if all we have to choose from is these two poles, then it appears that only a fool or a villain would choose war. The not-so-subtle message is that all reasonable people would champion an assimilationist model.

In 1915, Horace Kallen wrote an essay for *The Nation* entitled "Democracy versus the Melting Pot."[10] Kallen, of course, was a leading exponent of American pragmatism and one of the leading interpreters of Dewey and James in the first half of the twentieth century. In his essay, he provided a sharp contrast to a "shedding of differences" as the only possibility for the United States. Kallen argued that we should not aspire to a melting away of differences. Rather, he saw the persistence of ethnic groups and their distinctive traditions as a potential source of enrichment for the nation.

Kallen employed the metaphor of the symphony, noting that different instruments have different (but unequal?) roles and even sometimes blend into a harmonic whole. It was Kallen who introduced the concept of cultural pluralism into political theory, a *third way* that is neither assimilation nor enclaves always at the edge of warfare. Kallen's vision of a third option, a pluralism that eschews Pollyannish idealism and refuses to see strife-ridden enclaves as the only alternative to assimilation, rarely penetrates the current debates on pluralism (or multiculturalism). Thus, even in the United States, even for a nation of immigrants, the ideology and dominant public policy practice has been alternately to exclude or assimilate, rather than try to accommodate and extract value from difference.

Even though the debate has offered only the two alternatives, assimilation versus hostile enclaves, in the last two decades we have witnessed the emergence of a strong and newly integrated way of thinking about ethnic and cultural diversity where three factors are operating simultaneously:

1. the acknowledgment and affirmation of ethnic or cultural differences;
2. the development of political structures that reduce formal political domination by any one group; and
3. a notion that the public sphere is enriched by the combination of ethnic differentiation and participation in the commonweal.

Whether this is more than theory remains to be seen. Examples of successful plural societies are remarkably thin in the literature. In 1987, Harold Cruse published an interesting and important work with the subtitle *Blacks and Minorities in America's Plural Society.* Yet, the book was given a very misleading title, *Plural but Equal.*[11] Nothing in the text would so indicate, because it is very much an account of the lingering substantial inequalities among and between ethnic and racial groups in the United States. Cruse provides useful analyses of how and why different groups had different experiences in the stratified system, but in no way can the book be seen as providing evidence for a formulation of "plural but equal." For example, his discussion of the Chinese in Mississippi in the 1920s is an account of purposeful exceptionalism on the part of the Chinese, which allowed them to successfully circumnavigate the attempt by white Southerners to classify Chinese with blacks for the purposes of assigning them to schools.[12]

Further, in another book, by Cowan and Cowan, the discussion of Jewish economic success relies on the retelling of the now-familiar idea that a substantial portion of European Jews came to the United States with marketing and banking and entrepreneurial skills that well positioned them in an urbanizing and industrializing economy at the turn of the century.[13] In sharp contrast, American blacks, the main subject of Cruse's analysis, were overwhelmingly products of an agrarian and rural past, who after more than two centuries of slavery remain at the base of the nation's economic order.

There have also been recent attempts to lay some groundwork for a discussion of pluralism in an academic setting by Lawrence Levine and a few others.[14] Levine's title, *The Opening of the American Mind,* is an obvious broadside against Allan Bloom's attack on what he described as a dilution of the classical curriculum.

From the pluralistic perspective of this discussion, what we should find more instructive than examples from the literature are those socio-historical moments when groups do live side by side; share geographical, political, and economic space; and do more than just "get along." It now seems almost absurd to think of Beirut as such a model, but 25 years ago, it was widely touted as a flourishing example of pluralism. There are additional examples to be drawn from other parts of the world where Moslem Arabs, Jews, and Christians shared space. And of course, while we now turn to the Balkans as the limiting case of ethnic intolerance, there were decades in which several places in that region, including Sarajevo, looked like a pluralist success story.

It would seem that the greatest enemy of cultural and political pluralism is a destabilized political situation in which groups come to fear that one of them will gain power and dominate. The current situation in the former Yugoslavia, Malaysia after the withdrawal of the British, the Middle East after 1948, conflict between the Ibo and Yoruba in the Biafran war, and current tensions between Azerbaijanis and Armenians all have something in common: That is, the heightening of ethnic and racial tensions, sometimes leading to the outbreak of armed hostilities, was preceded by a period of relative calm and even pluralism.

Within the context of these examples, the "iron law of pluralism," of domination by a single group, may hold, but it is best placed along a continuum if we are to understand the dynamics and the variations that make for optimal circumstances. This would entail a minimal level of hierarchy, exploitation, and subordination of various groups, and a significant level of exchange. The barriers to achieving this are substantial. Brushfires that escalate into raging ethnic strife elicit moral exhortations (both glib and profound) to find a way to engage across cultural, religious, racial, ethnic, and linguistic differences. Moreover, the exhortation is to do more than simply live peacefully side by side—to elevate the human potential and experience by learning from each other, indeed to "celebrate difference." Yet, there is a poignant naivete in this version of multiculturalism, akin to Rodney King's plea of "can't we all get along?" Get along? The problem with social differentiation is that it is almost always subject to the iron law of pluralism and accompanied by a social stratification system that coordinates along those very borders of difference. Can not we all get along? On what terms, and on whose terms?

From Evolutionary Biology to Social Darwinism[15]

One of the most enduring truths in the study of human social life is that all societies are stratified. The unequal access to valuable resources can be based on something as simple as age or as complex as claims to spiritual or intellectual power. But as far back as recorded history permits us to garner evidence, we also know that humans have always tried to justify that stratification. In *The Republic*, Plato creates the "myth of the metals" to justify why only those "born gold" can become philosopher kings. The notion that power and privilege are inherited has a longer and wider history than the notion that power and privilege are *achieved*. Thus, the link between a theory of human biology and social theory has always been a significant force in the history of ideas, but it is only in the last 150 years that the connection has donned scientific clothing. At the core of this relatively recent development is the direct link between biological Darwinism and Social Darwinism.

Charles Darwin's *On the Origin of Species* is the Bible of evolutionary theory, at once a meticulous classification system of organisms and a theory of the evolving relationships between them. In its simplest form, the implications of the taxonomy are known even to some grade-school children: at the bottom of the rung are the single-celled amoebae; at the top of the heap is the magnificently complex human. In between are all the combinations and permutations and mutations that form an intricate hierarchy of organisms. It is intricate. It is most decidedly a hierarchy.[16]

What of humans? Once we get to the top rung of the ladder of species evolution, biological Darwinism trails off, and, like a relay sprinter in a race, huffing and puffing and tired, hands the baton on to the runner in the next leg. The baton was passed from biological Darwinism to Social Darwinism.

In the biological version of adaptation, species are ranked along a hierarchy of complexity in evolutionary adaptation, but what about rankings within species? Within, between, and among human groups, was there not also an evolutionary tree? As Darwin had done for biological Darwinism, the English social theorist Herbert Spencer would do for the canon of Social Darwinism. To better understand the climate in which scientific genetics germinated, it is necessary to rescue and restate two important features of late-nineteenth-century thought that have been largely forgotten. The first is that Spencer dominated the social thought of his age as few have ever done. By far the most popular nonfiction writer of his era, his ideas were so popular that more than 400,000 copies of his books were sold during his lifetime.[17] In the United States, by the turn of the century, Spencer was a dominant cultural figure for a wide range of politicians, intellectuals, educators, and public policy advocates.[18] Indeed, he was so influential that Oliver Wendell Holmes once sardonically turned to his colleagues on the Supreme Court to remind them that "Herbert Spencer did not write the U.S. Constitution."[19]

Although Darwin would ultimately distance himself from the more regressive social implications of Spencer's social evolutionary theory, Darwin once called Spencer "about a dozen times my superior."[20] While Charles Darwin set the stage, it was Spencer who would develop the key concepts that would apply evolutionary theory to humans. It was Spencer, for example, who coined the phrase "the survival of the fittest."[21] Herbert Spencer was not focusing his ideas on the animal kingdom, but on social life, human behavior, and the internal differences in evolution among humans.

As Humans Can Be Stratified in Evolutionary Development, so Can Cultures

Spencer's influence upon the newly emerging field of anthropology, the "study of man," was also overwhelming.[22] Not only are humans to be arrayed along a continuum of evolutionary development, but so are the races and the cultures, societies, tribes, and nations in which they live. At an individual level, the idea of a "savage" or a "primitive" was at one end of that continuum; at the other was the "civilized person." So, too, was there the notion of a primitive or savage society.

The fundamental basis of the continuum from savage to civilized, wrote Spencer, was the developmental stage of the brain. This was explained, in turn, by the way in which humans adapted to nature, and in particular, the seasons and the passage of time. The "primitive peoples" only had a sense of time relevant to such natural events as when birds migrate, or when fall or winter or spring begins. The more advanced and more "civilized" could encompass decades, even centuries in their thinking, planning, and "accumulation." As such, their brain capacity was vitally stimulated and, literally, enlarged. The longer the time sequence a human could encompass, said Spencer, the higher the level of intellectual development. At the bottom of the heap were the Australian Aborigines. Just above them were the Hottentots, who were judged one notch superior because they could use a combination of astrological and terrestrial phenomena to make adjustments to time sequences and changes.[23] Moving on up Spencer's social evolutionary ladder, next were the nomads, just a rung below the settled primitives who lived in thatched huts. Because they stored goods for future use, their conception of and relation to time were "more developed."

It followed that once selected individuals from "inferior cultures" came to live in "superior cultures," there would be a limit as to what their brains, of lower development capacity, could handle. Writing exactly a century before this claim would be made again by Arthur Jensen, Spencer noted in 1869 that black children in the United States could not keep up with whites because of the former's biological and genetically endowed limits, "their [blacks'] intellects being apparently incapable of being cultured beyond a particular point."[24]

This reached its logical culmination in the work of James George Frazer, who produced a prodigious six-volume work, *The Golden Bough,* that formally stratified cultures and societies along a continuum from simple to complex, from savage to civilized. Frazer posited a three-stage hierarchy—human societies evolve from magic, to religion, and finally, to science.[25] At the bottom of the hierarchy, of course, were "primitive cultures." This set of ideas about how cultures, and the peoples from those cultures, are "stratified" is lodged in the curricula of Western nations.[26] As we shall see, this has unsettling implications for proceeding toward a multicultural curriculum.

Given the historical and philosophical background discussed thus far, are we stuck at a multicultural impasse or is it possible to evolve beyond this point? To answer this question, let us first turn to an examination of the cross-cultural contacts that human social groups routinely exhibit. Because our topic is liberal education, we'll extend the argument to what has happened, or is happening, on our nation's campuses.

The Long Road: Intolerance to Enhancement

Intolerance

It may be useful, at least heuristically, to place the contacts between peoples from different cultures along a continuum. The first point could be called simply, "intolerance." That is an image easy for all to grasp because, as we have examined, the world is full of highly visible conflicts between groups who seem always willing to try to either conquer or obliterate their neighbors.

Yet, it is insufficient to point to slaughter or attempted genocide as if these activities were the sole measure of intolerance of racial, ethnic, and cultural differences in the contacts between groups. Humans are inventive in how they will display intolerance, ranging from the killing fields to the refusal to live or work side by side with "the other." For example, in the United States, white home owners routinely signed "restrictive covenants," agreeing not to sell their homes to blacks, up until 1948, when the Supreme Court declared these documents unconstitutional. These covenants were both legally binding and effective, and were also a symbolic measure of the intolerance of whites to racial integration.[27] They also had a counterpart in higher education. For blacks in the South, where most lived prior to 1948, there was a legal racial barrier to admission to most public colleges and universities. Even into the 1960s, the governor of Alabama would stand in a doorway to block the entrance of the single black admitted to the all-white University of Alabama.

The U.S. government would force an end to this kind of intolerance in higher education. Yet today's college students are unaware that the rhetoric of giving decision making back to the states, to "state's rights" and "get the government off our backs," were the rallying cries of white racists and conservatives across the nation, and particularly of the White Citizens Councils of the South between 1956 and 1967. Despite the fact that "liberal" has become a political pejorative, it was the liberals who led the fight to reduce racial intolerance in the United States.[28]

Intolerance? The golden age of U.S. higher education that Allan Bloom celebrates in *The Closing of the American Mind* was so deeply embedded with racial and ethnic intolerance that a Jew could not hold a professorship at Yale University until the 1930s.[29] And this was not limited to the private colleges. I have already mentioned the famous case of Alabama Governor George Wallace standing in the doorway to block racial integration, but it is less well known and appreciated that the state of Virginia paid full tuition, books, and fees for black students if they would leave the state and go elsewhere to school, thereby preserving the all-white character of its higher education system. Black students were not only subsidized if they went to traditionally black colleges; if a few could get into a state university in Michigan or California or Illinois, there were several Southern states willing to pick up the tab. Obviously, this required that the numbers of such students were very, very small. They were.

If we go back to the 1960s, the nation's system of higher education was de facto almost completely racially segregated: basically either all-white or all-black, with, at best, a 1 to 2 percent variation at some major institutions. Thus, the traditionally black colleges were routinely at least 99 percent black, and it was the rare traditionally white college that was less than 97 percent white. School segregation mirrored urban and suburban residential segregation.

Such was the situation that even a relatively small 2 to 4 percent change in these figures at elite colleges and universities was experienced as a shock wave that would reverberate through the entire institution, and thus into the public sphere. In 1960, blacks constituted only 4.3 percent of all college students in the United States, and most were enrolled in traditionally black colleges in the South. As late as 1967, blacks accounted for only 2.3 percent of enrollment at Ivy League colleges. And in the same year, 1967, black enrollment at "other prestigious institutions" was only 1.7 percent. By 1980, the proportion of blacks in the Ivy Leagues had more than doubled (from the 1967 figure), but still constituted only 5.8 percent of total enrollment.[30] Earlier, in 1975, the proportion of blacks in all postsecondary institutions had also more than doubled (from the 1960 figure) to reach 9.8 percent. By these figures, for the first time in history, blacks were "integrated" into mainly white institutions. Data from the American Council on Education's National Norms for Entering College Students reveal that in the fall of 1970, nearly 87 percent of college students in the United States were white. Nine percent were black, and the combined total of Asian-Americans, Native Americans, and "Others" was a mere 2.2 percent,[31] thus ending "intolerance" in higher education!

From *Intolerance* to *Tolerance*

When people are being massacred, raped, driven from their homes, and turned into starving refugees, *tolerance* becomes *vital*, in the very literal sense of the word. It is not something to be taken lightly or dismissed as "liberal pap" and "political correctness." In the context of massive slaughter, tolerance seems a desirable goal merely to stop the killing. Once arms are laid down and some measure of stability is achieved, groups turn to settling in or settling scores. If tolerance is achieved, it is no small accomplishment, but there will always be those who would like to see that "tolerance" revoked. For some, "peace without justice" is not worth it. The Truth Commission in South Africa is an attempt to settle in without settling old scores, to "tolerate" without getting even for the last half century of injustices of apartheid. Nelson Mandela has been heavily criticized by members of his own party, a substantial wing of the African National Congress, for leaning much more to the peace side (i.e., of tolerance) than to altering the imbalance in the justice equation. So *tolerance* will always have its price, its detractors, its suppressed memories—or those who would revivify those memories. Tolerance is a fragile peace, even more so in a democratic pluralism that navigates with blinders around issues of power and justice.

As noted earlier, because intolerance is not only about the killing fields, but also about restrictive covenants and blocking entry to work sites, educational institutions, and the corridors of power, it follows that tolerance will have its parallels and unfoldings in these arenas, as well. To be sure, when the Supreme Court struck down restrictive covenants in 1948, whites did not suddenly open up their neighborhoods. Informal "gentlemen's agreements" remained in force for decades. Yet whites did, in some instances, come to "tolerate" the sales of homes to nonwhites.[32]

From intolerance to tolerance in higher education? The parallels are there. White students learned to "tolerate" the few score students of color on their otherwise completely white campuses. In what I have called elsewhere Stage One (of a three-stage theory of diversity), white students had a choice: they could ignore the nonwhite students or they could try to engage them, either positively or negatively.[33] In any event, in higher education, from intolerance to tolerance may simply mean that administrators would not permit residence halls and campus buildings to be decorated with racist graffiti or swastikas painted on the doors of the Hillel Foundation.

From *Tolerance* to *Acceptance*

The next point along the continuum, where members of different groups move beyond mere tolerance of the others' existence, whether geopolitical or a neighborly version of detente, is *acceptance*, acceptance, for example, that the neighbor's differences are real, will not "go away," and need not be "converted" (religious) or "melted down" (cultural/ethnic) into a pot of indistinguishable homogeneity, consensus, likeness, sameness. What does it mean *to accept*, as beyond mere tolerance? The stony silence toward the "intruding neighbor from the village of otherness" is transmogrified into the sharing of a backyard barbecue, or perhaps the car pool, or maybe even the shared baby-sitter. That means literally that one is able and willing to *accept the difference* without attempting to change the other, to convert, to assimilate or homogenize into a likeness of the self, or of one's own group, through subtle controlling processes mired in unexamined ethnocentric assumptions. At the university, acceptance could and would come to mean the full range of college activities, including entry into fraternities and sororities.[34]

From *Acceptance* to *Appreciation*

The next point along the continuum is the *appreciation* of difference. It is in the realm of the sensual pleasures that we are most familiar with this quite positive experience of "the other." Food, music, the visual arts, and the like all come to mind as comfortable and readily available illustrations of how we can learn to appreciate the differences that come from "other" groups. The desire to "go out tonight and have some 'ethnic food'" is a staple of the experience. Indeed, the more we know, the more we prefer *authentic* ethnic food. And how do we know the food is authentic? We have a commonsense gauge—the density of people from that group who can "keep the cooks honest."

I shall return to the subject of appreciation of sensual pleasures when I turn to the curriculum. For the moment, it will suffice to place this matter of appreciation at a clear fourth marker on the continuum. Notice how far we have come from the killing, from the *intolerance* segment of the continuum. With *appreciation*, there is the strong experience that "the other group" has something to offer that my group does not. While that difference can be relegated to "ethnic food" and clothing, it is also the case that music, art, literature, dance, and other forms of cultural exchange can open new doors of contact that are enriching. If it is the difference, after all, that one comes to appreciate, then further exploration becomes an option.

In the academy, this type of appreciation has often been restricted to music and dance. The field of ethnomusicology began at the Los Angeles campus of the University of California in the 1950s as a serious attempt to better apprehend and appreciate the wide range of serious and enduring music from "other cultures" that were not rooted in Europe. Thus, ethnomusicology was contrasted to musicology. The latter was simply "the study of music," but primarily the classical tradition of serious music from Western Europe. *Ethno*musicology included everything "else"—from the *koto* of Japan to the *gamelan* of Indonesia, from the *sārangī* of India to the *didjeridoo* of the Australian Aborigines. The potential subject matter of "ethnomusicology" is therefore larger, deeper, and richer than the potential subject matter of "musicology." In a pluralist rendition, the study of musicology might well be enhanced, then, by the study of ethnomusicology. But lurking in the shadows of this *appreciation* is "the stratification of cultures."

From *Appreciation* to *Mutual Enhancement:* The Cultural Stratification Barrier Resurfaces

The last point along the continuum requires conscious acknowledgment both that no one society, no one culture "has it all," *and* that something is to be gained by learning and distilling and absorbing from other cultures. Indeed, because every culture has strengths, weaknesses, and blind spots, many strive for a common goal: (a) that the difference my group brings to the social or public arena potentially enhances that arena, and (b) that the difference that your group brings to the arena potentially enhances that arena, and thus (c) the possibility is there for *mutual enhancement*. With the sensual pleasures, that potential is understood: I teach you how to play and enjoy the music from my group, you teach me how to play and enjoy the music

from your group. Or either could learn from the other in completely different arenas. Both are enhanced by our different capacities and
different skills. Here, the critical issue emerges: different experiences
of the world produce different worldviews, perspectives, angles of
vision, and thus the potential for elevating the collective capacity to
analyze, problem solve, indeed, to think. In this sense, culture is not
static, but continually in the process of formation and re-formation.
So long as the discussion revolves around sensual pleasures, most can
at least entertain this idea. In the academy, the idea of mutual enhancement runs up against a profound barrier. It is the stratification of cultures, an idea so deeply embedded in Western thought that it is tak-
en for granted, unmarked, unexamined, and accepted even by those
who would argue against homogenized, assimilationist assumptions
of cultural relations. That is, if I think that my culture is superior to
yours, what have I got to learn from you? I may appreciate your food
and your music, but not your "way of thinking" or your perspective
on problem solving, certainly not your style of studying, communicating ideas, articulating concepts, elucidating theory, or, for example, proposing an alternative methodology or epistemology.

Indeed, if I come from what I believe to be a superior culture,
then even my toleration of your way of being (in the academic world)
is not a good thing, it is paternalistic and condescending. I should try
to get you to be more like me. *Mutual enhancement* isn't even on the
table for consideration. To return to Spencer, the "stratification of
cultures" is such a deeply embedded idea in Western thought that it
plays an important part in the curricular implications of this analysis.

Enhancement and Higher Education: Moving
Toward a Resolution

As we discussed the movement from intolerance to tolerance, we examined the issue of engagement. However, there is another issue here
that has important implications for the curriculum and otherwise.

Issues of access are quite different from issues of engagement. To
put it another way, "just because you have a ticket to the theater is no
guarantee that you'll enjoy the show." When students from groups

that have been historically excluded arrive in sufficient numbers to mobilize and challenge, they not only request inclusion as "admittees," but also inclusion into the curriculum. As an example, in the 1965-66 academic year, women constituted only 4 percent of the students studying for law degrees at U.S. law schools. By 1994-95, more than 44 percent of law students in the country were women, reflecting a tenfold increase over the last 30 years. With this substantial increase in the proportion of women and other previously under-represented groups in the student body, a *critical mass* is reached. The point at which this mass becomes "critical" is not absolute, but contingent upon the salient social, political, and cultural contexts. With the critical mass comes a transformation of the politics of identity and often an attendant political mobilization of the group—the development of social, political, and cultural advocacy organizations; challenges to the institution in terms of the gender and ethnic/racial composition of the faculty; and the importation and integration of curricula that address issues of gender and ethnic and racial stratification (including the deconstruction and reconstruction of traditional categories of knowledge).

The challenge to the curriculum from women has produced a number of new kinds of curricular responses and intellectual developments. To cite examples from but one field of study, these range from feminist jurisprudence to courses on Women and the Law. Even though there are far fewer students of color in law schools, their role in the push for curricular change has also been noteworthy, with a sufficient constituency to produce programs of study in Critical Race Theory, for example. Clinical programs now often reflect both of these new populations and their concerns—including programs that serve battered women, migrant workers, and other previously excluded groups.

One result has been that over the past two decades, institutions of higher education have experienced a profound discord about the meaning and implications of the new student body and its impact on the quality and content of the educational enterprise, including the shape and purpose of the curriculum and the very character of knowledge. From the perspective of the predominantly white and male senior faculty, current critiques of the orientation, bias, and focus of the academic curricula are frequently, even commonly, perceived as an assault—unwarranted "political" attacks on the core values of the institution.

In sharp contrast, to those who constitute the new and emerging critical mass of students, the calls for reform and curricular change are vital projects that give legitimate voice to the silenced and the ignored. With a level of moral authority and even indignation, they justify their demands and activities as imperatives to provide an arena for women and people of color. Moreover, their interests are not only in the content of the curriculum, but in the staffing of faculty and administration and in the funding priorities of the institution. To these advocates of new agendas and new social and cultural identities, the emerging critical mass, fueled by new student demographics, signals a welcome portent, a compelling change that is long overdue. They therefore deride the reactions of the predominantly white male professoriat as nothing more than an effort to sustain a period of white male dominance, patriarchy, and cultural colonialism reflected in scholarship over the past millennium.

Sometimes, within this conflict, neither side recognizes itself in the caricature provided by the opposition, and so has no use for serious engagement nor for dialogue about the other's version. In a classic case of figure and foreground, what is seen as an affirmation of new forms by the new student (assuming there are enough to achieve a critical mass) is seen as a reduction and diminution by those who experience themselves as guardians of the dominant values, paradigms, journals, and professional associations of scholars in the major disciplines. The effort to assert a relevant and culturally affirming agenda around curricular enrichment that extends beyond the Judeo-Christian European tradition is seen as an effort to dilute and politicize the dominant curriculum and to realign the personnel and governance of dominant institutions. In the sharpest conflicts, these competing points of view are presented without self-reflective distance as two holistic, elementary *essentialisms.*

While, when seen from afar, both essentialist views appear to be overstated and not amenable to compromise, the actual extent of curricular change is slow and limited. When compared to the remarkable changes in the composition of the undergraduate student population, changes in faculty hiring (of both women and people of color) have been quite slow. The tenured faculty across the nation tend to be overwhelmingly white and male (approximately 85 percent) across the full curriculum. And even when women, who have made the greatest strides in diversifying the faculty, are appointed to professorships, they have made negligible inroads in revamping the "core" curriculum.[35]

More Apparent Than Real?

The essentialist conflict is doubly unfortunate because it presupposes a stasis—both of mind-set and curriculum—that may not exist in fact. Where efforts have been made to incorporate multicultural elements into the existing curriculum, e.g., the American Cultures program at Berkeley, these changes have stimulated an infusion of new literary, historiographic, and social scientific perspectives into the study of the social sciences and humanities. While there are strident public voices opposing these developments, efforts to integrate a diversity of voices and viewpoints do not appear to most students or administrators, or even to most faculty, as a threat to the tradition and content of the enterprise of higher education. In part, this apparent ability of the dominant curriculum to absorb new sources, literature, narratives, methods, and voices is not the startling threat that has been portrayed, because it does not represent a sharp break from a unidimensional canon of scholarship that has been idealized by the defenders of the currently constituted canon.

In practice, the history of U.S. higher education, particularly of U.S. public higher education, reflects a process of considerable elasticity with continuing efforts and practices to incorporate new perspectives and canons into the core curriculum of the universities.[36] Indeed, it is perhaps only from the long historical view that we find the current "crisis of contestation" to be part of a deep and resonant continuity. In the first century and a half of the nation, colleges were private and Protestant denominational and saw their mission as combining elements of European classical education with moral and religious education. However, this version would be largely transformed over the next century and a half, eroded by the unrelenting realities of U.S. social philosophy in the eighteenth and early nineteenth centuries. The curriculum became both more secular and infused with the new sciences that developed and emerged, most especially by the middle of the nineteenth century. And the nature of these institutions shifted; in the late nineteenth century, public funds were extended to develop the land-grant institutions.

The gradual transformation of U.S. higher education has been a story of a continuous process in which colleges have adapted to changing social, nativistic, and scientific trends; this history shows that the last 50 years have involved an important but *continuous* extension of social enfranchisement. Inclusion in and access to higher education have mirrored enhanced participation in other realms of public life. The GI educational grants after World War II and the Korean War constituted a quantum leap in broadening higher education as an instrument of secondary social enfranchisement. Indeed, one irony of the current period is that many of the most passionate and public advocates for an unalterable canon are the sons and daughters of immigrants who attended colleges and universities when the canon was being stretched and tailored and altered by larger economic, demographic, and political forces. Even a cursory glance at the social history of higher education in the United States reveals that a singular core canon is a mythological construct.[37] It is myth because it is not tailored to the reality of the changing composition of the curriculum, the changing role of higher education, and the changing character of the student body. To return to an example we used earlier, as professional schools with a mandate to train students for a career, law schools are certain to face increasing pressures to be responsive and adaptive to these social transformations.

Resolution

We come finally to that point at which pragmatic learning, innovative pedagogy in liberal education, and the multicultural curriculum can converge. Under certain circumstances, these elements can come together to mitigate the barriers students from plural cultures have erected to seeing "mutual enhancement" as a possible outcome, helping them to overcome some of the deeply held assumptions that prevent them from coming together as equals. While I will rely primarily on findings from a study of student life and curricular issues conducted on the Berkeley campus of the University of California, the basic findings from this study have been replicated at the University of Michigan. The Berkeley campus provided a relatively unique situation for the study of racial and ethnic pluralism, because approximately one-third of the students are from Asian backgrounds, one-third of Northern or Western European ancestry, about 20 percent from Chicano/Latino backgrounds, and about 8 percent of African descent.

The study was conducted over a period of 26 months, from February 1989 through April 1991. Two hundred ninety-one students in 69 different groups were convened in two sequences of group interviews.[38] Lessons from the Berkeley study strongly suggest that students perceive each other, not simply approach each other, "from different backgrounds, races, and cultures"—through the lens of the social stratification of the larger society from which they come. That is, the Asian and white students tended to view the Chicano/Latino and black students as being "affirmative action" admittees, less deserving and less entitled to be on campus. The grounds for the Asian and white students' view is the assumption that the ordinal ranking of students at admission, based on a combination of grade-point average (GPA) and ranking on a standardized test, reflects their "entitlement" to be fully deserving citizens on campus.

In this kind of an atmosphere, it is difficult for these students to accept the idea that there could be "mutual enhancement" from exchange and engagement with "other" students from "culturally deprived" or "culturally inferior" or simply "less-well-prepared" backgrounds. Embedded in these assumptions is the legacy of the stratification of cultures. At best, these students can be appreciated for the different styles of music or dance that they bring, at worst, barely "tolerated." Mutual enhancement—the radical idea that students could learn from each other as equals—is far from being conceived or articulated.

Enter the pragmatic learning experience. When students are given problems to solve jointly—mandated to go out into the world with a group to learn and engage, and learn by engaging—there is a much greater possibility that these students will find that standardized test scores and high school GPAs become less salient. They learn to rely on each other for putting together different sets of competencies. And, in learning from direct experience, they come to understand how much they are learning from each other.

For example, one African-American student in the group studied said that he had spent three years at Berkeley and had never struck up an acquaintance with a member of any other group but his own. Then he said that one day a professor asked the students to break into small groups of three to discuss and solve a particular problem. Rather than leaving it up to the students, the professor assigned random numbers and forced a kind of interaction that had its own logic and legitimacy. "Forced" by legitimate educational requirements to discuss and interact, this student said he became friends with an Asian student, who, in turn, introduced him to a small circle of acquaintances that greatly broadened his intellectual experience of undergraduate life. This was not just about social interaction, but a broadened notion of what it meant to be educated.

If oriented pragmatically, this type of group learning is the edge of a wedge that has some chance of bringing together the ideas of Dewey, James, and G.H. Mead, discussed elsewhere in this volume, with a direct articulation of "the problem" of pluralism and the undertheorized binary conception (of perceived enclaves versus homogenized assimilation) addressed in this essay. If the iron law of pluralism sounds like a pessimistic version of the future, early returns on the lived experience of collective learning tell us that this may be both our best antidote and the fertile ground for our best hopes at mitigating the stratification of cultures.

Notes

1. This is an obvious takeoff on Michels's *Iron Law of Oligarchy*. Robert Michels was a political theorist at the turn of the century who put forward a theorem about how organizations work. Michels noted that whatever the form of organization, there was a tendency toward the concentration of power in a small group. This group he called "oligarchs" and thus the formulation, "Who says organization,

says oligarchy." This so-called "iron law" has been used, abused, and misused. For some, it was taken to be a single inevitability, and a justification for a lack of power-sharing, a top-down hierarchy of communication and control.

2. The form of this domination can vary, from forced assimilation to forced exclusion.

3. Arthur Schlesinger, Jr., *The Disuniting of America* (New York: W.W. Norton, 1992), 10.

4. Where those groups at the base are more likely to shed their differences as they climb upward. This is assimilation to the dominant group's language, religion, and culture. This kind of assimilation is more likely than the "melting pot" in which all groups equally shed differences. For an extended discussion of these two quite different forms of assimilation, see Lawrence Levine, *The Opening of the American Mind* (1996).

5. Dinesh D'Souza, *Illiberal Education: The Politics of Race and Sex on Campus* (New York: Vintage, 1992); Todd Gitlin, *The Twilight of Common Dreams: Why America Is Wracked by Culture Wars* (New York: Metropolitan Books, 1995).

6. John Rawls, *A Theory of Justice* (Cambridge, MA: Harvard University Press, 1971). See his Lecture I, "Fundamental Ideas" in *Political Liberalism* (New York: Columbia University Press, 1993) for the confession.

7. Rawls, *Political Liberalism*, 4. The qualifiers in this statement contain all the philosophical escape hatches and offer a hard look at the empirical reality and the lived experience of people residing in pluralistic societies: a) "just and stable society," b) "free and equal citizens," and c) "reasonable moral doctrines."

8. Joshua Cohen, "Moral Pluralism and Political Consensus," in David Copp and Jean Hampton, editors, *The Idea of Democracy* (Cambridge: Cambridge University Press, 1993).

9. Philosophers in this tradition resist "compromise" and want consensus to come from "reasoning" humans.

10. Horace Kallen, "Democracy Versus the Melting Pot," *The Nation* (February 18, 1915), 190 et seq.

11. Harold Cruse, *Plural but Equal: A Critical Study of Blacks and Minorities in America's Plural Society* (New York: Morrow, 1987).

12. Ibid., 295.

13. Neil M. Cowan and Ruth Schwartz Cowan, *Our Parents' Lives: The Americanization of Eastern European Jews* (New York: Basic Books, 1989).

14. Lawrence W. Levine, *The Opening of the American Mind: Canons, Cultures, and History* (Boston: Beacon, 1996). See also David A. Hollinger, *Postethnic America: Beyond Multiculturalism* (New York: Basic Books, 1995), which draws on Horace Kallen.

15. The following segment is excerpted from my essay, "Human Genetics, Evolutionary Theory, and Social Stratification," in Albert H. Teich and Mark S. Frankel, editors, *The Genetic Frontier: Ethics, Law, and Policy* (American Association for the Advancement of Science Press, 1994).

16. There are some missing links, and there are some leaps of faith; and indeed, as unreconstructed creationists (and not a few hard-nosed empiricists) are happy to point out, there is some faith.

17. According to Mark Haller, *Eugenics: Hereditarian Attitudes in American Thought* (New Brunswick, NJ: Rutgers University Press, 1965), 300,000 copies of Spencer's books were sold in the United States alone.

18. Richard Hofstadter, *Social Darwinism in American Thought* (Boston: Beacon, 1955).

19. Objecting to an opinion from the majority, Holmes's dissent included the statement "The Fourteenth Amendment does not enact Mr. Herbert Spencer's Social Statistics." William Seagle, *The History of Law* (New York: Tudor, 1946), 49.

20. This is from a letter written December 10, 1866, to Joseph Hooker [Francis Darwin, editor, *The Life and Letters of Charles Darwin* (New York: Basic Books, 1959), 2:239]. Four years later, Darwin would write in another letter to E. Lankester that "I suspect that hereafter he [Spencer] will be looked at as by far the greater living philosopher in England; perhaps equal to any that have lived." (Ibid., 2:301.)

21. Not aware of this history, current common sense and conventional wisdom unreflexively attribute this notion to Darwin because it is now also vital to the biological Darwinian theory of the evolutionary tree in the animal kingdom.

22. It is true that Spencer and Edward B. Tylor, the author of a similar treatise about the evolution of cultures, each claimed priority and accused the other of plagiarism. Nonetheless, it is without challenge that Spencer was the most influential social thinker of his era.

23. Herbert Spencer, *The Study of Sociology* (New York: D. Appleton & Co., 1899).

24. Arthur Jensen, "How Much Can We Boost IQ and Scholastic Achievement?" *Harvard Education Review* (Winter 1969). Spencer quoted in John S. Haller, Jr., *Outcasts from Evolution: Scientific Attitudes of Racial Inferiority, 1859-1900* (Urbana, IL: University of Illinois Press, 1971), p. 124.

25. Frazer did not posit a lockstep evolution. He acknowledged a zigzag path to "progress" and liked the metaphor of waves sweeping up the shoreline, ever constantly progressing even if receding at times.

26. Eric Ashby, *Universities: British, Indian, African, A Study of the Ecology of Higher Education* (Cambridge, MA: Harvard University Press, 1964).

27. Douglas Massey and Nancy Deuton, *American Apartheid: Segregation and the Making of the Underclass* (Cambridge, MA: Harvard University Press, 1993).

28. For an extensive treatment of how the newfound championing of a color-blind society through the lens of "individualism" is a political strategy that requires ignoring continuing structural inequalities, see Troy Duster, "Individual Fairness, Group Preferences, and the California Strategy," *Representations* (Summer 1996), 41–58.

29. For some remarkable reading on how Yale and other Ivy League universities were structurally intolerant of racial and ethnic differences, see Marcia Graham Synnott, *The Half-Opened Door: Discrimination and Admissions at Harvard, Yale, and Princeton, 1900–1970* (Westwood, CT: Greenwood, 1979) and Jerome Karabel, "Status, Group Struggle, Organizational Interests, and the Limits of Institutional Autonomy: The Transformation of Harvard, Yale, and Princeton, 1918–1940," *Theory and Society* (January 1984), 1–40.

30. David Karen, "The Politics of Class, Race, and Gender: Access to Higher Education in the United States, 1960–1986," *American Journal of Education* (February 1991), 208–37.
31. Alexander Astin, *What Matters in College? Four Critical Years Revisited* (San Francisco: Jossey-Bass, 1993).
32. Strike a blow on behalf of the color-blind society? Not quite so fast. Many of those homes were sold by a white who was angered by something his/her white neighbors had done, and so the selling was an act of revenge. More commonly, realtors would engage in "block busting," selling one property to a black, then telling whites in the neighborhood that the prices of their property would decline so they would sell at a low price to the realtor, who would then turn around and sell the houses for very much higher prices to the black middle-class families who had been unable to find such good housing stock. The realtors were the real beneficiaries.
33. Troy Duster, "The Diversity of California at Berkeley: An Emerging Reformulation of 'Competence' in an Increasingly Multicultural World," in Rebecca Thompson and Songeeta Tyagi, editors, *Beyond a Dream Deferred: Multicultural Education and the Politics of Excellence* (Minneapolis: University of Minnesota Press, 1993).
34. However, in the case of fraternities and sororities, the Procrustean bed of homogenization was always a lurking beast, and the "acceptance" of interracial, interethnic dating both the *bête blanc* and the shibboleth of acceptance.
35. Figures in this section were derived from *AALS Diversity Commission Report* (Washington, DC: Association of American Law Schools, in press).
36. W.B. Carnochan, *The Battleground of the Curriculum* (Stanford, CA: Stanford University Press, 1993).
37. Ibid.
38. For a detailed account of the methodology, see Duster, "The Diversity of California at Berkeley."

Biology, Pragmatism, and Liberal Education

ERNST MAYR

ALEXANDER AGASSIZ PROFESSOR
OF ZOOLOGY, EMERITUS, HARVARD UNIVERSITY

What would a biologist consider an indispensable component of liberal education? As far as education is concerned, I myself am what a paleontologist would call a "living fossil," a relic of times long past. I received a classical education at a German gymnasium where I had nine years of Latin, German, and mathematics, seven years of Greek and history, four years of French, and no English whatsoever; also a great deal of geography, together with one-year classes in various science subjects. Now, 75 years later, how do I evaluate such a strongly classics-based education? I still think it was very valuable, but I must admit that it crowded out some subjects that would have been even more important. Although I had lots of history, it was mostly dynastic history, and I had no courses in the social sciences, about democracy and citizenship or some other subjects valuable for daily life. But ignorance is met wherever we look, not only in Germany. What struck me most when I came to the United States in 1931 was the incredible ignorance of most Americans, including college graduates, about the rest of the world. Here we are, the most powerful nation, with interests in all parts of the world, and yet when the recent trouble in Yugoslavia broke out even the *New York Times* completely misrepresented the situation, ascribing genocidal activities to "the Yugoslav army" when every European knew that it was the Serbs who were to blame. No matter what else we may demand, a liberal education must eliminate that kind of ignorance, which is found in many areas. Let me only mention recent encounters between Creationists and Evolutionists.

I will return to this theme with some concrete suggestions as to the content of a liberal curriculum, but I want to begin by stating that it is the foremost task of liberal education to eliminate shameful ignorance. Liberal education should prepare a young American for adult life. That, broadly speaking, is what liberal education means. I fully realize that this is a vacuous statement until we list specifically the items this person needs.

Pragmatism

The evaluation of pragmatism is difficult for a nonprofessional because there is so much diversity within the concept. Some critics, for example, claim that James turned Peirce's ideas upside down. Dewey rejects teleology while Rorty accepts it. Lovejoy in 1908 distinguished 13 possible forms of pragmatism. Since then Rorty, Hilary Putnam, and others have added many more. By wielding Occam's razor, I distinguish for my own purposes only two kinds of pragmatism.

1.   There is epistemological pragmatism, according to which truth is established or determined by its efficacy in practical application, "that which works best."

Personally, I question the validity of epistemological pragmatism. In everyday life we find it most practical to act as if the earth were flat and as if the sun circled the earth, but neither assumption is true. In ordinary physics, Newton's equations are satisfactory, but, as Einstein has shown, they are not the ultimate truth. Truth in science is established by continuous testing, verification, and falsification. The pragmatic approach is adopted only when there are competing theories. As the philosopher Laudan has said, among several competing ones, that theory is the best which produces the best results.

Early in this century, the Mendelian geneticists and the Lamarckians argued about the correct theory of evolution. Most naturalists opted for Lamarckism because it was based on gradualism and naturalists had abundant evidence for their conclusion that evolution was gradual. Mendelian evolution, as proposed by Bateson, DeVries, and Johannsen, involved saltations and required the rejection of natural selection. One might therefore say that at that time Lamarckism was the pragmatist's choice of evolutionary theory. But this is true only when there are several seemingly equally well-supported theories competing with each other. Normally in science, pragmatism is not the way to truth, as Dewey recognized quite early in his career.

2.   Subjective or everyday pragmatism deals with personal actions and the adoption of value systems. Truth in the philosophical sense is not involved, but only the observable results of actions and of the application of values. The outcome of an action determines whether it is to be considered as constructive and useful. This kind of pragmatism is particularly useful in moral dilemmas.

It is now rather clear that the mistake made by the early pragmatists was to apply the same standards of finding truth to science and to ethics. Pragmatism is indeed a valuable approach in ethics, but it is not a suitable approach in science. However, it is a valuable guide in any kind of decision making in daily life.

There is only one subject matter in science where I apply pragmatism. It is the question of realism. I adopt commonsense realism because it works. I accept that there is an outside world and that it is more or less as our sense organs tell us. Of course, we realize that our sense organs are very inadequate. We can see neither ultraviolet nor infrared light. Our olfactory sense is scandalously poor as compared to most other mammals or most insects. However, natural selection has given us the sensory equipment to operate successfully in the world we live in.

I call this world, revealed to us by our sense organs and auxiliary instruments such as the microscope, the middle world. It extends from the atom to the solar system. Below is the world of the atom and elementary particles and above it is the world of the outer cosmos. The liberating consequence of the recognition of these two other worlds is that the subatomic and transgalactic worlds are of no relevance whatsoever to man. I know of no discovery in these two worlds that had any influence whatsoever on the biologist's understanding of the middle world. This means that the only world of any consequence for biology, anthropology, psychology, sociology, and the humanities is the middle world. Hence, the scholars in these fields occupy themselves exclusively with the middle world and do not feel in the least guilty about ignoring the other two worlds. This decision eliminates a huge number of actual and potential controversies.

Biology

I now come to my third theme: the science of biology. Until about 50 years ago, physics was the dominant science. Now it is said again and again, this is the age of biology. This change is not only due to the victorious march of molecular biology, but also to the working out of a unified theory of evolution that virtually ended all strife within evolutionary biology, as well as to advances in nearly all other branches of biology up to neurobiology. Related branches of science, such as anthropology and psychology, also have become increasingly biological.

The previous dominance of the physical sciences was reflected in the philosophy of science. From the Vienna Circle through Carnap, Hempel, Nagel, and Quine up to Popper and Kuhn, the philosophy of science was based on logic, mathematics, and physics. Now a philosophy of biology is developing, largely based on Darwinian thinking, moving in an entirely different direction. It reflects, among other things, the realization that theories in the physical sciences are usually based on laws but those in biology are based on concepts.

The importance of concepts cannot be exaggerated. Our own worldview, our *Weltanschauung,* is based on concepts, such as democracy, freedom, altruism, competition, progress, and responsibility. Concepts have a number of characteristics that have not yet been well articulated. One of them is the potential for change. Let me illustrate this with the concept of evolution. When Platonic essentialism was a dominant philosophy, evolution could take place only through the origin of a new essence. Evolution thus was a saltational process, jumping across a discontinuity. The transmutationism of the Mendelians (Bateson, DeVries, Johannsen) was based on essentialism.

This was followed by the proposal of transformationism, a new concept of evolution in which a particular object or entity gradually becomes transformed. Individual development from the fertilized egg to the adult was the classic illustration of transformationism, and the word evolution was first proposed for the development of the embryo. All so-called evolutions in the inanimate world, as in astronomy or geology, consist of either gradual or more or less explosive transformations of a concrete object. Lamarck's theory of evolution was a transformationist theory.

What Darwin proposed was an entirely new, third concept of evolution, based on his equally new concept of the biological population. Instead of recognizing classes, defined by a constant, sharply demarcated essence, Darwin recognized that every population of living organisms consists of unique, genetically different individuals, no two of which are the same, not even among the five or six billion human individuals. Evolution, in this case, is the replacement in each generation of a population of unique individuals by another such population.

I am presenting this case not as a lesson in evolutionary biology, but as an illustration of the change a concept may undergo in the course of time.

Let me single out two other important aspects of concepts. One is that a concept, in the course of time, may become obsolete. Supernatural powers was still a dominant concept in science at the time of the Scientific Revolution. It played a considerable role in Natural Theology and in the thinking of most philosophers until the time of Kant. It was, after 1859, a major obstacle for the adoption of Darwinian thought.

Another concept that is rapidly becoming obsolete is Platonic essentialism. This is the belief that the world consists of a limited number of classes, defined by their nature or essence, the members of each class being constant in time and identical with each other except for what the Scholastics called "accidents." This philosophy, going back to the thinking of the Pythagoreans and Plato, dominated not only philosophy but also the thinking of the common man. Racism is a typical essentialistic ideology. Essentialism is now increasingly replaced by Darwin's population thinking. These are two cases of concepts that have become obsolete or are on the way toward obsolescence. Others are vitalism, panpsychism, and Cartesian mechanism.

Another vitally important aspect of concepts is that a single term sometimes covers three, four, or five different concepts without the authors who use this term being aware of it. This is true, for instance, of the term *teleological.* There are five actual or potential phenomena or processes in nature that have been designated as teleological, but they are fundamentally different from each other. Let me mention only two of them. One involves teleonomic processes, that is, processes, behaviors, or activities coded in a genetic program and leading to a definite goal. The development of an individual from the fertilized egg, programmed in its genotype, is the most frequently described teleonomic activity. There is nothing mysterious, nothing transcendental, in such goal-finding behavior because not only the goal but also the pathway to it is contained in the genetic program. Teleonomic processes are totally acceptable to science and can ultimately be explained in terms of chemistry and physics.

However, particularly in philosophy, the term has been used most frequently for so-called "cosmic teleology." This is the postulate that there is some force in this world that leads it on toward progress and greater perfection. Cosmic teleology played a large role in pre-Darwinian thinking, for instance, in the philosophy of Immanuel Kant. All modern researchers in the physical and biological sciences have failed to find any evidence for the actual existence of such cosmic teleology. Various claims notwithstanding, Darwin clearly rejected it, and so did John Dewey after a certain amount of hesitation. On the other hand, Rorty has clearly expressed teleological sentiments; indeed, he stated "teleological thinking is inevitable."

On this occasion I want to rescue the reputation of Aristotle, who has often been called a cosmic teleologist. This, however, he was not, as clearly demonstrated by the recent Aristotle scholars Gotthelf, Lennox, Balme, and Nussbaum. Aristotle described the teleonomic processes that take place in embryonic development. Max Delbrück has pointed out that one achieves a remarkably modern account in Aristotle's embryological analyses if one translates his term *eidos* as "genetic program."

The use of the same term for entirely different processes has been the cause of many controversies in science and philosophy. Reduction, which has at least three different meanings, is another typical case.

Permit me to say a few words about Darwin's conceptual breakthroughs. I have already mentioned the replacement of the essence by the bio-population. Darwin was one of the first philosophers who credited chance with the importance it is now given in science and philosophy. He ended, Jacques Monod notwithstanding, the controversy over "chance or necessity." Darwin showed that in the first step of natural selection, the production of literally unlimited variability, chance is supreme. The second step, the actual selection, is an anti-chance process. Hence, the truth is that in selection both chance and necessity occur. There is no doubt that Darwin greatly contributed to the end of straight determinism. Furthermore, through his theory of common descent, Darwin led back to a single origin of life on earth, and this has now been confirmed by molecular biology, which has shown that all living organisms, down to the simplest bacteria, have the same genetic code and the same cellular mechanisms. It is curious how long, owing to the prominence of physicalism, it took to recognize Darwin's greatness as a philosopher.

In closing, let me now say a few words about John Dewey and his relation to some of the topics I have discussed.

Dewey and the Gap Between the Two Cultures

In addition to its monumental achievements, the Scientific Revolution of the seventeenth century created one serious problem for the Western world, the often-decried gap between science and the liberal arts (humanities). C.P. Snow, in his *Two Cultures*, has given us a vivid picture of this seemingly totally unbridgeable chasm. Dewey was keenly aware of this and he had a remarkably sound intuition when he thought Darwinism might help in building a bridge between the two cultures.

The time was not yet ripe for building such a bridge, and Dewey failed. Ninety years ago, the image of "science" was still that of the architects of the Scientific Revolution, including Galileo, Newton, and Descartes. For them, science was physics, mathematics, and logic, as it was for Snow as recently as 1959. But physics is only one science and not *the* science. In the nineteenth and twentieth centuries, another science developed, in many respects very different from physics, which was, in various ways, ideally suited to filling the gap between physics and the humanities and to forming a bridge. This science was biology. In a recent book, I have shown the many different ways biology forms such a bridge.[1] Indeed, certain biological disciplines are, to a great extent, actually closer to the humanities (particularly history) than to physics. Thus, there is an unbroken chain from the most mathematical and deterministic branches of physics to the "softest" branches of the humanities. Indeed, if we had to draw a line of demarcation between science and the humanities, we could make a good case for drawing it right through the middle of biology, placing evolutionary biology with the humanities. Evolutionary biology shares with history a number of attributes historians have always considered to be diagnostic of history: uniqueness of the treated entities, inability to predict, frequency of tentative (subjective) inferences, and relevance to religion and morality.[2]

In short, the demonstration by contemporary philosophers of biology, that biology is an autonomous science that shares a large number of concerns with the humanities, helps to solve many of the puzzles with which the humanities have struggled for many generations.[3] This is of the utmost importance for liberal education. Dewey groped for it unsuccessfully, but we now have the information to reach the goal he had in mind.

Dewey and Darwin

In 1909, Dewey wrote his famous paper, "The Influence of Darwinism on Philosophy." It was, of course, written to celebrate the one-hundredth anniversary of Darwin's birth and the fiftieth anniversary of the publication of *On the Origin of Species*. Ironically, the first two decades of the twentieth century saw about the lowest point in the prestige of Darwinism. The leaders of the new genetics, particularly the Mendelians—Bateson, DeVries, and Johannsen—but prior to 1910 also T. H. Morgan, rejected Darwinism and believed in saltational evolution, that is, evolution by major mutations. It was in those years that papers were published with titles such as "At the Deathbed of Darwinism." Remarkably, at exactly that period, Dewey declared himself a champion of Darwinism. Just exactly why did Dewey think that Darwin and Darwinism were so important?

We cannot answer this question until we have determined exactly what the word Darwinism meant to Dewey. As I recently showed,
there are at least seven different concepts of Darwinism in the literature.[4] At the present time, of course, Darwinism means an evolutionary theory based on the principle of natural selection. But at other
periods, the word meant rather different things. For instance, immediately after publication of *On the Origin of Species,* Darwinism meant
nothing more than a belief in evolution not guided by a supreme
being or any other supernatural factors. Therefore, the geologist
Charles Lyell and Darwin's friend T. H. Huxley were considered by
everyone to be Darwinians, even though neither accepted natural
selection. Under these circumstances, it becomes important to determine just exactly what John Dewey meant by Darwinism.

I cannot analyze Dewey's entire essay. However, it is quite clear that
he saw in Darwin a champion of anti-essentialism. "Up to now," said
Dewey, "the conception of *eidos*, species, a fixed form and a fixed cause,
is the central principle of knowledge as well as of nature. Upon it rested the logic of science. Change as change is mere flux and lapse."[5] For
Dewey, the gist of the Darwinian revolution was the introduction of
evolutionary change, the refutation of the fixed and constant. Because
this was already foreshadowed in the writings of Copernicus, Kepler,
Galileo, and their successors in astronomy and chemistry, said Dewey,

> Darwin would have been helpless in the organic sciences [without
> these predecessors]. The influence of Darwin upon philosophy resides
> in his having conquered the phenomenon of life for the principle of
> transition, and thereby freed the new logic for application to mind
> and knowledge and life. What he said of species, what Galileo had said
> of the earth, *e pur se muove,* he emancipated once for all, genetic and
> experimental ideas as an organum of asking questions and looking for
> explanations.[6]

Essentialism means constancy in all dimensions. All early evolutionists, for instance Lamarck, rejected fixity in the time dimension.
They accepted the idea that the essence changes over time. Darwin,
through his population principle, rejected constancy also in the geographical dimension. Even though Dewey accepted natural selection,

he made a number of statements indicating that he had not yet fully understood Darwin's population thinking.

Dewey was more or less a transformationist. Again and again he compared evolution to the development of the fertilized egg into an adult, but he realized that he had not yet grasped the whole of the story:

> Through a description of the ontogeny of the individual the whole miraculous tale is not yet told. The same glamour is enacted to the same destiny in countless millions of individuals so sundered in time, so severed in space, that they have no opportunity for mutual consultation and no means of interaction. This formal activity keeps individuals distant in space and remote in time to a uniform type of structure and function. This principle seemed to give insight into the very nature of reality itself. To it Aristotle gave the name *eidos*. This term scholastics translated as species.[7]

Here Dewey refers to what we now call the genetic program of a population or species. It is an anticipation of population thinking but not yet fully articulated.

Dewey completely rejected cosmic teleology, which was so popular among philosophers right up to his time. Here again, he followed Darwin. Alas, I don't have the time to develop this theme; and I would rather say a few words about Dewey and ethics.

In 1898, under the title "Evolution and Ethics," Dewey published an answer to T. H. Huxley's famous Romanes Lecture (1893) of the same title.[8] Right up to modern times, Huxley's lecture has been almost universally considered the authoritative view of ethics by a Darwinian. This, however, is a great mistake, as Dewey saw quite clearly. (Let me add parenthetically that Darwin, in 1871, in his *Descent of Man* stated that the possession of an ethical system was the most decisive difference between man and any animal.)[9] Ethics requires the high intelligence needed to be able to foresee the consequence of any action. This is one of the basic conditions for the development of ethics. If only the individual were the target of selection then indeed, as the opponents of Darwin claimed, only selfishness would be rewarded. However, primitive hominids and primitive men lived in small groups of hunter/gatherers, each group in severe competition with the others. Therefore, in addition to individual selection, the social group also became an object of selection. Those social groups have the greatest probability of survival and prosperity that have the most harmonious and altruistic interaction of the individuals of which the group is composed. Hence, contrary to the view expressed by many authors, there is indeed a selective premium placed on benign ethical behavior and a selection of those social groups that consisted of the most cooperative individuals. There is no difficulty in explaining the origin of human ethics in terms of Darwinian natural selection. Huxley, therefore, in rejecting natural selection as a nebulous "cosmic force," also rejected this ethical basis, a point Dewey saw clearly.

Throughout the second half of this paper, I have continuously dealt with concepts, their origins and changes. It is concepts that are the scaffolding of our *Weltanschauung*. It is the change of concepts that characterizes change in the *zeitgeist* of periods. It is the misunderstanding of concepts and the conflict among opposing concepts that is the cause of most strife in this world. If I were to suggest what should be emphasized more strongly in an up-to-date liberal education, it is more room in the curriculum for the study of the concepts that make up our *Weltanschauung* and a more fine-grained analysis of the concepts that are the basis of our belief in democracy.

Notes

1. E. Mayr, *This Is Biology* (Cambridge, MA: Harvard University Press, 1997).
2. E.H. Carr, *What Is History?* (London: Macmillan, 1961).
3. Mayr, *This Is Biology*.
4. E. Mayr, *One Long Argument* (Cambridge, MA: Harvard University Press, 1991).
5. John Dewey, "The Influence of Darwinism on Philosophy," in Martin Gardner, editor, *Great Essays in Science* (Buffalo, NY: Prometheus Books, 1994).
6. Ibid.
7. Ibid.
8. T.H. Huxley, *Evolution and Ethics* (London: Oxford University Press, 1893).
9. C. Darwin, *The Descent of Man* (London: Murray, 1871).

Liberal Education in Cyberia

PETER LYMAN
UNIVERSITY LIBRARIAN, UNIVERSITY OF CALIFORNIA, BERKELEY

The rational purport of a word or other expression lies exclusively in its conceivable bearing upon the conduct of life.
C. S. Peirce, *What Pragmatism Is*

Cyberia is the kind of place that Jane Addams would have liked to encounter while mapping the neighborhoods in Chicago, searching for resources that could be used to create an educational community.[1] Dining with John Dewey in Hull House, she might have described it as a living laboratory for community-based experiments in pragmatic cooperation. Dewey, in turn, might have asked whether Cyberia were a new and cosmopolitan kind of educational experiment, for it could be described as a kind of learning community now emerging on the Internet, a global information network originally designed for scientific research. If, as Dewey thought, learning develops from the everyday experiences that shape our habits of mind and character, perhaps Cyberia could replace schools as the focus of education reform, for information technologies are now becoming the dominant creators of the culture of everyday life.

The term "Cyberia" is intended not simply as a new name for information technology, signifying the economic dominance of science and technology in the late twentieth century, but to suggest that science and technology have become a dominant source of culture itself. This would be a fundamental change from 1931, the date of the first Rollins Conference and of the publication of *Philosophy and Civilization,* in which Dewey said:

The significant outward forms of the civilization of the western world are the product of the machine and its technology . . . . In its effect upon men's external habits, dominant interests, the conditions under which they work and associate, whether in the family, the factory, the state, or internationally, science is by far the most potent social factor in the modern world. It operates, however, through its undesigned effects rather than as a transforming influence on men's thoughts and purposes. This contrast between outer and inner operation is the great contradiction in our lives. Habits of thought and desire remain in substance what they were before the rise of science, while the conditions under which they take effect have been radically altered by science.[2]

The technology of Cyberia—information technology and biotechnology—is now being designed precisely to shape our "habits of thought and desire."

As Jane Addams would not have failed to notice, participants in Cyberia do not experience information as a "technology," but as a place and a community, a mode of communication and a possibility for collaborative thought, an invitation to pragmatic action, and a medium for a public life. Although information technologies are reshaping everyday life and culture, our intellectual universe still resembles Samuel Butler's *Erewhon,* a Luddite Utopia from which technology has been banned.[3] What, then, should be the relationship between Cyberia and institutions dedicated to liberal education, institutions that, in practice, often have taken the preindustrial City on the Hill as an ideal?

John Dewey called technology "a revolutionary transforming instrument," both because of its utility in improving the quality of life, and because of its method, a systematic experimental discipline of thought. Pragmatism was modeled on the experimental method, but not only because of the method's utility. Dewey believed that science and technology also transform the way we think about the future by creating new possibilities for life if, and only if, that is, they can be redirected from commercial to humanistic goals.[4] This was roughly the state of the dialogue between technology and pragmatic liberal education in 1931, and a prelude to the distinguished record of liberal arts colleges in educating scientists over the next three decades.

Information technologies are now transforming our understanding of human nature, both mind and body, and the way we practice the crafts of knowledge. As we observe Cyberia, we might congratulate Dewey on his prescience. Arturo Escobar, an anthropologist, defines it as the convergence of technology and culture: "Significant changes are taking place in both the character of technology and our understanding of it. Computer, information, and biological technologies are bringing about a fundamental transformation in the structure and meaning of modern society and culture."[5] Technology creates culture by making self and society, mind and body the objects of engineering, raising the question whether the traditional dualities between "man and nature," "science and culture," and "theory and practice" are becoming obsolete.

Cyberculture was invented when A.M. Turing distinguished between the machine and the logic of the machine—the program— forever changing technology by transforming mechanical repetition into a logic that can process symbols and thereby respond to context. The program is the culture of the machine, and, by analogy, program is to machine as mind is to body. It is this analogy of mind as computer code, and the analogy of DNA as genetic code shaping life forms, that is now changing our concept of thought.

If technology is changing our paradigm of knowledge, within what frame of reference might it be possible to have a liberal education in Cyberia? This is not simply a question of delivering education, but concerns the future content and organization of education itself, and the quality of life and learning that is its result. In the spirit of Jane Addams and Hull House, a resource map might be useful for discovering links between Cyberia and pragmatic liberal education. There is a resemblance between pragmatism and the culture that has shaped information technology, although the origins of Cyberia are not pragmatic. Rather there are common roots in another U.S. tradition that Charles Kettering described as "tinkering," a pragmatics of invention that Dewey admired and whose experimental temperament he tried to introduce into schools.

If describing the impact of technology on life is a first step in a pragmatic methodology, resource mapping cannot be purely empirical or simply utilitarian. In Dewey's words, "experience in its vital form is experimental, an effort to change the given; it is characterized by projection, by reaching forward into the unknown; connection with a future is its salient trait."[6] The search for liberal education in Cyberia will require just such a projection and connection with a future, one that places technology in service to a democratic society.

But Cyberia also implies a critique of schools, and indeed of all institutions that control access to knowledge in modern society, for communications technologies are designed to provide educational resources directly to learners at every state of life, in every place, at any time. This can be seen in a crude form in the saturation of everyday life by entertainment media and computerized information, and in the invention of the World Wide Web as a medium for the universal dissemination of opinion. It appears in a higher form in visions of a learning society, manifested in the idea of lifelong learning, of distance education and "virtual universities," and the futurist ideal of computerized workplaces in which workers are empowered to think and act creatively. Given that the pragmatic force of technological culture is changing every other institution in our society, can technology renew and enhance educational institutions, or will it replace institutions of higher education as we have known them?

The Learning Cultures of Cyberia

Modern information technology, a science that Norbert Weiner called *cybernetics,* was invented to serve the military need for *command and control.* Cybernetics was the information infrastructure of the military, successively becoming that of government and science; then of management of production and inventory in the economy; and very recently, through an unexpected metamorphosis, now adds computer intelligence to virtually every machine and provides a medium for mass communication and entertainment. We have all become used to cybernetic control, albeit implicitly, in the routines of everyday life. For example, cybernetics are present in the use of credit cards, digital documents that have turned credit into a liquid currency, thereby creating unprecedented freedom of movement, but at the same time acting as a surveillance technology, reporting our consumption patterns back to marketing companies.

Can technologies designed for control serve education? The metamorphosis to a medium for communication contains a new cultural ideal of democratic learning and community-based inquiry. Its pedagogy derives from the scientific laboratory, in the first instance, but also from the experimental practice of inventors, tinkerers, and *bricoleurs* as refracted through the social movements of the 1960s.[7] This is the culture of Silicon Valley, a vision of a learning society instantiated by entrepreneurs such as Steve Jobs and Bill Gates, both of whom dropped out of liberal arts colleges. This democratic, perhaps Utopian, tradition began with the design of the personal computer to empower the individual, not the organization, and with the subsequent development of the Internet to serve scientific research groups.

The Internet, connecting computers around the globe in a cosmopolitan fabric, is not cybernetic; it was designed as an egalitarian technology to manage technical expertise for collaborative scientific research, entrepreneur inventors, and university engineers. The Internet has now mutated into "the Web," a technology for electronic publishing and shared information that has become the foundation of a new kind of egalitarian society derived from the global scope of science. If it contains any discipline at all, it returns to the voluntary authority of a craft relationship in which a learner chooses to become an apprentice in order to learn under the guidance of a more skilled practitioner.

There are six aspects of the learning resources in Cyberia that may well be of relevance to a pragmatic liberal education: problem solving; heuristic teaching; iterative methods; collaborative work; a gift economy; and an understanding of community as diverse and cosmopolitan, not national or homogeneous.

1. Problem solving

Both problem solving and pragmatism derive from the experimental attitude of craft pedagogy, which understands learning to be derived from the experience of doing something. Dewey quoted C. S. Peirce's description of the pragmatic attitude of experimentation, "Whatever assertion you may make to him, he will either understand as meaning that if a given prescription for an experiment ever can be and ever is carried out in act, an experience of a given description will result, or else he will see no sense at all in what you say." Peirce continued by stating the essence of pragmatic philosophy, "The rational purport of a word or other expression lies exclusively in its conceivable bearing upon the conduct of life."[8]

As a learning activity, problem solving is experienced by the learner as a kind of play, that is, a free flow of experimental thinking. The difference between the pragmatic and Cyberian approaches lies in algorithmic thinking, for while pragmatism is broadly experimental, Cyberian problem solving uses mathematics as its model. Cyberian problem solving may be taught through games and simulations; the solution to the problem of the computer game is the discovery of its rules by inductive reasoning and experimentation. But problem solving is more than equations or games, for problems are best solved by inventing new tools, redefining the alternatives in the manner Dewey admired so much.

2. Heuristic teaching

The heuristic method places the student in the role of the discoverer of knowledge; the student is to *find out* rather than to be *told about* things. Heuristic teaching is designed to develop competency at the learner's pace; this transforms the student into an apprentice and the teacher into a coach. The art of heuristic teaching is to state the problem in a manner that can be solved. Thus, ideally, the teacher intervenes only to suggest alternative ways of stating the problem, or to transform questions into problems by suggesting a methodology for finding a solution, or to invent tools that do so.

3. Iterative methods

Iterative learning through problem solving is posed as an alternative to the abstract quality of school education, which perpetuates the opposition between culture and experience by empowering the teacher and devaluing the student's experience. Iterative learning proceeds via the progressive correction of error, unlike question-driven learning, which proceeds by seeking "right" answers. Error does not imply failure in iterative teaching. Thus, Seymour Papert designed the computer language *Logo* to teach children mathematics through an iterative and heuristic pedagogy, arguing that students most often do not learn mathematics because the subject is presented abstractly and error is treated as failure:

> Many children are held back in their learning because they have a model of learning in which you have either "got it" or "got it wrong." But when you learn to program a computer you almost never get it right the first time. Learning to be a master programmer is learning to become highly skilled at isolating and correcting "bugs," the parts that keep the program from working. The question to ask about the program is not whether it is right or wrong, but if it is fixable.[9]

The pedagogy of right and wrong stigmatizes error although, Papert argues, most skills involve practice and continuous improvement. From this point of view, schools as currently structured take on the discipline of the factory, with an emphasis on the accurate repetition of fragmented tasks.

4. Collaborative work

In Cyberia, the group is the primary focus of learning, not the individual. As an example, UNIX, the operating system for computer workstations upon which the Internet was built, was designed to be a communications medium for collaborative laboratory research. In this context, the coordination of the knowledge of a community is the precondition of discovery or learning. This is a "virtual" sense of community, as Cyberians have named it, connoting only that the individual's achievement is dependent upon the dynamics of the group; as such, it represents a fundamental evolution away from the Enlightenment ideal of the self-sufficient individual.[10] This is not to say that there is no individualism or competition in Cyberia, but that collaborative work is understood to be a resource for individual achievement.

5. Gift economy

Information is the glue of social life in Cyberia. On the Web, it is the currency of social life, a collective *public* property that is constantly evolving and thereby shaping the shared culture of the group. Thus, the economic structure of Cyberia is based on gift exchange, not a market economy; that is, the exchange of information is understood as a social relation, not an economic relation. Tacitly the idea of a gift economy constitutes a kind of theory of distributive justice for Cyberia, namely, that the Web constitutes a public domain within which everyone should have the right to equal access to free information.

6. Cosmopolitan community

The Web is the first global communications system built without government direction or control. As a social system, it is as cosmopolitan as the institution of science, in the image of which it was built. In fact, the cosmopolitan society of science may well be the most viable model of a public life in an information age because its sense of community is derived from membership in a shared professional practice, rather than from a place. In this community, historical continuity is maintained through the construction of a literature that includes not only the content of science, but a common system of discourse and rhetorical structure. Thus, part of the sense of community, as we shall see, is derived from the creation of new genres, based on multimedia, hypertext, and the Web.

In many respects each of these six ideas resonates with those of pragmatic educational philosophy; both share an emphasis on life experience, learning from doing, learning communities, and democracy. The difference, and this is a strategic difference, is that Cyberia is a free-form educational resource that is focused on providing information in a way that maintains a community of learners. The question, and this is a question now being actively debated, is whether Cyberia can serve as an infrastructure for a virtual education that is a substitute for school as a place.[11]

Experiments in Cooperation

Thinking about Cyberia as a virtual school might not seem strange to Dewey, who understood all institutions to be no more, and no less, than "experiments in cooperation," and every such experiment to require iterative improvement. Thus, three aspects of information exchange are emerging in Cyberia that hold promise for a pragmatic liberal education, yet each is incomplete unless a humanistic vision can replace the commercial exploitation now guiding their development.

1. *Hypertext.* Digital documents are creating new genres of literature, enabling knowledge to be custom crafted to the educational needs of the individual;
2. *Multimedia.* A new visual culture based on multimedia offers the possibility of combining the emotional impact of images, previously dedicated to entertainment, with the knowledge structures of print, making possible new modes of community experience;
3. *The Web.* The Web seems to make possible new kinds of social cooperation that might support new modes of education and civic participation in an information age.

Cyberia might become a new kind of public realm, one that enhances and renews political life in a market society in which consumption is replacing participation. But this is possible only if the emerging sense of community, new forms of literacy, visual culture, and new epistemologies can be linked to the deeper traditions of education and democratic culture represented by liberal education.

Hypertext: The New Rhetoric?

For an information society, Richard Lanham has redefined rhetoric, the art of persuasion, as the study of "structures of attention." This new rhetoric thus implies strategies for evaluating and using information in a world saturated with word, sound, and image, each designed to command our scarcest resource, our attention.[12] In our information-saturated world, the capacity to recognize and choose is an essential part of becoming a person. Thus, Lanham argues, a humanistic education that develops the "ability to manipulate symbolic reality" may be the best preparation for life in a technological society.

Hypertext is perhaps the first new genre in Cyberia, although Lanham and others argue that it echoes the medieval tradition of marginal commentary linking one text to another, and linking text to an oral tradition of reading aloud in groups. That is, the glosses on medieval manuscripts and hypertext share the characteristic of reflecting the way readers appropriate texts and the way a literature must be understood as both the product and producer of community.

Print reflects the world of the author, but hypertext reflects the world of the reader.[13] Print allows the writer to define the order of the text, and thereby the structure of attention of the reader. Authorship is reified by virtue of the fixed form of the printed page and by the legal right to ownership of the expression of an idea. In contrast, hypertext has a dialogical quality; the reader is empowered to create new texts by freely appropriating the writing of others, linking texts together in a personal way. The Web is a global network with millions of "pages" constructed using hypertext, allowing each writer to participate in a global conversation. Problem solving is the tacit structure of the Web: a learner asks a question by searching the Web for information, then reads and appropriates the information published by others, recreating it. Digital documents are more a performing art than a form of literature, a play of ideas and images with no authority or filter higher than the reader. In contrast to print, "publication" of hypertext simply involves the act of making a Web page accessible to others. In this sense, hypertext has no context, other than that given to it by a reader; every digital document is a unique performance.

What, then, has become of the idea of a text? D. F. Mckenzie, who explores the relation between the physical form of the book and its meaning, traces the etymology of the word text to "the Latin *texere*, 'to weave,' [which] therefore refers, not to any specific material as such, but to its woven state, the web or texture of the materials."[14] From a pragmatic point of view, this definition is important, because the idea of a text is extended beyond print to include all of the techniques with which a culture creates, records, and remembers knowledge. Because "content" cannot exist without a structure, the boundaries of what is communicated must reflect the medium itself.

The design of print and screen are not opposites, but neither are they the same.[15] Both computer screen and printed page hold texts, but with very different qualities and contexts. Each has *textures* as well as content, for the design of the medium is part of the message and shapes its meaning and use. The texture of the printed page is physical (light is reflected from the page), that of the screen is visual (light is projected from the screen). Print is a commodity with fixed material form given by the author; the organization of information on the screen is liquid, its form subject to the reader's control and imagination. In print, control over the reproduction and distribution of the page is separated from writing, but on the Web, every writer is both an author and a publisher.[16]

New forms of documents create the possibility of new kinds of social order.[17] Science became an institution when the circulation of letters evolved into the first scientific journal. The communication of scientific findings enabled the cumulative growth of scientific literature even though scientists were few and were located all over Europe. Today, electronic forms of communication make possible political resistance to repressive regimes, because they bypass the traditional government post, telegraph, and telephone bureaucracies. E-mail has created new kinds of social movements. As an example, Greenpeace can coordinate its members into a global community of shared interest without face-to-face meetings.

Both printed and digital texts enable communities to form and persist over time and distance, but they do so in different ways with important consequences for social structure. Because print instantiates the expression of an idea, ideas can be managed as a commodity in a marketplace and authors can be held responsible for the expression of an idea. But digital documents have no particular form or context; they are liquid, global, and ubiquitous.

Hypertext and other digital documents may combine the social aspect of conversation with the structure of print, but these are still primitive genres, and it is not clear what kind of collaborative action or social consensus they make possible. The creation of new genres with new capacities for teaching and learning is the most exciting aspect for pragmatic liberal education. Printed texts will no longer be the exclusive rhetorical focus of liberal education, although they are still essential. Every student must also be able to analyze the rhetorical structure of digital documents and be able to make decisions about the quality of information in a world without authors or authorities.

Multimedia: A Visual Culture?

Unfortunately, new technologies tend to be interpreted within the intellectual and social context of the established order. The printing press was used to reproduce medieval manuscripts until new kinds of social relations developed to take advantage of capabilities of the new medium. When this transition occurred, scientific journals made possible the institutionalization of science; newspapers the literate public; and government records the nation-state. In the past few decades, information technology has been defined as calculator (the origin of the name "computer"); as organizer of official records and clerical workers ("the electronic brain"); as typewriter and printer ("word processing"); as postal service ("electronic mail"); and as a medium for the reproduction of texts ("electronic publishing"). These print metaphors are tempting because they suggest that new technologies provide more efficient means to accomplish the distinctive functions of print, but will soon sound anachronistic as entirely new genres and social relations emerge from the new media.

Only now is information technology becoming a genuinely innovative medium for communication and visualization, one that makes possible new kinds of perception and thought and new kinds of social relations and groups. As a medium for visualization, information technology has changed science as fundamentally as did the telescope and microscope: by creating new kinds of data; new graphic representations of data (simulations, interactive models); new kinds of laboratory research (the "collaboratory," which enables scientists around the world to work with remote sensing data in a simulated lab); and new forms of data manipulation (the data base, the spreadsheet, electronic journals). The arts are beginning the same evolution from analog to digital expression, as computer simulation changes the nature and provenance of the image (the dinosaurs in *Jurassic Park*) and music.

Thus, students and citizens must be prepared to make aesthetic judgments about information, and more generally, develop appropriate visual literacy skills, for print literacy is of limited value when applied to visual culture. Visual literacy is important not just as a means of understanding experience, but as a way of informing our modes of action as well.

What, then, is the relationship between pragmatic liberal education and the visual media that saturate everyday life? This is not the same as asking, "What is the place of the arts in liberal education?" Our distinct educational and cultural problem is that "the arts" have been placed in the domain of entertainment. Dewey took this separation between aesthetic sensibility and pragmatic action as the core problem of his philosophy of art, saying, "to esthetic experience, then, the philosopher must go to understand what experience is."[18] Aesthetic judgment is inductive, the mode of reasoning by which we learn from experience, but it also links perception to the shared symbols and rituals that make social life possible. Thus, pragmatic liberal education might begin to explore the educational potential of visual culture, going beyond entertainment by linking the new media to education and democratic culture.[19]

Equally important, the aesthetics of visual culture must be linked to purposes beyond entertainment, or for that matter, beyond problem solving. As art historian Barbara Stafford has said of the evolution from a print to a visual multimedia culture, "all forms of graphic display will have to be reassociated with common rituals and public concerns."[20] This is the dimension of pragmatism that goes beyond experience to experimentation. Clearly the perceptual and emotional quality of visual media have had a powerful impact on popular culture, but this impact is only educational if there is "a connection with a future." Visual culture as entertainment and advertising turns the citizen into a consumer; a pragmatic visual culture goes beyond utility to a conception of public life in an information society.

What, then, is a visual language in democratic society; can multimedia become a public art form with educational potential? This question is particularly intriguing given the forms of graphic art available in Cyberia: simulation, animation, interactive graphics, and, perhaps, hypertext.

A Virtual Community?

Although computers are criticized for engendering social isolation and withdrawal, participants in Cyberia often describe it as a kind of community. This is not simply a matter of perspective, but a difference that bears on what community is and self might be in an information society.

It might seem paradoxical to find a sense of intimacy between people and computers, or to discover a sense of community in computer-mediated communication among people who have never met face to face. But we would not ordinarily find it useful to describe play as a "child/toy" relation nor making music as a "musician/instrument" relation, although it is possible to do so.

Sherry Turkle described the experiences of students working with computers in schools, and discovered a deep emotional and intellectual engagement that was a catalyst for psychological development and learning.[21] As with play or music, this engagement fostered a focused concentration marked by a loss of a sense of time, as does the exercise of any other skill. Erik Erikson described this kind of play as the recreation of the ego, "to synchronize the bodily and the social process with the self."[22] From a psychoanalytic point of view, this fusion fosters growth and personal change by providing a private space within which problems can be "worked through."

The concept of play thus suggests an analytic perspective on the experience of community in Cyberia: an engagement with tools that has the capacity to synchronize body, self, and society. As with play, computer-based communication is a skill that is practiced, an act of doing and making, a realm that requires the discipline of rules in order to produce a virtuoso performance, but that ultimately is governed by aesthetic judgment as is any other art form. Play is not only experienced in game environments, but in most kinds of engagement with interactive media. Here we gather together very different kinds of genres that produce very distinct kinds of social experiences: from *tools,* such as the computational machines that began this evolution;

to the workstations that are the instruments for collecting new kinds of data and analyzing and visualizing them in new ways; to *simulations,* the software that lands airplanes or provides geographic information systems that guide city planning; to *new media,* from a relatively primitive mode of sending messages such as e-mail, to a relatively powerful medium for publishing, such as the Web. Software is designed to solve specific problems, but its function often mutates in unexpected ways when it changes context; technology transfer is an organic, not a mechanical process. Thus far, education is adapting software built for very different purposes for new functions, for Cyberia is still experimental and its consequences are largely unknown.

Most striking, Cyberia is experienced as a kind of place, not a relationship to a machine. While it is possible to describe a child at play or a musician as isolated and withdrawn into a toy or instrument, at the same time play and music may seem to be intensely social experiences. Turkle, however, redefines the solitude of working with computers as *a new kind of private space,* not an anonymous experience of isolation in a mass medium.[23] Although both television and Cyberia are visual cultures within which fusion with an electronic image may be experienced, television is a mass broadcast medium that we consume, while Cyberia is a medium for participation, one that may be customized to the interests of the individual reader. Thus, children's television programs such as *Where in the World is Carmen Sandiego?* and the *Mighty Morphin' Power Rangers,* or for that matter MTV and most advertisements, have attempted to simulate the texture of computer games, because the sense of privacy and intimacy created by interactive computer media is so appealing to citizens of a mass society.[24] There is a fundamental difference in learning via television versus computer in that the fusion produced by television is essentially passive. Computer programs, in contrast, are essentially active, requiring that one engage in making something, which implies the possibility of developing and expressing a sense of self. And as with music, there is always a tacit social context, in that the computer simulates the presence of an other—a listener, an observer, a companion.

The anonymity of play often seems to free players from the social roles imposed by everyday life. That is, one chooses a *persona,* which allows for a certain playful risk taking.[25] A sense of community may be created by doing this role playing in adventure games called MUDs (multi-user domains) and MOOs (MUD object oriented). Most intriguingly, participants in virtual worlds often adopt another gender, race, and occupation so that social order and power are turned into a game. Some suggest that Cyberia enables children to free themselves from the social order that constrains communication in the classroom, because expression and participation are no longer embedded in the contexts of cultural domination that silence some and empower others. Similarly, social movements thrive in Cyberia, creating a domain of public discourse that is both political and private at the same time. This is not to say that Cyberia is a realm of pure democratic expression without social structure, for all communication is mediated by programmers, instantiating the cybernetic purposes for which technology has been designed; and by the editorial authority of those who define and govern the rhetorical structures and genres of this visual culture, such as List and Web managers, MOO "Avatars," and game "Wizards."

The elements of this virtual community, then, are interactivity and dialogue, a sense of privacy that encourages emotional engagement, an anonymity that encourages risk taking, and a sense of participation in a public space. This is not community in any traditional sense, although it may resemble the specifically disenchanted sense of the word which, John Rawls argues, is the only possibility in modern society, "a social union of social unions."[26] Both the new rhetoric, with its structures of attention, and the new visual culture, with the emotional power of images, are the components of Cyberia making possible a kind of community that seems otherwise to be missing from modern life. The important questions that a pragmatist must ask are when and how this experience contributes to learning, and if it does, can it do so beyond the realm of recreation or science, in education, the workplace, and the polity?

The Virtual Community?

Although Cyberia may be an imperfect educational vehicle that would benefit from a pragmatic connection to a future, it does offer some powerful resources for liberal education. As a vehicle for education, it is grounded in the individual's experience of learning, even if learning resembles recreation more than education. It creates a sense of individual privacy that is not inconsistent with a kind of participation in a broader community, even if this community is a disenchanted "social union of social unions." And it contains a principle of justice in the ideal of equal access to communication on a cosmopolitan scale, even if it does not address the issue of the content of education.

But Cyberia also raises questions about whether this experiment in cooperation that we refer to as institutions of higher education can be fixed. Is "technology" just another subject matter among many, or has it fundamentally changed our relationship to nature and our own patterns and habits of communication in a way that requires us to rethink the process, context, and content of learning?

Print made it possible to manage knowledge by centralizing the control of information in new kinds of institutions based on paper records. Law and bureaucracy are the essence of political order in the nation-state, and both are rhetorical systems based on print; currency, copyright, patent, and trademark are the authorized containers of the economic value of knowledge in the marketplace; professional certification and professional literature provide quality control for knowledge workers.

However, knowledge, the common currency of an information society, is liquid and cannot easily be regulated by institutions founded on the characteristics of print, a physical commodity. In Walter Wriston's words, "When the world's most precious resource is immaterial, the economic doctrines, social structures and political systems that evolved in a world devoted to the service of matter become rapidly ill suited to cope with the new situation. The rules and customs, skills and talents necessary to uncover, capture, produce, preserve, and exploit information are now mankind's most important rules, customs, skills and talents."[27] Although it might truly be said that Cyberia is an experiment, it is already irreversible.

Cyberia is an experiment in social order, for better or worse, either the "virtual community," the possibility of the end of the authority and power derived from centralized control of information, or a new

era of cybernetic control, through the surveillance of all transactions
in a market society. Dewey himself saw in technology the possibility
of a learning society free of the control of elites:

> If we go back centuries, we find a practical monopoly of learning . . . .
> Learning was a class matter. This was a necessary result of social con-
> ditions. There were not in existence any means by which the multi-
> tude could possibly have access to intellectual resources. These were
> stored up and hidden in manuscripts. Of these there were at least only
> a few, and it required long and toilsome preparation to be able to do
> anything with them. A high priesthood of learning, which guarded the
> treasury of truth and which doled it out to the masses under severe
> restrictions, was the inevitable expression of these conditions. But, as
> a direct result of the industrial revolution . . . this has been changed.
> Printing was invented, it was made commercial. Books, magazines,
> papers were multiplied and cheapened. As a result of the locomotive
> and telegraph, frequent, rapid, and cheap intercommunication by
> mail and electricity was called into being. Travel has been rendered
> easy, freedom of movement, with its accompanying exchange of ideas,
> indefinitely facilitated. The result has been an intellectual revolution.
> Learning has been put into circulation. While there still is, and prob-
> ably always will be, a particular class having the special business of
> inquiry in hand, a distinctively learned class is henceforth out of the
> question. It is an anachronism. Knowledge is no longer an immobile
> solid, it has been liquefied. It is actively moving in all the currents of
> society itself.[28]

The institutional order will not be the same in Cyberia. If knowledge is now a liquid, not a thing or located in a place, what is the
future of the educational institution? In an information society,
knowledge is not scarce, and the social strategy for education may
not necessarily require institutions or places in any traditional sense.
Peter Drucker observed long ago that management in a knowledge-
based economy will have to look much more like education than
the industrial discipline that governed manual labor.[29] More recently, Shoshanna Zuboff argued that computerized machines in the
workplace produce information to which the worker must respond,
thus the worker of the future must be educated to make judgments
and continuously learn.[30] As a consequence, corporate education is
the fastest-growing segment of education, and extension and dis-

tance education programs are bringing education into new social contexts. These experiments in the relation of theory and practice go far beyond the traditional educational contexts for practice in liberal education, the laboratory and field experience, to teach inductively, in the field, to everybody.

Perhaps the biggest threat raised by Cyberia is to the future of the educational institution as a context for teaching and learning—to the school, the college, and the university. This is not simply a consequence of the nature of work in an information society. It also reflects a theory of distributive justice that believes itself to be egalitarian by virtue of universal access and emphasis on the freedom of the learner. If a pedagogy of problem solving in a learner-centered community is now possible, it is no longer sufficient to think of education as a place, without, that is, specifying what it is about that place that enables people to learn better than they might in other contexts.

One of the historic missions of pragmatic liberal education has been teaching students how to be citizens in a democratic society. But it is no longer clear what it means to be a citizen in a consumer society that has begun to substitute markets for public institutions and saturates everyday life with mass media and advertising. To develop a new public realm, liberal education must link Cyberia to "common rituals and public concerns." How might Cyberia go beyond problem solving and universal access to information to a genuine conception of social justice?

Universal access is, of course, a precondition to the development of a public realm, but if it is necessary it is not necessarily sufficient. This is the defect in our current telecommunications policy, which understands the computer network to raise the same kind of policy issues as the telephone, broadcasting, and electrification. The issue of equal access is important, but without a conception of the public interest that guarantees citizens free access to the information they need to participate in governing themselves, or a medium for collective deliberation beyond political advertising, Cyberia does not meet the criteria for a true public forum.

Whatever its defects, Cyberia has created a new kind of public space for direct participation in public affairs within which new kinds of political association have begun to form. Nations that suppress dissent are forced to suppress a technology and mode of communication essential for the progress of science and education, which is a distinct disadvantage in economic and social development.

Ultimately, then, the core question for pragmatic liberal education is how to educate citizens for Cyberia, people capable of re-creating a public realm in which participation in a collaborative realm enhances the life of the individual and an economy in which the uses of technology are more than utilitarian.

Notes

1. Mary Jo Deegan, *Jane Addams and the Men of the Chicago School, 1892–1918* (New Brunswick, NJ: Transaction Books, 1988), 46–48. This paper is intended to be a kind of resource map of Cyberia, on the model of the Hull House maps and papers.
2. John Dewey, *Philosophy and Civilization* (New York: Minton, Balch & Company, 1931), 318.
3. Bruno Latour, *Aramis, or the Love of Teaching,* translated by Catherine Porter (Cambridge, MA: Harvard University Press, 1996), vii.
4. Charlene Haddock Seigfried, *Pragmatism and Feminism* (Chicago: University of Chicago Press, 1996), 184.
5. Arturo Escobar, "Welcome to Cyberia," *Current Anthropology* (June 1994), 211–31.
6. John Dewey, "The Need for a Recovery of Philosophy," *Creative Intelligence: Essays in the Pragmatic Attitude* (New York: Henry Holt and Company, 1917), 7.
7. See Peter Lyman, "Is Using a Computer Like Driving a Car, Reading a Book, or Solving a Problem? The Computer as Machine, Text, and Culture." In *Work and Technology in Higher Education: The Social Construction of Academic Computing* (Mahwah, NJ: Erlbaum, 1995), 19–36.
8. C.S. Peirce, "What Pragmatism Is," *Monist* (April 1905), 162. Cited by John Dewey in "The Development of American Pragmatism," *Philosophy and Civilization* (New York: Minton, Balch & Company, 1931), 14.
9. Seymour Papert, *Mindstorms: Children, Computers and Powerful Ideas* (New York: Basic Books, 1980), 23.
10. Richard Rorty, "The Priority of Democracy to Philosophy," in Merrill D. Peterson and Robert C. Vaughan, editors, *The Virginia Statute for Religious Freedom* (Cambridge: Cambridge University Press, 1988), 260, 273.
11. *New York Times,* September 25, 1996, B9.
12. Richard A. Lanham, *The Electronic Word: Democracy, Technology and the Arts* (Chicago: University of Chicago Press, 1993), 229.
13. Roger Chartier, *The Order of Books,* translated by Lydia G. Cochrane (Stanford, CA: Stanford University Press, 1994), 3.

14. D.F. Mckenzie, *Bibliography and the Sociology of Texts* (London: The British Library, 1986), 5.

15. Peter Lyman, "How is the Medium the Message?" *Computer Networking and Scholarly Communication in the 21st Century* (Albany: State University of New York Press, 1966).

16. Geoffrey Nunberg, "The Places of Books in the Age of Electronic Reproduction," in R. Howard Bloch and Carla Hesse, editors, *Future Libraries* (Berkeley: University of California Press, 1993), 13–37.

17. John Seely Brown and Paul Duguid, "The Social Life of Documents," *Release 1.0: Esther Dyson's Monthly Report* (New York: EDventure Holdings) October 11, 1995.

18. John Dewey, *Art as Experience*, in Jo Ann Boydston, editor, *John Dewey: The Later Works, 1925–1953*, Volume 10 (Carbondale: Southern Illinois University Press, 1987), 278.

19. Barbara Maria Stafford, *Good Looking: Essays on the Virtue of Images* (Cambridge, MA: MIT Press, 1996), 15–16.

20. Barbara Maria Stafford, *Artful Science: Enlightenment Entertainment and the Eclipse of Visual Education* (Cambridge, MA: MIT Press, 1994), 311.

21. Sherry Turkle, *The Second Self* (New York: Simon and Schuster, 1984).

22. Erik H. Erikson, *Childhood and Society* (New York: W.W. Norton, 1963), 209, 211.

23. Quoted in *The Future of Community and Personal Identity in the Coming Electronic Culture* (Washington, DC: Aspen Institute, 1995), 10.

24. Marsha Kinder, "Media Wars in Children's Electronic Culture: Domesticating the World with Carmen Sandiego and the Mighty Morphin' Power Rangers," *Proceedings of the Twenty-Ninth Annual Hawaii International Conference on System Sciences* (New York: IEEE Computer Society Press, 1996), 5:126–32.

25. Allucquere Rosanne Stone, "Will the Real Body Please Stand Up? Boundary Stories about Virtual Cultures," in Michael Benedikt, editor, *Cyberspace: First Steps* (Cambridge, MA: MIT Press, 1992), 81–118.

26. John Rawls, *A Theory of Justice* (London: Oxford University Press, 1973), 527, cited in Rorty, "The Priority of Democracy to Philosophy," 273, 282.

27. Walter Wriston, *The Twilight of Sovereignty: How the Information Revolution Is Transforming Our World* (New York: Charles Scribner's Sons, 1992), 19–20.

28. John Dewey, *The School and Society* (Chicago: University of Chicago Press, 1899), 16–17. Thanks to Robert Orrill for pointing out this passage and its significance.

29. Peter F. Drucker, *The Age of Discontinuity* (New York: Harper & Row, 1978).

30. Shoshanna Zuboff, *In the Age of the Smart Machine* (New York: Basic Books, 1988).

Placing Liberal Education in the Service of Democracy

Nicholas H. Farnham
Director, The Educational Leadership Program
of the Christian A. Johnson Endeavor Foundation

As other papers from this meeting have shown, considerations of pragmatism in liberal education inevitably bring John Dewey to the fore. Nowhere is the connection more appropriately evoked than in discussions about how better to place liberal learning in the service of democracy.

In his conclusion to a chapter in *Democracy and Education,* Dewey stated succinctly his view of democratic society and the type of education he believes can enable it to survive. As for the first, he says "a society which makes provisions for participation in its good of all its members on equal terms, and which secures flexible readjustment of its institutions is in so far democratic." Regarding the second, he states "such a society must have a type of education which gives individuals a personal interest in social relationships and control, and the habits of mind which secure social changes without introducing disorder."[1]

I know of no place where examination of these concepts is more interesting today than in the context of events in Eastern and Central Europe, where new post-Communist governments are attempting to reconstruct their institutions and are acutely in need of finding ways to instill the habits of mind in the citizenry to which Dewey was referring. I would like therefore to illustrate the relationship of liberal education to democracy by describing a conference I organized in the fall of 1996 in Budapest, for 60 rectors and senior faculty to discuss American-style concepts of liberal education, and the work that has come out of that meeting.

Because "liberal education" is a concept that eludes easy definition in the West, and has no counterpart in the East, it was important to begin in Budapest with a concrete definition of the term. The definition chosen was as follows:

> Liberal education can be described as education that fosters the development of intellectual curiosity, critical intelligence, judgment, imagination, and sympathy for the varieties of the human condition. It seeks to place students in the stream of history, to acquaint them with the methods of science, and to expose them to the power of the arts. At the same time it enhances in students an awareness of their own individual natures and motivations. In the United States its curriculum is often described as aiming at developing intellectual capacity through general knowledge, critical thinking, and problem solving. The way material is presented to students in liberal education programs is frequently cross-disciplinary, as one of its main concerns is to enable students to make connections between branches of knowledge.

This definition, which could be a composite of mission statements for liberal arts colleges across the United States, proved surprisingly resilient in the Eastern European context. In the course of the meeting, no one challenged its value, and more than one participant said that it was strikingly similar to his or her own articulation of hopes and expectations for educational change.

To an intellectual coming out from under 50 years of political and ideological repression, this definition as well as the idea that one can finally have free inquiry—and that free inquiry is a good thing for society—can be thrilling. You could feel the excitement in the voice of the president of Kiev's Mohyla Academy, for instance, when he spoke of the difference between the old Marxist curriculum and the new American undergraduate education he is adopting as being the difference between having to go down a long, narrow corridor with only two doors (and if you have ever been to Kiev, you know that it is poorly lit) and going into a large, airy room where there is freedom to move about and where one can choose different paths and precepts and emerge from several different exits. Liberty in the curriculum is a breathtaking idea. That such liberty could reinforce and even carry the weight of economic, political, and social liberty seems almost too good to be true.

Of course, there are more than a few reasons for educational leaders in Eastern and Central Europe to remain skeptical. The 20 presidents of U.S. liberal arts colleges who attended the meeting offered a number of realistic and hardly encouraging reports about the decline of political support for liberal education in their country, the difficulty of paying for it, the difficulty of finding shared values and curricular balance, as well as the difficulties of balancing access and excellence. But enthusiasm for the idea that new curricula are needed and might bring forth a new kind of leadership for political freedom and democracy, and that such curricula are related to the conditions of free inquiry, did not diminish in the course of the meeting. It reminded some American participants of the state of mind of intellectuals in the early American republic. It was the enthusiasm of the newly free reaffirming that freedom is a natural state for human beings. As a University of Warsaw leader put it in describing his recently begun experiment in interdisciplinary studies, "what we aimed at was creating space for individual responsibility, free choice, and the right to take risks for various talents and possibilities of the civilization. . . . Our access to 'liberal education' resembles to some degree the right of self-defense, which Cicero says is a law which comes to us not by education but by constitution, not by training but by intuition, a law which we possess not by instruction but which we sucked in at Nature's breast."

There was universal agreement at the Budapest meeting that it would be desirable to form some kind of continuing association that might encourage new liberal education experiments in the region and provide contact between efforts that have already begun. Among the latter are more than a few of unusual interest. Efforts at the University of Warsaw have resulted in the creation of an interdepartmental program of individual studies through the Center for Studies on the Classical Tradition. In Budapest, the Invisible College has been established to give extra preparation to future leaders by providing afterhours tutorials that are closely supervised and offering individualized study plans. At the Charles University in Prague, the Institute of Fundamental Learning was launched, in 1990, by former dissidents to counter Marxist influence in the curricula. It now offers tutorials and elective-based course structures leading to a B.A. degree following the American model. At Kiev's Mohyla Academy, the entire program has been overhauled to mirror the curricular flexibility of an American four-year liberal arts institution. And in troubled Bulgaria, several of the participants from the Budapest meeting, including the new minister of education, decided recently to begin Sofia University's first program of interdisciplinary seminars. Of course, these are small steps, but all of them represent significant new beginnings.

A committee was formed in Budapest to begin planning a new association "for the furtherance of liberal education and democratic values in post-Communist societies." It has decided to call itself *Artes Liberales,* as a way of associating itself with an educational tradition recognizable to everyone. Should anyone wonder about the societal purpose of the group, they only have to look at the statement of purpose that the group has recently formulated. This statement speaks as loudly and clearly about the connection between liberal education and democratic values as any that John Dewey could have formulated.

> Set free half a decade ago from the fetters of years of politicization and ideological abuse, our universities and colleges largely still remain in a critically weakened condition with respect to accepting the responsibilities of educating for democratic leadership. Yet it is clear that a free society can only remain so where its citizens are educated to accept the burdens of freedom and democracy. We are convinced that programs of liberal education that reach beyond preparing the student for specific tasks and imparting specific skills and that offer broad intellectual, historical, and cultural perspectives are of the utmost importance to the progress of our emerging democracies, the strengthening of our economies nationally and trans-nationally, and the development of the human potentiality of our citizenry. To this end *Artes Liberales* has been created to
>
> 1. encourage in our colleges and universities concrete experiments in teaching and learning that break the mold of premature and excessive specialization.
> 2. promote exchanges and cooperation on programs of liberal education and democratic leadership among scholars and institutions

in post-Communist countries, as well as with American scholars and institutions.

3. assist in the spread of new programs of liberal education that themselves avoid the dangers of political opportunism and militant nationalism.

4. advocate that opportunities be offered for students, as part of their education for leadership, to take individual responsibility for designing their own curriculum.

As the Iron Curtain recedes in memory, leaders on both sides of the former divide are finding that they must rethink many educational and governmental issues. We are no longer subject to nor in direct competition with a form of government that has absolute answers for everything from social welfare to the possibility of life after death. We in the United States rightly see this victory over the modern absolutist experiment called Communism as a reaffirmation of our pragmatic social values as much as a victory for our democratic form of government. Yet the meaning of this victory for the twenty-first century remains indistinct; with it comes a large measure of unpredictability in human affairs. Had the victory gone the way Marx so confidently predicted, you may be certain that the business of predicting would have been much easier; there would already be many volumes of forecasts ready to greet the new millennium. As it went, the world is not only surprised, but gently shocked by the predictive incapacity of liberal/democratic society. In this development may lie a principle on which leaders may build policies for the future. For educators, the unpredictability of social and economic life points toward liberal education as the best way to plan for the jobs that have not yet been invented.

It is therefore to be hoped that *Artes Liberales* will develop a new argument for liberal education and democratic values in Central and Eastern Europe and that some of its freshness may serve to help us in our own educational struggles.

Notes

1. John Dewey, *Democracy and Education* (New York: Macmillan, 1916), 99.

Education for a World Lived in Common with Others

LEE KNEFELKAMP
*PROFESSOR OF ADULT AND HIGHER EDUCATION,
TEACHERS COLLEGE, COLUMBIA UNIVERSITY*

CAROL SCHNEIDER
*EXECUTIVE VICE PRESIDENT, ASSOCIATION
OF AMERICAN COLLEGES AND UNIVERSITIES*

*Editor's note: Lee Knefelkamp and Carol Schneider were invited
to comment on the major themes of the colloquy dialogue. This
paper is based on the observations and remarks they offered at the
closing session of the colloquy.*

In her evocative treatise, *The Dialectic of Freedom,* Dewcyan philosopher Maxine Greene challenges educators to create authentic public spaces, spaces devoted to dialogue and possibility. The dialogue
that should take place in such spaces, she proposes, calls for "a special form of critical thinking . . . a powerful vision and reflection born
of an awareness of a world lived in common with others."[1]

The 1997 Rollins Colloquy, reprised in the chapters of this book,
rose elegantly to meet Greene's vision and standard, offering a distinctive, reflective, and illuminating moment of "dialogue and possibility." The colloquy and the papers gathered in this book provide a
framing window into a transformative century in the history of U.S.
higher education. They show us the paths taken and, equally important, the paths proposed but not taken, as educators constructed a
twentieth-century conception of liberal education. They take us, as

few academic gatherings do, to a deeper understanding of the values and assumptions that have profoundly shaped both the highest aspirations and the daily work of our educational communities.

Even more powerfully, however, the colloquy dialogue delineates, from a dozen different starting points, and through its joining of apparently quite disparate standpoints and conceptions, an emerging and important new direction for U.S. higher education. What is this new direction? In a sentence, it is a conception of education that holds at its core a vision of, and conscious preparation for, a "world lived in common with others."

Dewey, who is much cited in these pages, wrote that "the purpose of education was to create, in our students and in ourselves, the capacities for associative living."[2] The colloquy dialogue brings this purpose centrally into focus. Collectively, the ideas in these papers, which, in turn, reflect thousands of separate dialogues across the entire spectrum of contemporary higher education, provide a basic outline of what it would mean to take seriously the cultivation of developed capacities for a life lived in common with others. Such preparation includes, of course, the development of intellectual capacities, those habits of mind and the range of knowledge students need to live productively in a diverse and complex society. But these papers also highlight the affective domain and especially the interpersonal qualities that would enable students to hear one another, to respect one another's distinctiveness, to reach across differences without ignoring, silencing, or seeking to eliminate them. They underline, as well, the importance of what might be called behavioral capacities, those problem-solving and collaborative learning skills that are necessary to the building of community in a diverse democracy.

As Elizabeth Minnich's moving collage of social testaments from the early pragmatists beautifully attests, the proposal that education should prepare students for social engagement and commitment is, in and of itself, neither new nor unique to Dewey. A full century ago, pragmatists from William James to Jane Addams to Carter G. Woodson to W.E.B. du Bois called for an understanding of education that would develop the talents of ordinary human beings, from every race and every walk of life, and engage them centrally in public life,

collaborative work, moral action, and the redress of social inequities
and injustices. But this rich vision of what we might call a "societal turn"
toward democratic engagement and social reform was never adopted
by higher education. It is only now beginning to make a significant
claim on educators' imagination and activity. The colloquy's great contribution, we believe, is to make this claim central as well as visible and
to invite the academy to explore its implications and potential.

In this reflection on the larger implications of the colloquy dialogue as a whole, we will explore the contours of education for a world
lived in common with others and suggest what it might mean to adopt
this conception both for the future of the academy and for the societal role of our colleges and universities. We also bring to the surface
dimensions of this social and moral vision for the American academy that were, for the most part, embedded in rather than fully explored
in the colloquy dialogue. And finally, we offer our own suggestions
about commitments and directions that might capture in institutional
practices the full potential of the social and educational vision of
American pragmatism.

Paths Taken

The "Individualist" Turn in Twentieth-Century Higher Education

Bruce Kimball's provocative argument in "Toward Pragmatic Liberal Education" called the academy's attention to the curious neglect
of our major indigenous philosophical tradition through much of
the twentieth century's discourse about liberal education.[3] Kimball
also points us to what he argues is a new convergence between fundamental tenets of pragmatic thought and late-twentieth-century
trends toward higher education reform and renewal. In this new convergence, he proposes, we see the seeds of a distinctively American
vision of liberal education, a vision that is at once collaborative in
practice, constructivist in epistemology, and strongly animated by an
ethic of service and social responsibility.

Kimball's juxtaposition of previously separate discourses—philosophical and educational—has the fruitful effect of defamiliarizing
contours and features of the twentieth-century academy so utterly

taken for granted that they previously seemed facts of nature rather than the result of deliberate choice and social construction. As Ellen Lagemann's paper in this volume demonstrates, higher education did not simply overlook the educational prescriptions and social vision of Dewey, Addams, and other early American pragmatists. Those who wanted the academy to become directly involved in the work of building what Dewey calls a moral democracy came into direct conflict with the view that the academy should devote itself to the production of scientific and cultural knowledge. Proponents of the research agenda were better organized; the struggle was a rout. Control by academically structured departments over who and what counts as meritorious in the academy was the result and is still the most important social fact about U.S. higher education, as well as the most routinely cited frustration for virtually everyone who attempts institutional change or learning-centered reform.

This is not to say that pragmatic proposals and insights left no mark at all on the theory and practice of American liberal education. A comparison of the central tenets of the original 1931 Rollins Colloquy on Liberal Education, which Dewey attended, and those themes most enthusiastically endorsed in the present colloquy helps us see more exactly what was distilled and what was lost in higher education's transition from that legacy.

Dewey's educational philosophy holds in generative relationship five core ideas:

1. The distinctive worth and capacity of every individual;
2. The importance of educating each person to become significantly engaged in contexts of social action and experience;
3. The centrality, both for learning and for democracy, of each student's direct and collaborative involvement with core issues and challenges in the making of democratic community;
4. The belief that in democracy, as in science, it is the combination of multiple and different understandings that makes progress attainable; and
5. The insistence that this kind of learning is a lifelong endeavor and commitment, not a matter for schools alone.

While each of these tenets intersects with the others in Dewey's moral vision and recommended praxis, it is certainly possible to excerpt specific themes from the larger whole and to pursue them either in isolation or in fresh combination with other themes and agendas.

If we look back on the proceedings of the landmark 1931 Rollins Colloquy and compare the main points of discussion there with these core Deweyan tenets, several things stand out. The avowedly progressive institutions participating in that earlier dialogue focused intensely on the individual interests and development of each student. That distinctive individuality and uniqueness, participants held, must be prized and nurtured by the educational process. Moreover, those progressive institutions viewed extracurricular experience, hands-on learning, and reflection as important parts of their philosophy and effectiveness. They self-consciously compared themselves with more traditional institutions and presentational pedagogies whose approach they thought both rigid and stifling of intellectual curiosity and engagement.

But the 1931 proceedings are also striking for their lack of attention to the social agenda of the early pragmatists. Dewey's aim was a form of learning directly suited to the open-ended and collaborative task of building democracy as a participatory, moral, and justice-seeking framework for lives lived in common. But beyond the determination to liberate individuals from the constraints of lecture and recitation, there was little discussion in 1931 of higher education's responsibilities to aspirational democracy and almost none of the moral and social passion that characterizes a Jane Addams or a W.E.B. du Bois. Moreover, in its emphasis on cultivating the talents, interests, and unique accomplishments of the individual learner, this 1931 gathering gave short shrift to the interactive and collaborative concept of learning that was also fundamental to Dewey's educational philosophy.

Contemporary educational philosophers evidence a similar emphasis on the learning of the solitary individual, detached from specific social contexts or obligations. In *The Unschooled Mind,* Howard Gardner provides a contemporary distillation of progressive higher education's selective appropriation of Deweyan ideas. "I argue," Gardner asserts, "that the pursuit of individual understanding should be central throughout the educational enterprise." By understanding Gardner means the capacity of the individual learner "to apply facts, concepts, skills, and knowledge appropriately in new situations."[4]

Another contemporary depiction of the same selective appropriation from pragmatism is David Kolb's widely used experiential learning cycle. Kolb's model (see Figure 1) provides a rich explication of how students learn, capturing a movement from direct experience through reflection on the experience, to the generation of concepts and theoretical explanations, to an ability to use knowledge in active and intentional experimentation. This model, which is Deweyan both in its emphasis on direct experience and in its implicit incorporation of a scientific and experimental "method," also shows how more effective and varied pedagogies involving direct experience and experimentation, as well as analysis and abstraction, facilitate the very capacities of individual understanding that Gardner describes.

In each transition from the pragmatic vision, the distinguishing characteristic is a significant shift in focus and purpose away from

Figure 1. Educational Mission I: Individual Learning

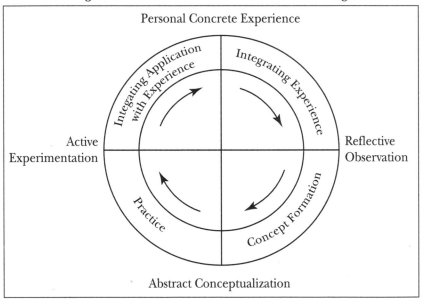

Source: Adapted from David Kolb, *Experiential Learning: Experience as the Source of Learning and Development* (Englewood Cliffs, NJ: Prentice Hall, 1984).

faculty-centered teaching toward student-centered learning. Each further instantiates a shift toward powerful forms of active learning, including hands-on experience, experimentation, critical reflection, and generalization. In the longer perspective of time, it is clear that this engaged and student-centered conception of learning has become, in the second half of the twentieth century, *the* primary progressive alternative to formalist, presentational modes of teaching and learning. Indeed, it is the elite alternative, the form of education most likely to be found at selective and residential liberal arts institutions.

This distillation from early pragmatic ideas is nonetheless an intensely individualized model, resolutely centered in and on the experience, interests, and unique understanding of the independent learner. As such, this conception fundamentally parts company with the dialogical, interactive foundations of the Deweyan vision of learning. In place of cooperative problem solving and an orientation toward social action and moral democracy, this individualized conception of learning leaves experiences of social connection and communal obligation essentially on the periphery, beyond the boundaries of the model. *How* the learner may choose to use the newly acquired understanding and intellectual power is an issue left, in this individualized learning model, absolutely elective to the learner.

Some may affirm this orientation, contending, as many proponents of liberal education do, that focus on individual uniqueness and accomplishments provides an incomparable education in personal freedom and responsibility. We, however, believe that an educational ethos of unencumbered individualism has a very high cost in the neglect and diminishment of democratic society. As Alexander Astin reminds elsewhere in this volume, "the biggest problem with contemporary civic life in America may be that too few of our citizens are actively engaged in efforts to effect positive social change even on the smallest scale." Surely there is a connection between this societal disengagement and an elite conception of learning as primarily a matter of individual preference, understanding, and development.

It is beyond the scope of this paper to explore the interplay between educational philosophy and societal ethos that underlies this individualized translation of an educational vision that was originally collaborative both in spirit and practice. But certainly this focus on the individual learner mirrors the historic American focus on rugged individualism—a freedom from restraint that holds out the promise of unlimited possibility for all who apply themselves. This belief in an unencumbered individualism continues to have great resonance in U.S. public culture, as the current national debate over affirmative action reminds us. Those who attack the role affirmative action has played in diversifying higher education do so in the name of American individualism—and a companion attachment to "merit"—and in explicit criticism of any attempt to consider how a particular individual's societal experiences and communal affiliations will *add* to the interactive and communal effectiveness of a learning environment as a whole.

Alternative Visions

Toward a Relational Pedagogy of Engagement and Service

For us, the great strength of this colloquy is the resonance with which both speakers and participants brought centrally into view an alternative and essentially collaborative educational vision, one that prepares learners for social involvement and action by immersing them in contexts of collaborative engagement, participatory democracy, and service learning. This collaborative and relational educational ethos resonates with Maxine Greene's crucial assertion that individual freedom is not "freedom from," but in fact, "freedom for" the acceptance of responsibilities, particularly those that accompany the realization that one lives one's life in the presence of others and in the context of the needs of others.

Clearly a conception of relational knowing is not original to this colloquy. Feminist scholars have long argued for more connected, communal, and responsive approaches to both learning and teaching. But the dialogue of this conference, led by prominent figures in all parts of higher education, surely attests that calls for connected and responsive learning have now moved from margin to center. Indeed, it was heartening to us as feminists who have worked closely with leaders in both gender and ethnic studies to see that the connections between learning and life so ardently and controversially developed through these fields are now being seriously recommended as high-priority and even salvational directions for the praxis of liberal education.

Nevertheless, the single dominant theme that reverberates as a constant refrain within the colloquy and this book is the endorsement of a pedagogy of engagement and service, through which students learn from direct action, from others in surrounding communities, and from one another as they reflect on their experiences in contexts of practice and service. Affirmation of service learning resonated from the start to the conclusion of the colloquy, and when participants were asked for a show of hands, most confirmed that service was already a formal or informal expectation at their institutions. Astin reinforced enthusiasm with evidence when he reported his new finding that participation in service learning experiences correlates positively with 35 different aspects of academic development, including academic outcomes, civic values, and life skills.

Figure 2 represents the emergent conception of knowing and knowledge suggested in the previous paragraphs. Here, we combine

Figure 2. Educational Mission II: Relational Learning

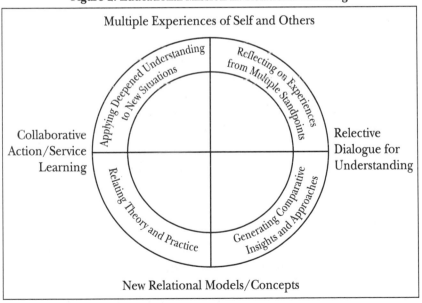

Source: Adapted from Patricia Hill Collins, *Black Feminist Thought: Knowledge, Consciousness, and the Politics of Empowerment* (New York: Routledge, 1990); Kolb, *Experiential Learning.*

Kolb's experiential learning cycle with the epistemology of feminist sociologist Patricia Hill Collins to depict a view of learning that is at its core interactive, collaborative, or as the Association of American Colleges and Universities' American Commitments National Panel on Diversity and Learning terms it, "relational." Our model is grounded not in one individual's learning experience alone, but in the joining of multiple and disparate experiences. What originally appeared in the Kolb model as an individualized process of experiencing, reflecting, conceptualizing, and experimenting is recast in this alternative model as fundamentally interactive and dialogical. Learning now involves the joining of multiple experiences and collaborative dialogue about the meanings of those experiences. In this model, new concepts or frameworks emerge from a serious engagement with perspectives and proposals that are both multiple and diverse.

These new concepts are not purely theoretical. Their purpose is to guide social experimentation and action; they will be tested against the demanding standard of their actual utility in solving problems and improving social practices. Because these guiding concepts and frameworks are socially negotiated, they have both the resilience and also the imperfection of ideas shaped in the give-and-take of disputation and competing interests. But whatever they lose in theoretical elegance and precision, they gain from the "buy-in" of those who must put the frameworks to actual use.

Crucially, in this model for relational learning, no student is left alone to consider whether and how to apply knowledge to practice. Because both concepts and applications are socially debated and negotiated, context and consequence are woven into their very fabric. The final test of theory becomes its usefulness in the intrinsically social contexts of actual practice.

Diversity is also an integral source of conceptual resilience in this relational model of knowing and knowledge. As we know from cognitive research, the more and more varied the concepts the mind takes in, the more complex and adequate are the frameworks produced for interpretation and understanding. In relational designs for learning, each participant encounters not only diverse and competing concepts, but also the frequently passionate convictions of peo-

ple who care about particular ideas and care about the actual uses to
which ideas will be put. Such encounters are anything but easy. But
they are essential in an adequate education for life and work in complex and increasingly intercultural communities. An integral dimension of relational learning is discovering how to deal simultaneously
with the inherent challenge of diverse and often-divided perspectives,
feelings, commitments, and positions.

Justice Seeking

Recovering the Early Pragmatists' Commitment to Aspirational Democracy

This more relational and practice-oriented conception of learning
recovers an important dimension of the Deweyan vision of learning
for a democratic society. It points us toward new standards of excellence in higher education that are fundamentally collaborative and
cooperative, and for that very reason far better suited than older models to be effective preparation for lives lived in common with others.
The academy would be much better able to articulate and advance—
in the courts and in the court of public opinion—the necessity of a
strong commitment to diverse educational communities if we had
long ago acknowledged society's fundamental dependence on communal and relational rather than individualized and competitive conceptions of excellence in learning.

At this point, however, we want to bring to the foreground another dimension of engaged and socially responsive learning, a dimension presented by several of the colloquy authors but not, we believe,
fully taken up or explored. The most important proposals in this
colloquy summon higher education to a moral encounter with the
unfinished agendas of equality and social justice that still await con-
certed commitment from both campus and society at this moment
in our history.

There is a crucial distinction between education that immerses
learners in contexts of practice or service, and education that presses the learner to take seriously the entire realm of democratic premises, principles, aspirations, and justice seeking. Both are important

and they are surely connected, but they are not the same. Service is the implicit social contract between each profession and the larger society. Every human being in every profession regularly struggles with the issue of providing effective service. Consider students who serve as reading tutors in schools. They provide a crucial service that opens doors and brings equal opportunity closer for those whom they help to learn. They may well serve in communities they have not previously visited and thereby foster significant and powerful new learning among all participants in the service experience. But providing the service, and even increasing the sum of human understanding, are different from pressing basic and fundamental questions about the radically unequal resources available to different public school systems in the first place.

These kinds of equity questions, these matters of differential resources, power, participation, and systemic advantage, confront our society—and each participant in it—at every turn. But the typical undergraduate rarely addresses them in the formal curriculum. We have left them, by default, in the hands of specialists and politicians. Few Americans are pleased with the result.

We believe, as the early pragmatists also believed, that education must help learners develop the knowledge, principles, and capacities to work generatively with the unresolved issues of equity and justice that continually confront us in our lives and in our work. It ought to be a crucial mission in liberal education to help learners identify and engage the often conflicting public assumptions that guide us, whether productively or not, in our struggles with particular issues of equity and fairness.

Elizabeth Minnich's talk threw open the question of higher education's responsibilities to democratic principles when she sketched her conception of "aspirational democracy"; ongoing social efforts began with the very founding of this nation to hold ourselves and our society fully accountable to such core principles as the dignity, equality, and potential contribution of all people, whatever their gender, race, ethnicity, or other communal identifications. The pragmatists were searingly aware, she reminds us, of the dangerously vast gulfs between rich and poor and of the desperation of lives lived in the tenements of our supposedly great cities. They called for forms of education that make these claims of aspirational democracy central to the educational process.

Collectively, the voices of the early pragmatists point us toward a morally engaged and justice-seeking conception of higher learning. From William James and Anna Julia Cooper we hear calls for the importance of including diverse and hitherto silenced perspectives in the search for adequate knowledge and understanding. "Neither the whole of truth, nor the whole of good, is revealed to any single observer," said James.[5] Pointing forcefully to the insight and understanding gained in the course of a seemingly ordinary and even insignificant life, James insists: "The subject knows a part of the world of reality which the judging spectator fails to see." "It is subversive of every human interest," said Cooper, denouncing the exclusion of women's views and voices, "that the cry of one-half the human family be stifled." But when woman's voice is added to public discourse, the advantage is not to women alone. "The darkened eye [of the complete human family] restored, every member rejoices with it."[6]

From Dewey, W.E.B. du Bois, and Fred Newton Scott, we encounter passionate calls for dismantling the social barriers that divide "rich and poor, men and women, noble and baseborn, ruler and ruled." "All children are the children of all. . . . The whole generation must be trained and guided and out of it as out of a huge reservoir must be lifted all genius, talent, and intelligence to serve all the world."[7]

In the worldview of these ardent reformers, it is not individual interests or inclinations alone that guide the design of the educational program. "The only question which concerns us here," says Carter G. Woodson in *The Mis-Education of the Negro*, "is whether these 'educated' persons are actually equipped to face the ordeal before them or unconsciously contribute to their own undoing by perpetuating the regime of the oppressor."[8] Educators must create social laboratories in which ordinary people research their own circumstances and assist one another in creating solutions, urged social activist Jane Addams, taking a position echoed, in treatise after treatise, by her friend John Dewey. We educate "the children of all," said du Bois, "to serve all the world."[9]

These voices from another time merge almost seamlessly with several colloquy presenters' own challenge to put the quality of democratic community squarely at the center of our concern and our educational practice.

Justice seeking, in the fullest vision of this dialogue about pragmatism and liberal education, is not, of course, simply something one does in the world "out there." As the early pragmatists realized, justice depends on and emerges ultimately from the quality of our interactions with and sense of responsibility to other human beings. A society riven by deep divisions is hard pressed to provide meaningful justice to all its citizens. If civic relationships are characterized by segregation, strangeness, and an assumption that some of us come from cultures that are intrinsically inferior, how is it possible to respond appropriately to the moral and social circumstances of one another?

In rebuttal, we offer our own proposal to further develop the interrelational educative processes in the service of the larger society. Our society is already at a significant point in redefining the educational role of our colleges and universities. Our campuses seek to move, as we observed above, from faculty-centered teaching to student-centered learning. But we propose an even richer ambition—the goal of becoming justice-centered communities in which learning fosters new capacities for engaged citizenship and aspirational or justice-seeking democracy. Our colleges and universities can literally become experiential learning centers where all members of the community are learning and practicing the capacities basic to the making of a just and equitable democracy. To the other, more familiar, tasks of identity and career development, values clarification, and intelligent reasoning, we now add the task of educating the engaged citizen, one who can conceptualize the relational aspects of self and society and who seeks to extend equity and justice in all aspects of daily life.

We depict this conception of education for engaged citizenship and justice seeking in Figure 3. Figures 2 and 3 are interrelated. Relational knowing, as we envision it, lays the foundation for justice seeking. But where Figure 2 emphasizes the connections between social contexts, knowledge production, and action, in Figure 3 we depict a more intentional focus on learning and capacities that are specifically important to the making of a just and diverse democracy. With Figure 3, therefore, we point higher education in the direction of *adding* to the curriculum and cocurriculum topics, forms of dialogue, and experiential learning that are explicitly tied to participatory democracy and significant issues of equity and justice.

There are two important educational premises embedded in this model for engaged citizenship and justice seeking. The first holds that we must provide learners with direct experiences of the kinds of applications we want them to make. A growing body of cognitive research tells us that students can learn to translate concepts and applications from one domain to another *provided that practice in such translation is provided and emphasized in the original learning context*. Higher education has long contended that, by developing students' rational capacities and societal knowledge, it prepares them for citizenship. We believe, however, that we will prepare learners more effectively for citizenship if they have direct and substantial opportunities to col-

Figure 3. Educational Mission III: Justice Seeking

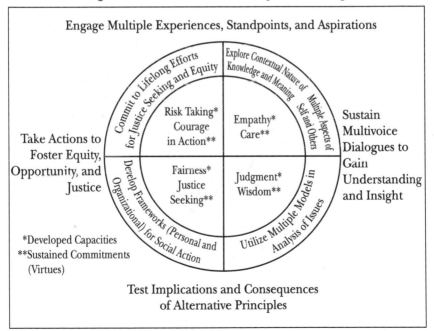

laboratively explore contested issues in contemporary society, and if they have opportunities to test, experientially as well as intellectually, the societal consequences of different policies and courses of action. In short, we want to move away from theory now, applications at some later date. Questions of equity and justice are simultaneously the most difficult, the most far-reaching, and the most basic issues we face in society. Students need to grapple with them extensively in the course of their undergraduate studies. These explorations must be multicultural. They cannot begin with the presupposition that the values, customs, and preferences of one or two groups are privileged while others must adjust to these prevailing expectations.

The second premise reflected in Figure 3 is that students' substantial immersion in topics, contexts, and socially negotiated choices involving justice and equity issues will result in development of capacities and commitments—virtues, if you will—that are basic to the goodness and vitality of democracy as a form of communal life. Hence, our model shows two levels of outcomes from each of the different kinds of learning that we recommend as preparation for democratic engagement and justice seeking. The first level is "developed capacities," a set of abilities that learners acquire through active practice under the guidance of a thoughtful mentor. These developed capacities include empathy, judgment, fairness, and risk taking. The second level, developed over the life span rather than from schooling alone, includes *sustained* commitments, capacities exercised so consistently and with sufficient quality that they can, in fact, be described as "virtues." Here we include capacities for care, wisdom, justice seeking, and courage.

We show these outcomes knowing that others will surely want to deliberate the particulars of our vision. But this is our point: our society is sorely in need, as we move into a new century and a new awareness of the United States as a nation drawn from many cultural traditions, of a strong dialogue about the kinds of capacities and virtues we must cultivate in our communities to make the full promise of democracy a lived experience for all our people.

From this perspective, every campus would devote substantial amounts of human energy and resources to justice-seeking activities that are basic to engaged and democratic citizenship. Dewey suggested that another term for an environment that fosters the capacities for associated living is "moral democracy," a society characterized by "free and open communication, unselfish and unself-seeking reciprocal relationships, and an interaction that contributes to mutual advantages."[10] Suppose we were to apply this concept to our colleges and universities, accepting as a principle the dictum that we should not ask of our students what we will not expect of ourselves. We would then accept the challenge of shaping our own communities as justice-seeking democracies and cultivating in ourselves as well as our students relational and justice-seeking ways of thinking and acting. We would invite every program, in ways appropriate to its subject matter, to make a fundamental commitment to relational ways of learning and to engagement with issues of equity, aspiration, and principle. Recognizing our intellectual and societal diversity as a precious educational resource, we would fully engage rather than tolerate the pluralism that is already present on our campuses. We would become communities that seek to educate about the aspirations as well as the inequities that pervade our world. We would hold out the expectation that a liberally educated individual, by definition, seeks and works to expand justice and equity in a world lived in common with others.

Clearly this is a different vision of education than the one to which most of us were exposed. But it is a vision that already has strong roots within the academy. The early pragmatists were defeated in their efforts to make our universities participatory communities, dedicated spaces in which the great issues of our time would be not only studied but fully addressed. But as Elizabeth Minnich has pointed out in her report for the American Commitments initiative, a new academy is already growing up within the walls of the old academy. In women's studies; ethnic studies; peace studies; environmental studies; science, technology, and values studies; cultural studies; interdisciplinary studies; continuing studies; and all the other "special" studies that now challenge and enliven our communities, we already find forms of learning that are fully involved with the larger society and with the moral and practical quandaries of our time.

To some, these new approaches to learning may seem supplementary and elective. But we believe, and the papers in this book affirm, that the engaged approach to knowledge encompassed in these fields has become the new frontier for liberal education.

Notes

1. Maxine Greene, *The Dialectic of Freedom* (New York: Teachers College Press, 1988).
2. John Dewey, "Creative Democracy: The Task Before Us," Debra Morris and Ian Shapiro, editors, *John Dewey: The Political Writings* (Indianapolis, IN: Hackett, 1993).
3. Bruce Kimball, "Toward Pragmatic Liberal Education," in Robert Orrill, editor, *The Condition of American Liberal Education: Pragmatism and a Changing Tradition* (New York: College Entrance Examination Board, 1995).
4. Howard Gardner, *The Unschooled Mind* (New York: Basic Books, 1991).
5. William James, "What Makes a Life Significant?" *Talks to Teachers on Psychology, and to Students on Some of Life's Ideals* (New York: W.W. Norton, 1958).
6. Anna Julia Cooper, *A Voice from the South* (New York: Oxford, 1988), 121.
7. W.E.B. du Bois, *Dark Water: Voices from Within the Veil* (New York: Schocken Books, 1972), 216–17.
8. Carter G. Woodson, *The Mis-Education of the Negro* (Trenton, NJ: Africa World Press, 1990).
9. du Bois, op. cit.
10. Dewey, "Creative Democracy," 270.

Afterword
Anchoring the Future
in the Past: 1931–1997

RITA BORNSTEIN

PRESIDENT, ROLLINS COLLEGE

B ruce Kimball's assertion that for the first time in our history a uniquely American form of liberal education is emerging came as a stunning idea to me, persuaded as I was by his earlier work, which suggested the continuing ascendancy of European traditions. Kimball's contention that the resurgent interest in John Dewey and pragmatism among American intellectuals is converging with current trends in liberal education provided an important historical connection with progressive education and a philosophical rationale for our efforts to rethink liberal education. Persistent questions about the value, relevance, and applicability of a liberal education have made such a rethinking necessary. My subsequent discussions with Bruce and with Bob Orrill led to The Rollins Colloquy, an extraordinary four-day conference about the future of liberal education from which the papers in this book are derived.

The search for an American approach to liberal education characterized a 1931 conference, "The Curriculum for the Liberal Arts College," chaired by John Dewey at Rollins College. At that gathering Dewey asked, "[H]ow shall we make the colleges count in developing a culture which is more truly indigenous, [which] . . . is not imported or exotic [but] grows out of American life?"[1]

The 17 prominent educators and writers who gathered in 1931 developed principles for liberal education that were a departure from the "conventional and traditional" European-style education characteristic of their own experiences. The conference emphasized student learning and the connections between liberal education, work, and democracy, and was historically situated in progressivism, the effort to reform American education and expand democracy in an increasingly urban, industrialized society. One of the participants, Goodwin Watson, a Teachers College professor, remarked, "[W]e must provide for students to have an actual part in dealing with [modern problems], to get . . . the feel of the fur on the tail of the world."[2]

Rollins President Hamilton Holt, a Yale-educated former newspaperman, convened the 1931 conference to identify principles that would support a revision of the traditional liberal arts curriculum. Holt had already garnered national attention for Rollins by creating a radically new student-centered approach to pedagogy called "The Conference Plan." An even more progressive educational experiment was launched two years later by a group of Rollins professors who founded Black Mountain College in North Carolina.

The 1931 conference became a significant part of the Rollins story, helping to define the College in that era as progressive in its curriculum and pedagogy. This legacy inspired successive faculties and presidents to remain committed to innovative programs and teaching, despite a return to a mainstream liberal education that mirrored the general eclipse of Dewey's ideas.

In the intervening years, at Rollins and other institutions, there have been curriculum modifications, innovations, and failures. In the 1960s and 1970s, many institutions, responding to social and intellectual discontent, experimented with "progressive" curricula and pedagogies. In 1977, John Brubacher noted that "[t]he task of undergirding liberal education with a pragmatic base has been approached" by connecting study with contemporary problems and by replacing "[t]he idea of a timeless curriculum, as invariant as human nature" with "an elective system more responsive to individual differences."[3]

The decade of the 1990s generated new pressures on the curriculum, based on changes in the organization and production of knowledge, institutional financing, enrollment patterns, and student interests. Dewey's statement at the 1931 curriculum conference applies as well to the end of the century: "[T]he conditions of American life

... in the last generation ... have changed so rapidly that the changes ... have outstripped the educational principles, philosophy, and practices of the college."[4]

The pragmatist approach to liberal education provides presidents and faculties with a useful perspective from which to re-envision the curriculum in response to the challenges of the twenty-first century. Liberal education can assume more direct responsibility for promoting democracy in a post–Cold War world. Academic learning can be enhanced through a wide range of practical experience and experimentation. And a liberal education can be entirely consistent with the preparation of students for careers in a global economy.

Despite the disinclination of arts and sciences professors to agree with the public's preference for education that prepares students for careers and citizenship, both curricula and pedagogical methods have been moving in this direction. "Culture wars" notwithstanding, our institutions have become more diverse, and our curricula more multicultural. General education and study in the disciplines are increasingly interdisciplinary. New technologies have given rise to creative, inquiry-based, and collaborative teaching methods. Experiences designed to help students apply their academic learning to work and community problems have proliferated: internships, jobs, tutoring, research, independent study, study abroad, community service. In addition, institutions themselves have become more service oriented.

To explore these transformational trends and to reconnect with the College's history, Rollins collaborated with the College Board to sponsor the February 1997 invitational colloquy, "Toward a Pragmatic Liberal Education: The Curriculum of the Twenty-First Century." The colloquy was modeled loosely on the 1931 curriculum conference, but had the added credibility of cosponsorship by the Association of American Colleges and Universities and the American Council of Learned Societies, as well as support from the Jessie Ball duPont Fund.

Most of the 50 institutions represented were characterized by their presidents, faculty, and academic administrators as having a traditional curriculum, but virtually all of the participants indicated that their curriculum has been under review in response to internal and external pressures.

Colloquy participants discussed the connection between philosophical pragmatism and liberal education more explicitly than did the conferees in 1931. The 1931 Rollins curriculum conference was part of a progressive social and education reform movement designed to improve the lives of an increasingly broad range of students and to prepare them for citizenship and work. While the philosophy of pragmatism was not discussed explicitly, Dewey's ideas permeated the discourse. Sixty-six years later, near the close of the century, concerns about industrialization had given way to anxiety about information technology, and the impetus toward mass education for Americans was succeeded by interest in education for global understanding. Although enthusiastic about cross-disciplinary research and learning, participants in The Rollins Colloquy were far more discipline bound than were their counterparts in 1931.

Despite the great differences in social and educational context, the curriculum issues debated in 1931 and 1997 show many similar concerns. The 1931 report urged that students have an understanding of the physical world and biological processes. Dewey stressed the importance of understanding the implications of technological change (at that time, the long-distance telephone, radio, electric lighting, and the automobile). By 1997, information technology had captured the collective imagination as having the potential for solving many educational and social problems, much as the belief in science dominated the earlier period.

Emblematic of the technological revolution that has occurred in this century, the 1931 curriculum conference yielded only a lengthy verbatim typed manuscript, while the verbatim transcription of the 1997 conference was uploaded twice a day to the Colloquy Web site, which also supplied an e-mail address for immediate feedback from interested individuals around the world.

The 1931 conferees advocated what was then a revolutionary notion: that the curriculum be broadened to encompass not only the traditional disciplines, but social problems and student interests. They also argued for a thinning of the traditional educational wall between the vocational and the cultural. And they recommended that students learn to use leisure time intelligently, with extracurricular activities considered a part of the educational experience. At the conclusion of the conference, Arthur Morgan, president of Antioch College, commented, "I believe this Conference . . . represent[s] a point of departure . . . from conventional outlook that will not be ignored."[5] However, this new perspective was indeed ignored as progressive education and pragmatism went into decline.

The 1997 colloquy participants described the contemporary pragmatist turn in liberal education as pervasive and significant. They also believed that their deliberations would not be ignored. The Colloquy did not seek to produce a set of specific recommendations for liberal education, but found what Lee Shulman called a "compelling convergence of thoughts, practices, of visions." The essays gathered in this book reflect that convergence and provide some of the most creative and provocative thinking about liberal education in recent years. They offer what participants in The Rollins Colloquy agreed was "a feast for the mind."

Most exciting is the potential for identifying and celebrating a uniquely American approach to liberal education, an acceptance of the influence of American experience, character, and thought. The new thinking about liberal education represented by The Rollins Colloquy will have its critics, but change in liberal education has been and continues to be inexorable. Lawrence Levine echoes Dewey's earlier comment by pointing out that "significant curricular changes are invariably and inextricably linked to significant changes in the general society and culture."[6]

Colloquy participants agreed that there are significant forces producing the need for change. These include the market, competition, cost, technology, and intellectual evolution in the disciplines. As impediments to change (also called forces for stability), participants noted departmental rigidity, finances, increased workload, faculty governance, fear of vocationalism, and inertia.

The need for change was elegantly expressed in a letter I received from Leon Lederman, Nobel laureate in physics and director emeritus of the Fermi National Accelerator Laboratory. Concerning the Colloquy, he wrote:

> We have watched the tuning of the education of our liberal arts grad-
> uates around the dean's table, a classical labor negotiation between
> campus powers. A from-the-ground-up, fresh, innocent review of what
> our graduates should know, what skills and modes of thinking will
> be imposed on them by the twenty-first century, is long overdue. . . .
> You might think of this [colloquy] as a warm-up for a six-week retreat
> on some irresistible mountain top in order to create the "Red Book"
> for the year 2000.

I take Lederman's charge seriously. Our problem in liberal education is that when we ask ourselves what our graduates should know
and what skills and modes of thinking they need, we do so within our
traditional frames of reference, habits, conventions, and power relations. With some notable exceptions, faculties are rarely successful in
their attempts to transform their curricula. However, if Kimball is correct in identifying a gathering consensus around a pragmatist turn
in liberal education, a collegial national conversation is merited to
explore pragmatism's utility in our efforts to rethink the curriculum.

Lederman suggests a leisurely conversation in an undisturbed
locale, unimpeded by institutional politics. Perhaps a national foundation will fund such an effort. Foundations might also support the
development, implementation, and assessment of curricular initiatives toward a pragmatic liberal education.

My hope is that the challenging proposals for liberal education
growing out of The Rollins Colloquy will become part of the vigor-
ous national debate on the future of the curriculum. For curricular
change to occur, ideas must be widely circulated and critiqued. A sustained forum for this discussion is best provided by the higher education associations and learned societies in their meetings, publications, and Web sites.

While the pace of change in higher education is often characterized as glacial, the very survival of liberal education is dependent
on our curricular and pedagogical responsiveness to the dramatic
social, technological, and cultural changes with which our graduates
will contend. Faculties must review their goals for students, the learning and experiences that comprise a liberal education within the tra-

ditions and culture of their institutions, and the means by which they evaluate their effectiveness.

These discussions and initiatives will not occur without controversy, but Dewey reminds us that controversy over the curriculum is neither negative nor recent: "All social movements involve conflicts which are reflected intellectually in controversies. It would not be a sign of health if such an important social interest as education were not also an arena of struggles, practical and theoretical."[7]

Notes

1. *Proceedings: Curriculum Conference,* vol. 2 (Winter Park, FL: Rollins College, January 19–24, 1931), 424.
2. *Proceedings,* vol. 1, 282.
3. John S. Brubacher, *On the Philosophy of Higher Education,* rev. ed. (San Francisco: Jossey-Bass, 1982), 85.
4. *Proceedings,* vol. 2, 422.
5. *Proceedings,* vol. 3, 830.
6. Lawrence W. Levine, *The Opening of the American Mind: Canons, Culture, and History* (Boston: Beacon Press, 1996), 67–68.
7. John Dewey, *Experience and Education* (1938; New York: Collier Books, 1963), 5.